CONTENTS

Key to Map Pages	2-3	Index to Streets, Towns, Villages, & selected Places of Interest	124-253
Large Scale City Centre	4-11		
Map Pages	12-123	Index to Hospitals & Hospices	254
		Index to Stations	255-256

Motorway	**M6**
A Road	
B Road	B3220
Dual Carriageway	
One-way Street	→
Traffic flow on A Roads is also indicated by a heavy line on the driver's left.	→
Restricted Access	
Pedestrianized Road	
Track / Footpath	=======
Railway	Level Crossing / Station / Tunnel
Metrolink (LRT)	
The boarding of Metrolink trains at stops may be limited to a single direction, indicated by the arrow.	
Built-up Area	MILL ST.
Map Continuation	86 Large Scale City Centre 8

House Numbers	13 8
'A' and 'B' Roads only	
Information Centre	🛈
National Grid Reference	³95
Police Station	▲
Post Office	★
Toilet	▽
with facilities for the Disabled	♿
Educational Establishment	
Hospital or Hospice	
Industrial Building	
Leisure or Recreational Facility	
Place of Interest	
Public Building	
Shopping Centre or Market	
Other Selected Buildings	

SCALE

Map Pages 12-123	Map Pages 4-11
1:14908 (4¼ inches to 1 mile)	1:10560 (6 inches to 1 mile)
0 ⅛ ¼ Mile	0 ⅛ Mile
0 100 200 300 Metres	0 100 200 300 Metres

Copyright of Geographers' A-Z Map Company Limited

Head Office :
Fairfield Road, Borough Green, Sevenoaks, Kent TN15 8PP
Telephone: 01732 781000 (Enquiries & Trade Sales)
01732 783422 (Retail Sales)
www.a-zmaps.co.uk
Copyright © Geographers' A-Z Map Co. Ltd.
Edition 2 2002, Edition 2A* (Part Revision) 2003

Ordnance Survey®
This product includes mapping data licensed from Ordnance Survey® with the permission of the Controller of Her Majesty's Stationery Office.

© Crown Copyright 2003. All Rights Reserved.
Licence number 100017302

D1427986

2 KEY TO MAP PAGES

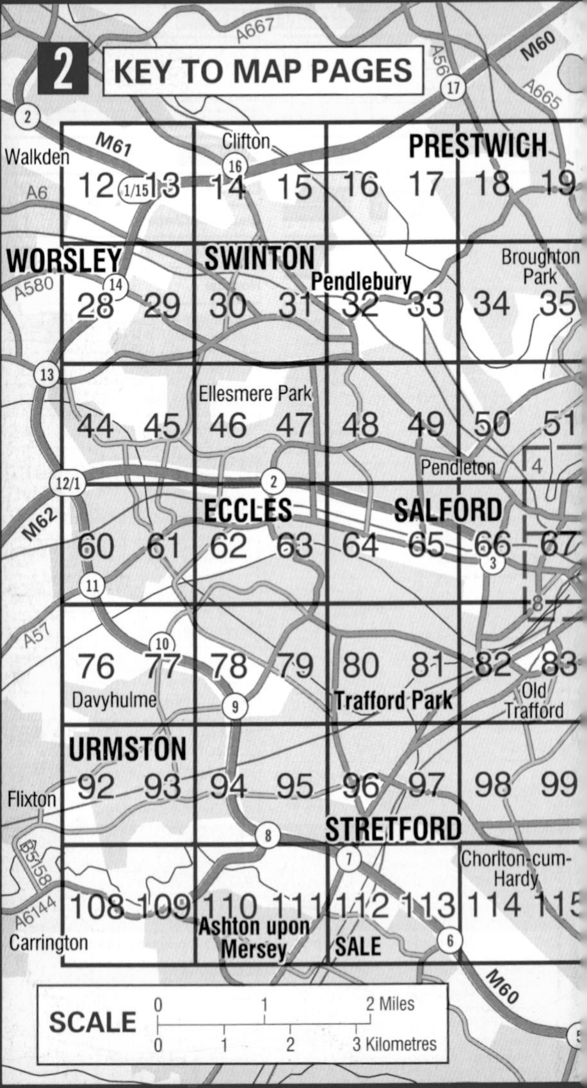

PRESTWICH

A667 · A56 · M60 · A665

Walkden	M61	Clifton (16)					
2	12 (1/15) 13	14	15	16	17	18	19

A6

WORSLEY — **SWINTON** — Broughton Park

A580

Pendlebury

28 (14) 29	30	31	32	33	34	35

(13)

Ellesmere Park

44	45	46	47	48	49	50	51

Pendleton · 4

(12/1)

ECCLES · (2) · **SALFORD**

M62

60	61	62	63	64	65	66	67

(11) · (3)

A57 · (10)

76	77	78	79	80	81	82	83

Davyhulme · (9) · **Trafford Park** · Old Trafford

URMSTON

Flixton

92	93	94	95	96	97	98	99

STRETFORD

(8) · (7) · Chorlton-cum-Hardy

A6144

108	109	110	111	112	113	114	115

Carrington · **Ashton upon Mersey** · **SALE** · (6) · M60

SCALE

0		1		2 Miles
0	1	2		3 Kilometres

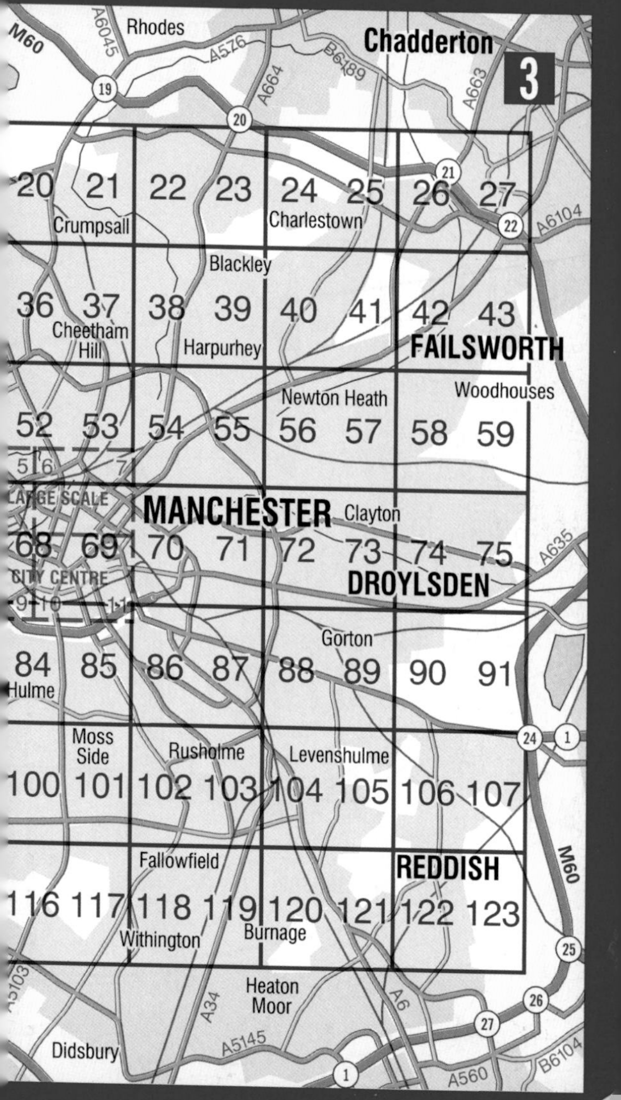
3
Chadderton
Rhodes
M60
A6045
A576
B6189
A664
A663
19
20
21
22
A6104
20
21
22
23
24
25
26
27
Crumpsall
Charlestown
Blackley
36
37
38
39
40
41
42
43
Cheetham Hill
Harpurhey
FAILSWORTH
Woodhouses
Newton Heath
52
53
54
55
56
57
58
59
5
6
7
LARGE SCALE
MANCHESTER
Clayton
68
69
70
71
72
73
74
75
A635
CITY CENTRE
DROYLSDEN
9
10
11
Gorton
84
85
86
87
88
89
90
91
Hulme
24
1
Moss Side
Rusholme
Levenshulme
100
101
102
103
104
105
106
107
Fallowfield
REDDISH
M60
116
117
118
119
120
121
122
123
Withington
Burnage
25
A5103
Heaton Moor
A34
A6
26
27
Didsbury
A5145
1
A560
B6104

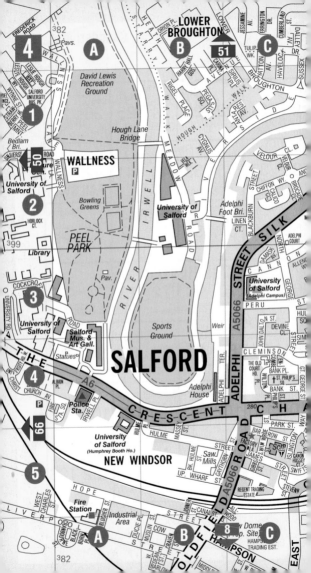

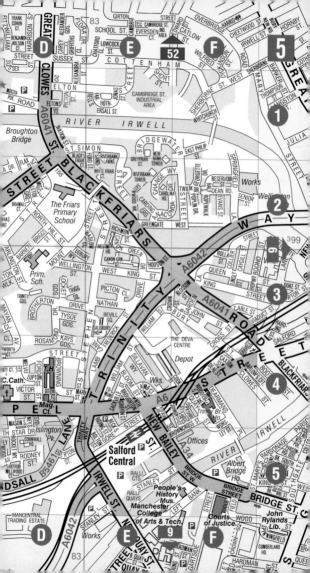

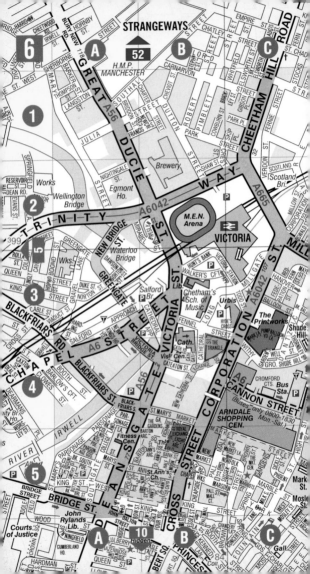

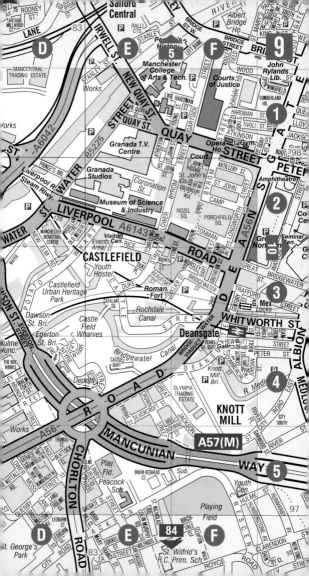

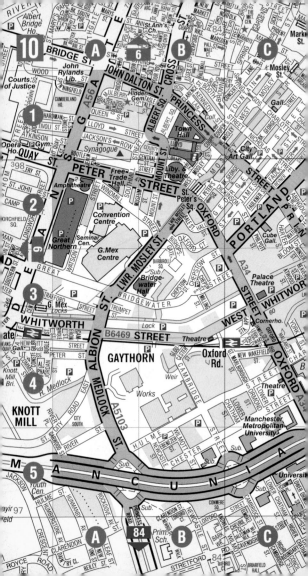

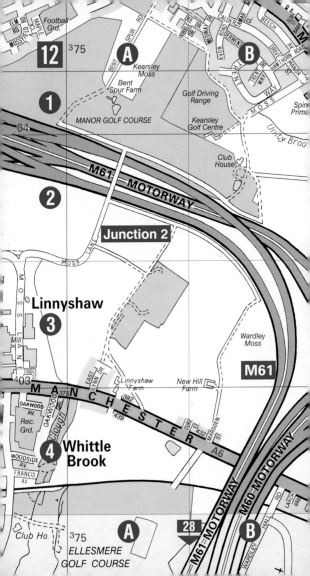

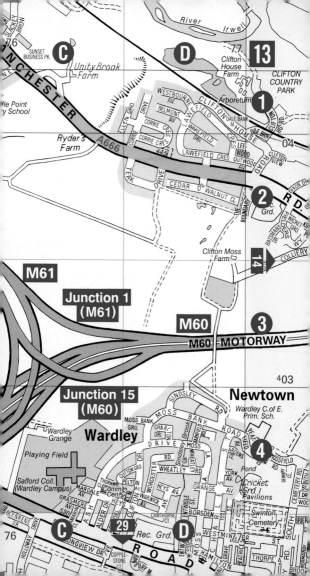

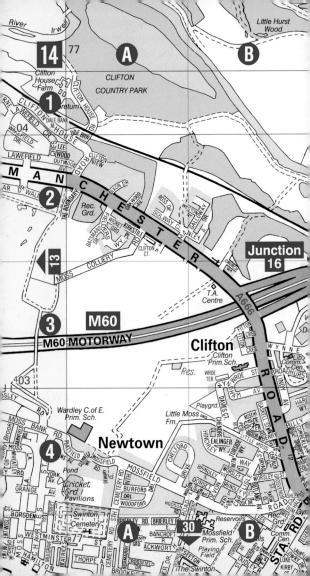

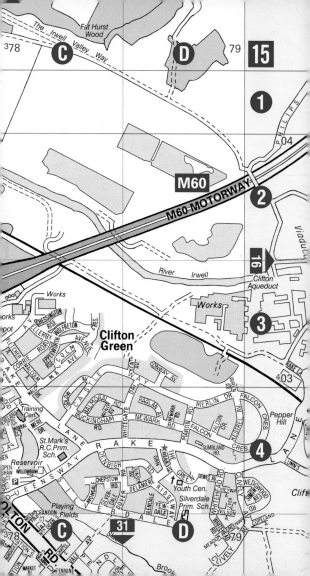

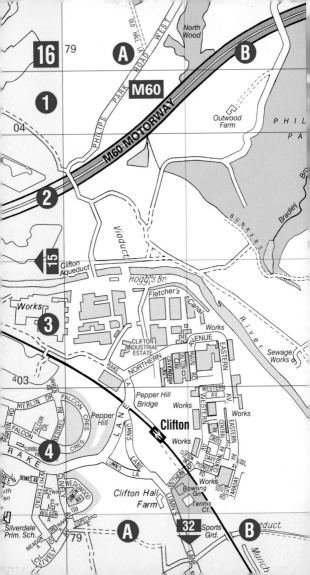

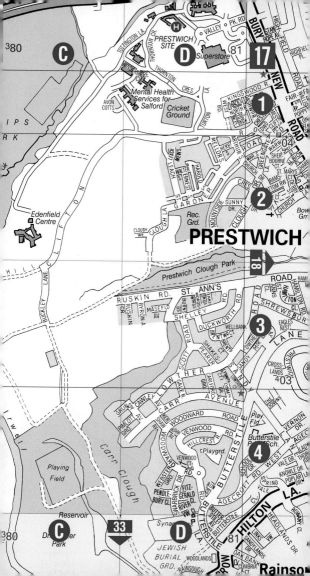

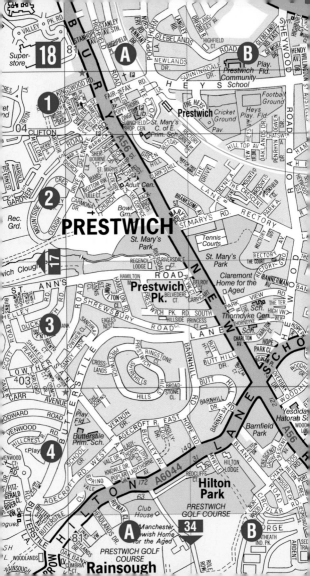

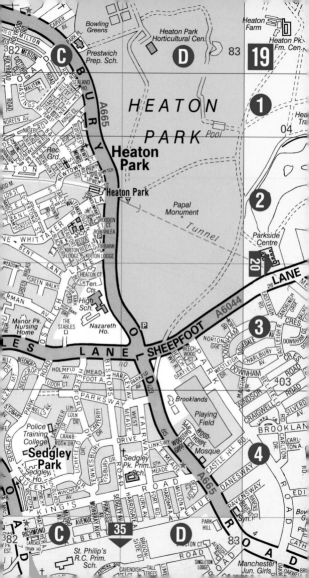

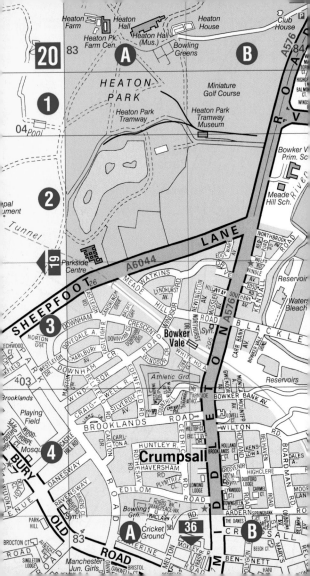

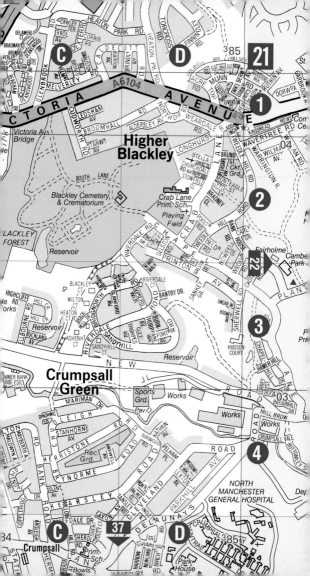

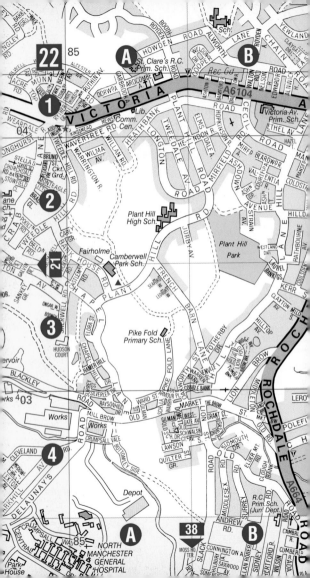

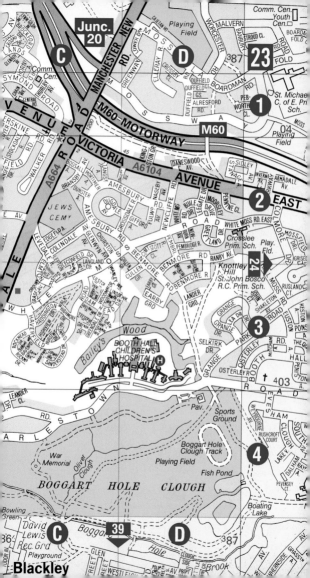

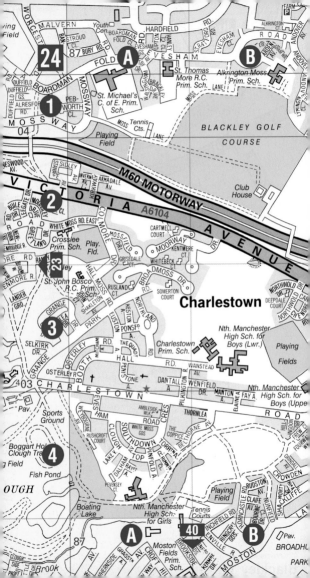

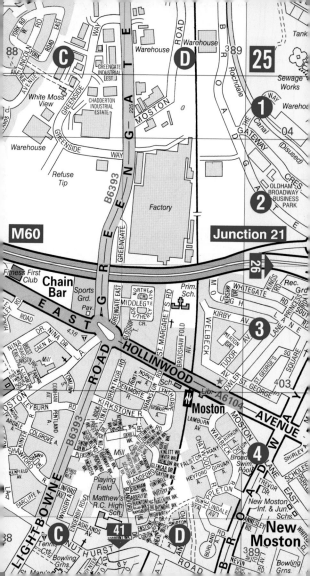

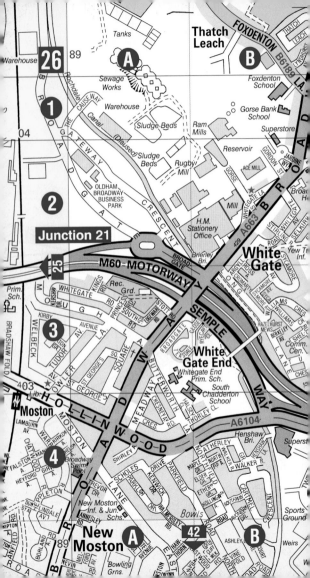

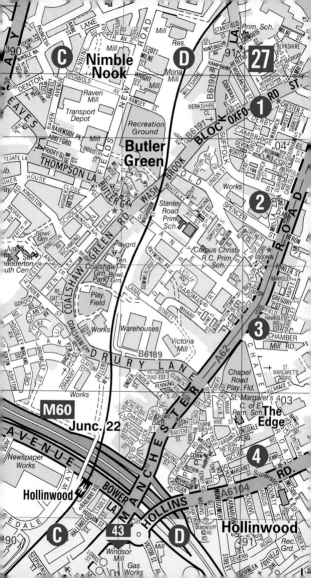

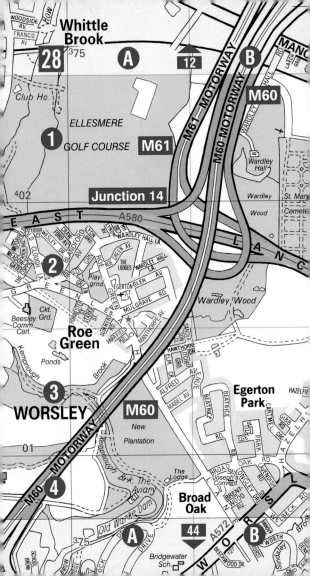

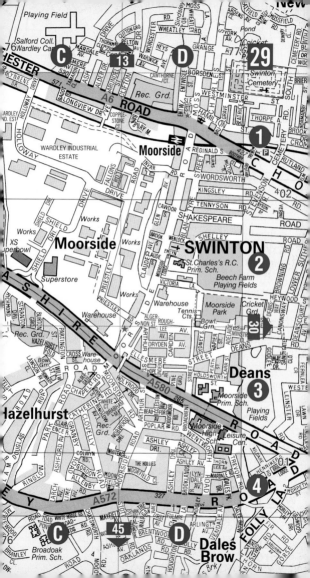

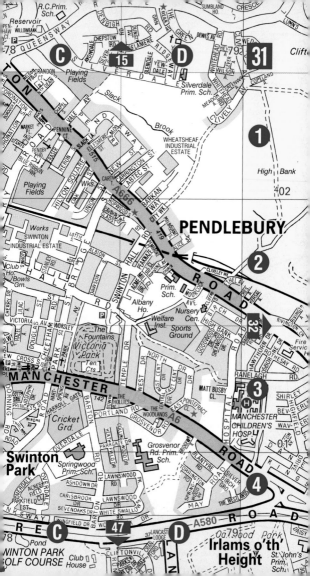

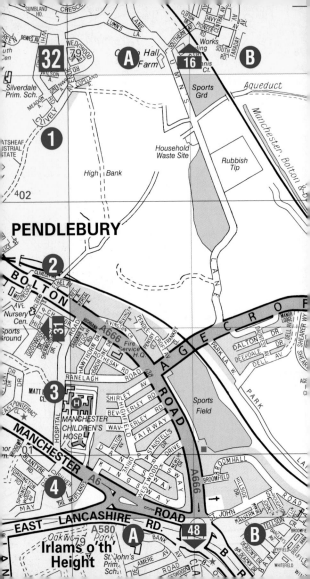

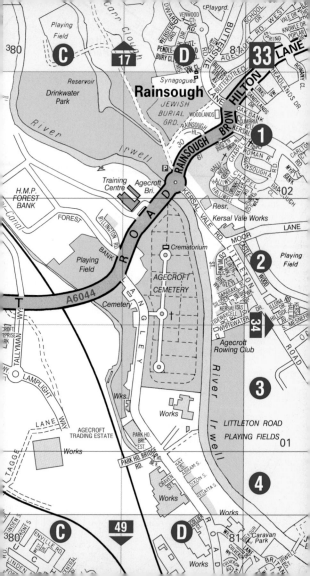

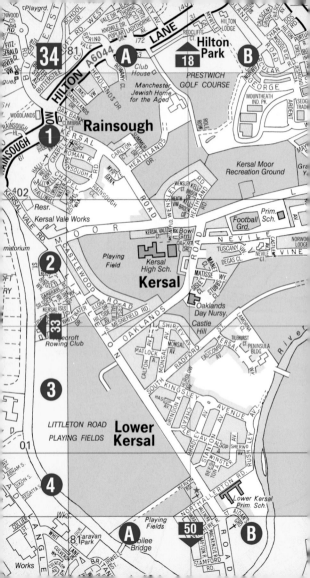

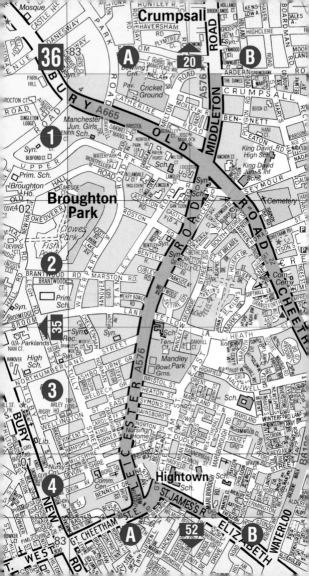

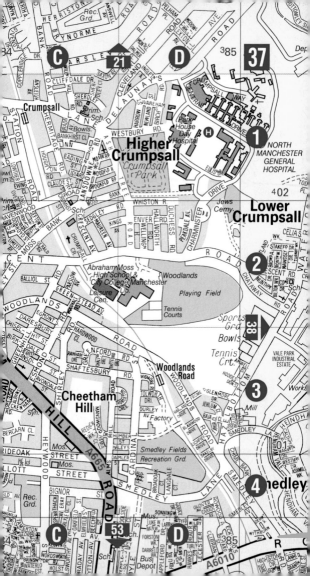

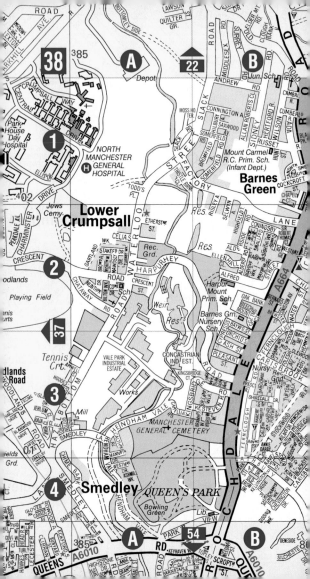

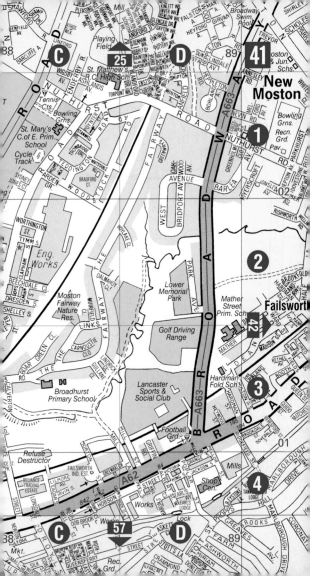

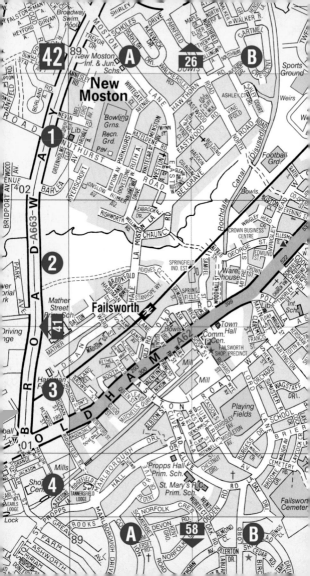

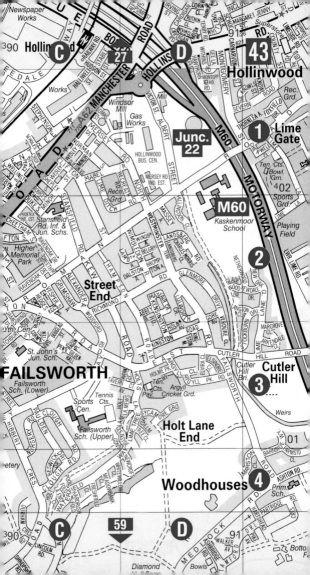

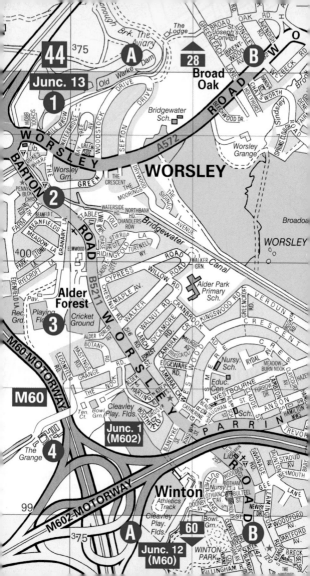

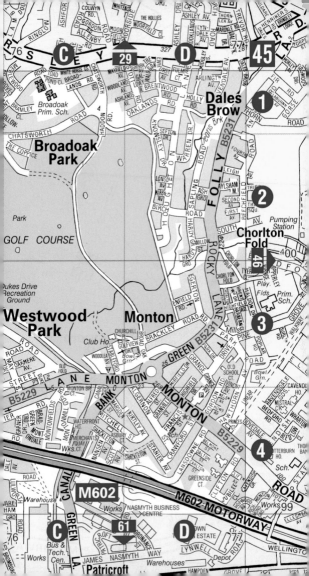

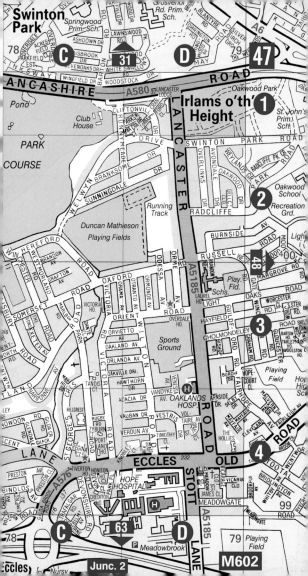

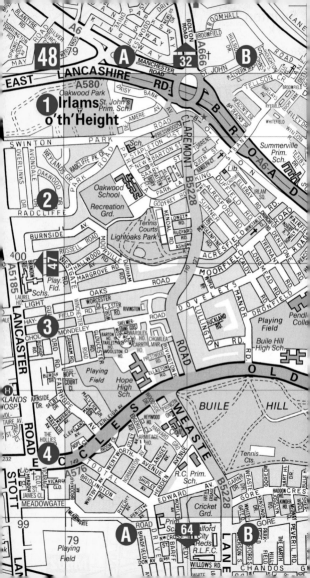

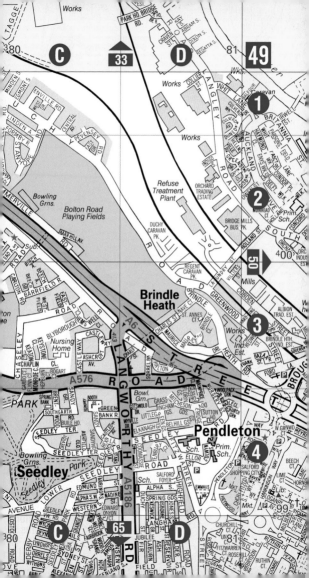

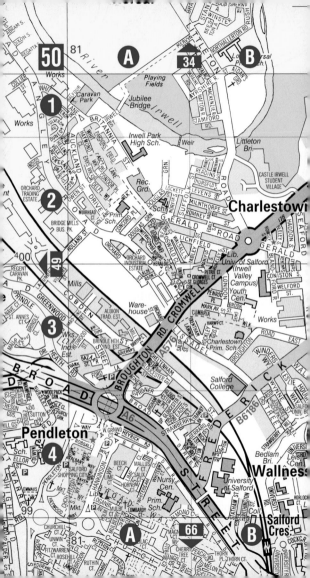

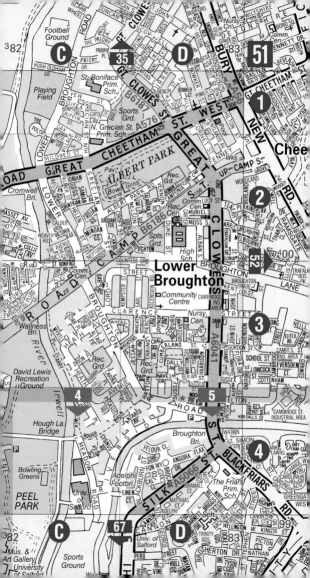

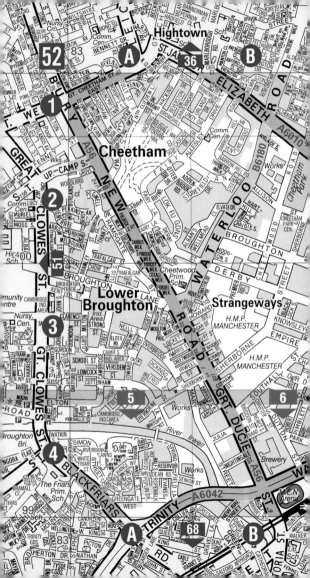

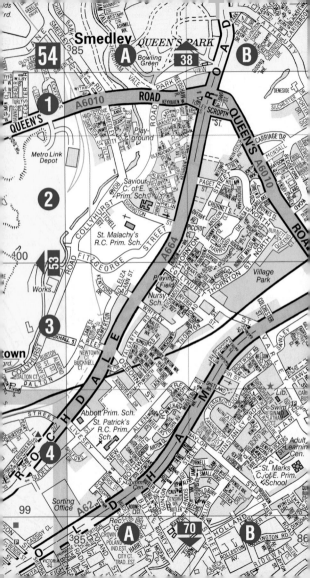

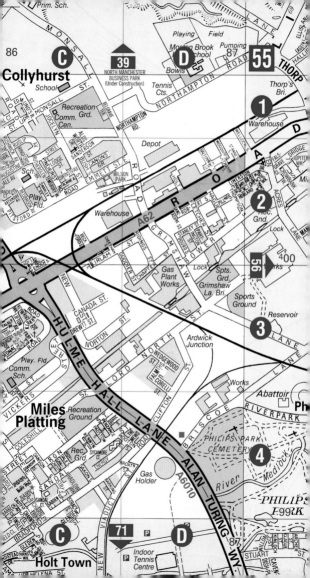

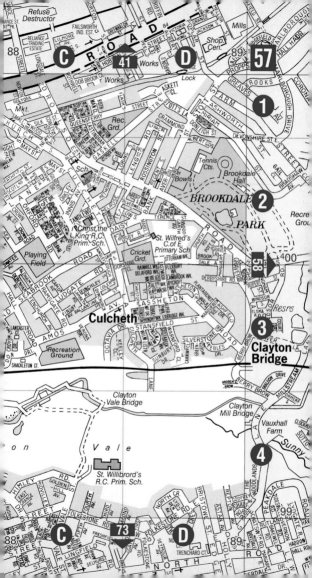

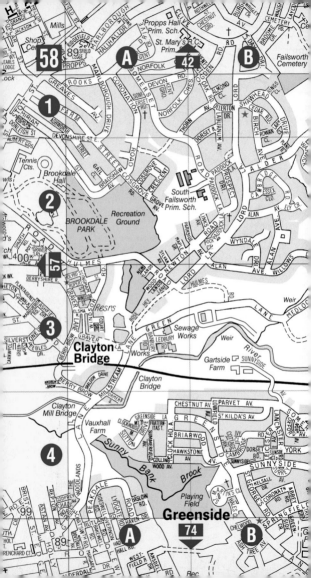

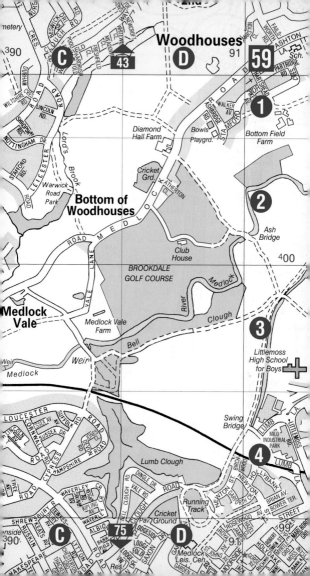

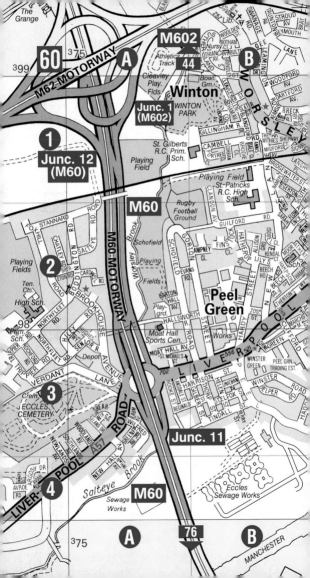

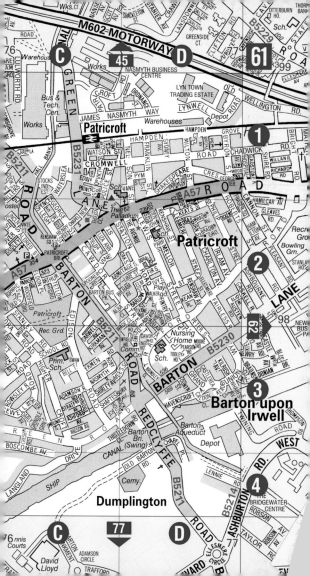

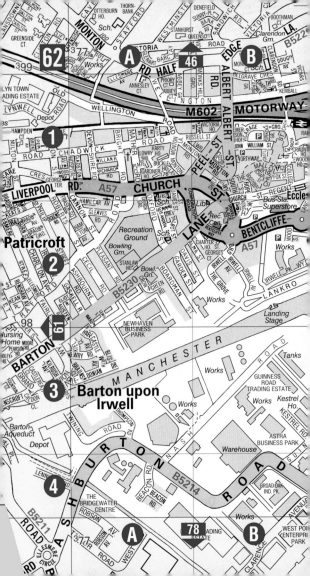

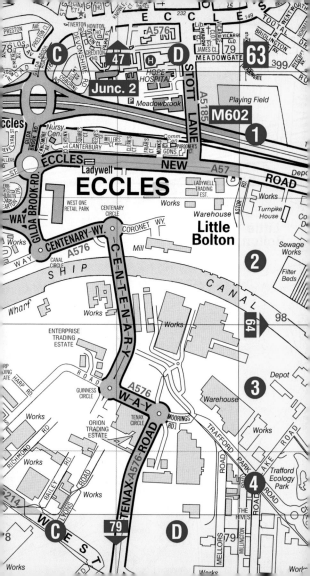

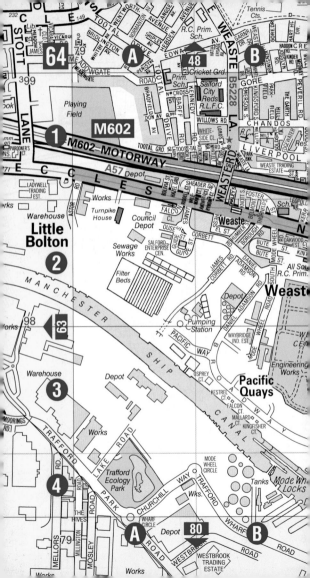

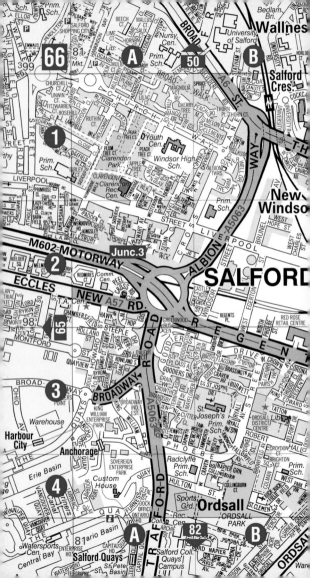

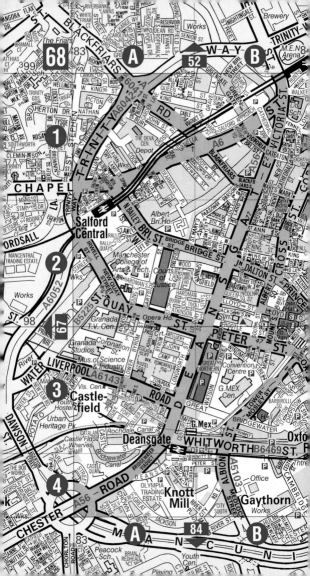

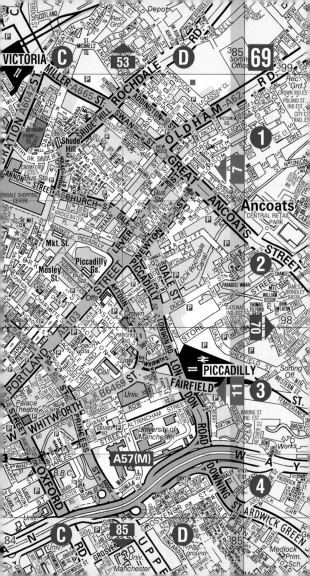

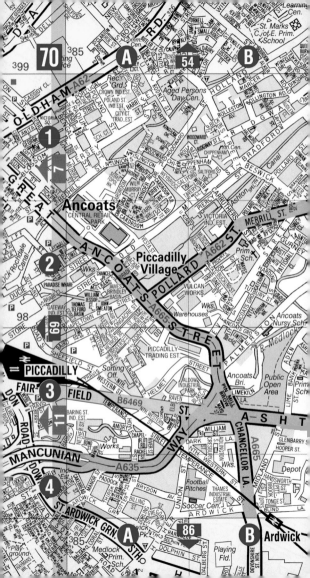

Holt Town

55

C

D

Gas Holder

River

Medlock

PHILIP

1399?

Indoor Tennis Centre

National Squash Centre

P

P

P

Running Track

Manchester City F.C. City of Manchester Stadium

Sportcity

Bedford

1

STUART

DISHPAN

CAVEN

ARCHE

BROOK

SCC

ALAN TURING WAY

ALAN TURING WAY

ROAD

ASHTON

Holt Town Bridge

Mary & Joseph Ho.

Medlock Valley High Sch.

Playing Fields

A662

NEW

VIKING

PARKE

HAVANA

MANILLA

ALBERT

Rec. Grd.

BLACKROCK

Ellinghm

Rec. Grd.

SILFIELD

TOWNLEY

CHARLESWORTH

BINGLE

MYRTLE ST.

HARRY THORNEY CROFT

WRIGHT ROBINSON CL

MANIPUR ST.

WYNNE

HARTWELL

HEY ST.

BRENNOCK

PENDLEGREEN

TYDD WK.

SHEFFRO

BELL

POPLAR ST

NORWAY ST.

LAIRBEL

REDVERS ST.

NANSEN ST.

GRIFFIN WK.

Ashbury Prim. Sch.

Beswick

Brigid's R.C. Sch.

72

F98

Gillingham

SLEDMERE

WORTH ST.

CRESCENT

Liby.

Shop. Cen.

Mkt.

3

BOSWORTH

Rec.

WES

ALAN TURING WAY

2

MAREE

GREY MARE

Ardwick

A635

OLD

ROAD

RONDIN

GIBSON

GORTON

ROAD

KAY ST.

DUDLEY

STREET

WOLVERTON

4

Ashbursys

REGAL IND. EST.

LANE

WAY

C

87

D

ANTHONY

WIGLEY ST.

MATHEWS ST.

STREET

VAUX INDUSTRIAL ESTATE

Works

87

MILES ST.

VAUGHAN

86

87

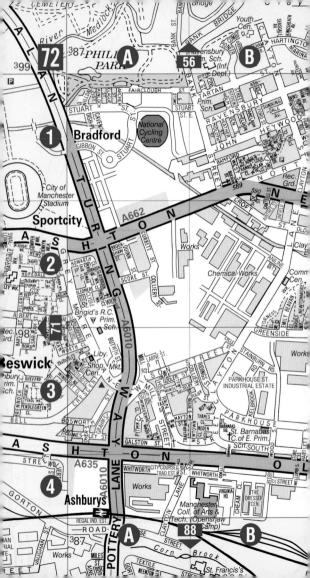

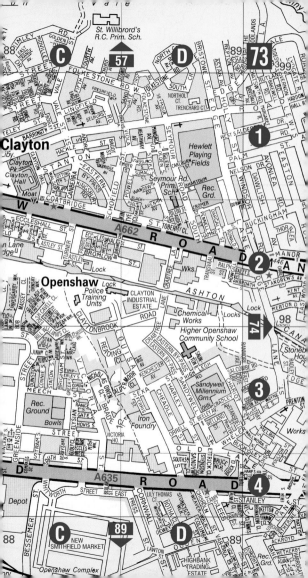

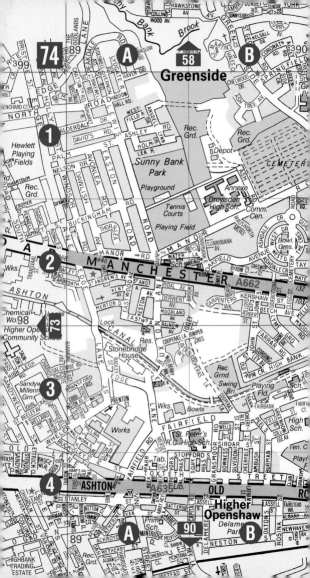

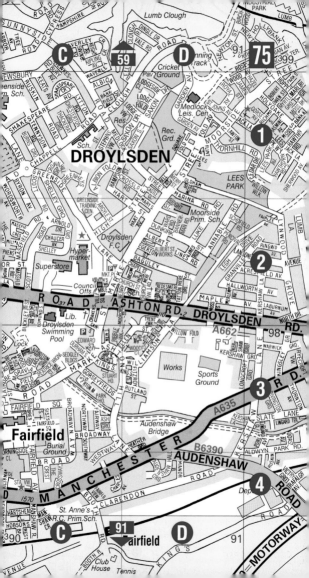

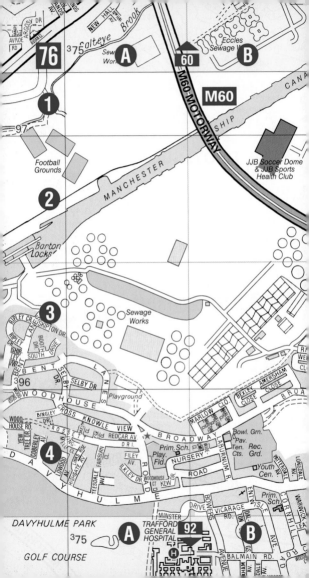

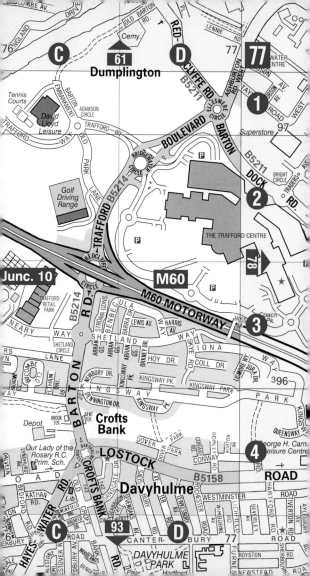

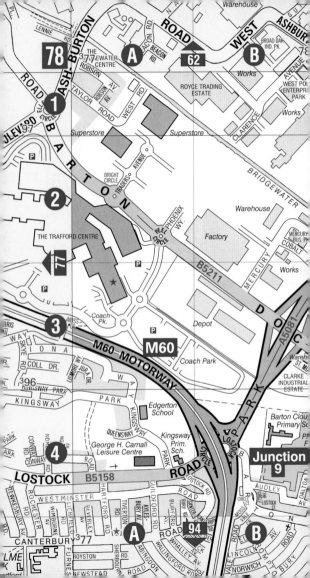

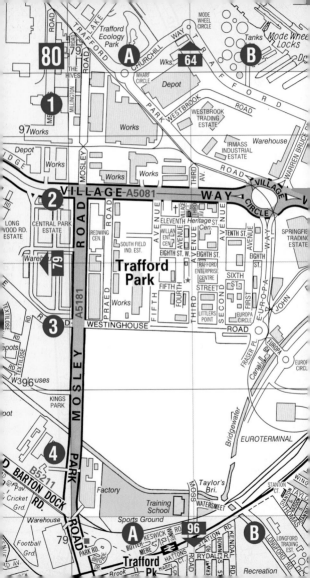

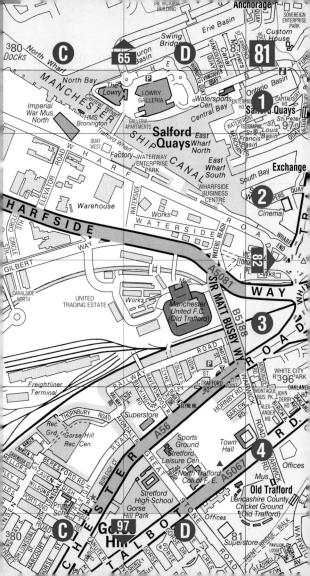

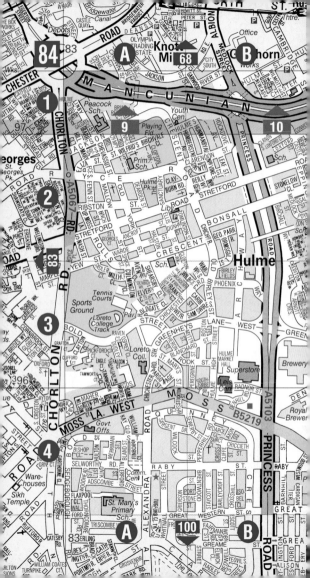

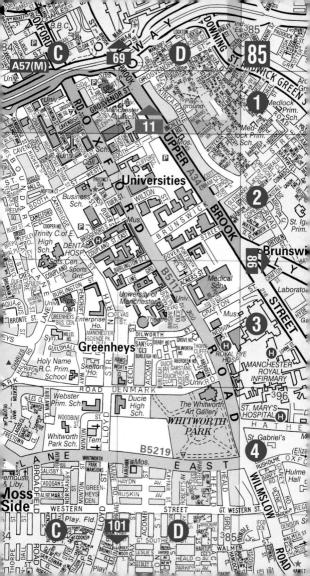

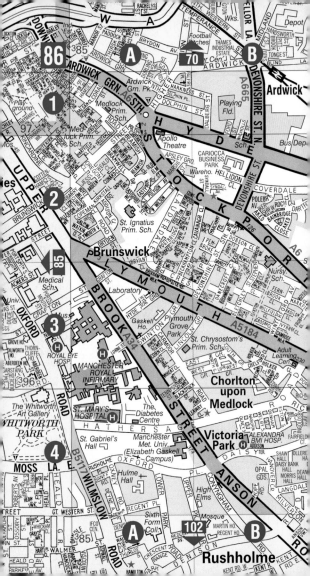

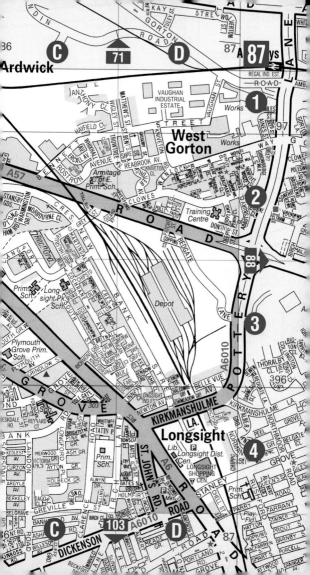

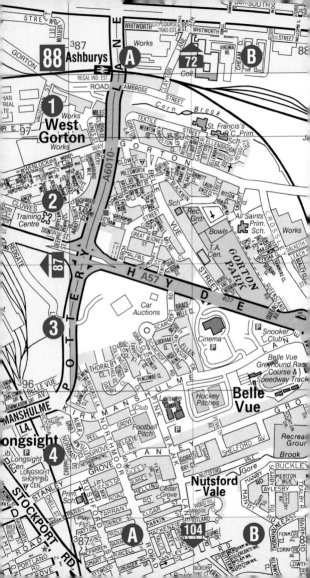

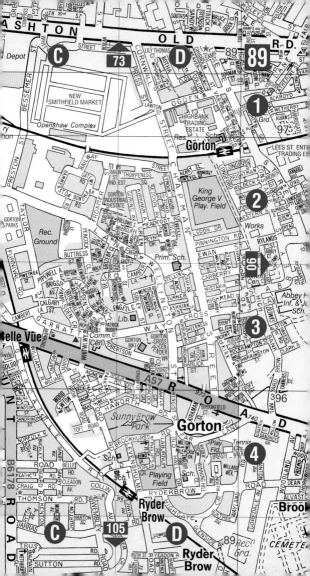

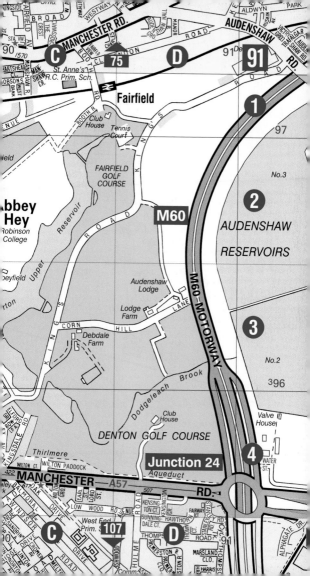

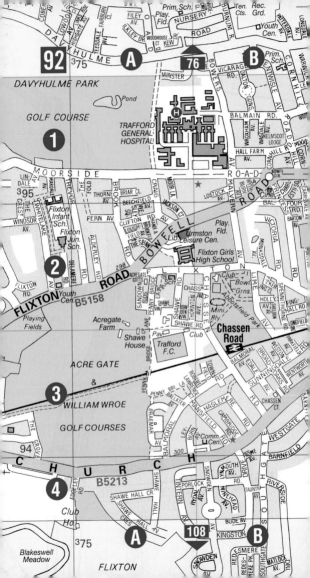

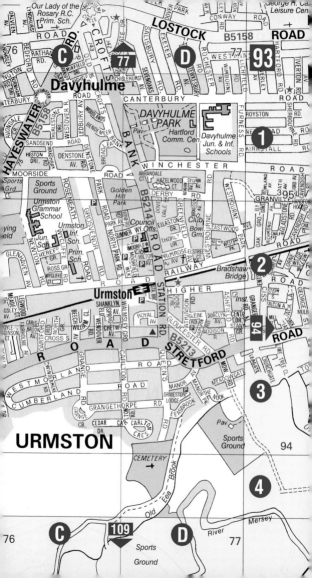

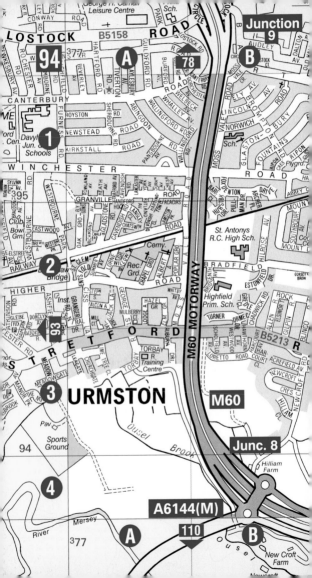

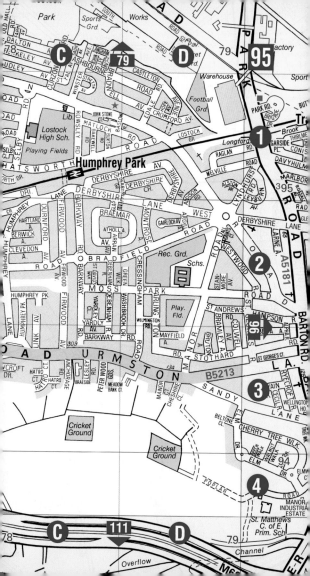

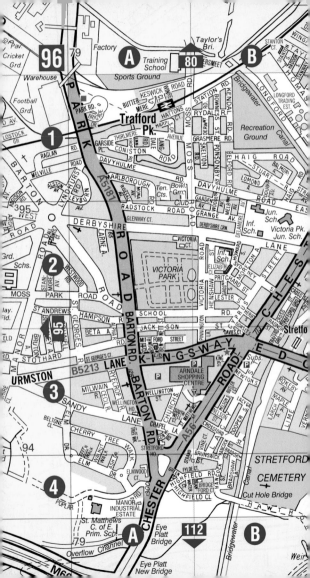

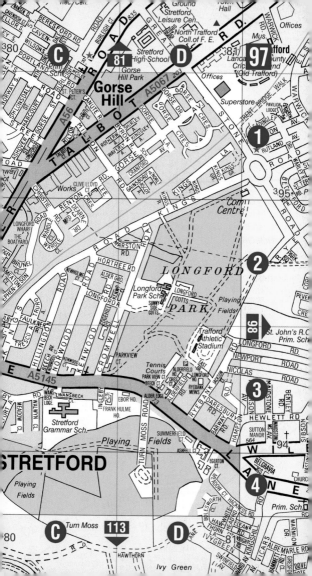

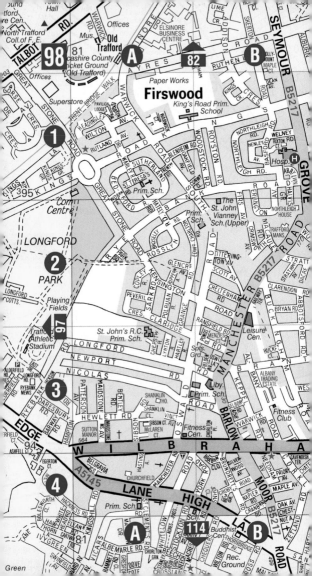

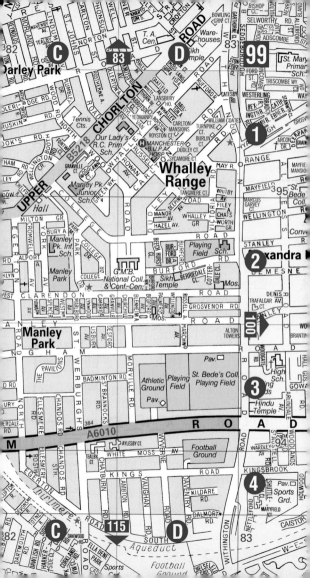

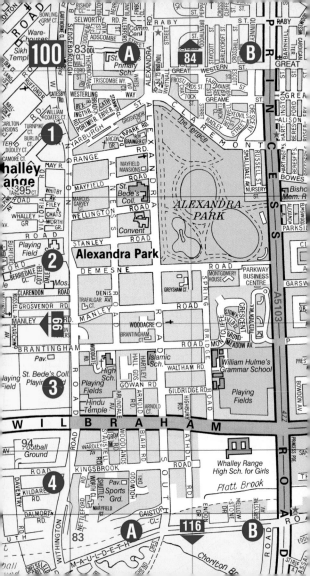

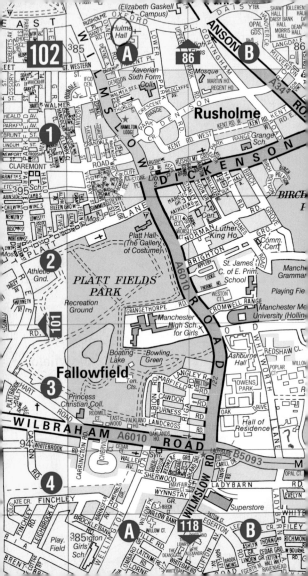

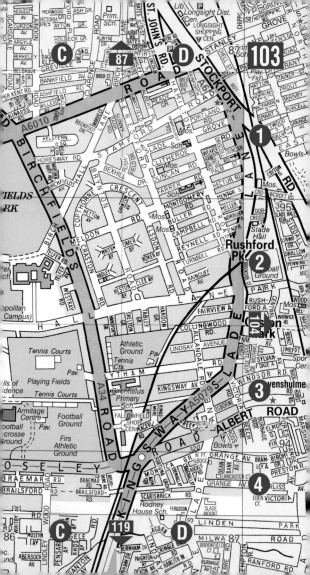

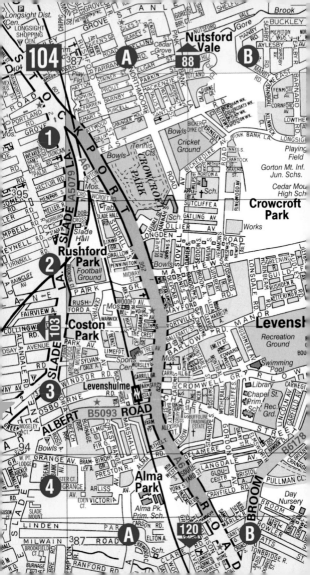

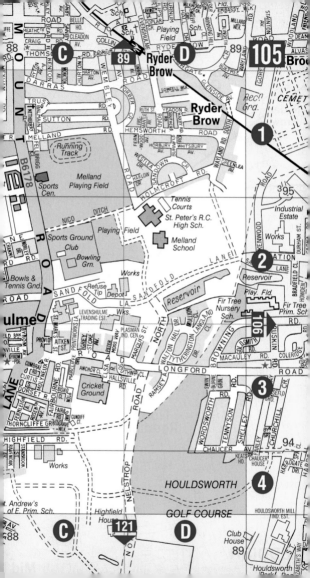

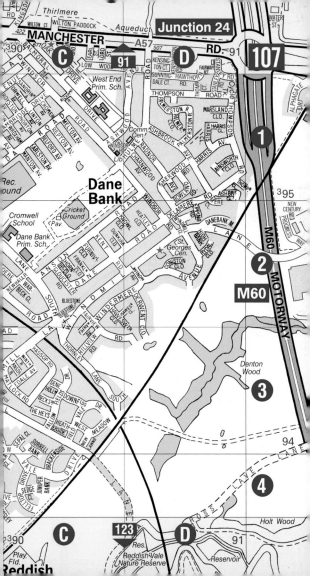

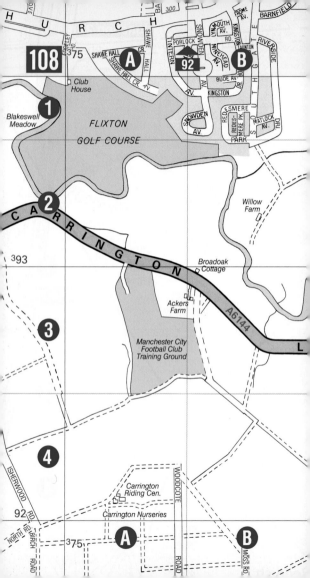

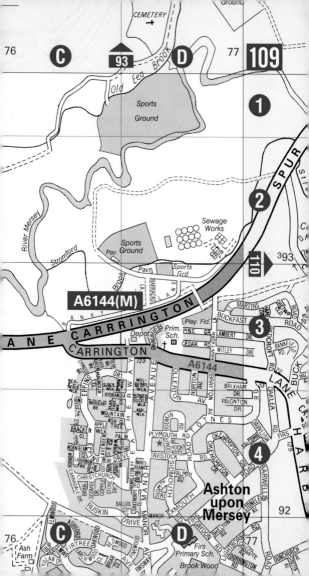

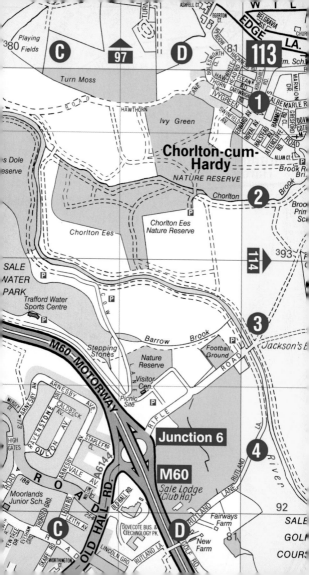

Chorlton-cum-Hardy

380 Playing Fields

C

97

D

Turn Moss

HAWTHORN

Ivy Green

's Dole Reserve

NATURE RESERVE

Chorlton

2

Chorlton Ees

Chorlton Ees Nature Reserve

114

393

SALE WATER PARK

Trafford Water Sports Centre

COW

Barrow Brook

Stepping Stones

Nature Reserve

Visitor Cen.

Picnic Site

Football Ground

Jackson's B

3

4

M60 MOTORWAY

ARNESBY AV

CALDBECK AV

RAVENSTONE AV

OULTON AV

STAPLE RD

ARNESVALE AV

HIGH GATES

173

A6144

Moorlands Junior Sch.

188

LEITH AV

YEW TREE AV

EVISHAM AV

WORTHINGTON CT

STAMFORD RD

LINCOLN GRO

OLD HALL RD

OUTHALL RD

DOVECOTE BUS. & TECHNOLOGY PK.

RUTLAND LA

Junction 6

M60

Sale Lodge (Club Ho)

RIFLE

RUTLAND ROAD

RUTLAND LANE

Fairways Farm

81

New Farm

GOLF RD

92

SALE GOLI COURSE

River

C

D

Brook Rd Bri.

Brook Prin Scl

ALBEMARLE ROAD

BELGRAVIA CHUF

WIL EDGE LA.

113

m. Sch.

1

IVYGREEN

EDWARD RD

ROYAL AV

HALSTED RD

ATTERCLIFFE

ALLAN CT.

DOVE COTI

ASHFELL CT.

EGERTON CT.

TURN

SWINFIELD AV

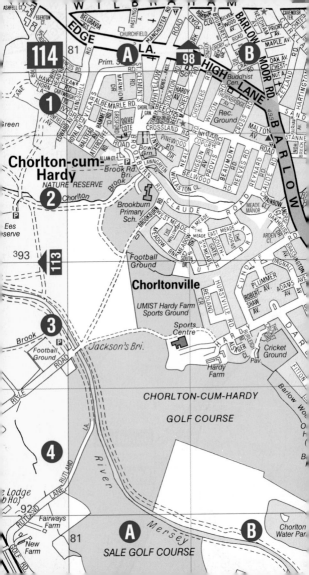

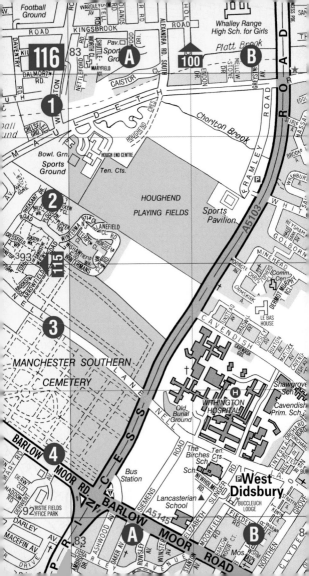

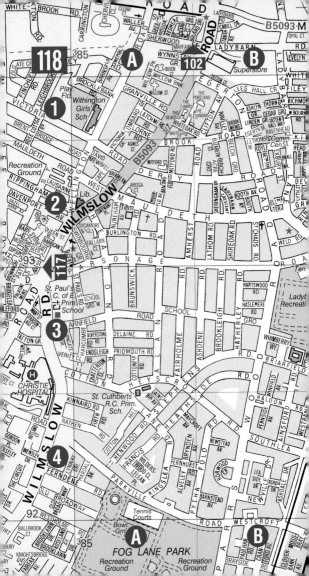

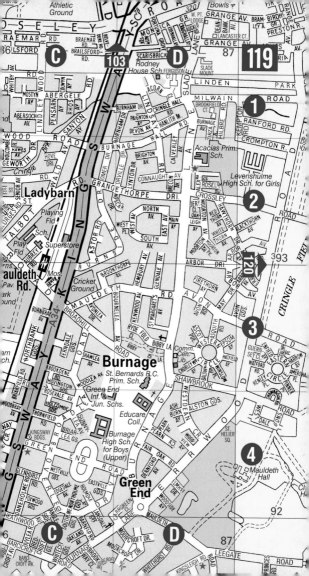

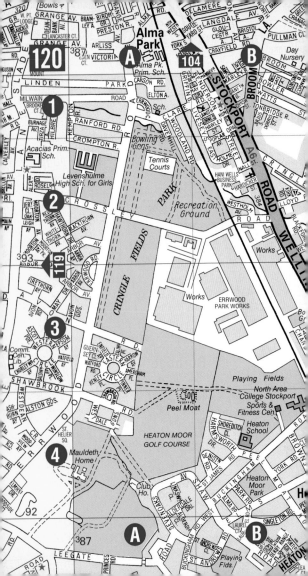

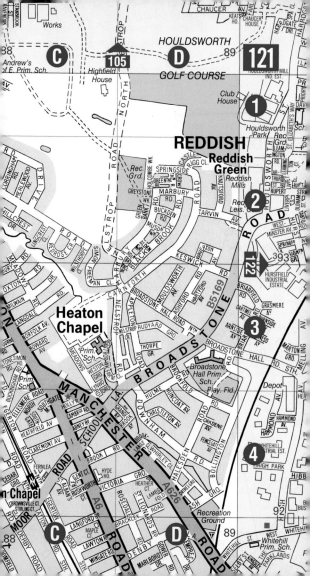

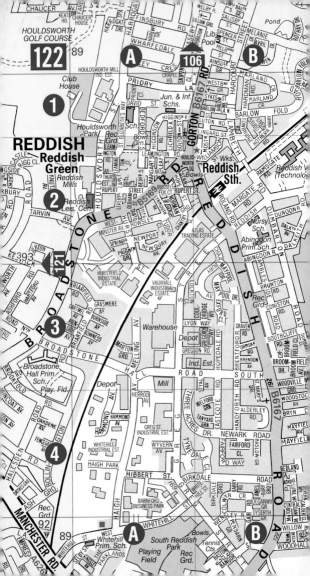

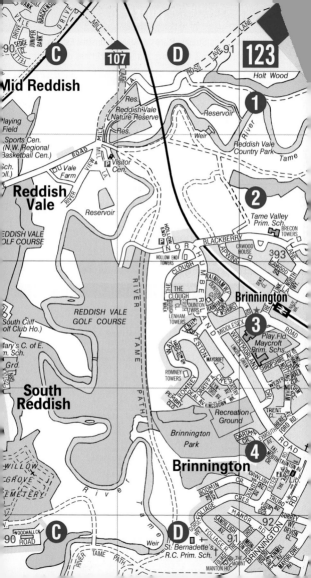

INDEX

Including Streets, Places & Areas, Industrial Estates,
Selected Flats & Walkways and Selected Places of Interest.

HOW TO USE THIS INDEX

1. Each street name is followed by its Posttown or Postal Locality and then by its
   map reference; e.g. Abbey Hey La. *Abb H* . . . . 3A **90** is in the Abbey Hey Postal
   Locality and is to be found in square 3A on page **90**.
   The page number being shown in bold type.

2. A strict alphabetical order is followed in which Av., Rd., St., etc. (though
   abbreviated) are read in full and as part of the street name;
   e.g. Alder Gro. appears after Alderglen Rd. but before Alderley Rd.

3. Streets and a selection of flats and walkways too small to be shown on the maps,
   appear in the index in *Italics* with the thoroughfare to which it is connected
   shown in brackets; e.g. *Abbeyfield Sq. Open* . . . . *3B 72 (off Herne St.)*

4. Places and areas are shown in the index in **blue type** and the map reference is to
   the actual map square in which the town centre or area is located and not to the
   place name shown on the map; e.g. **Abbey Hey** **2B 90**

5. An example of a selected place of interest is
   Abbotsfield Pk. Miniature Railway **2B 92**

6. Map references shown in brackets; e.g. Aberdaron Wlk. *M13* 1D **85** (5F **11**)
   refer to entries that also appear on the large scale pages **4-11**.

GENERAL ABBREVIATIONS

All : Alley	Ga : Gate
App : Approach	Gt : Great
Arc : Arcade	Grn : Green
Av : Avenue	Gro : Grove
Bk : Back	Ho : House
Boulevd : Boulevard	Ind : Industrial
Bri : Bridge	Info : Information
B'way : Broadway	Junct : Junction
Bldgs : Buildings	La : Lane
Bus : Business	Lit : Little
Cvn : Caravan	Lwr : Lower
Cen : Centre	Mc : Mac
Chu : Church	Mnr : Manor
Chyd : Churchyard	Mans : Mansions
Circ : Circle	Mkt : Market
Cir : Circus	Mdw : Meadow
Clo : Close	M : Mews
Comn : Common	Mt : Mount
Cotts : Cottages	Mus : Museum
Ct : Court	N : North
Cres : Crescent	Pal : Palace
Cft : Croft	Pde : Parade
Dri : Drive	Pk : Park
E : East	Pas : Passage
Embkmt : Embankment	Pl : Place
Est : Estate	Quad : Quadrant
Fld : Field	Res : Residential
Gdns : Gardens	Ri : Rise
Gth : Garth	Rd : Road

124 A-Z Mini Manchester & Salford

General Abbreviations

Shop : Shopping
S : South
Sq : Square
Sta : Station
St. : Street
Ter : Terrace
Trad : Trading
Up : Upper

Va : Vale
Vw : View
Vs : Villas
Vis : Visitors
Wlk : Walk
W : West
Yd : Yard

POSTTOWN AND POSTAL LOCALITY ABBREVIATIONS

Abb H : Abbey Hey
Ard : Ardwick
Ash L : Ashton-under-Lyne
Aud : Audenshaw
B'hth : Broadheath
Burn : Burnage
C'ton : Carrington
Chad : Chadderton
Chor H : Chorlton cum Hardy
Clay : Clayton
Col : Collyhurst
Crum : Crumpsall
Dent : Denton
Droy : Droylsden
Dun M : Dunham Massey
Eccl : Eccles
Fail : Failsworth
Fall : Fallowfield
Firs : Firswood
Gort : Gorton
Harp : Harpurhey
Heat C : Heaton Chapel
Hulme : Hulme
Kear : Kearsley
Lev : Levenshulme
Long : Longsight

Man S : Manchester Science Pk.
Midd : Middleton
Mile P : Miles Platting
Moss S : Moss Side
Most : Moston
New M : New Moston
Newt H : Newton Heath
Oldh : Oldham
Old T : Old Trafford
Open : Openshaw
P'wich : Prestwich
Redd : Reddish
Rom : Romiley
Rush : Rusholme
Sale : Sale
Salf : Salford
Stoc : Stockport
Stret : Stretford
Swin : Swinton
Traf P : Trafford Park
Urm : Urmston
Whal R : Whalley Range
W'fld : Whitefield
Wthtn : Withington
Wors : Worsley

A

Abberley Dri. *M40* 4D **25**
Abberton Rd. *M20* 3C **117**
Abbey Clo. *Stret* 1B **94**
Abbey Ct. *M18* 2A **90**
Abbey Ct. *Eccl* 1A **62**
Abbey Dri. *Swin* 1A **30**
Abbeyfield Sq. *Open* 3B **72**
              (off Herne St.)
Abbey Gro. *Chad* 2C **27**
Abbey Gro. *Eccl* 1A **62**
Abbey Hey 2B **90**
Abbey Hey La. *Abb H* 3A **90**
Abbey Hey La. *Open & M18* . . . 4A **74**
Abbey Lawn. *M16* 1B **98**
Abbey Rd. *Droy* 4B **58**
Abbey Rd. *Fail* 2D **43**
Abbey Rd. *Sale* 3C **111**

Abbeyville Wlk. *M15* 3A **84**
Abbeywood Av. *M18* 4A **90**
             (in two parts)
Abbotsbury Clo. *M12* 2A **88**
Abbots Clo. *Sale* 4B **112**
Abbots Ct. *Sale* 4B **112**
Abbotsfield Pk. Miniature
   Railway 2B **92**
Abbotsford Rd. *M21* 2B **98**
Abbotside Clo. *M16* 1D **99**
Abercarn Clo. *M8* 3C **37**
Abercrombie Ct. *Sale* 4B **112**
Aberdare Wlk. *M9* 1C **23**
         (off Brockford Dri.)
Aberdaron Wlk. *M13* 1D **85** (5F **11**)
Aberdeen. *Eccl* 1A **62**
         (off Monton La.)
Aberdeen Ho. *M15* 3D **85**
Aberdeen St. *M15* 3D **85**
Abergele Rd. *M14* 1C **119**

Abernant Clo. *M11* 2D **71**
Abersoch Av. *M14* 1C **119**
Abingdon Clo. *Chad* 2D **27**
Abingdon Rd. *Stoc* 2B **122**
Abingdon Rd. *Urm* 1A **94**
Abingdon St. *M1* 3C **69** (2C **10**)
Abinger Wlk. *M40* 3D **57**
Abney Rd. *Stoc* 4C **121**
Abraham Moss Leisure Cen. . . 2C **37**
Abram Clo. *M14* 3C **101**
Abram St. *Salf* 4D **33**
Absalom Dri. *M8* 2B **36**
Acacia Av. *Swin* 1A **46**
Acacia Dri. *Salf* 4D **47**
Acacia Gro. *Stoc* 4B **122**
Acacias. *Urm* 2A **94**
Academy Wlk. *M15* 3A **84**
Ace Mill. *Chad* 2B **26**
Acer Gro. *Salf* 3D **35**
Acheson St. *M18* 3D **89**
Ackers St. *M13* 3D **85**
Ackroyd Av. *M18* 2B **90**
Ackroyd St. *M11* 1A **90**
. . . . (in two parts)
Ackworth Rd. *Swin* 1A **30**
Acme Dri. *Swin* 2D **31**
Acomb St. *M14* 1D **101**
Acomb St. *M15* 3D **85**
Acorn Clo. *M19* 1D **119**
Acrefield Av. *Urm* 3B **94**
Acregate. *Urm* 2A **92**
Acregate Cotts. *Urm* 2A **92**
Acresfield Av. *Aud* 2D **75**
Acresfield Clo. *Swin* 4C **31**
Acresfield Rd. *Salf* 2B **48**
Acres Pass. *M21* 1A **114**
Acres Rd. *M21* 1A **114**
Acre St. *Chad* 4D **27**
Acre Top Rd. *M9* 1D **21**
Acton Av. *M40* 3B **56**
Acton Sq. *Salf* 1B **66** (4A **4**)
Adair St. *M1* 3A **70**
Adams Av. *M21* 3B **114**
Adamson Circ. *Urm* 1C **77**
Adamson Ho. *M16* 2B **82**
Adamson Rd. *Eccl* 3C **61**
Adamson Wlk. *M14* 1A **102**
Ada St. *M9* 1B **38**
Addenbrook Rd. *M8* 2A **52**
Addingham Clo. *M9* 1D **21**
Addington St. *M4* 1D **69** (3E **7**)
Addison Clo. *M13* 2A **86**
Addison Cres. *M16* 4B **82**
Addison Rd. *Stret* 1D **95**
Addison Rd. *Urm* 3D **93**
Addison Ter. *M14* 4B **86**
Adelaide St. *M8* 2B **52**
Adelaide St. *Eccl* 2D **61**
Adelaide St. *Swin* 3D **29**

Adelphi Ct. *Salf* 4D **51** (2C **4**)
Adelphi St. *Salf* 1D **67** (4C **4**)
Adelphi Ter. *Salf* 1C **67** (4B **4**)
Aden Clo. *M12* 3B **70**
Adlington Dri. *Stret* 4D **81**
Adlington St. *M12* 3B **70**
Admel Sq. *M15* 3C **85**
Adrian St. *M40* 3A **40**
Adscombe St. *M16* 4A **84**
Adstock Wlk. *M40* 4A **54**
Adstone Clo. *M4* 2B **70**
Adswood St. *M40* 1C **71**
Aegean Gdns. *Salf* 2C **51**
Agecroft Crematorium. *Salf* . . . 2D **33**
Agecroft Enterprise Pk. *Swin* . . 3B **32**
Agecroft Pk. Circ. *Swin* 3B **32**
Agecroft Rd. *Swin* 3A **32**
Agecroft Rd. E. *P'wich* 4A **18**
Agecroft Rd. W. *P'wich* 4D **17**
Agecroft Trad. Est. *Swin* 3C **33**
Agnes Clo. *Oldh* 2D **27**
Agnes Ct. *M14* 2A **118**
Agnes St. *M19* 2A **104**
Agnes St. *Salf* 3B **36**
Agnew Pl. *Salf* 3A **50**
Agnew Rd. *M18* 3C **89**
Aigburth Gro. *Stoc* 2A **106**
Ailsa Clo. *M40* 2B **54**
Ailsa Ct. *Salf* 2D **65**
. . . . (off Milford St.)
Aines St. *M12* 1A **88**
Ainsdale Av. *Salf* 1D **35**
Ainsdale Gro. *Stoc* 4B **106**
Ainsdale St. *M12* 2D **87**
Ainsford Rd. *M20* 4B **118**
Ainsley St. *M40* 2C **57**
Ainsty Rd. *M14* 4C **85**
Ainsworth Clo. *Dent* 1D **107**
Ainthorpe Wlk. *M40* 4A **54**
Aintree St. *M11* 2B **72**
Airton Clo. *M40* 4A **54**
Aitken St. *M19* 3C **105**
Aked Clo. *M12* 2B **86**
Alan Av. *Fail* 2B **58**
Alanbrooke Wlk. *M15* 3A **84**
Alan Rd. *M20* 3A **118**
Alan Turing Way. *M11* 4D **55**
Alba Clo. *Eccl* 2C **61**
Alban St. *Salf* 2D **51**
Albany Av. *M11* 1B **90**
Albany Rd. *M20* 3C **117**
Albany Ct. *Urm* 1B **92**
Albany Rd. *M21* 3B **98**
Albany Rd. *Eccl* 4B **44**
Albany Trad. Est. *M21* 3B **98**
Albany Way. *Salf* 4A **50**
Alba Way. *Stret* 3C **79**
Albemarle Av. *M20* 3C **117**
Albemarle Rd. *M21* 1A **114**

Albemarle Rd. *Swin* 3A **30**
Albemarle St. *M14* 4C **85**
Albert Av. *M18* 4B **90**
Albert Av. *P'wich* 1C **35**
Albert Av. *Urm* 2A **94**
Albert Fildes Wlk. *M8* 3B **36**
Albert Gdns. *M40* 2D **57**
Albert Gro. *M12* 4A **88**
(in two parts)
Albert Park 4C **117**
Albert Pk. Rd. *Salf* 2C **51**
Albert Pl. *M13* 1D **103**
Albert Rd. *M19* 3D **103**
Albert Rd. *Eccl* 4B **46**
Albert Sq. *M2* 2B **68** (1B **10**)
(in two parts)
Albert St. *M11* 2D **71**
Albert St. *Chad* 3D **27**
Albert St. *Droy* 2D **75**
Albert St. *Eccl* 1B **62**
Albert St. *Oldh* 1D **43**
Albert St. *P'wich* 2C **19**
Albert St. W. *Fail* 4D **41**
Albert St. Works. *Droy* 2D **75**
Albine St. *M40* 2D **39**
Albion Dri. *Droy* 1C **75**
Albion Fold. *Droy* 1C **75**
Albion Pl. *P'wich* 2A **18**
Albion Pl. *Salf* (M5) 1C **67** (4A **4**)
Albion Pl. *Salf* (M7) 2C **51**
Albion Rd. *M14* 3A **102**
Albion St. *M1* 4B **68** (4A **10**)
Albion St. *Fail* 3A **42**
Albion St. *Old T* 4D **83**
Albion St. *Swin* 2C **31**
Albion Towers. *Salf* 1B **66**
Albion Trad. Est. *Salf* 3A **50**
Albion Way. *Salf* 2B **66**
Albyns Av. *M8* 3C **37**
Alcester St. *Chad* 3C **27**
Alcester Wlk. *M9* 1A **22**
Alconbury Ct. *Droy* 3D **75**
(off Williamson La.)
Aldborough Clo. *M20* 3D **117**
Aldbourne Clo. *M40* 2B **54**
Aldcroft St. *M18* 2B **90**
Alden Wlk. *Stoc* 2D **121**
Alder Ct. *M8* 1B **36**
Alderdale Clo. *Stoc* 4A **120**
Alderdale Dri. *Droy* 1A **74**
Alderdale Dri. *Stoc* 4A **120**
Alder Dri. *Swin* 1C **29**
Alder Edge. *M21* 3D **97**
Alderfield Ho. *M21* 3D **97**
Alderfield Rd. *M21* 3D **97**
Alderford Pde. *M8* 4B **36**
(in two parts)
Alder Forest 3A **44**
Alder Forest Av. *Eccl* 3A **44**

Aldergate Ct. *Swin* 3C **29**
Aldergien Rd. *M8* 1B **52**
Alder Gro. *Stret* 2C **97**
Alderley Rd. *Stoc* 4B **122**
Alderley Rd. *Urm* 2A **92**
Alderman Sq. *M12* 3C **71**
Aldermary Rd. *M21* 4D **115**
Aldermoor Clo. *M11* 3C **73**
Alder Rd. *Fail* 2B **58**
Aldershot Wlk. *M11* 2D **71**
Alderside Rd. *M9* 2B **38**
Aldersley Av. *M9* 1D **21**
Alderson St. *Salf* 3A **50**
Alder St. *Eccl* 3A **44**
Alder St. *Salf* 1D **65**
Alderwood Wlk. *M8* 4B **36**
(off Dalmain Clo.)
Aldham Av. *M40* 3C **57**
Aldow Ind. Pk. *M12* 3A **70**
Aldred Clo. *M8* 4D **37**
Aldred St. *Eccl* 2C **61**
Aldred St. *Fail* 3A **42**
Aldred St. *Salf* 1B **66** (4A **4**)
Aldridge Wlk. *M11* 3D **71**
Aldsworth Dri. *M40* 1C **55**
Aldwych Av. *M14* 1D **101**
Aldwyn Pk. Rd. *Aud* 3D **75**
Alexander Av. *Fail* 2C **43**
Alexander Gdns. *Salf* 3D **51** (1D **5**)
Alexander Ho. *M16* 4A **82**
Alexander St. *Salf* 1C **65**
Alexandra Av. *M14* 2B **100**
Alexandra Ct. *Salf* 3A **66**
(off Rowland St.)
Alexandra Dri. *M19* 2D **119**
Alexandra Ho. *Eccl* 2C **61**
(off Liverpool Rd.)
Alexandra Park 2A **100**
Alexandra Rd. *M16* 1A **100**
Alexandra Rd. *Eccl* 2B **60**
Alexandra Rd. S. *M16* 1A **100**
Alexandra St. *Salf* 4D **51** (1D **5**)
Alexandra Ter. *M19* 3A **104**
Alexandra Ter. *Sale* 3C **111**
Alexandra, The. *M14* 1B **118**
Alford Av. *M20* 1C **117**
Alford Rd. *Stoc* 3B **120**
Alford St. *Oldh* 4D **27**
Alfred Av. *Wors* 3A **28**
Alfred James Clo. *M40* 4A **54**
Alfred St. *M9* 2B **38**
Alfred St. *Eccl* 4D **45**
Alfred St. *Fail* 2B **42**
Alfreton Wlk. *M40* 4A **40**
(off Thorpebrook Rd.)
Algernon St. *Eccl* 4D **45**
Algernon St. *Swin* 2D **29**
Alice St. *Swin* 2D **31**
Alison Kelly Clo. *M9* 2D **39**

Alison St. *M14* 1B **100**
Alker Rd. *M40* 4B **54**
Alkrington Ct. *Midd* 1B **24**
Allams St. *M11* 1C **71**
Allan Ct. *M21* 2A **114**
Allandale Cl. *Salf* 1A **36**
Allandale Rd. *M19* 3D **103**
Allan Roberts Clo. *M9* 1B **38**
Alldis Clo. *M12* 3C **87**
Allenby Rd. *Swin* 4C **29**
Allenby Wlk. *M40* 2A **54**
Allendale Wlk. *Salf* 1D **67** (3C **4**)
Allen Rd. *Urm* 2B **94**
Allerford St. *M16* 4A **84**
Allerton Wlk. *M13* 2D **85**
Allesley Dri. *Salf* 2A **52**
Allingham St. *M13* 4C **87**
Allington Dri. *Eccl* 3A **46**
Alliott Wlk. *M15* 3A **84**
Allison Gro. *Eccl* 2B **60**
Allison St. *M8* 2B **52**
Alloway Wlk. *M40* 4A **40**
All Saints Ct. *Stret* 2D **95**
All Saints St. *M40* 2C **57**
Allwood St. *Salf* 2C **67** (5B **4**)
Alma Ct. *M15* 4A **84**
Alma Park 4A **104**
Alma Rd. *M19* 4A **104**
Alma Rd. *Stoc* 4B **120**
Alma St. *Eccl* 2B **62**
Alma St. *Kear* 1B **12**
Alminstone Clo. *M40* 3D **57**
Almond Clo. *Fail* 1B **58**
Almond Clo. *Salf* 4A **50**
Almond Dri. *Sale* 3B **110**
Almond St. *M40* 3D **53** (1F **7**)
Alms Hill Rd. *M8* 4C **37**
Alness Rd. *M16* 1A **100**
Alnwick Rd. *M9* 1B **22**
Alperton Wlk. *M40* 3D **57**
Alphagate Dri. *Dent* 1D **107**
Alpha Pl. *M15* 4A **68** (4F **9**)
Alpha Rd. *Stret* 3A **96**
Alpha St. *Open* 4A **74**
Alpha St. *Salf* 4D **49**
Alpha St. W. *Salf* 4C **49**
Alphonsus St. *M16* 4C **83**
Alpine St. *M11* 1B **72**
Alpington Wlk. *M40* 4C **25**
Alport Av. *M16* 2C **99**
Alresford Rd. *Midd* 1D **23**
Alresford Rd. *Salf* 2B **48**
Alsager Clo. *M21* 3B **114**
Alsham Wlk. *M8* 1C **53**
Alsop Av. *Salf* 3B **34**
Alston Av. *Stret* 1D **95**
Alstone Rd. *Stoc* 3C **121**
Alston Gdns. *M19* 4D **119**
Alston Rd. *M18* 3A **90**

Altair Pl. *Salf* 3C **51**
Altcar Gro. *Stoc* 2A **106**
Altham Wlk. *M40* 4A **40**
         (off Craiglands Av.)
Althorpe Wlk. *M40* 3D **57**
Alton Sq. *Open* 1A **90**
Alton Towers. *M16* 3D **99**
Altrincham St. *M1* . . 3D **69** (3E **11**)
         (in two parts)
Alvan Sq. *M11* 1A **90**
Alvaston Rd. *M18* 4A **90**
Alveley Av. *M20* 4A **118**
Alverstone Rd. *M20* 3A **118**
Alworth Rd. *M9* 1B **22**
Alwyn Dri. *M13* 4C **87**
Amberley Rd. *Sale* 4A **110**
Amber St. *M4* 1C **69** (3D **7**)
Ambleside Rd. *Stoc* 3B **122**
Ambleside Wlk. *M9* 4A **24**
Ambrose Dri. *M20* 4A **116**
Ambrose Gdns. *M20* 4A **116**
Ambrose St. *M12* 1A **88**
Ambush St. *M11* 4B **74**
Amersham Clo. *Urm* 3B **76**
Amersham Pl. *M19* 3A **120**
Amersham St. *Salf* 2D **65**
Amesbury Gro. *Stoc* 4B **122**
Amesbury Rd. *M9* 2C **23**
Amherst Rd. *M20 & M14* . . . 2A **118**
Amory St. *M12* 3A **70**
Amos Av. *M40* 3C **57**
Amos St. *M9* 3D **39**
Amos St. *Salf* 1C **65**
Ampney Clo. *Eccl* 2B **60**
Amport Wlk. *M40* 4C **25**
Amwell St. *M8* 3D **37**
Anaconda Dri. *Salf* 4A **52** (2E **5**)
Ancaster Wlk. *M40* 4C **25**
Anchorage Quay. *Salf* 3A **66**
Anchorage Rd. *Urm* 3C **95**
Anchorage Wlk. *M18* 2C **89**
Anchor Clo. *M19* 3C **105**
Anchor Ct. *M8* 1B **36**
Anchorside Clo. *M21* 2B **114**
Ancoats. 1A **70** (5F **7**)
Ancoats Gro. *M4* 2B **70**
Ancoats Gro. N. *M4* 2B **70**
Ancroft St. *M15* 2A **84**
Andoc Av. *Eccl* 2C **63**
Andover Av. *Midd* 1B **24**
Andover St. *Eccl* 2C **61**
Andover Wlk. *M8* 1C **37**
Andre St. *M11* 1C **73**
Andrew Ct. *M20* 3D **117**
Andrew Rd. *M9* 1B **38**
Andrew's Brow. *M40* 3D **57**
Andrew St. *Fail* 2A **42**
Andy Nicholson Wlk. *M9* . . . 2D **39**
Anfield Rd. *M40* 1D **41**

Anfield Rd. *Sale* 4A **112**
Angela St. *M15*. 1D **83** (5D **9**)
Angel St. *M4*. 4C **53** (2D **7**)
Angel Trad. Est. *M4* 2D **7**
Angleside Av. *M19*. 4C **119**
Angora Dri. *Salf*. 4D **51** (2C **4**)
Aniline St. *M11* 2B **72**
Anita St. *M4*. 1D **69** (3F **7**)
Annable Rd. *M18*. 2A **90**
Annable Rd. *Droy*. 2D **75**
Annald Sq. *Droy*. 3C **75**
Anne Nuttall Rd. *M15* . . 1D **83** (5D **9**)
Annesley Ct. *Eccl*. 1A **62**
Annesley Gdns. *M18* 2D **89**
Annesley Rd. *M40*. 1A **42**
Annie Darby Ct. *M9* 3B **38**
Annie St. *Salf*. 1C **65**
Annisdale Clo. *Eccl*. 1B **60**
Annis St. *M9*. 2C **39**
Anscombe Clo. *M40*. 4B **54**
Anscombe Wlk. *M40* 4B **54**
Ansdell Av. *M21*. 1B **114**
Ansdell Dri. *Droy* 1A **74**
Ansdell Rd. *Stoc* 3C **107**
Ansdell St. *M8*. 3C **37**
Ansell Clo. *M18*. 2D **89**
Ansford Wlk. *M9* 4A **38**
    (off Hendham Va.)
Ansleigh Av. *M8*. 1C **37**
Anslow Clo. *M40* 2B **54**
Anson Av. *Swin* 1A **46**
Anson Rd. *M14* 4B **86**
Anson Rd. *Dent* 2C **107**
Anson Rd. *Swin*. 1A **46**
Anson St. *Eccl*. 4B **44**
Anson Vw. *M14* 1B **102**
Answell Av. *M8* 4C **21**
Antares Av. *Salf* 4D **51** (1C **4**)
Anthistle Ct. *Salf* 2B **64**
Anthony Clo. *M12* 1C **87**
Antilles Clo. *M12* 4A **88**
Anton Wlk. *M9*. 3B **38**
Apollo Theatre 2A **86**
Apollo Wlk. *M12* 2A **88**
Apperley Grange. *Eccl* 3A **46**
Appian Way. *Salf & Man*. 1A **52**
Appleby Av. *M12* 1B **104**
Appleby Lodge. *M14* 2B **102**
Applecross Wlk. *Open* 3C **73**
Appleford Dri. *M8* 1D **53**
Appleton Rd. *Stoc* 3D **121**
Apple Tree Ct. *Salf* 1A **66**
Apple Tree Wlk. *Sale*. 4C **109**
Apprentice Ct. *M9* 2C **39**
Apsley Gro. *M12* 2A **86**
Aquarius La. *Salf* 3C **51**
Aquarius St. *M15*. 3C **85**
Arbor Av. *M19*. 2D **119**
Arbor Dri. *M19*. 2D **119**

Arbor Gro. *Droy*. 4C **59**
Arbory Av. *M40*. 2B **40**
Arbour Clo. *Salf*. 4D **49**
Arbroath St. *M11*. 2D **73**
Arcade, The. *Stoc*. 4D **123**
Arcadia Sports Cen. 3A **104**
Archer Pl. *Urm*. 1B **94**
Archer St. *M11* 1A **72**
Archie St. *Salf* 1A **82**
Arcon Dri. *M16* 1A **100**
Ardale Av. *M40* 4C **25**
Ardcombe Av. *M9* 1A **22**
Arden Wlk. *M13* 2A **86**
Arden Av. *Midd* 1B **24**
Arden Ct. *M21* 2B **114**
Arden Gro. *M40*. 1C **41**
Ardens Clo. *Swin* 4D **13**
Arden St. *Chad* 3C **27**
Ardent Way. *P'wich* 1B **34**
Arden Wlk. *Sale* 4C **109**
Ardern Rd. *M8*. 4B **20**
Ardwick 4B **70**
Ardwick Grn. N. *M12* . . . 4A **70** (4F **11**)
Ardwick Grn. S. *M13* . . . 4A **70** (4F **11**)
Ardwick Sports Hall 3C **87**
Argosy Dri. *Eccl* 4A **60**
Argus St. *Oldh* 4D **27**
Argyle Av. *M14* 4C **87**
Argyle St. *M18*. 2D **89**
Argyle St. *Droy* 2C **75**
Argyle St. *Swin* 3A **30**
Argyll Av. *Stret*. 2D **95**
Argyll Clo. *Fail*. 3D **43**
Argyll Pk. Rd. *Fail* 3D **43**
Argyll Rd. *Chad* 3B **26**
Arkendale Clo. *Fail*. 3D **43**
Arkholme Wlk. *M40* 3B **40**
Arkley Wlk. *M13* 2D **85** (5F **11**)
Ark St. *M19* 2A **104**
Arkwright Way. *M4* 1C **69** (4C **6**)
    (off Arndale Shop. Cen.)
Arley Av. *M20* 4B **116**
Arley Ho. *Salf*. 3D **35**
Arley Moss Wlk. *M13*. . . 1D **85** (5F **11**)
Arlington Av. *P'wich*. 4C **19**
Arlington Av. *Swin*. 1D **45**
Arlington Rd. *Stret*. 2D **95**
Arlington St. *M8*. 2B **36**
Arlington St. *Salf* 1D **67** (3D **5**)
Arliss Av. *M19* 4A **104**
Armadale Av. *M9* 2A **24**
Armitage Cen. 3C **103**
Armitage Av. *M21* 4A **48**
Armitage Ho. *Salf*. 4A **48**
Armitage Owen Wlk. *M40*. 3A **40**
Armitage St. *Eccl*. 2C **61**
Armour Pl. *M9*. 4A **22**
Arndale Shop. Cen. *M4* . . 1C **69** (4C **6**)
Arndale Shop. Cen. *Stret* 3A **96**
Arnesby Av. *Sale* 4C **113**

Arne St. *Chad.*	1C **27**
Arnfield Rd. *M20*	3D **117**
Arnold Ct. *M16.*	3A **100**
Arnold Dri. *Droy.*	2C **75**
Arnold Rd. *M16*	3A **100**
Arnott Cres. *M15*	3B **84**
Arnside Av. *Stoc*	3D **121**
Arnside Dri. *Salf.*	4D **47**
Arnside Gro. *Sale.*	3D **111**
Arnside St. *M14.*	1D **101**
Arosa Ct. *M20*	2A **118**
Arran Av. *Stret*	2C **95**
Arrandale Ct. *Urm*	1D **93**
Arran Gdns. *Urm*	3C **77**
(in three parts)	
Arran St. *M40*	2D **39**
Arran St. *Salf.*	1D **51**
Arras Gro. *Dent*	1B **106**
Arreton Sq. *M14*	1B **102**
Arrowfield Rd. *M21*	2D **115**
Arrowsmith Wlk. M11	*2D **71***
(off Redfield Clo.)	
Arrow St. *Salf*	2D **51**
Arthur Millwood Ct.	
Salf	2D **67** (5D **5**)
Arthur Rd. *M16*	1C **99**
Arthur St. *Eccl*	2C **61**
Arthur St. *P'wich*	2D **17**
Arthur St. *Stoc.*	2A **122**
(Houldsworth St.)	
Arthur St. *Stoc.*	2A **122**
(Margaret St.)	
Arthur St. *Swin*	3D **29**
(in two parts)	
Arthur Ter. *Stoc.*	2A **122**
Artillery St. *M3*	3A **68** (2F **9**)
Arundale Av. *M16.*	3A **100**
Arundale Ct. M16	*3A **100***
(off Arundale Av.)	
Arundel Ct. *M9.*	1C **21**
Arundel St. *M15*	4D **67** (4D **9**)
Arundel St. *Swin*	1C **29**
Asbury Ct. *Eccl*	4C **45**
Ascension Rd. *Salf.*	3D **51**
Ascot Av. *Stret*	1D **97**
Ascot M. *Salf.*	1D **51**
Ascot Pde. *M19*	3D **119**
Ascot Rd. *M40.*	3B **56**
Ascot Wlk. *Salf*	2A **50**
Asgard Dri. *Salf.*	3C **67** (3B **8**)
Asgard Gro. *Salf*	3C **67** (3B **8**)
Ashbourne Gro. *Salf.*	3A **36**
Ashbourne Rd. *Eccl*	2A **62**
Ashbourne Rd. *Salf*	2A **48**
Ashbourne Rd. *Stret.*	4C **79**
Ashbridge. *Traf P*	2D **79**
(in two parts)	
Ashbridge Rd. *Fail*	1D **59**
Ashbrook Av. *Dent*	1D **107**
Ashbrook Clo. *Dent*	1D **107**
Ashbrook Farm Clo. *Stoc*	2B **106**
Ashbrook La. *Stoc*	2B **106**
Ashbrook St. *Open*	4C **75**
Ashburn Av. *M19.*	4D **119**
Ashburne Ho. M14.	*4B **86***
(off Conyngham Rd.)	
Ashburton Rd. W.	
Urm & Traf P	1D **77**
Ashbury Pl. *M40*	3C **55**
Ashcombe Wlk. M11	*2D **71***
(off Aldershot Wlk.)	
Ashcroft Av. *Salf*	3C **49**
Ashcroft St. *Chad.*	1C **27**
Ashdale Clo. *Stoc.*	4B **122**
Ashdale Cres. *Droy.*	2B **74**
Ashdale Dri. *M20.*	4B **118**
Ashdene Rd. *M20.*	3B **118**
Ashdown Av. *M9*	2B **22**
Ashdown Dri. *Swin*	4C **31**
Ashdown Gro. *M9*	2B **22**
Ashdown Ter. *M9.*	2B **22**
Ash Dri. *Swin.*	4C **13**
Ashenhurst Ct. *M9.*	3C **21**
Ashfell Ct. *M32.*	3D **97**
Ashfield Clo. *Salf.*	4C **49**
Ashfield Dri. *M40.*	3D **57**
Ashfield Gro. *M18*	4B **90**
Ashfield Rd. *M13.*	1C **103**
Ashfield Rd. *Sale*	4D **111**
Ashfield Rd. *Urm*	2D **93**
Ashfield Sq. *Droy.*	2B **74**
Ashfield St. *Oldh*	3D **27**
Ashford. *Sale*	4C **109**
Ashford Av. *Eccl.*	3C **61**
Ashford Av. *Stoc*	2B **106**
Ashford Av. *Swin*	4C **29**
Ashford Av. *M20*	2C **117**
Ashford Rd. *Stoc.*	3D **121**
Ashgill Wlk. M9	*3C **39***
(off Fernclough Rd.)	
Ash Gro. *M14*	4C **87**
Ash Gro. *Droy.*	3C **75**
Ash Gro. *Stoc.*	4D **121**
Ash Gro. *Stret*	4A **96**
Ash Gro. *Swin*	2D **45**
Ashill Wlk. *M3*	3A **68** (2F **9**)
Ashkirk St. *M18.*	3D **89**
Ashlands. *Sale*	4C **111**
Ashlands Av. *M40*	1C **41**
Ashlands Av. *Swin*	1C **45**
Ashlar Dri. *M12*	3B **70**
Ashleigh Gdns. M9.	*1A **38***
(off Slack Rd.)	
Ashley Av. *M16*	4D **83**
Ashley Av. *Swin.*	4D **29**
Ashley Ct. *M40*	1B **42**
Ashley Ct. *Swin*	4B **14**
Ashley Ct. Dri. *M40*	1B **42**

Ashley Cres. *Swin* 3D **29**
Ashley Dri. *Swin* 3D **29**
Ashley La. *M9* 2D **39**
Ashley Rd. *Droy* 1A **74**
Ashley St. *M4* 4D **53** (2E **7**)
Ashley St. *Salf* 1C **65**
Ashlyn Gro. *M14* 1B **118**
Ashmill Wlk. *M9* 4A **38**
Ashover Av. *M12* 2D **87**
Ashover St. *Stret* 1C **97**
Ashridge Dri. *Eccl* 3C **61**
Ash Rd. *Dent* 1B **106**
Ash Rd. *Droy* 1B **74**
Ash St. *Fail* 2A **42**
Ash St. *Harp* 3B **38**
Ash St. *Salf* 1D **65**
Ashton Cres. *Chad* 3C **27**
Ashton La. *Sale* 4B **110**
Ashton New Rd. *M11* 2C **71**
Ashton Old Rd. *M12 & M11* 3B **70**
Ashton Rd. *M9* 1B **22**
Ashton Rd. *Droy* 2D **75**
Ashton Rd. *Fail* 4D **43**
Ashton Rd. E. *Fail* 2B **42**
Ashton Rd. W. *Fail* 3A **42**
Ashton St. *M9* 2D **39**
Ashton St. *Chad* 3C **27**
Ashton upon Mersey 4D **109**
Ash Tree Av. *Droy* 1B **74**
Ash Tree Gro. *Droy* 4B **58**
Ash Tree Rd. *M8* 1C **37**
Ashurst *M11* 1B **72**
Ashville Ter. *M40* 1D **39**
Ash Wlk. *Sale* 4D **109**
Ashwater Wlk. *M9* 1C **23**
(off Brockford Dri.)
Ashwin Wlk. *M8* 4B **36**
(off Dalmain Clo.)
Ashwood Av. *M20* 4A **116**
Ashwood Av. *Dent* 1C **107**
Ashworth Clo. *Chad* 2D **27**
Ashworth St. *Fail* 1D **57**
Ashworth Vw. *Salf* 1B **82**
(off Ordsall Dri.)
Askett Clo. *M40* 1D **57**
Askrigg Wlk. *M13* 4D **87**
Aspinal St. *M14* 1A **102**
Aspull Wlk. *M13* 2A **86**
Asquith Rd. *M19* 3D **119**
Asquith St. *Stoc* 3B **106**
Assheton Cres. *M40* 3D **57**
Assheton Rd. *M40* 3D **57**
Assisi Gdns. *M12* 2B **88**
Astan Av. *Droy* 4D **57**
Astbury Av. *M21* 4C **115**
Astley St. *M11* 2C **73**
(in two parts)

Aston Av. *M14* 2B **100**
Astor Rd. *M19* 2C **119**
Astor Rd. *Salf* 2D **63**
Astra Bus. Pk. *Traf P* 3B **62**
Astral M. *M14* 1B **102**
Athenian Gdns. *Salf* 2C **51**
Atherfield Clo. *M18* 2B **90**
Atherley Gro. *M40 & Chad* 4B **26**
Atherstone Av. *M8* 4C **21**
Atherton Clo. *Fail* 2D **59**
Atherton St. *M3* 2A **68** (1E **9**)
Atherton St. *Eccl* 2B **60**
Atherton Way. *Eccl* 2B **60**
Athlone Av. *M40* 2A **40**
Athole St. *Salf* 2D **65**
Atholl Av. *Stret* 2C **95**
Athol Rd. *M16* 3A **100**
Athol St. *M18* 1A **106**
Athol St. *Eccl* 2B **60**
Athos Wlk. *M40* 4C **25**
Atkinson Ho. *Sale* 4D **111**
Atkinson Rd. *Sale* 3C **111**
Atkinson Rd. *Urm* 2D **93**
Atkinson St. *M3* 2A **68** (1F **9**)
Atlantic Wlk. *M11* 2D **71**
(off Seabright Wlk.)
Atlas Trad. Est. *Stoc* 2B **122**
Attercliffe Rd. *M21* 2A **114**
Attewell St. *Open* 3A **72**
Attleboro Rd. *M40* 3A **40**
Attlee Way. *M12* 2C **71**
Attwood St. *M12* 1A **104**
Atwood St. *M1* 3C **69** (3C **10**)
Aubrey Rd. *M14* 2C **119**
Aubrey St. *Salf* 4A **66**
Auburn Dri. *Urm* 3A **94**
Auburn Rd. *M16* 4B **82**
Auburn St. *M1* 2D **69** (1E **11**)
Auckland Dri. *Salf* 2A **50**
Auckland Rd. *M19* 4D **103**
Audax Wlk. *M40* 3B **56**
Auden Clo. *M11* 2D **73**
Auden Ct. *M11* 2D **73**
(off Auden Clo.)
Audenshaw Hall Gro. *Aud* 4D **75**
Audenshaw Rd. *Aud* 4D **75**
(in two parts)
Audlem Clo. *M40* 1B **70**
Audley Av. *Stret* 4B **78**
Audley Rd. *M19* 2B **104**
Audrey Av. *M18* 3A **90**
Audrey St. *M9* 3D **39**
Augustine Webster Clo. *M9* . . . 2C **39**
Augustus St. *M3* 3C **53** (1C **6**)
Augustus Way. *M15* 4D **83**
Austen Rd. *Eccl* 2D **61**
Auster Clo. *M14* 4C **101**
Austin Gro. *M19* 4D **103**
Avebury Clo. *Salf* 4B **36**

Avenham Clo. *M15* 3A **84**
Avenue, The. *Eccl.* 2D **61**
Avenue, The. *Salf.* 2C **51**
Averill St. *M40* 2D **57**
Aveson Av. *M21* 3B **114**
Avian Clo. *Eccl.* 4A **60**
Avian Dri. *M14* 4D **101**
Aviemore Wlk. *M11* 3C **73**
Avonbrook Dri. *M40* 4B **26**
Avon Cotts. *P'wich* 1C **17**
Avon Ct. *M15* 2D **83**
Avondale. *Swin* 4C **15**
Avondale Cres. *Urm* 1C **93**
Avondale Dri. *Salf* 2D **47**
Avondale Rd. *Stret* 4C **81**
Avondale St. *M8* 3C **37**
Avon Gdns. *M19* 3A **120**
Avonlea Dri. *M19* 3C **119**
Avonlea Rd. *Droy* 1A **74**
Avon Rd. *M19* 3D **119**
Avon Rd. *Kear* 1B **12**
Avril Clo. *Stoc* 4B **106**
Avro Clo. *M14* 3D **101**
Avroe Rd. *Eccl* 4A **60**
Axbridge Wlk. *M40* 1B **70**
Axford Clo. *Salf* 4B **36**
Axon Sq. *M16* 4B **84**
Aycliffe Av. *Chor H.* 4D **115**
Aylcliffe Gro. *Long* 1C **103**
Aylesbury Av. *Urm* 4A **78**
Aylesbury Clo. *Salf* 2A **66**
Aylesby Av. *M18* 4B **88**
Aylesby Ct. *M21* 3D **99**
Aylesford Rd. *M14* 1B **102**
Aylestone Wlk. *M40* 3A **40**
Aylsham M. *Swin* 2D **45**
Ayres Rd. *M16* 4A **82**
Ayrshire Rd. *Salf* 1B **50**
Aysgarth Av. *M18* 3A **90**
Ayton Ct. *M16* 4D **83**
Ayton Gro. *M14* 4C **87**
Aytoun St. *M1* 2C **69** (1D **11**)
Azalea Av. *M18* 2D **89**

Bk. Acton St. *M1* 3D **69** (2E **11**)
Bk. Ashley St. *M4* 4D **53** (2E **7**)
Bk. Balloon St. *M4* 1C **69** (3C **6**)
Bk. Bank St. *M8* 3C **53**
Bk. Bridge St. *M3* 2B **68** (5A **6**)
Bk. Camp St. *Salf* 2D **51**
Bk. Chapel St. *M19* 3A **104**
Bk. Chapel St. *Eccl* 1B **62**
Bk. China La. *M1* 2D **69** (1E **11**)
Bk. College Land. *Salf* 4A **6**
Bk. Dashwood Rd. *P'wich* 1A **18**
Bk. Deacon's Dri. *Salf* 1B **48**

Bk. Deyne Av. *P'wich* 2B **18**
Bk. Duncan St. *Salf* 3C **35**
Bk. Elsworth St. *M3* 4C **53** (1C **6**)
Bk. Federation St. *P'wich* 1D **17**
Backford Wlk. *M20* 2C **117**
Bk. Garden St. *Salf* 1A **68** (4F **5**)
Bk. George St. *M1* 3C **69** (2C **10**)
                              (in two parts)
Bk. Hamilton St. *Salf* 3D **35**
Bk. Hampson St. *M40* 3B **54**
Bk. Hilton St. *Salf.* 3D **35**
Bk. Hope St. *Salf* 3D **35**
Bk. Howe St. *Salf.* 3C **35**
Bk. Hulme St. *Salf.* 2C **67** (5B **4**)
Backmill St. *M4* 2A **70**
Back Piccadilly.
    M4 & M1. . . . . . . 2C **69** (5D **7**)
Bk. Pool Fold. *M2* 2B **68** (5B **6**)
Bk. Quay St. *M3* 2A **68** (1E **9**)
Bk. Red Bank. *M4* 4C **53** (1D **7**)
Bk. Roman Rd. *Salf* 1A **52**
Bk. St Georges Rd. *M4* . . 4D **53** (2F **7**)
Bk. South Pde. *M3* 2B **68** (5A **6**)
Bk. Spear St. *M1* 1D **69** (4E **7**)
Back St. *P'wich* 1D **17**
Bk. Thomas St. *M4* 1C **69** (4D **7**)
Backton Pl. *M40.* 3B **54**
Bk. Tootal Rd. *Salf* 1B **64**
Bk. Turner St. *M4* 1C **69** (4D **7**)
Bacup St. *M40.* 2A **40**
Badby Clo. *M4* 2B **70**
Baden St. *M11.* 3C **71**
Badminton Rd. *M21* 3C **99**
Bagot St. *M11* 1C **73**
Bagot St. *Swin* 1C **29**
Baguley St. *Droy* 2D **75**
Baildon St. *M40.* 1A **40**
Bailey Rd. *Traf P* 4C **63**
Bailey St. *M11.* 2D **73**
Bailey St. *P'wich* 1C **19**
Bails, The. *Salf.* 1C **51**
Bainbridge Clo. *M12.* 2B **86**
Bain St. *Swin* 3B **30**
Bainton Wlk. *M9* 1A **22**
Baird St. *M1* 3D **69** (2F **11**)
Bakewell Rd. *Droy* 1A **74**
Bakewell Rd. *Eccl.* 3C **61**
Bakewell Rd. *Stret* 1C **95**
Bakewell St. *M18.* 4C **89**
Bala Clo. *Salf.* 1A **66**
Baldwin Rd. *M19* 3D **119**
Bale St. *M2.* 3B **68** (2B **10**)
Balfour Gro. *Stoc* 3B **106**
Balfour Rd. *Urm.* 2B **92**
Balfour St. *M8.* 2C **37**
Balfour St. *Salf.* 1A **50**
Balham Wlk. *M12* 2D **87**
Ballantine St. *M40.* 3C **57**
Ballater Av. *Urm.* 3A **92**

Ballater Wlk. *M8*. 3B **36**
Ballbrook Av. *M20* 4C **117**
Ballbrook Ct. *M20* 4D **117**
Balleratt St. *M19* 3A **104**
Balliol Ct. *Sale* 4D **109**
Balliol St. *M8* 2C **37**
Balliol St. *Swin* 2A **30**
Balloon La. *M4* 3C **6**
Balloon St. *M4* 1C **69** (3C **6**)
Balmain Av. *M18* 1C **105**
Balmain Rd. *Urm* 1B **92**
Balmfield St. *M8* 2C **53**
Balmforth St. *M15* 4D **67** (4D **9**)
Balmoral Av. *Stret* 1B **96**
Balmoral Av. *Urm* 3B **92**
Balmoral Ct. *M8* 1B **20**
Balmoral Dri. *Dent* 4C **91**
Balmoral Grange. *P'wich* . . 3A **20**
Balmoral Ho. *Eccl.* 1C **61**
　　　　　(off Queen Victoria St.)
Balmoral Rd. *M14* 4B **102**
Balmoral Rd. *Swin* 4C **15**
Balmoral Rd. *Urm* 3A **92**
Balmoral St. *M18* 4C **89**
Balsam Clo. *M13* 1A **86** (5F **11**)
Baltic St. *Salf* 1C **65**
Baltimore St. *M40* 2D **55**
Bamford Rd. *M9* 1B **22**
Bamford St. *M11* 1B **72**
Banbury M. *Swin* 1D **31**
Banbury Rd. *Fail* 3A **58**
Banbury Rd. *Midd* 1D **23**
Bancroft Rd. *Swin* 1A **30**
Banff Rd. *M14* 4A **86**
Bangor Rd. *M15* 3D **83**
Bangor St. *Stoc* 4B **122**
Bank Bri. Rd. *M11* 4B **56**
Bankfield Av. *M13* 1C **103**
Bankfield Av. *Droy* 1C **75**
Bankfield Rd. *Sale* 3A **110**
Bankfoot Wlk. *M8* 2C **53**
　　　　　(off Alderglen Rd.)
Bankhall Wlk. *M9* 3C **39**
　　　　　(off Broadwell Dri.)
Bankhirst Clo. *Crum* 1C **37**
Bank Ho. Rd. *M9* 2D **21**
Bank La. *Swin & Salf* 2B **48**
Bankley St. *M19* 3A **104**
Bankmill Clo. *M13* . . 1D **85** (5F **11**)
Bank Pl. *Salf* 1D **67** (4C **4**)
Bank Rd. *M8* 4C **21**
Bankside Ct. *M12* 4B **88**
Bank St. *M7* 2B **36**
Bank St. *M11* 4A **56**
　　　　　(in two parts)
Bank St. *Droy* 3B **74**
Bank St. *Sale* 4A **112**
Bank St. *Salf* 1D **67** (4C **4**)
Banky La. *Sale* 3C **109**

Bannatyne Clo. *M40* 1A **42**
Bannerdale Clo. *M13* 4D **87**
Bannerman Av. *P'wich* 3B **18**
Bannerman Rd. *Droy* 2D **75**
Bannerman St. *Salf* 3A **36**
Banner Wlk. *M11* 2D **71**
Bantry Dri. *M9* 3D **21**
Baptist St. *M4* 4D **53** (2E **7**)
Barbeck Clo. *M40* 4C **55**
Barbican St. *M20* 2D **117**
　　　　　(in two parts)
Barbirolli Mall. *M4* 1C **69** (4C **6**)
　　　　　(off Arndale Shop. Cen.)
Barbirolli Sq. *M2* 3B **68** (3B **10**)
　　　　　(off Lwr. Mosley St.)
Barbon Wlk. *M4* 1A **70**
Barcicroft Rd. *M19 & Stoc* . . 4C **119**
Barcicroft Wlk. *M19* 4C **119**
Barclay Dri. *Eccl* 4A **46**
Barclays Av. *Salf* 1B **48**
Barcliffe Av. *M40* 4C **25**
Barcombe Clo. *Urm* 1B **94**
Barcombe Wlk. *M9* 3B **38**
　　　　　(in two parts)
Bardsley Av. *Fail.* 3B **42**
Bardsley St. *M40* 2D **57**
Bardsley St. *Chad.* 3B **26**
Barff Rd. *Salf.* 1A **64**
Baric Clo. *Eccl* 2B **62**
Baring St. *M1* 3D **69** (3F **11**)
Baring St. Ind. Est. *M1.* . . 3A **70** (3F **11**)
Barkan Way. *Swin* 2D **31**
Barkers La. *Sale* 4B **110**
Barker St. *M3* 4B **52** (1A **6**)
Barking St. *M40* 4C **55**
Bark Wlk. *M15* 2B **84** (5B **10**)
Barkway Rd. *Stret* 2C **95**
Barkworth Wlk. *M40* 1B **56**
Barlby Wlk. *M40* 1B **56**
Barlea Av. *M40* 1D **41**
Barleycroft St. *M16* 4B **84**
Barlow Fold Rd. *Stoc* 1B **122**
Barlow Hall Rd. *M21* 4C **115**
Barlow La. *Eccl* 1C **61**
Barlow La. N. *Stoc* 1B **122**
Barlow Moor 4C **115**
Barlow Moor Ct. *M20.* 4B **116**
Barlow Moor Rd. *M21 & M20* . . 3B **98**
Barlow Pl. *M13* 1A **86**
Barlow Rd. *Lev.* 3A **104**
Barlow Rd. *Salf* 2C **67** (1B **8**)
Barlow Rd. *Stret* 4D **81**
Barlow's Cft. *Salf* 1A **68** (4F **5**)
Barlow St. *Eccl* 2D **61**
Barlow Ter. *M13*. 1A **86** (5F **11**)
　　　　　(off Wadeson Rd.)
Barlow Ter. *M21* 4C **115**
　　　　　(off Barlow Hall Rd.)
Barlow Wlk. *Stoc* 1B **122**

Barmouth St. *M11* 3D **71**
Barmouth Wlk. *Oldh.* 4D **27**
Barnard Rd. *M18* 1B **104**
Barnby St. *M12* 1A **104**
Barnes Green 1B **38**
Barnett Av. *M20.* 3D **117**
Barnett Dri. *Salf* 1D **67** (3D **5**)
Barnfield. *Urm* 3B **92**
Barnfield Clo. *Salf* 2D **65**
Barnfield Cres. *Sale* 3B **110**
Barnfield Rd. *M19* 4C **119**
Barnfield Rd. *Swin.* 4D **13**
Barnford Bus. Pk. *Stoc.* 4A **122**
Barnhill Av. *P'wich* 4B **18**
Barnhill Dri. *P'wich.* 4B **18**
Barnhill Rd. *P'wich.* 3A **18**
Barnhill St. *M14.* 4B **84**
Barnsdale Dri. *M8* 1C **53**
Barnsfold Av. *M14* 1A **118**
Barnside Way. *Fail* 4D **43**
Barnstaple Dri. *M40* 1A **54**
Barnstead Av. *M20.* 4B **118**
Barnston Av. *M14* 2D **101**
Barnswell St. *M40* 2C **57**
Barn Wlk. *Open* 1A **90**
Barnway Wlk. *M40.* 4C **25**
Baroness Gro. *Salf.* 3C **51**
Barons Ct. *Fail* 4D **41**
Barracks La. *Sale* 3D **109**
Barrack St. *M15* 1D **83** (5C **8**)
Barra Dri. *Urm* 3D **77**
Barrass St. *M11* 1D **89**
Barrfield Rd. *Salf.* 3C **49**
Barr Hill Av. *Salf.* 2C **49**
Barrhill Clo. *M15* 2A **84** (1E **9**)
Barrington Av. *Droy.* 2B **74**
Barrington St. *M11* 1C **73**
Barrow Hill Rd. *M8.* 2B **52**
Barrow St. *Salf.* 2D **67** (5C **4**)
Barr St. *Kear.* 1B **12**
Barry Ct. *M20* 3D **117**
Barry Lawson Clo. *M8* 3B **36**
Barry Rd. *Stoc.* 4B **122**
Bartlett St. *M11* 4B **72**
Barton Arc. *M2* 2B **68** (5B **6**)
(off Deansgate)
Barton Av. *Urm* 2B **92**
Barton Bus. Pk. *Eccl.* 2C **61**
Barton Dock Rd.
  Urm & *Stret* 2A **78**
Barton Embkmt. *Urm.* 1C **77**
Barton Hall Av. *Eccl* 2A **60**
Barton Ho. *Salf.* 3A **48**
Barton La. *Eccl.* 3D **61**
Barton Rd. *Eccl.* 2C **61**
Barton Rd. *Stret.* 4B **78**
Barton Rd. *Swin.* 3C **31**
Barton Rd. *Urm.* 4C **77**
Barton Rd. *Wors.* 2A **44**

Barton Sq. *M2.* 2B **68** (5A **6**)
Barton St. *M3* 3A **68** (3F **9**)
(in two parts)
Barton St. *Swin.* 4B **14**
Barton Upon Irwell 3D **61**
Barway Rd. *M21* 3D **97**
Barwell Clo. *Stoc.* 4B **106**
Barwell Rd. *Sale.* 4A **110**
Basechurch Wlk. *M12* 2D **87**
(off Skarratt Clo.)
Basford Rd. *M16.* 1B **98**
Basildon Clo. *M13* 3B **86**
Basil St. *M14* 1A **102**
Baslow Av. *M19.* 2B **104**
Baslow Gro. *Stoc.* 4B **122**
Baslow Rd. *Droy.* 4A **58**
Baslow Rd. *Stret.* 1C **95**
Baslow St. *M11.* 2C **71**
Basset Av. *Salf.* 2C **51**
Basten Dri. *Salf.* 1A **52**
Batchelor Clo. *M21.* 2A **116**
Bates St. *M13* 4D **87**
Bath Cres. *M16* 3C **83**
Batley St. *M9.* 2C **39**
Batsmans Dri. *Swin* 2A **14**
Battersby St. *M11.* 4A **74**
Batty St. *M8.* 2A **54**
Baxter St. *Oldh* 4D **27**
Baycliffe Wlk. *M8.* 4B **36**
Baydon Av. *Salf.* 4B **36**
Bayfield Gro. *M40* 1A **40**
Baynard Wlk. *M9.* 2D **21**
Baysdale Wlk. *M11* 2D **71**
Bayston Wlk. *M12* 2D **87**
(off Wenlock Way)
Bayswater Av. *M40.* 3B **56**
Bay Tree Av. *Wors* 2A **44**
Baywood St. *M9.* 2B **38**
Bazaar St. *Salf.* 3A **50**
Beacon Rd. *Traf P* 4A **62**
Beaconsfield *M14* 2A **118**
Beadham Dri. *M9.* 1C **21**
Beale Gro. *M21* 4B **98**
Bealey Clo. *M18.* 3B **88**
Beaminster Wlk. *M13.* 3A **86**
Beamish Clo. *M13* 2A **86**
Beanfields. *Wors* 2A **44**
Beanfield Ter. *Wors* 2A **44**
Beard Rd. *M18.* 4C **89**
Beard St. *Droy.* 2B **74**
Beardwood Rd. *M9* 2B **22**
Beatrice Av. *M18.* 4B **90**
Beatrice Rd. *Wors* 3B **28**
Beatrice St. *Swin.* 1D **29**
Beatrice Wignall St. *Droy.* 3C **75**
Beattock Clo. *M15.* 1D **83** (5D **9**)
Beaufort Av. *M20.* 4C **117**
Beaufort Av. *Swin* 3D **29**
Beaufort St. *M3* 3A **68** (3E **9**)

Beaufort St. *Eccl*	4B **44**
Beaufort St. *P'wich*	2C **19**
Beaumaris Clo. *M12*	2D **87**
Beaumont Rd. *M21*	2B **114**
Beaver St. *M1*	3C **69** (3C **10**)
Bebbington St. *M11*	2C **73**
Beckenham Rd. *M8*	3C **37**
Becket Av. *Salf*	4A **36**
Beckett St. *M18*	4C **89**
Beckfoot Dri. *M13*	1C **103**
Beckford St. *M40*	2C **55**
Beckhampton Clo. *M13*	3A **86**
Beckley Av. *P'wich*	4A **18**
Beckside. *Stoc*	3C **107**
Beck St. *M11*	4A **74**
Beck St. *Salf*	1A **68** (4E **5**)
Bedfont Wlk. M9	*1C 39*
(off Polworth Rd.)	
Bedford Av. *M16*	2D **99**
Bedford Av. *Swin*	3A **30**
Bedford Ct. *Salf*	1D **35**
Bedford Rd. *M16*	1A **98**
Bedford Rd. *Eccl*	4A **46**
Bedford Rd. *Urm*	4C **77**
Bedford Rd. *P'wich*	1C **19**
Bedford St. *Stoc*	1A **122**
(in two parts)	
Bednal Av. *M40*	3C **55**
Bedwell St. *M16*	1B **100**
Beech Av. *Droy*	2B **74**
Beech Av. *Kear*	1B **12**
Beech Av. *Salf*	3C **49**
Beech Av. *Stret*	3C **97**
Beech Av. *Urm*	2C **93**
Beech Clo. *P'wich*	3C **19**
Beech Ct. *M8*	1B **36**
Beech Ct. *M14*	4A **102**
Beech Ct. *M32*	3D **97**
Beech Ct. *Salf*	4A **50**
Beechcroft. *P'wich*	3C **19**
Beechcroft Clo. *M40*	4B **54**
Beechdale Clo. *M40*	2C **41**
Beecher Wlk. M9	*4B 38*
(off Kelvington Dri.)	
Beeches, The. *Eccl*	4B **46**
Beechfield Av. *Urm*	1A **92**
Beechfield Rd. *Swin*	2D **45**
Beechfield St. *M8*	1C **53**
Beech Gro. *M14*	2B **118**
Beech Gro. *Salf*	3C **49**
Beech Ho. *Eccl*	2B **60**
Beech Hurst Clo. *M16*	2D **99**
Beech M. *M21*	1B **114**
Beech Mt. *M9*	2B **38**
Beech Range. *M19*	3A **104**
Beech Rd. *M21*	1A **114**
Beech Rd. *Sale*	4B **112**
Beech St. *Chad*	3D **27**
Beech St. *Eccl*	2B **60**
Beech St. *Fail*	2A **42**
Beech St. *Swin*	3B **30**
Beech Tree Bank. *P'wich*	2A **18**
Beech Wlk. *Stret*	3A **96**
Beechwood Av. *M21*	2C **115**
Beechwood Av. *Stoc*	4B **122**
Beechwood Ct. *P'wich*	3D **19**
Beechwood Dri. *Wors*	1B **44**
Beechwood Gro. *M9*	3C **39**
Beechwood Rd. *P'wich*	3D **19**
Beede St. *Open*	3B **72**
Beeley St. *Salf*	2B **50**
Beeston Av. *Salf*	4B **34**
Beeston St. *M9*	2C **39**
Beeth St. *M11*	1D **89**
Beeton Gro. *M13*	4C **87**
Beetoon Wlk. M4	*2A 70*
(off Cardroom Rd.)	
Beever St. *M16*	3C **83**
Begonia Wlk. *M12*	2D **87**
Belding Av. *M40*	1B **42**
Beldon Rd. *M9*	2D **21**
Belfield Rd. *P'wich*	3A **20**
Belfield Rd. *Stoc*	1B **106**
Belford Av. *Dent*	1C **107**
Belford Rd. *Stret*	1B **96**
Belfort Dri. *Salf*	3B **66** (3A **8**)
Belgate Clo. *M12*	4A **88**
Belgrave Av. *M14*	1C **103**
Belgrave Av. *Fail*	2D **43**
Belgrave Cres. *Eccl*	1B **62**
Belgrave Rd. *M40*	1A **42**
Belgrave Ter. *M40*	1C **55**
Belgravia Gdns. *M21*	4A **98**
Belhaven Rd. *M8*	4B **20**
Belhill Gdns. *Salf*	4D **49**
Bellamy Ct. *M18*	2A **90**
(in two parts)	
Bell Clough Rd. *Droy*	4D **59**
Bell Cres. *M11*	3C **71**
Belle Vue	3B **88**
Belle Vue Av. *M12*	3D **87**
Belle Vue Greyhound	
Race Track	3B **88**
Belle Vue Leisure Cen.	4A **88**
Belle Vue Speedway Track	3B **88**
Belle Vue St. *M12*	2A **88**
Bellew St. *M11*	3C **71**
Bellis Clo. *M12*	2C **71**
Bellott St. *M8*	4C **37**
Bellscroft Av. *M40*	3B **40**
Bell St. *Droy*	1D **75**
Bell Ter. *Eccl*	3C **61**
Belmont Av. *Salf*	1C **63**
Belmont Av. *Swin*	1D **13**
Belmont Rd. *Sale*	3C **111**
Belmont Rd. *M16*	3D **83**
Belmont St. *Eccl*	4D **45**
Belmont St. *Eccl*	2B **64**

Belmont Wlk. *M13* 2A **86**
Belmore Av. *M8* 1B **36**
Belper Rd. *Eccl* 3B **60**
Belper Wlk. *M18* 2C **89**
Belroy Ct. *P'wich* 3B **18**
Belsyde Wlk. *M9* *3C **39***
(off Craigend Dri.)
Belthorne Av. *M9* 4A **24**
Beltone Clo. *Stret* 3D **95**
Belton Wlk. *M8* 1C **53**
Belvedere Av. *Stoc* 2B **106**
Belvedere Ct. *P'wich* 3A **18**
Belvedere Rd. *M14* 4C **103**
Belvedere Rd. *Salf* 4A **50**
Belvedere St. *Salf* 4B **50**
Belvoir Av. *M19* 2A **104**
Belwood Rd. *M21* 2B **114**
Bembridge Clo. *M14* 1A **102**
Bemsley Pl. *Salf* 3A **66**
Benbecula Way. *Urm* 3C **77**
Benbow Av. *M12* 3D **87**
Benbow St. *Sale* 4D **111**
Bendall St. *Open* 3A **74**
Bendemeer. *Urm* 1C **93**
Bendix St. *M4* 1D **69** (3E **7**)
(in two parts)
Benedict Clo. *Salf* 2C **51**
Benfield Av. *M40* 4C **25**
Benfleet Clo. *M12* 2A **88**
Bengain. Salf *1D **51***
(off Murray St.)
Bengal St. *M4* 1D **69** (3F **7**)
Benhale Wlk. M8 . . . . *1C **53***
(off Tamerton Dri.)
Benin Wlk. *M40* 2C **57**
Benjamin Wilson Ct. Salf . 3D **51** (1D **5**)
(off Fitzwilliam St.)
Benmore Rd. *M9* 2D **23**
Bennett Dri. *Salf* 4A **36**
Bennett Rd. *M8* 1B **36**
Bennett St. *M12* 2C **87**
Bennett St. *Stret* 3A **96**
Bennon Clo. *Salf* 4A **36**
Benson Clo. *Salf* 2A **52**
Ben St. *M11* 1B **72**
Bentcliffe Way. *Eccl* 2B **62**
Bentinck Ind. Est. *M15* 5C **8**
Bentinck St. *M15* 1D **83** (5C **8**)
Bent La. *M8* 3B **36**
Bent La. *P'wich* 2C **19**
Bent Lanes. *Urm* 3A **76**
Bentley Ct. *Salf* 2A **36**
Bentley Rd. *M21* 3A **98**
Bentley Rd. *Salf* 2A **36**
Benton St. *M9* 3D **39**
Bent Spur Rd. *Kear* 1A **12**
Bent St. *M8* 3C **53**
Bent Ter. *Urm* 4C **77**
Bentworth Wlk. *M9* 3C **39**

Benville Wlk. *M40* 1B **56**
(off Troydale Dri.)
Berberis Wlk. *Sale* 3C **109**
Beresford Ct. *M20* 4C **117**
Beresford Cres. *Stoc* 1A **106**
Beresford Rd. *M13* 1D **103**
Beresford Rd. *Stret* 4C **81**
Beresford St. *M14* 1B **100**
Beresford St. *Fail* 3A **42**
Berger St. *M40* 2D **57**
Bergman Wlk. M40 . . . . *1B **56***
(off Harmer Clo.)
Berigan Clo. *M12* 3C **87**
Berkeley Av. *M14* 4C **87**
Berkeley Av. *Chad* 3B **26**
Berkeley Av. *Stret* 4C **79**
Berkeley Ct. *M8* 1A **36**
Berkley Av. *M19* 3A **104**
Berkshire Clo. *Chad* 1D **27**
Berkshire Pl. *Oldh* 1D **27**
Berkshire Rd. *M40* 4B **54**
Bermondsay St. *Salf* 3B **66**
Bernard St. *M9* 2B **38**
Berriedale Clo. *M16* 2D **99**
Berrie Gro. *M19* 1B **120**
Berry Brow. *M40* 3D **57**
(in two parts)
Berry St. *M1* 3D **69** (3F **11**)
Berry St. *Eccl* 3B **60**
Berry St. *Swin* 4B **14**
Bertha St. *M11* 4B **72**
Bertram St. *M12* 2A **88**
Berwick Av. *Urm* 2C **95**
Berwyn Av. *M9* 1D **21**
Bessemer St. *M11* 1C **89**
Beswick 3A **72**
Beswick Dri. *Fail* 4C **43**
Beswick Row. *M4* 4C **53** (2C **6**)
Beswick St. *M4* 1B **70**
Beswick St. *Droy* 2D **75**
Beta Av. *Stret* 3A **96**
Bethel Av. *Fail* 3A **42**
Bethesda Ho. *M7* 2A **36**
Bethnall Dri. *M14* 3C **101**
Betley Rd. *Stoc* 3B **106**
Betley St. *M1* 3A **70**
Bettwood Dri. *M8* 4B **20**
Betty's Fitness Cen. 3A **98**
Betula Gro. *Salf* 3D **35**
Beulah St. *M11* 4C **73**
Bevan Clo. *M12* 2C **71**
(in two parts)
Bevendon Sq. *Salf* 4A **36**
Beverdale Clo. *M11* 3A **72**
Beveridge St. *M14* 1C **101**
Beverley Av. *Urm* 4A **78**
Beverley Rd. *Swin* 3A **32**
Beverley St. *M9* 1C **39**
Beverly Rd. *M14* 2B **118**

Beverston Dri. *Salf* 1A **52**
Bevill Sq. *Salf* 1A **68** (3E **5**)
Bewley Wlk. *M40* 4A **40**
Bexhill Dri. *M13* 1C **103**
Bexington Rd. *M16* 1A **100**
Bexley Clo. *Urm* 4B **76**
Bexley Sq. *Salf* 1D **67** (4D **5**)
Bexley Wlk. M40 . . . . *1B* **56**
(off John Foran Clo.)
Beyer Clo. *M18* 3C **89**
Bibby La. *M19* 3D **119**
(in two parts)
Bickerdike Av. *M12* 1B **104**
Bickerdyke Ct. *M12* 1B **104**
Bickerton Ct. *Chad* 3D **27**
Biddisham Wlk. *M40* 2B **54**
(in two parts)
Bidston Av. *M14* 2D **101**
Bigginwood Wlk. M40 . . . . *3A* **40**
(off Halliford Rd.)
Bignor St. *M8* 4C **37**
Bilbrook St. *M4* 4D **53** (1E **7**)
Billing St. *M12* 4A **70**
Billington Rd. *Swin* 2C **33**
Bill Williams Clo. *M11* 3C **73**
Billy La. *Swin* 4B **14**
Billy Meredith Clo. *M14* 1C **101**
Billy Whelan Wlk. *M40* 2B **56**
Bilsland Wlk. *M40* 2C **57**
Bilton Wlk. *M8* 2A **38**
Bincombe Wlk. *M13* 3A **86**
Bindloss Av. *Eccl* 4C **47**
Bindon Wlk. M9 . . . . *3D* **38**
(off Carisbrook St.)
Bingham St. *Swin* 2B **30**
Bingley Clo. *M11* 3D **71**
Bingley Dri. *Urm* 4A **76**
Bingley Wlk. *Salf* 2D **33**
Binns Pl. *M4* 2D **69** (5F **7**)
Binstead Clo. *M14* 1C **103**
Birchacre Gro. *M14* 2B **118**
Birchall Way. *M15* 2B **84**
Birch Av. *M16* 4A **82**
Birch Av. *Fail* 1B **58**
Birch Av. *Salf* 2C **49**
Birch Av. *Stoc* 4B **120**
Birch Ct. *M13* 1C **103**
Birch Dri. *Swin* 2D **31**
Birchenall St. *M40* 2D **39**
Birchenlea St. *Chad* 3C **27**
Birches, The. *Sale* 4A **110**
Birchfields Av. *M13* 1C **103**
Birchfields Rd. *M13 & M14* . . . 1C **103**
Birch Gro. *M14* 1B **102**
Birch Hall La. *M13* 2C **103**
Birchington Rd. *M14* 1C **117**
Birchin La. *M4* 2C **69** (5D **7**)
Birchin Pl. M4 . . . . 2C **69** (5D **7**)
(off Birchin La.)

Birch La. *M13* 1C **103**
Birchleaf Gro. *Salf* 1A **64**
Birch Polygon. *M14* 1B **102**
Birch Rd. *M8* 1D **37**
Birch Rd. *C'ton & B'hth* 4A **108**
Birch Rd. *Swin* 2D **45**
Birch St. *M12* 2A **88**
Birch St. *Droy* 2D **75**
Birchvale Clo. *M15* 2A **84** (5F **9**)
Birchwood. *Droy* 4D **59**
Birdhall Gro. *M19* 4A **104**
Birkdale Gro. *Eccl* 1B **62**
Birkdale Gro. *Stoc* 4B **122**
Birkdale Pl. *Sale* 3B **110**
Birkdale Rd. *Stoc* 4A **122**
Birkdale St. *M8* 3C **37**
Birley Ct. *Salf* 1A **66**
Birley Fields. *M15* 3B **84**
Birtles Av. *Stoc* 1B **106**
Birtley Wlk. *M40* 4A **54**
Birt St. *M40* 3B **54**
Birwood Rd. *M8* 4D **21**
Biscay Clo. *M11* 2D **71**
Bishop Clo. *M16* 4A **84**
Bishop Marshall Clo.
M40 . . . . 2B **54**
Bishop Rd. *Salf* 3D **47**
Bishopscourt. *Salf* 2C **35**
Bishopsgate. *M2* 3B **68** (2B **10**)
Bishops M. *Sale* 3A **110**
Bishops Rd. *P'wich* 3C **19**
Bishopton Clo. *M19* 3C **105**
Bispham Av. *Stoc* 2B **106**
Bispham St. *M40* 3A **36**
Blackberry La. *Stoc* 2D **123**
Black Brook Rd. *Stoc* 2D **121**
Blackburn Gdns. *M20* 4C **117**
Blackburn Pl. *Salf* 2C **67** (1A **8**)
Blackburn St. *P'wich* 2C **19**
Blackburn St. *Salf* 4D **51** (2C **4**)
Blackcroft Clo. *Swin* 2A **30**
Blackett St. *M12* 3B **70**
Blackfield La. *Salf* 2C **35**
(in two parts)
Blackfields. *Salf* 2C **35**
Blackford Rd. *Stoc* 2B **120**
Blackford Wlk. *M40* 4B **54**
Black Friar Ct. *Salf* 1D **5**
Blackfriars Rd. *Salf* 4A **52** (2D **5**)
Blackfriars St. *Salf* 1B **68** (4A **6**)
Blackhill Clo. *M13* 1D **85** (5F **11**)
Blackley. 1C **39**
Blackley Ct. *M9* 3C **21**
Blackley Crematorium. *M9* 2C **21**
Blackley New Rd. *M9* 3B **20**
Blackley Pk. Rd. *M9* 1B **38**
Blackley St. *M16* 3C **83**
Blacklock St. *M8* 3B **52**

Blackpool St. *M11* 1D **73**
(Powell St.)
Blackpool St. *M11* 1C **73**
(Walsden St.)
Blackrock St. *M11* 2D **71**
Blackstock St. *M13* 4A **86**
Blackstone Wlk. *M9* 4B **38**
Blackthorn Av. *M19* 2A **120**
Blackwell Wlk. *M4* *1A* **70**
(off Cardroom Rd.)
Blackwin St. *M12* 2A **88**
Blairhall Av. *M40* 3A **40**
Blair Rd. *M16* 3A **100**
Blair St. *M16* 3D **83**
Blakedown Wlk. *M12* *3C* **87**
(off Cochrane Av.)
Blakemore Wlk. *M12* 2C **71**
Blakey St. *M12* 4A **88**
Blanchard St. *M15* 3A **84**
Bland Clo. *Fail* 3A **42**
Blandford Av. *Wors* 2A **28**
Blandford Dri. *M40* 4D **25**
Blandford Rd. *Eccl* 1B **60**
Blandford Rd. *Salf* 2B **50**
Bland Rd. *P'wich* 4B **18**
Bland St. *M16* 4A **84**
Blanefield Clo. *M21* 2A **116**
Blantyre Rd. *Swin* 4D **31**
Blantyre St. *M15* 4D **67** (4D **9**)
Blantyre St. *Eccl* 4A **44**
Blantyre St. *Swin* 2D **29**
Blanwood Dri. *M8* 3D **37**
Blaydon St. *M1* 3D **69** (2E **11**)
Bledlow Clo. *Eccl* 4A **46**
Blencarn Wlk. *M9* 4B **38**
Blendworth Clo. *M8* 3B **36**
Blenheim Av. *M16* 2D **99**
Blenheim Ct. *M9* *1C* **21**
(off Deanswood Dri.)
Blenheim Rd. *Old T* 1A **98**
Bletchley Clo. *M13* 3B **86**
Blinco Rd. *Urm* 3B **94**
Blind La. *M12* 4B **70**
Blisworth Av. *Eccl* 3A **62**
Blisworth Clo. *M4* 2B **70**
Block La. *Chad* 1D **27**
Blodwell St. *Salf* 1D **65**
Bloom St. *M1* 3C **69** (3C **10**)
(in two parts)
Bloom St. *Salf* 1A **68** (4E **5**)
Blossom St. *M4* 1D **69** (4F **7**)
Blossom St. *Salf* 1A **68** (3F **5**)
Bloxham Wlk. *M9* 3D **23**
Blucher St. *M12* 2C **87**
Blucher St. *Salf* 2C **67** (1A **8**)
Blue Bell Av. *M40* 1A **40**
Blue Ribbon Wlk. *Swin* 1C **31**
Bluestone Rd. *M40* 2A **40**
Bluestone Rd. *Dent* 2C **107**

Bluestone Ter. *Dent* 2C **107**
Blyborough Clo. *Salf* 3C **49**
Blyton St. *M15* 3D **85**
Boad St. *M1* 3D **69** (2F **11**)
Boardman Fold Clo. *Midd* 1A **24**
Boardman Fold Rd. *Midd* 1D **23**
Boardman Rd. *M8* 4B **20**
Boardman St. *Eccl* 2A **62**
Boar Grn. Clo. *M40* 3C **41**
Boatyard, The. *Stret* 2C **97**
Bobbin Wlk. *M4* *2D* **71**
(off Cardroom Rd.)
Bob Massey Clo. *Open* 2C **73**
Boddington Rd. *Eccl* 2A **60**
Bodley St. *M11* 1C **73**
Bodmin Cres. *Stoc* 4D **123**
Bodmin Rd. *Sale* 4D **109**
Bodney Wlk. *M9* 3D **21**
Bodyline Health &
Fitness Cen. 4C **111**
Bodyshapers Fitness Club 3B **98**
Bogart Ct. *Salf* 3C **49**
Boland Dri. *M14* 4A **102**
Bold Row. *Swin* 3B **30**
Bold St. *Hulme* 3A **84**
Bold St. *Moss S* 4A **84**
Bold St. *Swin* 4B **14**
Bolesworth Clo. *M21* 1D **113**
Bolivia St. *Salf* 1A **64**
Bollin Clo. *M15* 2D **83**
Bollin Ct. *M15* 2D **83**
Bollington Rd. *M40* 1B **70**
Bollington Rd. *Stoc* 4D **121**
Bollin Ho. *Salf* *2C* **51**
(off Lwr. Broughton Rd.)
Bollin Wlk. *Stoc* 4B **122**
Bolney Wlk. *M40* 3B **54**
Bolton Clo. *P'wich* 4D **17**
Bolton Rd. *Salf* 1B **48**
Bolton Rd. *Swin* 4B **14**
Bolton St. *Salf* 2A **68** (5E **5**)
Bolton St. *Stoc* 2A **122**
Bombay Sq. *M1* *3C* **69** (3D **11**)
(off Bombay St.)
Bombay St. *M1* 3C **69** (3D **11**)
Bonchurch Wlk. *M18* 2B **88**
Bondmark Rd. *M18* 2C **89**
Bond Sq. *Salf* 4A **36**
Bond St. *M12* 3A **70** (3F **11**)
Bonhill Wlk. *M11* 1B **72**
Bonsall St. *M15* 2B **84**
Bookham Wlk. *M9* 2C **39**
Boond St. *M4* 2B **70**
Boond St. *Salf* 1A **68** (3F **5**)
Booth Av. *M14* 2B **118**
Boothby Ct. *Swin* 1D **29**
Boothby Rd. *Swin* 1A **30**
Booth Clibborn Ct. *Salf* 2D **35**
Booth Dri. *Urm* 3A **76**

Boothfield. *Eccl* 4A **44**
Booth Hall Rd. *M9* 3A **24**
Booth La. *M9* 2C **21**
Boothman Ct. *Eccl* 4B **46**
Booth Rd. *M16* 1C **99**
Booth Rd. *Aud* 4C **75**
Booth Rd. *Sale* 3D **111**
Boothroyden Rd. *M9* 1A **22**
Booth St. *M2* 2B **68** (1B **10**)
Booth St. *Fail* 3A **42**
Booth St. *Salf* 1B **68** (4A **6**)
Booth St. E. *M13* 2D **85** (5D **11**)
Booth St. W. *M15* 2C **85**
Boothway. *Eccl* 1B **62**
Bootle St. *M2* 2B **68** (1A **10**)
Bordale Av. *M9* 3D **39**
Bordan St. *M11* 3D **71**
Boringdon Clo. *M40* 1B **56**
Borland Av. *M40* 1D **41**
Borough Av. *Swin* 1C **31**
Borough Rd. *Salf* 2B **64**
Borsden St. *Swin* 4D **13**
Borwell St. *M18* 2D **89**
Boscombe Av. *Eccl* 3C **61**
Boscombe St. *M14* 2D **101**
Boscombe St. *Stoc* 2B **106**
Boslam Wlk. *M4* 1A **70**
(off Salford Av.)
Bosley Av. *M20* 1C **117**
Bossall Av. *M9* 2C **23**
Bostock Wlk. *M13* . . . 1D **85** (5F **11**)
Boston Clo. *Fail* 1B **42**
Boston Ct. *Salf* 3C **65**
Boston St. *M15* 3B **84**
Bosworth St. *M11* 3A **72**
Botanical Av. *M16* 3A **82**
Botanical Ho. *M16* 3A **82**
Botany Rd. *Eccl* 3A **44**
Botha Clo. *M11* 4D **73**
Botham Clo. *M15* 3B **84**
Botham Ct. *Eccl* 4B **44**
Bothwell Rd. *M40* 4A **54**
Bottesford Av. *M20* 4B **116**
Bottomley Side. *M9* 4A **22**
Bottom of Woodhouses 2C **59**
Bouley Wlk. *M12* 2A **88**
Boundary La. *M15* 2C **85**
Boundary Rd. *Swin* 1B **30**
Boundary St. *M12* 3A **88**
Boundary St. E. *M13* 1C **85** (5D **11**)
Boundary St. W. *M15* 2C **85** (5C **10**)
(in two parts)
Boundary, The. *Swin* 2D **13**
Bourdon St. *M40* 4B **54**
Bourget St. *M8* 2B **36**
Bourne Av. *Swin* 3B **30**
Bourne Dri. *M40* 1B **40**
Bourne Ho. *Salf* 1D **65**
Bournelea Av. *M19* 3D **119**

Bourne St. *Chad* 4D **27**
Bournville Av. *Stoc* 4A **122**
Bournville Gro. *M19* 3B **104**
Bourton Dri. *M18* 4B **88**
Bowden Rd. *Swin* 3C **31**
Bowden Vw. *Urm* 2A **92**
Bowdon Av. *M14* 3B **100**
Bower La. *Chad* 4C **27**
Bowers Av. *Urm* 4B **76**
Bower St. *Newt H* 2D **55**
Bower St. *Salf* 3A **36**
Bower St. *Stoc* 2B **106**
Bower Ter. *Droy* 4D **59**
Bowes St. *M14* 1B **100**
Bowfell Circ. *Urm* 1B **92**
Bowfell Gro. *M9* 2D **21**
Bowfell Rd. *Urm* 2A **92**
Bowfield Wlk. *M40* 2C **57**
Bowgreen Wlk. *M15* 2D **83**
Bowker Bank Av. *M8* 4B **20**
Bowker Bank Ind. Est. *M8* . . . 3C **21**
Bowker Ct. *Salf* 1D **51**
Bowker St. *Salf* 4D **35**
Bowker Va. Gdns. *M9* 3B **20**
Bowland Av. *M18* 4C **91**
Bowland Rd. *Dent* 1D **107**
Bow La. *M2* 2B **68** (1B **10**)
Bowler's Leisure Cen. 2C **79**
Bowler St. *Lev* 1B **120**
Bowling Grn. Ct. *M16* 4D **83**
Bowling Rd. *M18* 1A **106**
Bowling St. *Chad* 4D **27**
Bowmeadow Grange. *M12* . . . 4D **87**
Bowmead Wlk. *M8* 4B **36**
(off Ermington Dri.)
Bowness Av. *Stoc* 3A **122**
Bowness Dri. *Sale* 4B **110**
Bowness St. *M11* 4B **74**
Bowness St. *Stret* 1B **96**
Bowscale Clo. *M13* 4D **87**
Bow St. *M2* 2B **68** (5A **6**)
Bowyers St. *M14* 2C **119**
Boxgrove Rd. *Sale* 4B **110**
Boxgrove Wlk. *M8* 1C **53**
Boxtree Av. *M18* 4D **89**
Box Works, The. *M15* . . . 4D **67** (4D **9**)
Boyd St. *M12* 1A **88**
Boyer St. *M16* 3B **82**
Boyle St. *M8* 1D **53**
Brabham Clo. *M21* 4B **98**
Brabham M. *Swin* 3C **29**
Bracewell Clo. *M12* 3A **88**
Brackenbury Wlk. *M15* 3C **85**
Bracken Clo. *Sale* 4C **109**
Brackenside. *Stoc* 4C **95**
Brackley Av. *M15* 1D **83** (5C **8**)
Brackley Dri. *Midd* 1A **24**
Brackley Lodge. *Eccl* 4B **46**
Brackley Rd. *Eccl* 3D **45**

Brackley Rd. *Stoc.* 4D **121**
Bracknell Dri. *M9* 3C **21**
Bradburn Av. *Eccl* 2D **61**
Bradburn Clo. *Eccl.* 1D **61**
Bradburn Gro. *Eccl.* 2D **61**
Bradburn St. *Eccl.* 2D **61**
Bradburn Wlk. M8 . . . . *1D 53*
　　　　　　　　　(off Moordown Clo.)
Bradden Clo. *Salf* 2A **66**
Braddon Av. *Urm* 2D **93**
Braddon St. *M11* 2C **73**
Brade Clo. *M11* 3C **73**
Bradfield Av. *Salf* 1A **64**
Bradfield Clo. *Stoc.* 2A **106**
Bradfield Rd. *Urm & Stret* 2B **94**
Bradford St. *M4.* 2A **70**
Bradford 1D **71**
Bradford Ct. *M40.* 1C **41**
Bradford Rd. *M40* 1B **70**
Bradford Rd. *Eccl.* 3A **46**
Bradgreen Rd. *Eccl.* 4C **45**
Bradley Av. *Salf* 3B **34**
Bradley La. *Stret* 2C **111**
Bradley's Ct. *M1* 2D **69** (5E **7**)
Bradley St. *M1.* 4E **7**
Bradney Clo. *M9* 2D **21**
Bradshaw Clo. *M20.* 2D **117**
Bradshaw Av. *Fail.* 2A **58**
Bradshaw Fold Av. *M40* 3D **25**
Bradshaw La. *Stret.* 3B **96**
Bradshaw St. *M4.* 1C **69** (3C **6**)
Bradshaw St. *Salf.* 1A **52**
Bradshaw St. N. *Salf.* 3D **35**
Bradstock Rd. *M16* 1A **100**
Bradstone Rd. *M8* 2B **52**
Bradwell Av. *M20.* 3B **116**
Bradwell Av. *Stret.* 1C **95**
Bradwen Av. *M8.* 1C **37**
Braemar Av. *Stret.* 2C **95**
Braemar Av. *Urm* 3A **92**
Braemar Ct. *M9* 1C **21**
Braemar Rd. *M14.* 4C **103**
　　　　　　　　　(in two parts)
Braeside. *Stret.* 3C **95**
Bragenham St. *M18.* 3C **89**
Brailsford Rd. *M14.* 4C **103**
　　　　　　　　　(in two parts)
Brakenhurst Dri. *Salf* 1B **52**
Braley St. *M12.* 4D **69** (4F **11**)
Bramall Ct. *Salf.* 4D **51** (2D **5**)
Bramble Av. *Salf* 4C **67** (4A **8**)
Bramble Wlk. *Sale* 4C **109**
Bramfield Wlk. *M15* 1D **83** (5D **9**)
Bramhall St. *M18.* 3A **90**
Bramhope Wlk. *M9* 3B **38**
Bramley Av. *M19* 4A **104**
Bramley Av. *Stret.* 2D **95**
Bramley Clo. *Swin* 1C **45**
Bramley Meade. *Salf* 3D **35**

Bramley St. *Salf.* 3A **52**
Brampton Wlk. *M40.* 1B **56**
Bramwell Dri. *M13.* 2A **86**
Brancaster Rd. *M1* 4C **69** (4D **11**)
Brandish Clo. *M13.* 3B **86**
Brandon Av. *Dent.* 1B **106**
Brandon Av. *Eccl.* 2C **47**
Brandon Rd. *Salf.* 3D **47**
Brandram Rd. *P'wich* 2C **19**
Brandsby Gdns. *Salf.* 3A **66**
Brankgate Ct. *M20.* 4C **117**
Branksome Av. *P'wich* 2A **18**
Branksome Dri. *Salf.* 2C **47**
Bransby Av. *M9* 2C **23**
Branscombe Dri. *Sale.* 4C **109**
Bransford Rd. *M11* 3A **74**
Bransford Rd. *Urm.* 4C **77**
Branson St. *M40.* 1B **70**
Branston Rd. *M40* 4D **25**
Brantingham Ct. *M16.* 3A **100**
Brantingham Rd.
　　M21 & Whal R 3B **98**
Brantwood Ct. *Salf.* 2D **35**
Brantwood Rd. *Salf.* 2D **35**
Brantwood Ter. *M9.* 3D **39**
Brassica Clo. *Eccl.* 3A **44**
Brassington Av. *M21* 2B **114**
Brassington Av. *Salf.* 3B **66**
Bratton Wlk. *M13.* 2B **86**
Braunston Clo. *Eccl* 3A **62**
Braxton Wlk. *M9* 2C **39**
Bray Av. *Eccl* 4B **44**
Brayside Rd. *M20 & M19.* 4B **118**
Brayton Av. *Sale.* 3D **109**
Brazennose St. *M2* 2B **68** (1A **10**)
Brazil Pl. *M1.* 3C **69** (3D **11**)
Brazil St. *M1.* 3C **69** (3D **11**)
Bread St. *M18* 2A **90**
Brechin Wlk. *Open* 2C **73**
Breck Rd. *Eccl* 1B **60**
Brecon Av. *M19* 2D **119**
Brecon Wlk. *Oldh.* 4D **27**
Bredbury Rd. *M14.* 2D **101**
Breeze Mt. *P'wich* 4B **18**
Brendon Av. *M40.* 3A **40**
Brendon Av. *Stoc.* 3B **122**
Brenley Wlk. M9. . . . . *2B 38*
　　　　　　　　　(off Maybrook Wlk.)
Brennan Clo. *M15* 3C **85**
Brennan Ct. *Oldh* 4D **27**
Brennock Clo. *M11* 3D **71**
Brentbridge Rd. *M14* 1D **117**
Brentfield Av. *M8* 4B **36**
Brentford Rd. *Stoc.* 3B **122**
Brentford St. *M9* 3C **39**
Brentnor Rd. *M40* 4C **25**
Brentwood. *Sale.* 4C **111**
Brentwood. *Salf.* 4C **49**
Brentwood Av. *Urm* 2D **93**

Brentwood Av. *Wors.* 4B 28
Brentwood Ct. *P'wich.* 3D 17
Brentwood Dri. *Eccl.* 3D 45
Brentwood Rd. *Swin* 1D 45
Brentwood St. *M16* 4B 84
Brereton Rd. *Eccl.* 2A 60
Breslyn St. *M3* 4B 52 (2B 6)
Brethren's St. *Droy.* 3C 75
Brettargh St. *Salf.* 3A 50
Brewer St. *M1* 2D 69 (5E 7)
Brewster St. *M9.* 2B 38
Brian Av. *Droy.* 4D 59
Brian Redhead Ct. *M15* 5B 8
Briar Clo. *Sale* 4C 109
Briar Clo. *Urm* 1A 92
Briarfield Hall. *M15* 5C 10
Briarfield Rd. *M20 & M19* 3B 118
Briarfield Rd. *Stoc* 3A 122
Briar Hill Ct. Salf *4A 50*
(off Briar Hill Way)
Briar Hill Way. *Salf.* 4A 50
Briarlea Gdns. *M19* 4C 119
Briarwood Av. *Droy.* 4A 58
Brickley St. *M3* 4C 53 (1B 6)
Brick St. *M4* 1C 69 (4D 7)
Bridcam St. *M8* 2C 52
Briddon St. *M3* 4B 52 (1A 6)
(in two parts)
Brideoak St. *M8* 3C 37
Bridgeford Ct. *Stret* 4B 96
Bridgeford St. *M15* 2C 85
Bridgelea Rd. *M20* 3D 117
Bri. Mills Bus. Pk. *Salf* 2D 49
Bridgend Clo. *M12.* 2A 88
Bridgenorth Av. *Urm* 2B 94
Bridge St. *Droy* 3A 74
Bridge St. *Salf* 2A 68 (5F 5)
Bridge St. *Swin* 2C 31
Bridge St. W. *Salf.* 2A 68 (5F 5)
Bridgewater Cen., The. *Urm* 4A 62
Bridgewater Circ. *Urm* 2D 77
Bridgewater Hall 3B 10
Bridgewater Hall. M1 . . . . 3B 68 (3A 10)
(off Gt. Bridgewater St.)
Bridgewater Pl. *M4* 2C 69 (5C 6)
Bridgewater Rd. *Swin* 3D 31
Bridgewater St. *M3* 3A 68 (3E 9)
(in two parts)
Bridgewater St. *Eccl.* 1B 60
Bridgewater St. *Sale.* 4D 111
Bridgewater St. *Salf.* 4A 52 (1E 5)
Bridgewater St. *Stret* 2C 97
Bridgewater Viaduct.
 M15. . . . . 4A 68 (4F 9)
Bridgewater Way. *M16* 3B 82
Bridgnorth Rd. *M9.* 3C 21
Bridlington Av. *Salf.* 4A 48
Bridlington Clo. *M40* 1C 57
Bridport Av. *M40* 2D 41

Bridson St. *Salf* 2C 65
Briercliffe Clo. *M18* 2D 89
Brierfields. Fail. *3C 43*
(off Brierley Av.)
Brierley Av. *Fail* 3B 42
Brierley Rd. E. *Swin* 1A 30
Brierley Rd. W. *Swin* 1A 30
Brigade Dri. *Stret* 1A 96
Brigadier Clo. *M20.* 3D 117
Brigantine Clo. *Salf* 3A 66
Briggs Rd. *Stret.* 4D 81
Briggs St. *Salf.* 4D 51 (2D 5)
Brigham St. *M11* 3C 73
Bright Circ. *Urm* 2A 78
Brightman St. *M18* 2D 89
Brighton Av. *M19.* 2D 119
Brighton Av. *Salf* 4A 36
Brighton Av. *Stoc.* 2B 106
Brighton Ct. *Salf.* 4B 66
Brighton Gro. *M14.* 2B 102
Brighton Gro. *Sale* 4C 111
Brighton Pl. *M13* 2D 85
Brighton Range. *M18* 4B 90
Brighton St. *M4.* 4C 53 (1D 7)
Bright Rd. *Eccl.* 1A 62
Brightstone Wlk. *M13* 4C 87
Bright St. Chad 2C 27
Bright St. *Droy.* 2D 75
Brightwell Wlk. M4 . . . . . 1D 69 (4E 7)
(off Foundry La.)
Brigsteer Wlk. M40 . . . . 2B 54
(off Thornton St. N.)
Brigstock Av. *M18* 3C 89
Brimfield Wlk. *M40* 1C 57
Brimpton Wlk. M8 . . . . 1B 52
(off Kenford Wlk.)
Brindale Rd. *Stoc.* 4D 123
Brindle Clo. *Salf.* 3D 49
Brindle Heath **3D 49**
Brindle Heath Ind. Est. *Salf.* . . . 3A 50
Brindle Heath Rd. *Salf* 3D 49
Brindle Pl. *M15* 2C 85
Brindley Av. *M9* 1D 21
Brindley Av. *Sale* 3A 112
Brindley Clo. *Eccl.* 3D 61
Brindley Lodge. *Swin* 4A 30
Brindley Rd. *M16.* 3B 82
Brindley St. *Eccl.* 4B 44
Brindley St. *Swin* 4B 14
(in two parts)
Brinklow Clo. *M11* 4A 74
Brinnington **4D 123**
Brinnington Rd. *Stoc* 4D 123
Brinsop Sq. *M12* 2B 88
Brinston Wlk. *M40* 3A 40
Brinsworth Dri. *M8* 1C 53
Brisbane St. *M15* 3D 85
Briscoe La. *M40.* 4D 55
Bristol Av. *M19* 4B 104

Bristol Ct. *Salf* 1A **36**
Bristol St. *Salf* 3A **36**
Bristowe St. *M11* 4D **57**
Britannia Rd. *Sale* 4D **111**
Britannia St. *Salf* 1A **50**
Britnall Av. *M12* 3C **87**
Britwell Wlk. *M8* *2A 38*
(off Mawdsley Dri.)
Brixham Dri. *Sale* 3D **109**
Brixham Rd. *M16* 4B **82**
Brixham Wlk. *M13* 3A **86**
Brixton Av. *M20* 3C **117**
Brixworth Wlk. *M9* *3C 23*
(off Greendale Dri.)
Broadacre Rd. *M18* 1A **106**
Broadbent St. *Swin* 3D **29**
Broad Ees Dole
    Nature Reserve 2B **112**
Broadfield Gro. *Stoc* 1A **106**
Broadfield Rd. *M14* 4C **85**
Broadfield Rd. *Stoc* 1A **106**
Broadgate. *Chad* 3A **26**
Broadgate. *Midd & Chad* 1D **25**
Broadgate Mdw. *Swin* 3B **30**
Broadgate Wlk. *M9* *2C 39*
(off Roundham Wlk.)
Broadhaven Rd. *M40* 3B **54**
Broadhill Rd. *M19* 3C **119**
Broadhurst Av. *Swin* 3B **14**
Broadlands Rd. *Wors* 1C **45**
Broadlands Wlk. *M40* 4A **40**
Broadlea. *Urm* 1C **93**
Broadlea Rd. *M19* 4C **119**
Broadmeadow Av. *M16* 3B **100**
Broadmoss Dri. *M9* 3A **24**
Broadmount Ter. *Oldh* *2D 27*
(off Devon St.)
Broad Oak 4B **28**
Broadoak Ct. *M8* 4D **37**
Broad Oak Ind. Pk. *Traf P* 4B **62**
Broadoak Park 2C **45**
Broad Oak Pk. *Eccl* 3D **45**
Broad Oak Rd. *Wors* 4B **28**
Broadoaks Rd. *Sale* 4C **111**
Broadoaks Rd. *Urm* 3B **92**
Broad Rd. *Sale* 4A **112**
Broadstone Clo. *P'wich* 3A **18**
Broadstone Hall Rd. N. *Stoc* . . . 3D **121**
Broadstone Hall Rd. S. *Stoc* . . . 3D **121**
Broadstone Rd. *Stoc* 3D **121**
Broad St. *Swin & Salf* 1B **48**
(in two parts)
Broad Wlk. *Salf* 4A **50**
Broadway. *M40 & Chad* 1D **41**
Broadway. *Chad* 2B **26**
Broadway. *Droy* 4C **75**
Broadway. *Fail* 3D **41**
Broadway. *Sale* 4C **111**
Broadway. *Salf* 3B **64**

Broadway. *Urm* 4A **76**
Broadway Clo. *Urm* 3C **77**
Broadway Ind. Est. *Salf* 3A **66**
Broadway N. *Droy* 3C **75**
Broadwell Dri. *M9* 3C **39**
Broadway Swimming Pool 4A **26**
Brocade Clo. *Salf* 4D **51** (2C **4**)
Brock Clo. *M11* 4D **73**
Brockford Dri. *M9* 1C **23**
Brocklebank Rd. *M14* 1A **118**
Brocklehurst St. *M9* 2A **40**
Brockley Av. *M14* 2D **101**
Brock St. *M1* 2D **69** (5F **7**)
Brockton Wlk. *M8* 2C **37**
Brocton Ct. *Salf* 1D **35**
Brodick St. *M40* 2D **39**
Brodie Clo. *Eccl* 1B **60**
Brogan St. *M18* 3D **89**
Bromborough Av. *M20* 1C **117**
Bromfield Av. *M9* 1B **38**
Bromley St. *M4* 4D **53** (1E **7**)
Bromley St. *Chad* 3C **27**
Bromlow St. *M11* 2C **73**
Brompton Av. *Fail* 2D **43**
Brompton Rd. *M14* 2D **101**
Brompton Rd. *Stret* 1B **94**
Bromsgrove Av. *Eccl* 1C **61**
Bromshill Dri. *Salf* 1A **52**
Bromwich Dri. *M9* 3B **39**
Bronte St. *M15* 3C **85**
Brook Av. *M19* 2B **104**
Brook Av. *Droy* 2B **74**
Brook Av. *Stoc* 4D **121**
Brook Av. *Swin* 3B **30**
Brookburn Rd. *M21* 2A **114**
Brook Ct. *Salf* 1C **35**
Brookdale Av. *M40* 2D **57**
Brookdale St. *Fail* 3A **42**
Brookdene Rd. *M19* 3C **119**
Brookfield. *P'wich* 2B **18**
Brookfield Av. *M21* 2C **115**
Brookfield Av. *Salf* 4A **48**
Brookfield Av. *Urm* 2A **92**
Brookfield Clo. *P'wich* 2B **18**
Brookfield Ct. *M18* 4D **89**
Brookfield Ct. *M19* 1D **119**
Brookfield Dri. *Swin* 1A **30**
Brookfield Gro. *M18* 4D **89**
Brookfield Rd. *M8* 1C **37**
Brookfield Rd. *Eccl* 3B **44**
Brookfold. *Fail* 2A **42**
Brookfold Rd. *Stoc* 3D **121**
Brook Green 4A **90**
Brook Grn. La. *M18* 1B **106**
Brookhead Av. *M20* 2B **116**
Brookhill St. *M40* 4C **55**
Brookhouse Av. *Eccl* 2A **60**
Brookhurst Rd. *M18* 4D **89**
Brooklands Av. *M20* 3C **117**

Brooklands Clo. *Stoc*	4D **121**
Brooklands Ct. *M8*	4B **20**
Brooklands Dri. *Droy*	4D **59**
Brooklands Rd. *P'wich & M8*	4A **20**
Brooklands Rd. *Stoc*	2A **106**
Brooklands Rd. *Swin*	4D **29**
Brooklawn Dri. *M20*	4D **117**
Brookleigh Rd. *M20*	3B **118**
Brooklyn Av. *M16*	2C **99**
Brooklyn Ct. *M20*	2A **118**
Brook M. *M14*	1B **118**
Brook Rd. *M14*	2A **118**
Brook Rd. *Stoc*	4C **121**
(in two parts)	
Brook Rd. *Urm*	1A **92**
Brooks Dri. *Fail*	1A **58**
Brookshaw St. *M11*	2A **72**
Brookside Ct. *M19*	2A **104**
Brookside Dri. *Salf*	1D **35**
Brookside Rd. *M40*	1A **40**
Brook's Rd. *M16*	1C **99**
Brookstone Clo. *M21*	3D **115**
Brook St. *M1*	4C **69** (4D **11**)
Brook St. *Fail*	4C **41**
Brook St. *Sale*	4A **112**
Brook St. *Salf*	3B **50**
Brook St. *Swin*	2D **29**
Brook Ter. *M12*	1D **103**
Brook Ter. *Urm*	4C **77**
Brookthorpe Av. *M19*	3C **119**
Brook Vs. *M9*	3C **39**
Brookway Clo. *M19*	4C **119**
Brookwood Av. *M8*	2A **38**
Broom Av. *M19*	4B **104**
Broom Av. *Salf*	2A **36**
Broom Av. *Stoc*	3B **122**
Broom Cres. *Salf*	4A **48**
Broomedge. *Salf*	2D **35**
Broome Gro. *Fail*	4B **42**
Broomfield. *Salf*	1B **48**
Broomfield. *Swin*	4B **32**
Broomfield Clo. *Stoc*	3B **122**
Broomfield Dri. *M8*	3B **36**
Broomfield Dri. *Stoc*	3B **122**
Broomfield Rd. *Stoc*	4C **121**
Broomhall Rd. *M9*	1C **21**
Broomhall Rd. *Swin*	4B **32**
Broomhill Ho. *Dent*	1D **107**
(off Thompson Ct.)	
Broom La. *M19*	1B **120**
Broom La. *Salf*	2D **35**
Broom St. *Swin*	3B **30**
Broomwood Wlk. *M15*	2C **85** (5C **10**)
(off Chevril Clo.)	
Broseley Rd. *M16*	2A **98**
Brotherton Clo. *M15*	2D **83** (5C **8**)
Brotherton Dri. *Salf*	1D **67** (3D **5**)
Brough St. *M11*	4A **74**
Broughton La. *Salf & M8*	2D **51**
(in two parts)	
Broughton Park	1D **35**
Broughton Recreation Cen.	2D **51**
Broughton Rd. *Salf*	3A **50**
Broughton Rd. E. *Salf*	3B **50**
Broughton St. *M8*	2B **52**
Broughton Swimming Pool	1D **51**
Broughton Trade Cen. *Salf*	3D **51**
Broughton Vw. *Salf*	4B **50**
Browfield Av. *Salf*	4B **66**
Brownacre St. *M20*	3D **117**
Brownbank Wlk. *M15*	3B **84**
(off Greenthorn Wlk.)	
Brown Ct. *M4*	1C **69** (4C **6**)
(off Arndale Shop. Cen.)	
Browncross St. *Salf*	2A **68** (5F **5**)
Browning Av. *Droy*	2C **75**
Browning Rd. *Stoc*	3D **105**
Browning Rd. *Swin*	2A **30**
Browning St. *M15*	2D **83**
Browning St. *Salf*	1D **67** (4D **5**)
Brownslow Wlk. *M13*	1D **85** (5F **11**)
Brownson Wlk. *M9*	2C **39**
Brown St. *M2*	2C **69** (1B **10**)
Brown St. *Fail*	3A **42**
Brown St. *Salf*	2D **65**
Brownsville Ct. *Stoc*	4C **121**
Brownsville Rd. *Stoc*	4B **120**
Brow, The. *M9*	4B **22**
Brow Wlk. *M9*	3B **22**
Broxton St. *M40*	4D **55**
Broxwood Clo. *M18*	3D **89**
Bruce Wlk. *M11*	4D **73**
Brundrett's Rd. *M21*	4B **98**
Brunel Av. *Salf*	2B **66**
Brunel Clo. *Stret*	2C **97**
Brunet Wlk. *M12*	2D **87**
(off Skarratt Clo.)	
Bruno St. *M9*	2D **21**
Brunswick	2A **86**
Brunswick Rd. *M20*	3A **118**
Brunswick St. *M13*	2D **85** (5F **11**)
Brunswick St. *Stret*	4B **96**
Brunton Rd. *Stoc*	3B **122**
Brunt St. *M14*	1D **101**
Bruton Av. *Stret*	3D **95**
Brutus Wlk. *Salf*	1A **52**
Bryan Rd. *M21*	2B **98**
Bryant Clo. *M13*	2A **86**
Bryceland Clo. *M12*	3C **71**
Brydon Av. *M12*	4A **70**
Brydon Clo. *Salf*	1A **66**
Brynden Av. *M20*	4A **118**
Bryn Dri. *Stoc*	4B **122**
Brynford Av. *M9*	1C **21**
Brynorme Rd. *M8*	4C **21**
Brynton Rd. *M13*	1C **103**
Bryson Wlk. *M18*	3C **89**

Buccleuch Lodge. M20. . . . . . . 4B **116**
Buchanan St. Swin. 1B **30**
Buchan St. M11. . . . . 1B **72**
Buckden Rd. Stoc 2D **121**
Buckfast Clo. M21. . . . . 3B **98**
Buckfast Rd. Sale. 3D **109**
Buckfast Wlk. Salf 4A **36**
Buckfield Av. Salf. 4B **66** (4A **8**)
Buckfield Dri. Salf 4B **66**
Buckhurst Rd. M19 . . . . 3A **104**
Buckingham Av. Salf 1B **64**
Buckingham Rd. M21. . . . . 2B **98**
Buckingham Rd. Droy 2A **74**
Buckingham Rd. P'wich 4B **18**
Buckingham Rd. Stoc. 4B **120**
     (in two parts)
Buckingham Rd. Stret 3D **81**
Buckingham Rd. Swin 4C **15**
Buckingham Rd. W. Stoc 4A **120**
Buckingham St. Salf. 2D **65**
Buckland Av. M9 . . . . 3C **21**
Buckland Rd. Salf. 3B **48**
Buckland St. M4. . . . . 2B **70**
Buck La. Sale 3A **110**
Buckle Ho. Eccl 1A **62**
Buckley Av. M18 . . . . 4C **89**
Buckley La. W'fld 3C **17**
Buckley Rd. M18 . . . . 4B **88**
Buckley St. Droy 2C **75**
Buckley St. Open 3D **73**
Buckley St. Stoc. 2A **106**
Bucklow Av. M14 . . . . 3D **101**
Bucknell Ct. M40 . . . . . . 3A **54** (1F **7**)
Buckthorn Clo. M21. . . . . 2D **115**
Buddleia Gro. Salf 4D **35**
   (off Bk. Hilton St.)
Bude Av. Stoc 4D **123**
Bude Av. Urm. 1B **108**
Budsworth Av. M20 . . . . 2D **117**
Budworth Gdns. Droy 2D **75**
Buerton Av. M9 . . . . 1C **21**
Buffalo Ct. Salf. 3C **65**
Buffoline Trad. Est. Lev. 3B **104**
Bugle St. M15 & M1 . . . . 4A **68** (4F **9**)
Buile Dri. M9 . . . . 2D **23**
Buile Hill Dri. Salf. 4B **48**
Buile Ho. Salf. 4C **49**
Buile St. Salf 3A **36**
Buller Rd. M13. . . . . 2D **103**
Buller St. Droy 3D **75**
Bullfinch Wlk. M21. . . . . 2D **115**
Bulteel St. Eccl 4B **44**
Bunkers Hill. W'fld 2B **16**
Bunsen St. M1 . . . . 2D **69** (5E **7**)
Bunyard St. M8 . . . . 1D **53**
Burbridge Clo. M11 . . . . 3C **71**
Burcot Wlk. M8 . . . . 3A **52**
Burdale Dri. Salf. 3D **47**
Burdett Way. M12 . . . . 3C **87**

Burdith Av. M14. . . . . 2C **101**
Burford Av. M16 . . . . 2D **99**
Burford Av. Urm. 4A **78**
Burford Dri. M16. . . . . 2D **99**
Burford Dri. Swin. 4A **14**
Burford Rd. M16 . . . . 2D **99**
Burford Wlk. M16 . . . . 2D **99**
Burgess Dri. Fail. 3B **42**
Burgin Wlk. M40 . . . . 2A **54**
Burland Clo. Salf 2A **52**
Burleigh Ct. Stret 4C **81**
Burleigh Ho. M15. . . . . 3D **85**
Burleigh M. M21 . . . . 3B **114**
Burleigh Rd. Stret 1C **97**
Burleigh St. M15 . . . . 3D **85**
Burlin Ct. M16. . . . . 1D **99**
Burlington Pl. M15. . . . . 3C **85**
   (off Burlington St.)
Burlington Rd. M20 . . . . 2A **118**
Burlington Rd. Eccl 3A **46**
Burlington St. M15. . . . . 3C **85**
Burlington St. E. M15. . . . . 3D **85**
Burman St. M11 & Droy. 4B **74**
Burnage 4C **119**
Burnage Av. M19. . . . . 1D **119**
Burnage Hall Rd. M19 . . . . 2C **119**
Burnage La. M19. . . . . 4C **119**
Burnage Range. M19. . . . . 3A **104**
Burnbray Av. M19 . . . . 3C **119**
Burnell Clo. M40 . . . . 4B **54**
Burnett Av. Salf 3B **66**
Burnett Clo. M40. . . . . 2B **54**
Burnfield Rd. M18 . . . . 1D **105**
Burnfield Rd. Stoc 1A **106**
Burnham Av. Stoc 3B **106**
Burnham Dri. M19. . . . . 1D **119**
Burnham Dri. Urm 1C **93**
Burnley St. Fail. 2C **43**
Burns Av. Swin 1D **29**
Burns Clo. M11. . . . . 2D **71**
Burns Gdns. P'wich 3D **17**
Burns Gro. Droy. 1C **75**
Burnside Av. Salf 2D **47**
Burnside Av. Stoc. 3A **122**
Burnside Dri. M19 . . . . 2C **119**
Burnthorp Av. M9 . . . . 3D **21**
Burntwood Wlk. M9 . . . . 2A **54**
   (off Naunton Wlk.)
Burrows Av. M21 . . . . 3B **114**
Burslem Av. M20 . . . . 4C **101**
Burstead St. M18. . . . . 1A **90**
Burstock St. M4 . . . . 4D **53** (1E **7**)
Burston St. M18. . . . . 2C **89**
Burtinshaw St. M18. . . . . 3D **89**
Burton Av. M20 . . . . 3C **117**
Burton Gro. Wors. 2C **29**
Burton M. M20. . . . . 4B **116**
Burton Rd. M20. . . . . 4B **116**
Burton St. M40 . . . . 3D **53** (1F **7**)

Burton Wlk. *Salf* 1D **67** (3C **4**)
Burtree St. *M12* 2A **88**
Bury Av. *M16* 2C **99**
Bury New Rd. *Salf* 2C **35** (1A **6**)
Bury New Rd. *W'fld & P'wich* . . . 1A **18**
Bury Old Rd. *P'wich & Salf* 1C **19**
Bury Pl. *M11* 1C **73**
Bury St. *Salf* 1A **68** (3F **5**)
Bushgrove Wlk. *M9* 1B **22**
(off Claygate Dri.)
Bushmoor Wlk. *M13* 3B **86**
Bushnell Wlk. *M9* 1B **22**
(off Eastlands Rd.)
Bush St. *M40* 2C **55**
Bushton Wlk. *M40* 2A **54**
Bushway Wlk. *M8* 1D **53**
(off Moordown Clo.)
Bute St. *M40* 2D **39**
Bute St. *Salf* 2B **64**
Butler Ct. *M40* 4A **54**
Butler Ct. *Stret* 3B **96**
Butler Green 2C **27**
Butler Grn. *Chad* 2C **27**
Butler La. *M4* 4A **54**
Butler St. *M4* 4A **54**
Butman St. *M18* 3E **90**
Butter La. *M3* 2B **68** (5A **6**)
Buttermere Av. *Swin* 4B **30**
Buttermere Clo. *Stret* 1A **96**
Butterstile Av. *P'wich* 4D **17**
Butterstile Clo. *P'wich* 1D **33**
Butterstile La. *P'wich* 4D **17**
Butterwick Clo. *M12* 1B **104**
Butterworth La. *Chad* 3A **26**
Butterworth St. *M11* 3A **72**
Butt Hill Av. *P'wich* 3B **18**
Butt Hill Ct. *P'wich* 3B **18**
Butt Hill Dri. *P'wich* 3B **18**
Butt Hill Rd. *P'wich* 3B **18**
Buttress St. *M18* 2C **89**
Buxton Av. *M20* 3B **116**
Buxton La. *Droy* 3A **74**
Buxton Rd. *Stret* 1C **95**
Buxton St. *M1* 3D **69** (3F **11**)
Bycroft Wlk. *M40* 3D **57**
Byrom Av. *M19* 3C **105**
Byrom Ct. *Droy* 2B **74**
Byrom Pde. *M19* 3C **105**
Byrom Pl. *M3* 2A **68** (1F **9**)
Byrom St. *M3* 3A **68** (2F **9**)
(in two parts)
Byron St. *Old T.* 4D **83**
Byron St. *Salf* 3A **66**
Byron Av. *Droy* 1C **75**
Byron Av. *P'wich* 3D **17**
Byron Av. *Swin* 2A **30**
Byron Gro. *Stoc* 3A **106**
Byron Rd. *Stret* 1D **97**
Byron St. *Eccl* 1D **61**

Byron St. *Oldh* 4D **27**
Bywell Wlk. *M8* 3B **36**
(off Levenhurst Rd.)
Bywood Wlk. *M8* 2A **52**

C

*C*ablestead Wlk. *M11* 3D **71**
(off Ranworth Clo.)
Cable St. *M4* 1D **69** (3E **7**)
Cable St. *Salf* 1A **68** (3F **5**)
Cabot St. *M13* 2D **85**
Caddington Rd. *M21* 1C **115**
Cadleigh Wlk. *M40* 3A **40**
Cadmium Wlk. *M18* 4C **89**
Cadogan Pl. *Salf* 1A **36**
Cadogan St. *M14* 4C **85**
Cadum Wlk. *M13* 2A **86**
Caen Av. *M40* 3C **25**
Cairn Dri. *Salf* 2C **51**
Cairn Wlk. *M11* 2D **71**
Caistor Clo. *M16* 1A **116**
Cajetan Ho. *Midd* 1D **23**
Cakebread St. *M12* 4A **70** (4F **11**)
Calbourne Cres. *M12* 1B **104**
Caldbeck Av. *Sale* 4C **113**
Caldecott Rd. *M9* 1C **21**
Calderbrook Wlk. *M9* 3B **38**
Calder Clo. *Stoc* 4B **122**
Calder Dri. *Kear* 1B **12**
Calder Dri. *Swin* 1A **30**
Calder Ho. *Salf* 2C **51**
Calder St. *Salf* 3D **67** (3C **8**)
Caldervale Av. *M21* 4C **115**
Caldon Clo. *Eccl* 3D **61**
Caldwell St. *Stoc* 3B **106**
Caldy Rd. *Salf* 3B **48**
Caledon Av. *M40* 2A **40**
Caledonian Dri. *Eccl* 3A **62**
Caledonia Way. *Stret* 3C **79**
Caley St. *M1* 4C **69** (4C **10**)
Calgary St. *M18* 3C **89**
Calico Clo. *Salf* 4D **51** (2C **4**)
California Fitness Cen. 5D **7**
Callingdon Rd. *M21* 4D **115**
Callum Wlk. *M13* 2A **86**
Calluna M. *M20* 4C **117**
Calthorpe Av. *M9* 3A **38**
Calton Av. *Salf* 3A **34**
Calver Av. *Eccl* 3C **61**
Calverley Av. *M19* 2D **119**
Calverton Dri. *M40* 3C **41**
Calvert St. *Salf* 1B **64**
Calver Wlk. *M40* 4A **54**
Calvine Wlk. *M40* 4A **54**
Cambell Rd. *Eccl* 1B **60**
Cambert La. *M18* 3C **89**
(Garratt Way)

Cambert La. *M18* 3D **89**
(Wellington St.)
Camberwell St. *M8* 3C **53**
Camborne St. *M14* 1D **101**
Cambrai Cres. *Eccl* 3A **44**
Cambrian St. *M40 & M11* . . . 1C **71**
Cambridge Av. *M16* 2C **99**
Cambridge Dri. *Dent* 1C **107**
Cambridge Gro. *Eccl* 1B **62**
Cambridge Ind. Area. *Salf* . . . 3D **51**
(in two parts)
Cambridge Rd. *M9* 1B **38**
Cambridge Rd. *Droy* 4B **58**
Cambridge Rd. *Fail* 2B **58**
Cambridge Rd. *Stoc* 4C **121**
Cambridge Rd. *Urm* 3B **92**
Cambridge St.
M1 & M15 . . . . 4B **68** (4B **10**)
(in two parts)
Cambridge St. *Oldh* 1D **27**
Cambridge St. *Salf* 3A **52** (1E **5**)
Cambridge St. Ind. Area.
Salf 3A **52** (1E **5**)
(Cambridge St.)
Cambridge St. Ind. Area.
Salf 4A **52** (1E **5**)
(Short St.)
Camdale Wlk. *M8* *4B* **36**
(off Ermington Dri.)
Camden Av. *M40* 3C **57**
Camelford Clo. *M15* 2C **85**
Camelia Rd. *M9* 3A **38**
Cameron St. *M1* . . . 3B **68** (3A **10**)
Camley Wlk. *M8* 1D **53**
(off Appleford Dri.)
Campanula Wlk. *M8* 1C **53**
(off Magnolia Dri.)
Campbell Rd. *M13* 2D **103**
Campbell Rd. *Swin* 4A **30**
Campbell St. *Stoc* 3B **106**
Campfield Av. *M3* 3F **9**
Campion Wlk. *M11* 3D **71**
Camponia Gdns.
Salf 2D **51**
Camp St. *M3* 3A **68** (2F **9**)
Camp St. *Salf* 2C **51**
Camrose Wlk. *M13* 3B **86**
Canada St. *M40* 3C **55**
Canal Bank. *Eccl* 4C **45**
(in two parts)
Canal Circ. *Eccl* 2C **63**
Canal Side. *Eccl* 4C **45**
Canalside N. *Traf P.* 3C **81**
Canal St. *M1* 3C **69** (2D **11**)
Canal St. *Chad* 3D **27**
Canal St. *Droy* 3C **75**
Canal St. *Salf* 2C **67** (5B **4**)
Canberra St. *M11* 1C **73**
Candleford Rd. *M20* 3D **117**

Cannon Ct. *Salf* 1B **68** (4B **6**)
(off Cateaton St.)
Cannon St. *M4* 1C **69** (4C **6**)
Cannon St. *Eccl* 2A **62**
Cannon St. *Salf* 1D **67** (3C **4**)
Canon Grn. Ct. *Salf* 1A **68** (3E **5**)
Canon Grn. Dri. *Salf* 4A **52** (2E **5**)
Canon Hussey Ct. *Salf* 5C **4**
Canons Gro. *M40* 2C **55**
Canonsleigh Clo. *M8* 2A **52**
Canonsway. *Swin* 2A **30**
Canterbury Dri. *P'wich* 4C **19**
Canterbury Gdns. *Salf* 1C **63**
Canterbury Rd. *Urm* 1C **93**
Cantrell St. *M11* 2B **72**
Canute Ct. *Stret* 1C **97**
Canute Rd. *Stret* 1C **97**
Canute St. *Salf* 1B **66**
Capella Wlk. *Salf* 3C **51**
Cape St. *M20* 2A **118**
Capital Ho. *Salf* 1A **82**
Capital Quay. *Salf* 1A **82**
Capital Rd. *M11* 1B **90**
Capricorn Way. *Salf* 3C **51**
Capstan St. *M9* 2C **39**
Captain Wlk. *Salf* *3B* **66**
(off Robert Hall St.)
Caradoc Av. *M8* 4D **37**
Carberry Rd. *M18* 3D **89**
Carbis Wlk. *M8* 2A **52**
Cardale Wlk. *M9* *3B* **38**
(off Conran St.)
Carden Av. *Swin* 3D **29**
Carder Clo. *Swin* 3A **30**
Cardiff Clo. *Oldh* 4D **27**
Cardiff St. *Salf* 3A **36**
Cardigan Rd. *Oldh* 4D **27**
Cardigan St. *Salf* 1C **65**
Cardigan Ter. *M14* 4B **84**
Cardinal St. *M8* 4D **37**
Carding Gro. *Salf* 4A **52** (2E **5**)
Cardroom Rd. *M4* 1A **70**
Cardus St. *M19* 3A **104**
Cardwell Rd. *Eccl* 2A **60**
Carey Clo. *Salf* 3D **51** (1D **5**)
Carey Wlk. *M15* *3B* **84**
(off Arnott Cres.)
Carfax St. *M18* 3D **89**
Cargate Wlk. *M8* 1B **52**
Carib St. *M15* 3B **84**
Carill Av. *M40* 1A **40**
Carill Dri. *M14* 4B **102**
Carina Pl. *Salf* 3C **51** (1B **4**)
Cariocca Bus. Pk. *M12* 2B **86**
Cariocca Bus. Pk. *Mile P* . . . 4B **54**
Carisbrook Av. *Urm* 2C **93**
Carisbrook Dri. *Swin* 4C **31**
Carisbrook St. *M9* 3B **38**
Carlburn St. *M11* 1D **73**

Carley Gro. *M9* 2D **21**
Carlford Gro. *P'wich*. 3D **17**
Carlisle St. *Oldh*. 2D **27**
(in two parts)
Carlisle St. *Swin*. 4B **14**
Carlton Av. *Fall*. 1D **101**
Carlton Av. *Firs*. 4B **82**
Carlton Av. *P'wich*. 4A **20**
Carlton Ct. *P'wich* 1A **34**
Carlton Cres. *Urm*. 3D **93**
Carlton Dri. *P'wich*. 4A **20**
Carlton Mans. *M16* 1D **99**
Carlton Range. *M18*. 4B **90**
Carlton Rd. *M16* 1D **99**
Carlton Rd. *Sale*. 3C **111**
Carlton Rd. *Salf*. 3C **49**
Carlton Rd. *Urm*. 3D **93**
Carlton St. *M16*. 4C **83**
Carlton St. *Eccl*. 4D **45**
Carlyle Clo. *M8* 1C **53**
Carmel Av. *Salf* 3C **67** (3A **8**)
Carmel Clo. *Salf*. 3C **67** (3A **8**)
Carmoor Rd. *M13* 3A **86**
Carnaby St. *M9* 1D **39**
Carna Rd. *Stoc*. 2A **106**
Carnarvon St. *M3* 3B **52** (1B **6**)
Carnarvon St. *Oldh* 4D **27**
Carnarvon St. *Salf* 3A **36**
Carnegie Av. *M19*. 3B **104**
Carnforth Rd. *Stoc*. 3D **121**
Carnforth St. *M14*. 1D **101**
Carnoustie Clo. *M40*. 3C **41**
Carnwood Clo. *M40*. 3D **57**
Carolina Ho. *Salf* 4A **52** (2E **5**)
Caroline Dri. *M4*. 2A **70**
Caroline St. *Salf*. 3A **52**
Caronet Way. *Salf* 2D **63**
Carpenters La. *M4*. 1C **69** (4D **7**)
Carpenters Wlk. *Droy*. 2B **74**
Carradale Dri. *Sale* 4C **109**
Carradale Wlk. *M40* 4A **40**
Carr Av. *P'wich* 4D **17**
Carr Bank Av. *M9*. 3B **20**
Carrgreen Clo. *M19*. 4D **119**
Carriage Dri. *M40*. 2B **54**
Carriage St. *M16*. 3D **83**
Carrigart. *P'wich* 3B **18**
Carrill Gro. *M19*. 3A **104**
Carrill Gro. E. *M19*. 3A **104**
Carrington Ho. *Salf* 3A **48**
Carrington La. *C'ton & Sale* . . 2A **108**
Carrington Rd. *M14* 4A **102**
Carrington Spur. *Sale & Urm* . . 3C **109**
Carrington St. *Chad*. 3D **27**
Carrington St. *Swin*. 1D **31**

Carrington Ter. *Swin*. 1C **31**
(off Carrington St.)
Carron Av. *M9*. 1D **39**
Carroway St. *M40* 2C **55**
Carr St. *Swin* 3D **29**
Carrsvale Av. *Urm* 1B **92**
Carruthers St. *M4* 1B **70**
Carslake Rd. *M40*. 2B **54**
Carson Rd. *M19*. 1A **120**
Carstairs Clo. *M8*. 3B **36**
Carter St. *Salf* 2D **51**
Carthorpe Arch. *Salf*. 2D **65**
Cartmel Av. *Stoc* 3A **122**
Cartmel Cres. *Chad* 4B **26**
Cartmel Ct. *M9* 2A **24**
Cartmel Wlk. *M9* 3B **38**
(in two parts)
Cartwright Rd. *M21* 1D **113**
Carver Av. *P'wich* 1C **19**
Carver Clo. *M16*. 3B **82**
Carver St. *M16*. 3B **82**
Carver Wlk. *M15* 3B **84**
(off Arnott Cres.)
Carville Rd. *M9* 3B **24**
Cascade Dri. *Salf* 2A **52**
Cashmoor Wlk. *M12* 2C **87**
Cass Av. *Salf* 3A **66**
Cassandra Ct. *Salf*. 3C **67** (3B **8**)
Cassidy Clo. *M4*. 1D **69** (3F **7**)
Cassidy Ct. *Salf* 3C **65**
Casson St. *Fail*. 3B **42**
Castle Clo. *Droy*. 1D **75**
Castle Courts. *Salf* 2B **66**
Castledene Av. *Salf*. 4C **49**
Castlefield. 3A **68** (3E **9**)
Castle Field 3A **68**
Castlefield Av. *Salf* 2A **36**
Castlefield Gallery 4A **68** (4F **9**)
(off Hewitt St.)
Castlefield Vis. Cen. . . . 3A **68** (2E **9**)
Castleford Wlk. *M21* 2D **115**
Castle Hill Rd. *P'wich*. 4D **19**
Castle Irwell Student Village.
Salf. 2B **50**
Castlemere Rd. *M9* 3A **22**
Castlemoor Av. *Salf* 2B **34**
Castle Quay. *M15*. 4A **68** (4E **9**)
Castlerea Clo. *Eccl*. 3D **61**
Castlerigg Clo. *Heat C* 2D **121**
Castle St. *M3*. 3A **68** (3E **9**)
Castle St. *Eccl* 1B **62**
Castleton Av. *Stret*. 4D **79**
Castleton Rd. *Salf* 1A **36**
Castleton Wlk. *M11* 2D **71**
Castleway. *Salf*. 3C **49**
Castle Way. *Swin* 4C **15**
Castlewood Rd. *Salf*. 2A **34**
Catalan Sq. *M3* 3A **68** (3E **9**)

Cateaton St. *M3*. 1B **68** (4B **6**)
Caterham St. *M4*. 2B **70**
Catesby Rd. *M16*. 1D **99**
Catfield Wlk. *M15*. 1D **83** (5D **9**)
Cathedral App. *Salf*. 1B **68** (3B **6**)
Cathedral Gates. *M3*. 1B **68** (4B **6**)
Cathedral St. *M4*. 1B **68** (4B **6**)
Cathedral Yd. *Salf*. 1B **68** (4B **6**)
Catherine Rd. *M8*. 1A **36**
Catherine Rd. *Swin*. 3C **29**
Catherine St. *M11*. 1A **90**
Catherine St. *Eccl*. 4A **44**
Catherston Rd. *M16*. 1A **100**
Catlow La. *M4*. 1C **69** (4D **7**)
Catlow St. *Salf*. 3A **52** (1F **5**)
Cattlin Way. *Oldh*. 4D **27**
Causeway, The. *Chad*. 1A **26**
Cavalier St. *M40*. 1B **70**
Cavanagh Clo. *M13*. 2B **86**
Cavell St. *M1*. 2D **69** (5E **7**)
(off Newton St.)
Cavell Way. *Salf & M6*. 2A **66**
Cavendish Av. *M20*. 3B **116**
Cavendish Av. *Swin*. 3A **16**
Cavendish Ct. *M9*. 1C **21**
(off Deanswood Dri.)
Cavendish Ct. *Salf*. 1D **35**
Cavendish Ct. *Stret*. 4C **81**
Cavendish Ct. *Urm*. 2A **94**
(off Cavendish Rd.)
Cavendish Gdns. *M20*. 3B **116**
Cavendish Gro. *Eccl*. 4A **46**
Cavendish Ho. *Eccl*. 3A **46**
Cavendish Pl. *M11*. 1A **72**
Cavendish Pl. *Swin*. 2C **31**
Cavendish Rd. *M20*. 3B **116**
Cavendish Rd. *Eccl*. 4A **46**
Cavendish Rd. *Salf*. 1C **35**
Cavendish Rd. *Stret*. 4C **81**
Cavendish Rd. *Urm*. 2A **94**
(in two parts)
Cavendish Rd. *Wors*. 4B **28**
Cavendish St. *M15*. 2C **85** (5C **10**)
(in two parts)
Cavendish Ter. *M21*. 4B **98**
Cavenham Wlk. *M9*. 3A **38**
(off Hendham Va.)
Caversham Dri. *M9*. 2C **39**
Cawdor Ho. *Eccl*. 3D **61**
(off Enfield Clo.)
Cawdor Rd. *M14*. 3A **102**
Cawdor St. *M15*. 1D **83** (5C **8**)
Cawdor St. *Eccl*. 2C **61**
Cawdor St. *Swin*. 2D **29**
Cawley Av. *P'wich*. 4D **17**
Cawley Ter. *M9*. 1C **21**
Cawood Ho. *Rom*. 2D **123**
Cawood Sq. *Stoc*. 3D **123**
Cawston Wlk. *M8*. 1C **53**

Cawthorne Ct. *Swin*. 1D **29**
Caxton Rd. *M14*. 3D **101**
Caxton St. *Salf*. 4F **5**
Caygill St. *Salf*. 1A **68** (3F **5**)
Caythorpe St. *M14*. 1C **101**
Cayton St. *M12*. 1A **104**
Cecil Gro. *M18*. 3D **89**
Cecil Rd. *M9*. 1B **22**
Cecil Rd. *Eccl*. 2A **62**
Cecil Rd. *Stret*. 3A **96**
Cecil St. *M15*. 3D **85**
Cedar Ct. *M14*. 3A **102**
Cedar Dri. *Droy*. 1D **75**
Cedar Dri. *Swin*. 2D **13**
Cedar Dri. *Urm*. 3C **93**
Cedar Gro. *M14*. 1B **118**
Cedar Gro. *Stoc*. 4C **121**
Cedar Pl. *Salf*. 3C **51**
Cedar Rd. *Fail*. 1B **58**
Cedar Rd. *Sale*. 3D **109**
Cedric Rd. *M8*. 4A **20**
Cedric St. *Salf*. 1B **64**
Celia St. *M8*. 2A **38**
Cemetery Rd. *Droy*. 2B **74**
Cemetery Rd. *Fail*. 4B **42**
Cemetery Rd. *Salf*. 2C **65**
Cemetery Rd. N. *Swin*. 4A **14**
Cemetery Rd. S. *Swin*. 1A **30**
Centaur Clo. *Swin*. 4B **14**
Centaur Way. *M8*. 3B **36**
Centenary Circ. *Salf*. 2C **63**
Centenary Way. *Salf*. 2C **63**
Central Av. *M19*. 2A **104**
Central Av. *Salf*. 1C **49**
Central Av. *Swin*. 4B **16**
Central Dri. *M8*. 1D **37**
Central Dri. *Stoc*. 4B **122**
Central Dri. *Swin*. 3D **31**
Central Dri. *Urm*. 2D **93**
Central Ho. *M9*. 1C **23**
Central Library 3B **68** (2B **10**)
Central Pk. Est. *Traf P*. 2D **79**
Central Retail Pk. *M4*. . . . 2A **70** (5F **7**)
Central Rd. *M20*. 4C **117**
Central St. *M2*. 2B **68** (1B **10**)
Centrepoint. *Traf P*. 3C **79**
Centurion Gro. *Salf*. 1A **52**
Century St. *M3*. 3A **68** (3F **9**)
Ceylon St. *M40*. 1A **56**
Chadderton Ind. Est. *Midd*. . . . 1C **25**
Chadderton St. *M4*. 1D **69** (3E **7**)
Chaddesley Wlk. *M11*. 3D **71**
Chadkirk Clo. *M14*. 1D **101**
Chadwick Rd. *Eccl*. 1A **62**
Chadwick Rd. *Urm*. 2B **94**
Chadwick St. *Swin*. 2B **30**
Chain Bar. 3C **25**
Chainhurst Wlk. *M13*. . . . 2A **86** (5F **11**)
(off Weald Clo.)

Chain Rd. *M9* 1B **22**
Chain St. *M1* 2C **69** (1C **10**)
Chain Wlk. *M9* 1C **23**
Chalcombe Grange. *M12* 4D **87**
Chale Clo. *M40* 4B **54**
Chalfont Av. *Urm* 2A **94**
Chalfont Dri. *M8* 3C **37**
Chalfont Ho. *Salf* 1D **65**
Challenor Sq. *M12* 2A **88**
Chamber Rd. *Oldh* 3D **27**
Chambersfield Ct. *Salf* 2D **65**
Champneys Wlk. *M9* 4B **38**
Chancel Av. *Salf* 3C **67** (3A **8**)
Chancellor La. *M12* 3B **70**
Chancel Pl. *M1* 2A **70**
Chancery La. *M2* 2B **68** (1B **10**)
Chancery Pl. *M2* 2B **68** (1B **10**)
Chandlers Point. *Salf* 3D **65**
Chandlers Row. *Wors* 2A **44**
Chandos Gro. *Salf* 1B **64**
Chandos Rd. *M21* 3C **99**
Chandos Rd. *P'wich* 4B **18**
Chandos Rd. *Stoc* 3B **120**
Chandos Rd. S. *M21* 4C **99**
Change Way. *Salf* 4A **52** (2E **5**)
Chantry Clo. *Stoc* 2A **122**
Chantry Wlk. *M8* 3B **36**
Chapel Ct. *M9* 1B **38**
Chapel Ct. *Sale* 3A **110**
Chapelfield Rd. *M12* 3A **70**
Chapel Gro. *Urm* 2A **94**
Chapelhill Dri. *M9* 3A **22**
Chapel Ho. *Stoc* 1A **122**
Chapel La. *M9* 2D **21**
Chapel La. *Stret* 3A **96**
Chapel Pl. *Urm* 3D **61**
Chapel Rd. *Oldh* 3D **27**
Chapel Rd. *P'wich* 1D **33**
Chapel Rd. *Sale* 4D **111**
Chapel Rd. *Swin* 3C **29**
Chapel St. *Droy* 2D **75**
Chapel St. *Eccl* 2C **61**
Chapel St. *Lev* 3A **104**
Chapel St. *P'wich* 2A **18**
Chapel St. *Salf* 1D **67** (4C **4**)
Chapel St. *Swin* 1C **31**
Chapel Ter. *M20* 2D **117**
Chapeltown St. *M1* . . . 3D **69** (2F **11**)
Chapel Wlk. *Eccl* 1B **62**
Chapel Wlk. *P'wich* 2A **34**
Chapel Walks. *M2* 2B **68** (5B **6**)
Chapel Walks. *Sale* 4D **111**
Chaplin Clo. *Salf* 3C **49**
Chapman M. *M18* 3D **89**
(in two parts)
Chapman St. *M18* 2D **89**
Chappell Rd. *Droy* 1C **75**
Chapter St. *M40* 3D **55**
Charfield St. *M40* 2D **57**

Chariot St. *Open* 3D **73**
Charlbury Av. *P'wich* 3A **20**
Charlbury Av. *Stoc* 2B **122**
Charles Av. *Aud* 4C **75**
Charles Halle Rd. *M15* 3C **85**
Charles Morris Clo. *Fail* 2D **43**
Charles Morris Ho. *Fail*. *3C 43*
(off Gildenhall)
Charles St. *M1* 4C **69** (4C **10**)
Charles St. *Droy* 2A **74**
Charles St. *Salf* 3D **49**
(in two parts)
Charles St. *Swin* 1D **29**
Charleston Sq. *Urm* 1B **92**
Charlestown **3A 24**
(Manchester)
Charlestown **2B 50**
(Salford)
Charlestown Rd. *M9* 4B **22**
Charlesworth St. *M11* 3D **71**
Charley Av. *Salf* 3D **51**
Charlotte St. *M1* 2C **69** (1C **10**)
Charlton Av. *Eccl* 2D **61**
Charlton Av. *P'wich* 3B **18**
Charlton Ct. *P'wich* 3B **18**
Charlton Dri. *Sale* 4A **110**
Charlton Dri. *Swin* 4D **13**
Charlton Pl. *Ard* 4D **69** (4F **11**)
Charlton Rd. *M19* 2B **104**
Charminster Dri. *M8* 2D **37**
Charminster M. *Swin* 4B **30**
Charnley Clo. *M40* 4C **55**
Charnley Wlk. *M40* 4C **55**
Charnwood Av. *Dent* 1D **107**
Charter Ho. *Eccl* 2B **62**
Charter St. *M3* 4B **52** (1B **6**)
Chartwell Clo. *Salf* 1D **65**
Chaseley Rd. *Salf* 3C **49**
Chase St. *M4* 4C **53** (1D **7**)
Chase, The. *Wors* 2A **44**
Chassen Av. *Urm* 2A **92**
Chassen Ct. *Urm* 3B **92**
Chassen Rd. *Urm* 2B **92**
Chataway Rd. *M8* 2A **38**
Chatburn Rd. *M21* 4C **99**
Chatfield Rd. *M21* 4B **98**
Chatford Clo. *Salf* 3A **52** (1E **5**)
Chatham Clo. *M20* 3C **117**
Chatham Gro. *M20* 3C **117**
Chatham Rd. *Gort* 1A **106**
Chatham Rd. *Old T*. 1C **99**
Chatham St. *M1* 2D **69** (1E **11**)
Chatley Rd. *Eccl* 2A **60**
Chatley St. *M3* 3B **52** (1B **6**)
Chatsworth Av. *P'wich* 2B **18**
Chatsworth Clo. *Droy* 4D **57**
Chatsworth Clo. *Urm* 2A **94**
Chatsworth Ct. *M9*. *1C 21*
(off Deanswood Dri.)

Chatsworth Cres. *Stret* 1B **94**
Chatsworth Gro. *M16.* 2D **99**
Chatsworth Rd. *M18* 3C **89**
Chatsworth Rd. *Droy.* 1A **74**
Chatsworth Rd. *Eccl.* 3B **46**
Chatsworth Rd. *Stret* 1C **95**
Chatsworth Rd. *Wors.* 1B **44**
Chatterton Clo. *M20* 3A **118**
Chattock St. *M16* 1A **100**
Chatwood Rd. *M40* 4D **25**
Chaucer Av. *Droy.* 2C **75**
Chaucer Av. *Stoc.* 3D **105**
Chaucer Ho. *Stoc.* 4A **106**
Chaucer Wlk. *M13* 2A **86**
Chauncy Rd. *M40* 2A **42**
Chaytor Av. *M40* 3A **40**
Cheadle Av. *Salf.* 3A **34**
Cheadle St. *M11* 3D **73**
Cheam Clo. *M11* 4B **72**
Cheapside. *M2* 2B **68** (5B **6**)
Cheddar St. *M18* 3D **89**
Cheeryble St. *Droy & M11* 3B **74**
            (in two parts)
Cheetham. 1B **52**
Cheetham Hill. 3C **37**
Cheetham Hill Rd.
  M4, M3 & M8 . . . . . 4C **53** (1C **6**)
Cheetham Hill Rd. *M8* 2B **36**
Cheetham Pde. *M8.* 2B **36**
Cheetham Pk. Cen. *M8.* 2B **52**
Cheetham Rd. *Swin.* 3C **31**
Cheetham St. *M40* 2C **55**
Cheetham St. *Fail.* 2C **43**
            (in two parts)
Cheetwood Rd. *M8* 3B **52**
Cheetwood St. *M8* 3A **52** (1F **5**)
Chelbourne Dri. *Oldh* 4D **27**
Cheldon Wlk. *M40* 1C **57**
Chelford Clo. *M13* 3B **86**
Chelford Dri. *Swin.* 4A **14**
Chelford Rd. *M16.* 1C **99**
Chell St. *M12.* 4D **87**
Chelmsford Av. *M40.* 3B **56**
Chelsea Rd. *M40* 2B **56**
Chelsfield Gro. *M21* 1D **115**
Chelston Av. *M40.* 4D **25**
Cheltenham Cres. *Salf.* 2A **36**
Cheltenham Dri. *Sale* 4A **112**
Cheltenham Rd. *M21* 2B **98**
Cheltenham St. *Salf.* 3A **50**
Chelwood Dri. *Droy.* 1B **74**
Chendre Clo. *Swin.* 4B **14**
Chendre Rd. *M9.* 3B **24**
Cheney Clo. *M11.* 1D **89**
Chepstow Rd. *M21.* 3A **98**
Chepstow Rd. *Swin.* 4C **15**
Chepstow St. *M1.* 3B **68** (3B **10**)
Chepstow St. S. *M1.* . . . 3B **68** (3B **10**)
Chequers Rd. *M21.* 1B **114**

Cheriton Av. *Sale* 4A **112**
Cherry Dri. *Swin* 2C **31**
Cherry St. *P'wich* 1C **19**
Cherryton Wlk. *M13.* 2A **86**
Cherry Tree Ct. *Salf* 1A **66**
Cherry Tree Wlk. *Stret* 3A **96**
Chertsey Clo. *M18* 3A **90**
Cherwell Clo. *Oldh* 1D **43**
Chesham Ho. *Salf* 2D **65**
Chesham Rd. *Eccl* 3C **61**
Cheshill Ct. *Salf* 4B **36**
Cheshire Clo. *Stret.* 3D **95**
Cheshire Gdns. *M14.* 3C **101**
Chesney Av. *Chad* 4A **26**
Chesshyre Av. *M4* 2B **70**
Chessington Ri. *Swin.* 3C **15**
Chester Av. *Urm* 1A **94**
Chester Rd.
  M16 & M15 . . . . . 3B **82** (5B **8**)
Chester Rd. *Stret & M16* 2A **112**
Chester St.
  M15 & M1 . . . . . 1B **84** (5B **10**)
Chester St. *Oldh.* 1D **27**
Chester St. *P'wich.* 1A **18**
Chester St. *Swin* 3A **30**
Chesterton Gro. *Droy.* 1C **75**
Chestnut Av. *M21.* 1B **114**
Chestnut Av. *Droy.* 4A **58**
Chestnut Gro. *Fail.* 4B **42**
Chestnut Rd. *Eccl.* 3A **44**
Chestnut St. *Chad.* 3B **26**
Chesworth Ct. *Droy.* 2B **74**
Chesworth Wlk. *M15* 2A **84** (5E **9**)
     (off Jackson Cres.)
Chetham Clo. *Salf* 1B **82**
Chetham's Library 1B **68** (3B **6**)
     (off Long Millgate)
Chetwynd Av. *Urm* 3C **93**
Chetwynd Clo. *Sale* 3A **110**
Chevassut St. *M15.* 2A **84** (5E **9**)
Chevington Dri. *M9* 4B **38**
Cheviot Clo. *Salf.* 4C **49**
Cheviot St. *M3.* 1B **6**
Chevril Clo. *M15* 2C **85** (5C **10**)
Chevron Clo. *Salf.* 1B **66**
Chichester Rd. *M15* 3A **84**
     (Bold St.)
Chichester Rd. *M15* 2B **84**
     (Old Birley St.)
Chichester Rd. S. *M15* 4A **84**
Chidlow Av. *M20* 2C **117**
Chiffon Way. *Salf.* 4D **51** (2C **4**)
Chilcombe Wlk. *M9* 1C **23**
     (off Brockford Dri.)
Chilcote Av. *Sale* 4A **110**
Chilham Rd. *Eccl.* 3B **46**
Chilham St. *Swin.* 4A **30**
Chiltern Dri. *Swin.* 1B **46**
Chilworth St. *M14* 2D **101**

Chime Bank. *M8* 3D **37**
China La. *M1* 2D **69** (1E **11**)
Chinese Arts Cen. 4D **7**
Chingford Wlk. *M13* 4D **87**
      (off Bates St.)
Chinley Av. *M40* 2A **40**
Chinley Av. *Stret* 4C **79**
Chinley St. *Salf* 2B **50**
Chinwell Vw. *M19* 3A **104**
Chippenham Ct. *M4* 1B **70**
Chippenham Rd. *M4* 1A **70**
Chipping Sq. *M12* 4D **87**
Chipstead Av. *M12* 3C **87**
Chirton Wlk. *M40* 3A **40**
Chiselhurst St. *M8* 2C **37**
Chisholm St. *Open* 4D **73**
Chisledon Av. *Salf* 4B **36**
Chislehurst Av. *Urm* 1C **93**
Choir St. *Salf* 3A **52**
Cholmondeley Rd. *Salf* 3D **47**
Chomlea Mnr. *Salf* 3A **48**
Choral Gro. *Salf* 2A **52**
Chorley Rd. *Swin* 1A **30**
Chorley St. *Stret* 4D **81**
Chorley Wood Av. *M19* 3D **119**
Chorlton-cum-Hardy 3A **82**
Chorlton Ees
   Nature Reserve 2D **113**
Chorlton Fold 3D **45**
Chorlton Fold. *Eccl* 2D **45**
      (in two parts)
Chorlton Grn. *M21* 1A **114**
Chorlton Leisure Cen. 3B **98**
Chorlton Pl. *Chor H* 3B **98**
Chorlton Rd.
   M16 & M15 . . . . . . 4D **83** (5D **9**)
Chorlton St. *M1* 3C **69** (2D **11**)
Chorlton St. *M16* 3C **83**
Chorlton upon Medlock 3B **86**
Chorltonville 3B **114**
Chorlton Water Pk. 4B **114**
Christ Chu. Av. *Salf* . . . 1B **66** (4A **4**)
Christchurch Rd. *Sale* 4C **109**
Christie Fields Office Pk. *M21* . . 4D **115**
Christie Rd. *Stret* 1C **97**
Christleton Av. *Stoc* 4D **121**
Christopher St. *M40* 3D **57**
Christopher St. *Salf* 2B **66**
Chudleigh Rd. *M8* 4C **21**
Church Av. *M40* 2C **57**
Church Av. *Salf* 1B **64**
Churchdale Rd. *M9* 2D **21**
Church Dri. *P'wich* 2A **18**
Churchfield. *M21* 4A **98**
Churchfield Rd. *Salf* 2B **48**
Churchfields. *Sale* 3D **109**
Churchfield Wlk. *M11* 3A **72**
     (off Outrington Dri.)
Churchgate. *Urm* 3A **94**

Churchgate Bldgs. *M1* 3A **70**
Church Grn. *Salf* 4D **49**
Church Gro. *Eccl* 2A **62**
Churchill Av. *M16* 2D **99**
Churchill Ct. *Salf* 1D **65**
Churchill Cres. *Stoc* 3A **106**
Churchill Pl. *Eccl* 3C **45**
Churchill Way. *Salf* 1A **66**
Churchill Way. *Traf P* 4A **64**
Church La. *M9* 3C **39**
     (Kingscliffe St.)
Church La. *M9* 2B **38**
     (Water St.)
Church La. *Burn* 3D **119**
Church La. *P'wich* 2A **18**
Church La. *Sale* 3A **110**
Church La. *Salf* 1C **35**
Church Rd. *Eccl* 1B **62**
Church Rd. *Urm* 4A **92**
Churchside Clo. *M9* 4B **22**
Church St. *M4* 1C **69** (4D **7**)
Church St. *Droy* 2D **75**
Church St. *Eccl* 1A **62**
     (in three parts)
Church St. *Fail* 2B **42**
Church St. *Salf* 4D **49**
Church St. *Stret* 3A **96**
Church St. *Swin* 2D **31**
     (Bolton Rd.)
Church St. *Swin* 2A **30**
     (Chorley Rd.)
Church Ter. *Sale* 3C **111**
Church Vw. *Droy* 2D **75**
Church Vw. *Fail* 2B **42**
Church Wlk. *Swin* 3B **14**
Churnet St. *M40* 2B **54**
Churston Av. *M9* 2C **23**
Churton Av. *M14* 2D **101**
Churton Rd. *M18* 1C **105**
Cicero St. *M9* 2D **39**
Cinder St. *M4* 1A **70** (3F **7**)
Cipher St. *M4* 4A **54**
Circle Ct. *Stret* 4B **78**
Circle S. *Traf P* 2C **81**
Circle, The. *Stret* 4B **78**
Circuit, The. *M20* 4D **117**
Circular Rd. *M20* 4D **117**
Circular Rd. *P'wich* 4B **18**
Ciss La. *Urm* 2A **94**
Citrus Way. *Salf* 1A **66**
City Course Trad. Est. *Open* . . . 4A **72**
City Ct. Trad. Est. *M4* 1A **70**
City of Manchester Stadium 1D **71**
     (Manchester City)
City Pk. Bus. Village. *M16* 3B **82**
City Point. *M32* 3D **81**
City Rd. *M15* 2C **83** (5D **9**)
City Rd. E. *M15* 4B **68** (4A **10**)
City S. *M15* 4B **68** (4A **10**)

City Wlk. *Swin* 2D **31**
Clacton Wlk. M13. . . . . 2A **86**
        (off Kirkstall Sq.)
Clague St. *M11* 1A **72**
Claife Av. *M40* 4B **24**
Clandon Av. *Eccl* 1B **60**
Clapham St. *M40* 2C **41**
Clara St. *Oldh* 2D **27**
Claremont Av. *M20* 4C **117**
Claremont Av. *Stoc* 4C **121**
Claremont Range. *M18* 4B **90**
Claremont Rd. *M16 & M14.* . . . 1A **100**
Claremont Rd. *Sale* 4D **111**
Claremont Rd. *Salf.* 1B **48**
Claremont St. *Fail.* 2B **42**
Clarence Av. *Traf P.* 1B **78**
Clarence Rd. *M13* 1C **103**
Clarence Rd. *Stoc* 4B **120**
Clarence Rd. *Swin* 3C **29**
Clarence St. *M2.* . . . 2B **68** (1B **10**)
Clarence St. *Salf* 3D **51**
Clarendon Cres. *Eccl* 4B **46**
Clarendon Cres. *Sale* 4B **112**
Clarendon Recreation Cen. . . 1A **66**
Clarendon Rd. *M16* 2C **99**
Clarendon Rd. *Aud.* 4C **75**
Clarendon Rd. *Eccl.* 4B **46**
Clarendon Rd. *Sale.* 4B **112**
Clarendon Rd. *Swin* 2B **30**
Clarendon Rd. W. *M21* 2B **98**
Clarendon St. *M15.* 2B **84** (5A **10**)
        (in two parts)
Clarendon Wlk. *Salf* 1A **66**
Clare Rd. *M19* 1A **120**
Clare St. *M1* 4D **69** (4F **11**)
Claribel St. *M11* 3C **71**
Claridge Rd. *M21* 2A **98**
Clarion St. *M4* 4A **54**
Clark Av. *M18* 3A **90**
Clarke Av. *Salf* 1B **82**
Clarke Ind. Est. *Stret* 3B **78**
Clark's Hill. *P'wich* 2A **18**
        (in two parts)
Clatford Wlk. M9 . . . . 3B **38**
        (off Fernclough Rd.)
Claude Av. *Swin* 2D **29**
Claude Rd. *M21* 2A **114**
Claude St. *M8* 1C **37**
Claude St. *Eccl.* 4B **44**
Claude St. *Swin* 2D **29**
Claxton Av. *M9.* 3B **22**
Clay Bank. *Droy.* 2B **74**
Claybrook Wlk. *M11.* 2A **72**
Clayburn Rd. *M15* 2A **84**
Claycourt Av. *Eccl* 3B **44**
Claygate Dri. *M9* 1B **22**
Clayhill Wlk. *M9.* 1C **39**
Claymore St. *M18* 2A **90**
Claythorpe Wlk. *M8* 4A **20**

Clayton 1C **73**
Clayton Bridge 3A **58**
Claytonbrook Rd. *M11.* 2C **73**
Clayton Clo. *M15* 3A **84**
Clayton Community Farm 2C **73**
        (off Turner St.)
Clayton Hall Rd. *M11.* 1C **73**
Clayton Ind. Est. *M11.* 2D **73**
Clayton La. *M11.* 3B **72**
Clayton La. S. *M11.* 1A **88**
Clayton St. *M11* 4B **56**
        (in two parts)
Clayton St. *Chad* 3C **27**
Clayton St. *Fail.* 3B **42**
Cleadon Av. *M18* 4C **89**
Cleavley St. *Eccl.* 1B **60**
Clee Av. *M13* 2D **103**
Cleethorpes Av. *M9* 3D **21**
Clegg St. *Droy* 2B **74**
Clematis Wlk. *Swin* 4A **14**
Clement Ct. M11 . . . . 4B **74**
        (off Toxteth St.)
Clementine Clo. *Salf.* 1B **66**
Clements St. *M11* 1A **90**
Clement Stott Clo. *M9* 2D **23**
Clement St. *Chad.* 3D **27**
Cleminson St. *Salf.* 1D **67** (4C **4**)
Clerk's Ct. *Salf.* 1D **63**
Clevedon Av. *Urm* 2C **95**
Clevedon St. *M9.* 3C **39**
Cleveland Av. *M19* 2B **104**
Cleveland Av. *Salf.* 4A **48**
Cleveland Clo. *Swin* 4C **15**
Cleveland Rd. *M8.* 1D **37**
Cleveleys Av. *M21* 1C **115**
Cleveleys Gro. *Salf.* 3A **36**
Cleworth St. *M15* 1D **83** (5C **8**)
Cleworth Wlk. *M15* 1D **83** (5C **8**)
Clibran St. *M8* 1D **53**
Cliff Av. *Salf.* 1C **51**
Cliff Cres. *Salf.* 3D **35**
Cliffdale Dri. *M8.* 1C **37**
Cliff Grange. *Salf.* 3D **35**
Clifford Ct. *M15* 3A **84**
Clifford St. *M13.* 2D **85** (5E **11**)
Clifford St. *Eccl* 3B **60**
Clifford St. *Swin.* 2D **31**
Cliff, The 3C **35**
Clifton 3B **14**
Clifton Av. *M14* 1B **118**
Clifton Av. *Eccl.* 4D **45**
Clifton Clo. *M16.* 3D **83**
Clifton Country Pk. 1A **14**
Clifton Ct. *Swin* 2A **14**
Clifton Dri. *Swin.* 1D **29**
        (Manchester Rd.)
Clifton Dri. *Swin.* 4A **16**
        (Western Av.)
Clifton Green 3D **15**

Clifton Gro. *Old T.* 3D **83**
Clifton Gro. *Swin* 4D **13**
Clifton House Arboretum 1D **13**
Clifton Ho. Rd. *Swin* 1D **13**
Clifton Ind. Est. *Swin* 3A **16**
Clifton Pl. *P'wich* 1A **18**
Clifton Rd. *M21* 4C **99**
Clifton Rd. *Eccl* 4D **45**
Clifton Rd. *Urm* 2A **92**
Clifton Rd. *W'fld & P'wich* 2C **17**
Clifton St. *Fail* 1C **43**
Clifton St. *Mile P* 4D **55**
Clifton St. *Old T.* 3D **83**
Clifton Vw. *Swin* 2A **14**
Clifton Vs. *Fail* 1C **43**
Cliftonville Dri. *Swin & Salf* . . . 1C **47**
Clinton Av. *M14* 2B **100**
Clinton Gdns. *M14* 2C **101**
Clinton Ho. *Salf* 2D **65**
Clippers Quay. *Salf* 2A **82**
Clitheroe Rd. *M13* 1D **103**
Clito St. *M9* 2D **39**
Cliveley Wlk. *Swin* 2D **31**
Clive Lloyd Ct. *Stret* 1C **97**
Clively Av. *Swin* 4D **15**
Clive Rd. *Fail* 3A **42**
Clive St. *M4.* 4D **53** (2E **7**)
Clivewood Wlk. *M12* 2C **87**
Clivia Gro. *Salf* 4D **35**
Cloak St. *M1* 4C **69** (4D **11**)
Clock Ho. Av. *Droy* 4A **58**
Clockhouse M. *Droy* 4A **58**
Clock St. *Chad* 4D **27**
Cloister St. *M9* 2D **39**
Clopton Wlk. *M15* 2A **84** (5F **9**)
(Birchvale Clo.)
Clopton Wlk. *M15* 2A **84**
(Rolls Cres.)
Clough Bank. *M9* 4B **22**
Clough Dri. *P'wich* 2D **17**
Cloughfield Av. *Salf* 3B **66** (3A **8**)
Clough La. *P'wich* 2D **17**
Clough Rd. *M9* 2D **39**
Clough Rd. *Droy* 1C **75**
Clough Rd. *Fail* 3C **43**
Clough Side. *M9* 1D **39**
Clough St. *M40* 3C **57**
Clough, The. *Stoc* 3D **123**
Cloughton Wlk. *M40* 2D **57**
Clough Top Rd. *M9* 4A **24**
Clough Wlk. *P'wich* 2D **17**
Clough Wlk. *Stoc* 3D **123**
Clovelly Rd. *M21* 1C **115**
Clovelly Rd. *Swin* 3C **29**
Clovelly St. *M40* 2D **57**
Cloverbank Av. *M19* 4B **118**
Clowes St. *M12* 2D **87**
(in two parts)
Clowes St. *Chad* 4D **27**

Clowes St. *Salf* 1A **68** (4F **5**)
Club St. *M11* 4B **74**
Clumber Rd. *M18* 4B **90**
Clyde Rd. *M20* 4B **116**
Clydesdale Gdns. *M11* 2A **72**
Clyne Ho. *Stret* 4D **81**
Clyne St. *Stret* 3D **81**
Coalbrook Wlk. *M12* 3C **71**
(off Aden Clo.)
Coalburn St. *M12* 2A **88**
Coalshaw Grn. Rd. *Chad* 3C **27**
Coatbridge St. *M11* 1C **73**
Cobalt Av. *Urm* 2B **78**
Cobb Clo. *M8.* 3A **20**
Cobble Bank. *M9* 3A **22**
Cobden Cen., The. *Salf* 2D **65**
Cobden St. *M9.* 2C **39**
Cobden St. *Salf* 3A **50**
Coberley Av. *Urm* 4A **76**
Cob Hall Rd. *Stret* 3A **96**
Cobham Av. *M40* 4C **25**
Cobourg St. *M1.* 3D **69** (2E **11**)
Coburg Av. *Salf* 3D **51**
Cochrane Av. *M12* 3C **87**
Cockcroft Rd. *Salf* 1B **66** (3A **4**)
Cockcroft St. *M9* 1B **38**
Coconut Gro. *Salf* 1B **66**
Coddington Av. *Open* 3A **74**
Cody Ct. *Salf* 3C **65**
Coghlan Clo. *M11* 1B **72**
Coke St. *Salf* 2B **36**
Colborne Av. *Eccl* 1B **60**
Colborne Av. *Stoc.* 1B **106**
Colbourne Av. *M8* 1B **36**
Colby Wlk. *M40* 3A **40**
Colchester Av. *P'wich* 4C **19**
Colchester St. *M40* 3B **54**
Colclough Clo. *M40* 4B **40**
Coldstream Av. *M9.* 2B **22**
Colebrook Dri. *M40* 4A **40**
Coleby Av. *Old T.* 4C **83**
Coleridge Clo. *Stoc.* 3A **106**
Coleridge Rd. *M16.* 1C **99**
Coleridge Rd. *Stoc.* 3A **106**
Coleridge St. *M40* 3C **57**
Coleridge Way. *Stoc* 3A **106**
Coleshill St. *M40* 4C **55**
Colesmere Wlk. *M40* 1D **41**
Cole St. *M40* 2D **39**
Colgate Cres. *M14* 4D **101**
Colgate La. *Salf* 2A **82**
Colgrove Av. *M40.* 4C **25**
Colina Dri. *Salf.* 2A **52**
Colindale Av. *M9* 2C **23**
Colin Murphy Rd. *M15.* . . . 2A **84** (5E **9**)
Coll Dri. *Urm* 3D **77**
College Av. *Droy.* 3B **74**
College Cft. *Eccl* 1B **62**
College Rd. *M16* 2C **99**

College Land. *M3* 2B **68** (5A **6**)
College Rd. *M16* 2C **99**
College Rd. *Eccl* 1C **63**
Colley St. *Stret* 3D **81**
Collie Av. *Salf* 2C **51**
Collier St. *Salf* 3A **68** (3F **9**)
    (Bridgewater St.)
Collier St. *Salf* 1D **49**
    (Langley Rd. S.)
Collier St. *Salf* 1A **68** (3F **5**)
    (Rolla St.)
Collier St. *Swin* 3A **30**
Colliery St. *M11* 2A **72**
    (in two parts)
Collin Av. *M18* 4C **89**
Collingburn Av. *Salf* 4B **66**
Collingburn Ct. *Salf* 4B **66**
Collingham St. *M8* 3D **53**
Collington Clo. *M12* 3A **88**
Collingwood Av. *Droy* 4A **58**
Collingwood Dri. *Swin* 3D **31**
Collingwood Rd. *M19* 3D **103**
Collyhurst 2B **54**
Collyhurst Rd. *M40* 3D **53** (1F **7**)
Collyhurst St. *M40* 3A **54**
Colman Gdns. *Salf* 4B **66**
Colmore Dri. *M9* 2A **24**
Coltness Wlk. *M40* 2C **57**
Columbia Av. *M18* 4B **90**
Columbine St. *Open* 1D **89**
Colwell Av. *Stret* 3D **95**
Colwell Wlk. *M9* 1D **21**
Colwood Wlk. M8 . . . . 1B **52**
    (off Elizabeth St.)
Colwyn Av. *M14* 1C **119**
Colwyn Cres. *Stoc* 4B **122**
Colwyn Rd. *Swin* 3C **29**
Colwyn St. *Salf* 4D **49**
Combe Clo. *M11* 4B **56**
Combermere Av. *M20* 2C **117**
Como Wlk. *M18* 2B **88**
Compass St. *Open* 4C **73**
Compstall Av. *M14* 2D **101**
Compstall Gro. *M18* 2A **90**
Comus St. *Salf* 3C **67** (2A **8**)
Concastrian Ind. Est. *M9* 3A **38**
Concert La. *M2* 2C **69** (1C **10**)
Concil St. *M15* 2C **85** (5C **10**)
Concord Pl. *Salf* 2A **50**
Condor Pl. *Salf* 2A **50**
Condor Wlk. M13 . . . . 2A **86**
    (off Cumbrian Clo.)
Conewood Wlk. *M13* 2A **86**
Congleton Av. *M14* 2C **101**
Congou St. *M1* 3A **70** (2F **11**)
Coningsby Dri. *M9* 2B **38**
Coniston Av. *M9* 2B **38**

Coniston Clo. *Dent* 2D **107**
Coniston Rd. *Stoc* 3B **122**
Coniston Rd. *Stret* 1A **96**
Coniston Rd. *Swin* 4B **30**
Coniston Rd. *M40* 2C **57**
Coniston St. *Salf* 3B **50**
Conmere Sq. *M15* 1B **84** (5B **10**)
Connaught Av. *M19* 2D **119**
Connie St. *M11* 3C **73**
Connington Av. *M9* 1B **38**
Conquest Clo. *M12* 2D **87**
Conran St. *M9* 3B **38**
Constable St. *M18* 2A **90**
Constance Gdns. *Salf* 2D **65**
Constance St. *M15* 4A **68** (4F **9**)
Contact Theatre 3D **85**
Conway Av. *Swin* 3D **15**
Conway Clo. *M16* 1A **98**
Conway Rd. *Urm* 4D **77**
Conyngham Rd. *M14* 4B **86**
Cooke St. *Fail* 2B **42**
Cook St. *Eccl* 1C **61**
Cook St. *Salf* 1A **68** (4F **5**)
Coomassie St. *Salf* 4D **49**
Coopers La. *Droy* 3A **74**
    (in three parts)
Co-operation St. *Fail* 1B **42**
Co-operative St. *Salf* 1D **65**
Cooper Ho. *M15* 2C **85**
Cooper La. *M9* 1B **22**
Cooper St. *M2* 2B **68** (1B **10**)
    (in two parts)
Cooper St. *Stret* 3B **96**
Coop St. *M4* 1D **69** (3E **7**)
Cope Clo. *M11* 1A **90**
Copeland Av. *Swin* 1A **32**
Copeman Clo. *M13* 2A **86**
Copgrove Rd. *M21* 2B **114**
Copley Rd. *M21* 2A **98**
Copperas St. *M4* 1C **69** (4D **7**)
Copperways. *M20* 4C **117**
Coppice, The. *M9* 4A **24**
Coppice, The. *P'wich* 2A **18**
Coppice, The. *Swin* 2C **45**
Coppice, The. *Wors* 2A **28**
Copping St. *M12* 2D **87**
Coppleridge Dri. *M8* 1C **37**
Copplestone Ct. *Wors* 1C **29**
Copplestone Dri. *Sale* 4C **109**
Copson St. *M20* 2D **117**
Copthall La. *M8* 2B **36**
Copthorne Cres. *M13* 2C **103**
Coral St. *M13* 1A **86** (5F **11**)
Coram St. *M18* 2B **90**
Corbett St. *M11* 2A **72**
    (in two parts)
Corbridge Wlk. *M8* 1D **53**
Corby St. *M12* 2A **88**
Cordingley Av. *Droy* 3B **74**

Cordova Av. *Dent* 1B **106**
Corelli St. *M40*. 3D **55**
Corinthian Av. *Salf* 2C **51**
Corkland Rd. *M21* 4B **98**
Cork St. *M12* 3B **70**
Corley Wlk. *M11* 2D **71**
Cormallen Gro. *Fail*. 3C **43**
Cormorant Wlk. *M12* 2A **88**
Cornbrook 4D **67** (5C **8**)
Cornbrook Arches.
 M15 . . . . 1C **83** (5B **8**)
Cornbrook Ct. *M15* 2D **83**
Cornbrook Gro. *M16* 3D **83**
Cornbrook Pk. Rd.
 M15 . . . . 2C **83** (5B **8**)
Cornbrook Rd. *M15* 5A **8**
Cornbrook St. *M16* 3D **83**
 (in two parts)
Cornbrook Way. *M16*. 3D **83**
Corn Clo. *M13* 3A **86**
Cornell St. *M4* 1D **69** (3F **7**)
Cornerhouse 3C **10**
Cornet St. *Salf* 1D **51**
Cornford Av. *M18*. 1B **104**
Cornhill Av. *Urm* 1B **92**
Corn Hill La. *Aud* 3C **91**
Cornhill Rd. *Urm* 4B **76**
Corn St. *Fail* 4C **41**
Cornwall Av. *M19*. 1B **120**
Cornwall Ct. *M18* *2D **89***
 (off Keary Clo.)
Cornwall Cres. *Stoc* 3D **123**
Cornwall Ho. *Salf* 5D **5**
Cornwall Rd. *Droy* 4C **59**
Cornwall St. *M11* 4D **73**
Cornwall St. *Eccl* 2C **61**
Cornwall St. *Oldh* 1D **27**
Cornwood Clo. *M8* 3B **36**
Coronation Bldgs. *M4* 3D **53** (1E **7**)
Coronation Rd. *Droy* 4B **58**
Coronation Rd. *Fail* 1A **58**
Coronation Sq. *M12* 3A **70**
Coronation St. *M11* 3C **73**
Coronation St. *Salf* 3B **66** (2A **8**)
Coronation St. *Swin* 1C **31**
Corporation Rd. *Eccl* 1A **62**
Corporation Rd. *M4* 1B **68** (4B **6**)
Corporation Yd. *Redd*. 4B **106**
Corran Clo. *Eccl* 1B **60**
Corrie Cres. *Kear* 1D **13**
Corrie Dri. *Kear* 2D **13**
Corrie Rd. *Swin* 3C **15**
Corrigan St. *M18* 2A **90**
Corringham Rd. *M19* 2C **121**
Corris Av. *M9* 1C **21**
Corston Wlk. *M40* 1B **56**
Corwen Clo. *Oldh*. 4D **27**
Corwen St. *M9*. 2C **39**
Cosgrove Cres. *Fail* 2A **58**

Cosgrove Rd. *Fail*. 2A **58**
Costabeck Wlk. *M40* 3D **57**
Coston Park 2A **104**
Cotall Wlk. *M8* 3A **52**
Cotham St. *M3* 3B **52** (1A **6**)
Cotswold Av. *Chad*. 1C **27**
Cotswold Clo. *P'wich* 1C **19**
Cotswold Dri. *Salf* 4D **49**
Cottage Wlk. *Droy* 4B **58**
Cottam Gro. *Swin*. 3C **31**
Cottenham La. *Salf* 3A **52** (1E **5**)
Cottenham St. *M13* 2D **85**
Cotterdale Clo. *M16*. 2D **99**
Cotteridge Wlk. *M11* 3D **71**
Cotter St. *M12*. 4A **70**
Cottesmore Dri. *M8* 2A **38**
Cottingham Rd. *M12* 2C **87**
Cottonfield Rd. *M20*. 3A **118**
Cotton Hill. *M20*. 4A **118**
Cotton La. *M20* 3A **118**
Cotton Mill Cres. *Oldh* 2D **27**
Cotton St. *M4* 1D **69** (4F **7**)
Cottonwood Dri. *Sale* 4C **109**
Cottrill St. *Salf* 1B **66**
Coulsden Dri. *M9*. 3B **22**
Coulton Wlk. *Salf* 1D **65**
Councillor St. *M12* 2C **71**
Countess Gro. *Salf* 2D **51**
Countess Pl. *P'wich* 2C **19**
Counthill Dri. *M8* 4A **20**
County St. *M2* 2B **68** (1B **10**)
County St. *Oldh* 4D **27**
Coupland St. *M15* 3C **85**
Coupland St. E. *M15* 2C **85**
Courier St. *M18* 2A **90**
Court Dri. *M40*. 3A **58**
Courtfield Av. *M9* 2B **22**
Courts Vw. *Sale* 4A **112**
Court, The. *P'wich* 3B **18**
Courtyard, The. *Salf* 2C **35**
Covall Wlk. *M8* 1D **53**
Coverdale Cres. *M12* 2B **86**
Cowan St. *M40* 1B **70**
Cowburn St. *M3* 4B **52** (1B **6**)
Cowesby St. *M14*. 1C **101**
Cow La. *Fail* 3A **42**
Cow La. *Sale* 3C **113**
Cow La. *Salf* 2C **67** (1B **8**)
Cowley St. *M40*. 1C **57**
Cowling St. *Swin* 2D **33**
Cowper Wlk. *M11* 2D **71**
Crabbe St. *M4*. 4C **53** (1D **7**)
Crab La. *M9*. 2D **21**
Crabtree La. *M11*. 3D **73**
 (in two parts)
Cradley Av. *M11*. 3D **73**
Craig Av. *Urm* 1A **92**
Craigend Dri. *M9* 3C **39**
Craighall Av. *M19*. 4D **103**

Craigie St. *M8* 2B **52**
Craiglands Av. *M40* 4A **40**
Craignair Ct. *Swin* 3A **32**
Craig Rd. *M18* 4C **89**
Craigwell Rd. *P'wich* 4A **20**
Craigwell Wlk. *M13* . . . 1D **85** (5E **11**)
Cramer St. *M40* 2D **55**
Crammond Clo. *M40* 1D **57**
Cranage Rd. *M19* 4B **104**
Cranbourne Rd. *Chor H* 4B **98**
Cranbourne Rd. *Old T* 4C **83**
Cranbourne St. *Salf* 2C **67** (1A **8**)
Cranbrook Dri. *P'wich* 4C **19**
Cranbrook Rd. *M18* 1A **106**
Cranbrook Rd. *Eccl* 3A **44**
Cranby Village. *M1* 3D **11**
Crandon Ct. *Swin* 4C **15**
Crane St. *M12* 3A **70**
Cranfield Clo. *M40* 1B **70**
Cranford Av. *M20* 4B **118**
Cranford Av. *Sale* 3A **112**
Cranford Av. *Stret* 1D **97**
Cranford Clo. *Swin* 1D **47**
Cranford Ho. *Eccl* 4B **46**
Cranleigh Dri. *Sale* 4C **111**
Cranlington Dri. *M8* 1B **52**
Cranmere Av. *M19* 2C **105**
Cranswick St. *M14* 1C **101**
Crantock St. *M12* 1B **104**
Cranwell Ct. Droy *3D **75***
             (off Williamson La.)
Craston Rd. *M13* 2C **103**
Craunton Ho. *Eccl* 1B **62**
Craven Av. *Salf* 3B **66**
Craven Dri. *Salf* 2A **82**
Cravenhurst Av. *M40* 3B **56**
Craven Pl. *M11* 1C **73**
Craven Rd. *Stoc* 3B **122**
Craven Rd. *Droy* 2C **75**
Craven St. *Salf* (M5) . . . 2C **67** (1B **8**)
Craven St. *Salf* (M6) 4D **33**
Cravenwood Rd. *M8* 2C **37**
Crawford Av. *Wors* 2A **28**
Crawford St. *M40* 2C **57**
Crawford St. *Eccl* 4D **45**
Crawley Av. *Eccl* 4C **47**
Craydon St. *Open* 3B **72**
Crayfield Rd. *M19* 4B **104**
Crayford Rd. *M40* 3B **56**
Cray Wlk. *M13* 1D **85** (5E **11**)
Crediton Clo. *M15* 3B **84**
Crediton Ho. Salf *4C **47***
             (off Devon Clo.)
Creel Clo. *M9* 2D **21**
Cremer Ho. Eccl *1C **63***
            (off Trevelyan St.)
Cresbury St. *M12* 3B **70**
Crescent Av. *M8* 2C **37**
Crescent Av. *P'wich* 4B **18**

Crescent Av. *Swin* 2A **32**
Crescent Ct. *M21* 3D **97**
Crescent Gro. *M19* 3A **104**
Crescent Gro. *P'wich* 4B **18**
Crescent Range. *M14* 1A **102**
Crescent Rd. *M8* 2B **36**
Crescent Rd. *Chad* 4A **26**
Crescent St. *M8* 2A **38**
Crescent, The. *M19* 3A **104**
Crescent, The. *Droy* 2B **74**
Crescent, The. *P'wich* 2B **18**
Crescent, The. *Salf* 1B **66** (4A **4**)
Crescent, The. *Urm* 2A **92**
Crescent, The. *Wors* 2A **44**
Cressfield Way. *M21* 2D **115**
Cressingham Rd. *Stret* 2D **95**
Cressington Clo. *Salf* 1C **65**
Cresswell Gro. *M20* 4C **117**
Crest St. *M3* 4C **53** (1B **6**)
Crest, The. *Droy* 4C **75**
Crestwood Wlk. *M40* 1A **54**
Cricceith St. *M16* 4B **84**
Cricket Gro., The. *M21* 3B **114**
Crimsworth Av. *M16* 2B **98**
Crinan Wlk. *M40* 4B **54**
Cringleford Clo. *M12* 3D **87**
Cringle Hall Rd. *M19* 1D **119**
Cringle Rd. *M19* 2B **120**
Criterion St. *Stoc* 2B **106**
Crocker Wlk. *M9* 3C **39**
Crocus Wlk. Salf *4D **35***
             (off Hilton St.)
Croft Bank. *M18* 3A **90**
Croft Bank. *Salf* 2C **51**
Crofters Hall Wlk. M40 . . . . *3B **40***
             (off Kenyon La.)
Cft. Hill Rd. *M40* 1A **40**
Crofton St. *M14* 1D **101**
Crofton St. *Old T* 4D **83**
Crofts Bank. **4C 77**
Crofts Bank Rd. *Urm* 4C **77**
Croft St. *M11* 2B **72**
Croft St. *Fail* 1C **43**
Croft St. *Salf* 2C **51**
Cromarty Av. *Chad* 3B **26**
Cromarty Wlk. *M11* 2D **71**
Cromer Av. *M20* 3D **117**
Cromer Av. *Dent* 1C **107**
Cromer St. *M11* 2D **73**
Cromford Av. *Stret* 1D **95**
Cromford Ct. M4 . . . . *1C **69** (4C **6***)
       (off Arndale Shop. Cen.)
Cromford Courts. *M4* 1C **69** (4C **6**)
Cromhall Wlk. *M16* 1C **53**
Cromhurst St. *M8* 1C **37**
Crompton Ho. *Swin* 2A **30**
Crompton Rd. *M19* 2A **120**
Crompton St. *Swin* 2A **30**
Cromwell Av. *M16* 2C **99**

Cromwell Ct. *Salf* 3B **50**
Cromwell Gro. *M19* 3A **104**
Cromwell Gro. *Salf.* 2C **51**
Cromwell Range. *M14* 2B **102**
Cromwell Rd. *Eccl* 1C **61**
Cromwell Rd. *P'wich* 2C **19**
Cromwell Rd. *Salf* 3A **50**
Cromwell Rd. *Stret.* 3C **97**
Cromwell Rd. *Swin* 1A **30**
Crondale Wlk. *M13* *2A 86*
(off Watkin Clo.)
Crondall St. *M14* 1C **101**
Cronshaw St. *M19* 1B **120**
Crookhill Dri. *M8* 3B **36**
Croom Wlk. *M40* 1B **70**
Crosby Rd. *M40.* 2C **57**
Crosby Rd. *Salf* 2B **48**
Crosfield Gro. *M18* 3D **89**
Crossbank Clo. *M13.* 3B **86**
Crossby Clo. *Midd* 1D **23**
Crosscliffe St. *M16* 4B **84**
Crossdale Rd. *M9* 2D **23**
Crossfell Av. *M9.* 1D **21**
Crossfield Dri. *Swin* 1A **30**
Crossford Ct. *Sale* 3A **112**
Crossford St. *Stret.* 3B **96**
Crosshill St. *M16* 4B **84**
Cross Keys St. *M4.* 1D **69** (3E **7**)
Cross Knowle Vw. *Urm.* 4A **76**
Crossland Rd. *M21* 1A **114**
Crossland Rd. *Droy* 1D **75**
Crosslands. *P'wich* 3A **18**
Cross La. *M18.* 3D **89**
Cross La. *Salf* 2A **66**
Crossley Ct. *M4* *2B 70*
(off Merrill St.)
Crossley Rd. *M19 & Stoc.* . . . 2D **119**
Crossley Rd. *Sale.* 3C **111**
Crossley St. *M18.* 2B **88**
Crossmead Dri. *M9* 1C **23**
Cross Rd. *M21.* 1B **114**
Cross St. *M2.* 2B **68** (1B **10**)
Cross St. *Old T* 3D **83**
Cross St. *Sale* 4D **111**
Cross St. *Salf.* 1A **68** (4F **5**)
Cross St. *Stret.* 2B **96**
Cross St. *Swin.* 4B **16**
Cross St. *Urm* 3C **93**
Cross St. *Wors* 3C **29**
Crossway. *Droy* 4C **75**
Croston Wlk. *M11* 2C **71**
Croughton Clo. *M11.* 1D **89**
Crowbank Wlk. *M40.* 2A **56**
Crowborough Wlk. *M15* *3B 84*
(off Botham Clo.)
Crowcroft Park 1A **104**
Crowcroft Rd. *M13 & M12.* . . 1A **104**
Crowden Rd. *M40* 4B **24**
Crowley Rd. *M9.* 2D **39**

Crown Bus. Cen. *Fail* 2B **42**
Crowngreen Rd. *Eccl* 2A **62**
Crownhill Ct. Droy *1C 75*
(off Chappell Rd.)
Crownhill Dri. *Droy* 1C **75**
Crown Ind. Est. *M4* 1A **70**
Crown La. *M4.* 4C **53** (2D **7**)
Crown Point Av. *M40* 2C **57**
Crown Sq. *M3.* 2A **68** (1F **9**)
Crown St. *M15* 4A **68** (4E **9**)
Crown St. *M40.* 2C **57**
Crown St. *Fail* 2B **42**
Crown St. *Salf.* 1A **68** (3E **5**)
Crowther Av. *Salf.* 3A **66**
Crowther St. *M18* 3D **89**
Crowthorn Rd. *Stoc.* 2D **121**
Croxdale Wlk. M9. . . . . *1B 22*
(off Claygate Dri.)
Croxton Wlk. *M13* 2A **86** (5F **11**)
Croydon Ct. *Salf.* 3B **66**
Croydon Dri. *M40* 3B **56**
Crumpsall 1B **36**
Crumpsall Cres. *M8* 2C **37**
Crumpsall Green 4C **21**
Crumpsall La. *M8.* 1B **36**
Crumpsall Va. *M9* 4A **22**
Crumpsall Way. *M8* 1D **37**
Cube Gallery. 2C **10**
Cubley Rd. *Salf* 2A **36**
Cuddington Av. *M20.* 1C **117**
Cudworth Rd. *M9.* 1C **21**
Culand St. *M12* 2C **87**
Culcheth 2C **57**
Culcheth La. *M40.* 2C **57**
Culcombe Wlk. *M13.* 3A **86**
Culford Clo. *M12* 3C **87**
Culgaith Wlk. *M9* 3B **38**
Cullen Gro. *M9* 2D **23**
(in two parts)
Cullercoats Wlk. *M12* 1B **104**
Culmington Clo. *M15* 3A **84**
Culross Av. *M40.* 1A **42**
Culvercliff Wlk. *M3.* 3A **68** (2F **9**)
Culverden Av. *Salf* 1D **49**
Culverden Wlk. *Salf* 1D **49**
Culverwell Dri. *Salf.* 1B **66**
Cumberland Av. *Stoc* 4D **123**
Cumberland Av. *Swin* 4B **14**
Cumberland Ho. *M3.* . . . 2A **68** (1A **10**)
Cumberland Rd. *M9.* 1B **38**
Cumberland Rd. *Urm* 3C **93**
Cumberland St. *Salf* 3D **51** (1C **4**)
Cumbrae Gdns. *Salf.* 2B **64**
Cumbrae Rd. *M19* 3C **105**
Cumbria Ct. *P'wich* 1A **34**
Cumbrian Clo. *M13* 2A **86**
Cumbria Wlk. *Salf* 3B **50**
Cunard Clo. *M13* 2A **86**
Cundiff Ct. *M19* 3C **105**

Cundiff Rd. *M21* 3B **114**
Curlew Wlk. *M12* 3C **87**
Curtels Clo. *Wors.* 3C **29**
Curtis St. *M19* 3C **105**
Curzon Av. *M14* 4C **87**
Curzon Rd. *Sale.* 4D **111**
Curzon Rd. *Salf.* 3D **35**
Curzon Rd. *Stret.* 1C **95**
Cuthbert Av. *M19.* 2B **104**
Cuthbert Bus. Cen. *M11.* 4C **73**
  (off Ashton Old Rd.)
Cuthill Wlk. *M40.* 3D **57**
Cutland St. *M40.* 1A **56**
Cutler Hill 3D **43**
Cutler Hill Rd. *Fail.* 3D **43**
Cutter Clo. *Salf.* 3A **66**
Cycle St. *M11* 3B **72**
Cyclone St. *M11* 3D **71**
Cygnus Av. *Salf.* 4C **51** (1B 4)
Cypress Rd. *Droy.* 4C **59**
Cypress Rd. *Eccl.* 3A **44**
Cypress St. *M9* 3B **38**
Cypress Wlk. *Sale* 3C **109**
Cyprus Clo. *Salf.* 2D **65**
Cyprus St. *Stret.* 2B **96**
Cyril St. *M14* 1D **101**
Cyrus St. *M40* 1B **70**

D

Daccamill Dri. *Swin* 3B **30**
Dacre Av. *M16.* 2B **98**
Dagenham Rd. *M14.* 4A **86**
Dagenham Rd. Ind. Est.
  M14. . . . . 1A **102**
  (off Denison St.)
Dagnall Av. *M21.* 3B **114**
Daimler St. *M8.* 4C **37**
Dainton St. *M12.* 4B **70**
Daintry Clo. *M15.* 2B **84** (5A 10)
Daisy Av. *M13.* 4C **87**
Daisy Bank. *M40* 2C **57**
Daisy Bank Av. *Swin & Salf.* . . . 1A **48**
Daisy Bank Hall. *M14.* 4B **86**
Daisy Bank Rd. *M14.* 4B **86**
Dakerwood Clo. *M40.* 2C **57**
Dakota Av. *Salf.* 3C **65**
Dakota S. *Salf.* 3D **65**
Dalbeattie St. *M9.* 1C **39**
Dalberg St. *M12.* 1B **86**
Dalbury Dri. *M40.* 2A **54**
Dalby Av. *Swin.* 3A **30**
Dale Av. *Eccl.* 4C **45**
Dale Bank M. *Swin.* 1D **13**
Daleford Sq. *M13.* . . . 1D **85** (5F **11**)
Dalehead Clo. *M18.* 2B **90**
Dales Av. *M8* 4B **20**
Dales Brow. 1D **45**

Dales Brow. *Swin.* 4D **29**
Dalesman Clo. *M9* 2D **39**
Dales Pk. Dri. *Swin* 4D **29**
Dale St. *M1* 2C **69** (5D **7**)
  (in two parts)
Dale St. *Swin.* 4A **30**
Dalham Av. *M9* 4A **24**
Dalkeith Av. *Stoc* 2B **122**
Dalkeith Rd. *Stoc.* 2B **122**
Dalkeith St. *M18.* 2B **88**
Dallas Ct. *Salf.* 3C **65**
Dalley Av. *Salf.* 3D **51** (1C **4**)
Dalmahoy Clo. *M40.* 2C **41**
Dalmain Clo. *M8* 4B **36**
Dalmain Wlk. M8 . . . . 4B **36**
  (off Dalmain Clo.)
Dalmorton Rd. *M21.* 1D **115**
Dalny St. *M19* 3B **104**
Dalston Av. *Fail.* 2D **43**
Dalton Av. *M14* 2C **101**
Dalton Av. *Stret.* 4B **78**
Dalton Av. *Swin* 3A **16**
Dalton Ct. *M4.* 3D **53** (1F **7**)
Dalton Dri. *Swin.* 3B **32**
Dalton Gdns. *Urm* 1B **92**
Dalton Rd. *M9.* 1B **22**
Dalton St. *M4 & M40.* 3D **53** (1F **7**)
Dalton St. *Eccl.* 4D **45**
Dalton St. *Fail.* 2A **42**
Dalton St. *Sale.* 3A **112**
Dalveen Av. *Urm* 4C **77**
Damask Av. *Salf.* 1D **67** (3C **4**)
Dameral Clo. *M8* 4C **37**
Dam Head Dri. *M9.* 3C **23**
Damien St. *M12.* 2A **104**
Danby Wlk. M9 . . . . 1C **39**
  (off Polworth Rd.)
Dancehouse Theatre. 4C **10**
Dane Bank 2D **107**
Danebank M. *Dent* 2D **107**
Danebank Wlk. *M13.* . . . 1D **85** (5F **11**)
Danecroft Clo. *M13* 3B **86**
Danefield Rd. *Sale.* 3A **112**
Daneholme Rd. *M19* 4C **119**
Dane M. *Sale.* 3D **111**
Dane Rd. *Dent.* 2C **107**
Dane Rd. *Sale.* 3A **112**
Dane Rd. Ind. Est. *Sale.* 3A **112**
Danesmoor Rd. *M20.* 4C **117**
Danes Rd. *M14* 2B **102**
Danes, The. *M8* 1B **36**
Dane St. *M11.* 1A **90**
Danesway. *P'wich* 4D **19**
Danesway. *Swin.* 3A **32**
Daneswood Av. *M9* 2D **23**
Danett Clo. *M12.* 2B **88**
Dane Wlk. *Stoc* 4B **122**
Danforth Gro. *M19.* 1B **120**
Daniel Adamson Rd. *Salf.* . . . 2B **64**

Danson St. *M40*. 4C **55**
Dantall Av. *M9*. 3A **24**
Dante Clo. *Eccl*. 3C **47**
Dantzic St. *M4*. 1C **69** (4C **6**)
Dapple Gro. *M11*. 3A **72**
Darcy Wlk. *M14*. 4C **85**
Daresbury Rd. *M21*. 3D **97**
Daresbury St. *M8*. 2C **37**
Darfield Wlk. *M40*. 4B **54**
Dargai St. *M11*. 2D **73**
Dargle Rd. *Sale*. 3D **111**
Dark La. *M12*. 3B **70**
Darlbeck Wlk. *M21*. 4C **115**
Darley Av. *M21 & M20*. 3B **114**
                              (in two parts)
Darley Av. *Eccl*. 3C **61**
Darley Park 4C **83**
Darley Rd. *M16*. 1C **99**
Darley St. *M11*. 2D **71**
Darley St. *Stret*. 4B **80**
Darlington Rd. *M20*. 3C **117**
Darliston Av. *M9*. 1C **21**
Darlton Wlk. *M9*. 2C **39**
Darnall Av. *M20*. 1C **117**
Darncombe Clo. *M16*. 4B **84**
Darnley St. *M16*. 4D **83**
Darras Rd. *M18*. 1C **105**
Darrell Wlk. *M8*. 1D **53**
Dartford Av. *Eccl*. 1B **60**
Dartford Av. *Stoc*. 4D **123**
Dartford Clo. *M12*. 2B **86**
Dartford Rd. *Urm*. 3C **93**
Dartmouth Cres. *Stoc*. 4D **123**
Dartmouth Rd. *M21*. 1C **115**
Darton Av. *M40*. 4B **54**
Darwell Av. *Eccl*. 3C **61**
Darwen St. *M16*. 3C **83**
Dashwood Rd. *P'wich*. 1A **18**
Dashwood Wlk. *M12*. 2A **88**
Dauntesy Av. *Swin*. 3B **32**
Davenham Rd. *Sale*. 3A **110**
Davenham Rd. *Stoc*. 2B **106**
Davenhill Rd. *M19*. 1A **120**
Davenport Av. *M20*. 2D **117**
Davenport St. *Droy*. 2A **74**
Davenport Ter. *M9*. 2C **39**
Daventry Rd. *M21*. 4D **99**
David Lloyd Leisure Cen. 1C **77**
David M. *M14*. 2A **118**
David Pegg Wlk. *M40*. 1B **56**
David's Rd. *Droy*. 1A **74**
David St. *Stoc*. 1A **122**
Davies Ct. *Stret*. 3B **96**
Davies Sq. *M14*. 4C **85**
Davis Hall. *M14*. 4B **86**
Davis St. *Eccl*. 2A **62**
Davy Av. *Swin*. 4B **16**
Davyhulme 1D **93**
Davyhulme Circ. *Urm*. 4C **77**

Davyhulme Rd. *Stret*. 1A **96**
Davyhulme Rd. *Urm*. 4A **76**
Davyhulme Rd. E. *Stret*. 1B **96**
Davy St. *M40*. 3D **53** (1F **7**)
Dawlish Av. *Droy*. 1A **74**
Dawlish Av. *Stoc*. 4D **123**
Dawlish Rd. *M21*. 1C **115**
Dawlish Rd. *Sale*. 4A **110**
Dawnay St. *M11*. 3B **72**
Dawson St. *M3*. 3D **67** (3C **8**)
Dawson St. *Salf*. 1B **68** (3A **6**)
Dawson St. *Swin*. 2C **31**
Day Dri. *Fail*. 4B **42**
Deacon Av. *Swin*. 1A **30**
Deacon's Dri. *Salf*. 1B **48**
Deal Av. *Stoc*. 4D **123**
Deal Clo. *M40*. 2D **57**
Deal St. *Salf*. 1A **68** (4F **5**)
Dean Av. *Newt H*. 4B **40**
Dean Av. *Old T*. 1B **98**
Deanbank Av. *M19*. 4D **103**
Dean Brook Clo. *M40*. 3B **40**
Dean Clo. *M15*. 2D **83**
Dean Ct. *M15*. 2D **83**
Deanery Gdns. *Salf*. 2D **35**
Dean Hall. *M14*. 4B **86**
Dean La. *M40*. 4B **40**
Dean Rd. *M18*. 4A **90**
Dean Rd. *Salf*. 4A **52** (2F **5**)
Deans 3A **30**
Deanscourt Av. *Swin*. 3A **30**
Deansgate. *M15 & M3*. . . 4A **68** (4F **9**)
                              (in two parts)
Deansgate Quay. *M3*. 4F **9**
Deansgate, The. *M14*. 1A **118**
Deans Rd. *Swin*. 3D **29**
Deans Rd. Ind. Est. *Swin* 3D **29**
Dean St. *M1*. 2D **69** (5E **7**)
Dean St. *Fail*. 3A **42**
Deansway. *Swin*. 2A **30**
Deanswood Dri. *M9*. 1C **21**
Deanwater Clo. *M13*. . . . 1D **85** (5F **11**)
Deanwater Ct. *Stret*. 4A **96**
Deanway. *M40*. 2A **40**
Dearden Wlk. *M15*. 2A **84**
Dearman's Pl. *M3*. 1A **68** (4F **5**)
Dearne Dri. *Stret*. 2C **97**
Debdale 4B **90**
Debdale Av. *M18*. 4B **90**
Debdale La. *M18*. 4B **90**
Debdale Outdoor Cen. 4A **90**
Debenham Av. *M40*. 3C **57**
Debenham Rd. *Stret*. 2C **95**
Dee Dri. *Kear*. 1B **12**
Deepcar St. *M19*. 2A **104**
Deepdale Av. *M20*. 4C **101**
Deepdale Clo. *Stoc*. 3B **106**
Deepdale Ct. *M9*. 3B **24**
Deepdale Dri. *Swin*. 3B **32**

Deepdene St. *M12* 2D **87**
Deeping Av. *M16* 2D **99**
Deerfold Clo. *M18* 3D **89**
Deerhurst Dri. *M8* 1B **52**
Deeroak Clo. *M18* 2B **88**
(in two parts)
Deerpark Rd. *M16* 1A **100**
Deer St. *M1* 3A **70**
Deganwy Gro. *Stoc* 4B **122**
Degas Clo. *Salf* 2B **34**
Deighton Av. *M20*. 4C **101**
Delacourt Rd. *M14* 1C **117**
Delafield Av. *M12* 2A **104**
Delaford Wlk. *M40* 3D **57**
Delahays Range. *M18* 4B **90**
Delaine Rd. *M20* 3A **118**
Delamere Av. *Salf.* 1A **48**
Delamere Av. *Stret* 2B **96**
(in two parts)
Delamere Av. *Swin* 4D **15**
Delamere Ct. *M9* 1C **21**
Delamere Rd. *M19* 3B **104**
Delamere Rd. *Dent.* 2D **107**
Delamere Rd. *Urm* 2A **92**
Delamere St. *M11* 1B **90**
Delaunays Rd. *M8 & M9* 1C **37**
Delaunays Rd. *Sale* 4B **110**
Delaware Wlk. *M9* 3B **38**
Delft Wlk. *Salf* 2A **50**
Dell Av. *Swin* 3B **32**
Dellcot Clo. *P'wich* 4D **19**
Dellcot Clo. *Salf.* 2D **47**
Delside Av. *M40*. 2A **40**
Delta Martial Arts, Gym &
    Fitness Cen. 1A **30**
Delta Wlk. *M40* 3A **40**
Delvino Wlk. *M14*. 4C **85**
Demesne Rd. *M16* 2A **100**
Denbigh Pl. *Salf*. 1A **66**
(in two parts)
Denbigh Rd. *Swin* 4C **15**
Denbigh Wlk. *M15* 3A **84**
Denbury Wlk. M9 . . . . *4A **38***
(off Westmere Dri.)
Denby La. *Stoc* 4D **121**
Dencombe St. *M13* 4D **87**
Denefield Pl. *Eccl* 4B **46**
Dene Hollow. *Stoc* 3C **107**
Deneside. *M40*. 1B **54**
Deneside Wlk. M9 . . . . *2C **39***
(off Dalbeattie St.)
Denes, The. *Stoc* 3B **106**
Denewell Clo. *M13*. 2B **86**
Denham St. *M13* 4B **86**
Denhill Rd. *M15*. 4B **84**
Denis Av. *M16*. 2A **100**
Denison Rd. *M14*. 1A **102**
Denison St. *M14* 1A **102**
Deniston Rd. *Stoc* 4B **120**

Denman Wlk. *M8* 4B **36**
(off Ermington Dri.)
Denmark Rd. *M15* 4B **84**
Denmark Rd. *Sale* 3D **111**
Denmore Rd. *M40* 3D **25**
Dennington Dri. *Urm* 4C **77**
Dennison Av. *M20* 2D **117**
Densmead Wlk. *M40* 4A **54**
Densmore St. *Fail.* 3B **42**
Denstone Av. *Eccl* 4A **46**
Denstone Av. *Urm* 1C **93**
Denstone Rd. *Salf* 2B **48**
Denstone Rd. *Stoc* 3B **106**
Denstone Wlk. M9 . . . . *3C **3***
(off Woodmere Dri.)
Dent Clo. *Stoc* 3D **123**
Denton La. *Chad* 1C **27**
Denver Av. *M40* 4B **54**
Deramore St. *M14* 1D **101**
Derby Av. *Salf* 1C **65**
Derby Gro. *M19* 3B **104**
Derby Ho. *M15* 3D **85**
Derby Range. *Stoc* 4B **120**
Derby Rd. *M14*. 2A **118**
Derby Rd. *Sale*. 3A **110**
Derby Rd. *Salf & M6* 2C **65**
Derby Rd. *Stoc.* 4C **121**
Derby Rd. *Urm* 1D **93**
Derbyshire Av. *Stret* 1C **95**
Derbyshire Cres. *Stret* 1D **95**
Derbyshire Grn. *Stret* 2B **96**
Derbyshire Gro. *Stret* 1C **95**
Derbyshire La. *Stret* 2A **96**
Derbyshire La. W. *Stret* 1C **95**
Derbyshire Rd. *M40*. 3D **57**
Derbyshire St. *M11* 4C **73**
Derby St. *M8* 2A **52**
Derby St. *Chad* 3D **27**
Derby St. *Fail.* 1C **43**
Derby St. *Oldh* 1D **27**
Derby St. *P'wich* 2A **18**
Derg St. *Salf* 1D **65**
Dermot Murphy Clo. *M20*. 3B **116**
Dernford Av. *M19*. 4D **119**
Derville Wlk. M9 . . . . *2B **38***
(off Alderside Rd.)
Derwent Av. *M21* 4D **115**
Derwent Av. *Droy*. 2A **74**
Derwent Clo. *Chor H* 4D **115**
Derwent Clo. *Dent* 2D **107**
Derwent Dri. *Kear*. 1B **12**
Derwent Ind. Area.
    Salf 4C **67** (3B **8**)
Derwent Rd. *Stret* 1B **96**
Derwent St. *M8* 1A **54**
Derwent St. *Droy* 2D **73**
Derwent St. *Salf* 3C **67** (3B **8**)
Desford Av. *M21* 3C **99**
Destructor Rd. *Swin*. 1A **30**

De Trafford Ho. *Eccl.* 2D **61**
(off Fintry Gro.)
Dettingen St. *Salf.* 1B **48**
Deva Cen., The. *Salf.* 1A **68** (4F **5**)
Deva Ct. *M16.* 3C **83**
Devas St. *M15.* 3D **85**
(in two parts)
Deverill Av. *M18.* 4B **90**
Devine Clo. *Salf.* 1D **67** (3C **4**)
Devon Av. *M19.* 1D **119**
Devon Clo. *Salf.* 4C **47**
Devon Clo. *Stoc.* 4D **123**
Devon Rd. *Droy.* 4C **59**
Devon Rd. *Fail.* 1A **58**
Devonshire Clo. *Urm* 2A **94**
Devonshire Ct. *Salf.* 2D **35**
Devonshire Pl. *P'wich* 1A **18**
Devonshire Rd. *M21* 4C **99**
Devonshire Rd. *Eccl.* 1A **62**
Devonshire Rd. *Salf.* 4C **47**
Devonshire St. *M12* 2B **86**
Devonshire St. *Salf.* 4D **35**
Devonshire St. E. *Fail.* 1D **57**
Devonshire St. N. *M12.* 4B **70**
Devonshire St. S. *M13.* 3B **86**
Devon St. *Oldh* 2D **27**
(in two parts)
Devon St. *Swin* 4B **14**
Dewar Clo. *M11.* 2A **72**
Dewberry Clo. *Swin* 4A **14**
Dewes Av. *Swin* 4D **15**
Dewey St. *M11* 1D **89**
Dewhurst St. *M8* 3B **52**
Dexter Rd. *M9* 1C **21**
Deyne Av. *M14.* 4A **86**
Deyne Av. *P'wich* 2B **18**
Deyne St. *Salf.* 1C **65**
Dickenson Rd.
    M14 & M13 . . . . 1A **102**
Dickens Rd. *Eccl.* 2D **61**
Dickinson St. *M1.* 3B **68** (2B **10**)
Dickinson St. *Salf.* 3A **52** (1F **5**)
Didley Sq. *M12* 2A **88**
Didsbury Ct. *M20.* 4D **117**
Digby Wlk. M11. . . . . 2D **71**
(off Albert St.)
Digsby Ct. *M20* 4D **117**
Dillicar Wlk. *M9* 3B **38**
Dillmoss Wlk. *M15.* 2D **83**
Dillon Dri. *M12* 3C **87**
Dilston Clo. *M13* 2A **86**
Dilworth Ho. *M15* 3D **85**
Dilworth St. *M15* 3D **85**
Dingle Dri. *Droy.* 4D **59**
Dinnington Dri. *M8* 1B **52**
Dinorwic Clo. *M8.* 4C **21**
Dinsdale Clo. *M40.* 1B **70**
Dinslow Wlk. *M8* 3B **36**
Dinting Av. *M20.* 2C **117**

Dinton Ho. *Salf.* 2D **65**
(off Buckingham St.)
Dinton St. *M15* 5B **8**
Dipton Wlk. *M8* 1A **54**
(off Smedley Rd.)
Disley Av. *M20.* 3B **116**
Dixon Av. *Salf* 4A **36**
Dixon Dri. *Swin* 2A **14**
Dixon St. *M40.* 4B **40**
(in two parts)
Dixon St. *Salf.* 4D **33**
Dob Brook Clo. *M40.* 1C **57**
Dobcross Clo. *M13* 2A **104**
Dobroyd St. *M8* 2C **37**
Dobson Clo. *M13.* 2B **86**
Dobson Ct. *M40.* 3B **56**
Dock Office. *Salf* 4A **66**
Doddington La. *Salf.* 3A **66**
Dodd St. *Salf.* 1B **64**
Doe Brow. *Swin* 1A **14**
Dolbey St. *Salf.* 2C **65**
Dolefield. *M3.* 2A **68** (5F **5**)
Dollond St. *M9.* 1C **39**
Dolman Wlk. *M8* 4B **36**
Dolphin Pl. *M12.* 1A **86**
Dolphin St. *M12.* 1A **86**
Dolwen Wlk. *M40.* 2B **56**
Dome, The. *Urm* 2D **77**
(off Trafford Cen., The)
Domett St. *M9.* 4A **22**
Donald St. *M1.* 3C **69** (3D **11**)
Don Av. *Salf.* 1A **64**
Doncaster Av. *M20.* 2C **117**
Donhead Wlk. *M13* 2A **86**
Donleigh St. *M40.* 1D **57**
Donnington Rd. *M18* 3A **90**
Donnison St. *M12* 2D **87**
Donovan St. *M40.* 3A **54**
Dorchester Av. *P'wich* 4C **19**
Dorchester Av. *Urm* 1B **94**
Dorchester Rd. *Swin* 4B **30**
Dorclyn Av. *Urm* 2D **93**
Doric Clo. *M11* 2D **71**
Dorking Av. *M40* 3B **56**
Dorlan Av. *M18* 4B **90**
Dorman St. *M11* 4D **73**
Dorman St. *M18.* 3D **89**
Dorning Rd. *Swin.* 3C **31**
Dorning St. *Eccl.* 2D **61**
Dornton Wlk. M8 . . . . 4B **36**
(off Waterloo Rd.)
Dorothy St. *M8* 3B **36**
Dorrington Rd. *Sale* 4D **109**
Dorris St. *M19.* 1B **120**
Dorset Av. *M14* 2C **101**
Dorset Av. *Aud.* 3D **75**
Dorset Rd. *M19.* 3C **105**
Dorset Rd. *Droy.* 4B **58**
Dorset Rd. *Fail.* 1B **58**

Dorset St. *Oldh* 1D **27**
Dorset St. *Stret* 3B **96**
Dorset St. *Swin* 4B **14**
Dorsey St. *M4* 1D **69** (4E **7**)
Dorstone Clo. *M40* 3C **57**
Dorwood Av. *M9* 1A **22**
Dougall Wlk. M12 . . . . *2A 88*
(off Bridgend Clo.)
Doughty Av. *Eccl* 4B **46**
Douglas Av. *Stret* 1B **96**
Douglas Grn. *Salf* 2A **50**
Douglas Rd. *Wors* 3C **29**
Douglas St. *M40* 3A **40**
Douglas St. *Fail* 3C **43**
Douglas St. *Salf* 4D **35**
Douglas St. *Swin* 3C **31**
Douglas Wlk. *Sale* 4C **109**
Doulton St. *M40* 2C **41**
Dounby Av. *Eccl* 4B **44**
Douro St. *M40* 2D **55**
Dovecote Bus. & Technology Pk.
Sale 4D **113**
Dovecote M. *M21* 1A **114**
Dovedale Av. *M20* 2C **117**
Dovedale Av. *Droy* 1A **74**
Dovedale Av. *Eccl* 4A **46**
Dovedale Av. *P'wich* 3A **20**
Dovedale Av. *Urm* 2D **93**
Dovedale St. *Fail* 3A **42**
Doveleys Rd. *Salf* 3B **48**
Doveridge Gdns. *Salf* 4D **49**
Dover Pk. *Urm* 4D **77**
Dover Rd. *Swin* 4C **15**
Dover St. *M13* 2D **85**
Dover St. *Eccl* 1B **60**
Dover St. *Stoc* 2A **122**
Dovestone Wlk. *M40* 1A **42**
Doveston Gro. *Sale* 3D **111**
Doveston Rd. *Sale* 3D **111**
Dove Wlk. *M8* 2D **53**
Downgate Wlk. *M8* 1C **53**
Downfields. *Stoc* 3C **107**
Downham Cres. *P'wich* 3D **19**
Downham Gdns. *P'wich* 3A **20**
Downham Gro. *P'wich* 3A **20**
Downham Rd. *Stoc* 4D **121**
Downing St. *M1* 4D **69** (4F **11**)
Downing St. Ind. Est. *Ard* 4F **11**
Downley Dri. *M4* 1A **70**
Downs, The. *P'wich* 4A **18**
Drayton Wlk. *M16* 3D **83**
Drefus Av. *M11* 1C **73**
Dresden St. *M40* 2C **41**
Dresser Cen., The. *Open* 4B **72**
Drewett St. *M40* 3C **55**
Driffield St. *M14* 1C **101**
Driffield St. *Eccl* 3C **61**
Drill Wlk. M4 . . . . *1A 70*
(off Kirby Wlk.)

Drinkwater Rd. *P'wich* 1D **33**
Driscoll St. *M13* 1D **103**
Drive, The. *P'wich* 2B **18**
Drive, The. *Salf* 1C **35**
Drive, The. *Stoc* 4D **123**
Droitwich Rd. *M40* 3B **54**
Dronfield Rd. *Salf* 3B **48**
Droylsden **2C 75**
Droylsden Rd. *M40* 1C **57**
Droylsden Rd. *Aud* 2D **75**
Droylsden Swimming Pool. . . **2C 75**
Drury La. *Chad* 3C **27**
Drury St. *M19* 3A **104**
Dryad Clo. *Swin* 4B **14**
Drybrook Clo. *M13* 3C **87**
Dryden Av. *Swin* 3D **29**
Dryden Rd. *M16* 1C **99**
Dryden St. *M13* 2A **86**
Drygate Wlk. M9 . . . . *3C 39*
(off Bentworth Wlk.)
Dryhurst Wlk. *M15* 2C **85**
Drywood Av. *Wors* 2A **44**
Ducal St. *M4* 4D **53** (1E **7**)
Duchess Rd. *Crum* 2D **37**
Duchy Bank. *Salf* 1B **48**
Duchy Cvn. Pk. *Salf* 2D **49**
Duchy Rd. *Salf* 1C **49**
Duchy St. *Salf* 4D **49**
Ducie Av. *M15* 3D **85**
Ducie Cres. *M15* 3D **85**
Ducie Gro. *M15* 3D **85**
(Denmark Rd.)
Ducie Gro. *M15* 3D **85**
(Oxford Rd.)
Ducie Pl. *Salf* 2C **67** (1A **8**)
Ducie St. *M1* 2D **69** (1E **11**)
Duckworth Rd. *P'wich* 3D **17**
Dudley Clo. *M15* 3A **84**
Dudley Ct. *M16* 1D **99**
Dudley Rd. *M16* 2D **99**
Dudley Rd. *Sale* 3A **112**
Dudley Rd. *Swin* 1B **30**
Dudley St. *Eccl* 2C **61**
Dudley St. *Salf* 3A **36**
Dudlow Wlk. *M15* 2D **83**
Duffield Ct. *M15*. 3C **85**
Duffield Ct. *Midd* 1D **23**
Duffield Gdns. *Midd* 1D **23**
Duffield Rd. *Midd*. 1D **23**
Duffield Rd. *Salf* 2B **48**
Dugdale Av. *M9* 2C **23**
Duke Ct. *M16* 1D **83**
Duke Pl. *M3* 3A **68** (3E **9**)
Duke St. *M3* 3A **68** (3E **9**)
Duke St. *Eccl* 3C **45**
Duke St. *Fail* 2C **43**
Duke St. *Salf* (M3) 1B **68** (3A **6**)
Duke St. *Salf* (M7) 2D **51**
Duke St. *Wors* 4A **12**

Duke's Wharf. *Wors* 2A **44**
Dulford Wlk. *M13* 3A **86**
(off Plymouth Gro.)
Dulgar St. *Open* 3B **52**
Dulverton St. *M40* 1B **56**
Dulwich St. *M4* 4D **53** (1E **7**)
Dumbarton Clo. *Stoc* 3B **122**
Dumbarton Rd. *Stoc* 2B **122**
Dumbell St. *Swin* 4B **14**
Dumber La. *Sale* 3B **110**
Dumplington **4D 61**
Duncan Edwards Ct. *M40*. 2B **56**
(off Mitchell St.)
Duncan Edwards Ho. *Salf*. 4D **49**
(off Sutton Dwellings.)
Duncan Rd. *M13* 1D **103**
(in two parts)
Duncan St. *Salf* (M5) . . . 3C **67** (2A **8**)
Duncan St. *Salf* (M7) 4C **35**
Dunchurch Rd. *Sale* 4A **110**
Dun Clo. *Salf*. 1D **67** (3C **4**)
Duncombe Dri. *M40*. 3B **40**
Duncombe St. *Salf*. 1A **52**
Dundee. *Eccl* 1A **62**
(off Monton La.)
Dunedin Dri. *Salf* 1D **49**
Dunham St. *M15* 2A **84**
Dunkerley Av. *Fail.* 3B **42**
Dunkerleys Clo. *M8* 2B **36**
Dunkirk Clo. *Dent*. 2C **107**
Dunkirk St. *Droy* 2D **75**
Dunley Clo. *M12* 3A **88**
Dunlop St. *M3*. 2B **68** (5A **6**)
Dunmere Wlk. *M9* 4A **38**
(off Hendham Va.)
Dunnerdale Wlk. *M18*. 3C **89**
Dunoon Rd. *Stoc*. 2B **122**
Dunoon Wlk. *M9* 3B **38**
Dunsley Av. *M40*. 4D **25**
Dunsmore Clo. *M16*. 4D **83**
Dunstable St. *M19* 3B **104**
Dunstan Ct. *M40* 2A **40**
Dunster Av. *M9* 2C **23**
Dunster Av. *Stoc*. 4D **123**
Dunster Av. *Swin* 4D **15**
Dunston St. *M11* 3C **73**
Dunton Grn. *Stoc*. 3D **123**
Dunton Towers. *Stoc* 3D **123**
(off Dunton Grn.)
Dunworth St. *M14* 1D **101**
Durant St. *M4* 4D **53** (2E **7**)
Durham Av. *Urm* 1A **94**
Durham Clo. *Swin* 4B **14**
Durham Cres. *Fail* 4C **43**
Durham Rd. *Salf* 3A **48**
Durham St. *M9* 3C **39**
Durham St. *Droy* 3C **75**
Durham St. *Oldh* 2D **27**
(in two parts)
Durham St. *Stoc* 2A **106**
Durley Av. *M8* 3D **37**
Durling St. *M12* 1A **86**
Durnford Av. *Urm*. 2C **95**
Durrington Wlk. *M40* 3C **25**
(off Moston La.)
Dutton St. *M3*. 4B **52** (1B **6**)
Duxford Lodge. *M8* 4B **20**
Duxford Wlk. *M40* 3C **25**
Dyche St. *M4* 4D **53** (3D **7**)
Dyche St. Trad. Est. *M4* 2E **7**
Dyer St. *M11* 3A **72**
Dyer St. *Salf* 4C **67** (4B **8**)
Dymchurch St. *M40*. 3C **57**
Dyserth Gro. *Stoc* 4B **122**

E

Eades St. *Salf*. 4A **50**
Eadington St. *M8*. 1C **37**
Eagar St. *M40* 4C **41**
Eagle Ct. *M15* 3A **84**
Eagle Dri. *Salf* 2A **50**
Eagles Nest. *P'wich* 3A **18**
Eagle St. *M4* 1C **69** (3D **7**)
Ealing Av. *M14*. 2A **102**
Ealinger Way. *Swin* 4B **14**
Ealing Pl. *M19* 3A **120**
Eamont Wlk. *M9* 3B **38**
Earby Gro. *M9*. 3D **23**
Earls Lodge. *Fail* 4D **41**
Earlston Av. *Dent* 1C **107**
Earl St. *Dent* 4C **91**
Earl St. *P'wich*. 2C **19**
Earl St. *Salf* 3D **51**
Earl's Way. *Fail.* 4D **41**
Earlswood Wlk. *M18* 2C **89**
Earl Wlk. *M12* 3D **87**
Easington Wlk. *M40*. 4A **40**
East Av. *M19* 2D **119**
Eastburn Av. *M40*. 4A **54**
E. Central Dri. *Swin* 3D **31**
Eastcombe Av. *Salf*. 3B **34**
Eastcote Av. *Open* 3A **74**
Eastcote Rd. *Stoc*. 4B **122**
Eastcourt Wlk. *M13* 2A **86**
East Dri. *M32*. 3D **97**
East Dri. *Salf* 2C **49**
East Dri. *Swin* 3D **31**
Eastern Av. *Swin* 3B **16**
(in two parts)
Eastern By-Pass. *M11* 3D **73**
(Crabtree La.)
Eastern By-Pass. *M11* 1C **73**
(Stanton St.)
Eastern Circ. *M19*. 3A **120**
Eastfield. *Salf*. 3C **49**
Eastfield Av. *M40*. 4C **55**

Eastford Sq. *M40* 3A **54**
E. Garth Wlk. *M9* 3C **23**
E. Grange Av. *M11* 4C **57**
East Gro. *M13* 3A **86**
Eastham Av. *M14* 3D **101**
Easthaven Av. *M11* 4C **57**
Eastholme Dri. *M19* 2B **120**
Easthope Clo. *M20* 2D **117**
E. Lancashire Rd. *Wors* 2A **28**
Eastlands Rd. *M9* 1B **22**
Eastleigh Av. *Salf* 2A **36**
Eastleigh Dri. *M40* 4B **54**
Eastleigh Rd. *P'wich* 3A **20**
(in two parts)
E. Lynn Dri. *Wors* 3A **12**
East Meade. *M21* 2B **114**
East Meade. *P'wich* 4D **19**
East Meade. *Swin* 4A **30**
Eastmoor Dri. *M40* 3D **57**
E. Newton St. *M4* 4A **54**
Eastnor Clo. *M15* 2D **83**
Easton Rd. *Droy* 1A **74**
E. Ordsall La. *Salf* 2D **67** (1C **8**)
Eastpark Clo. *M13* 2A **86**
E. Philip St. *Salf* 4A **52** (1F **5**)
East Rd. *Gort* 1B **104**
East Rd. *Long* 1A **104**
East Rd. *Stret* 4D **79**
Eastry Av. *Stoc* 3D **123**
E. Union St. *M16* 2C **83**
Eastville Gdns. *M19* 4C **119**
Eastwood. *M14* 3A **102**
Eastwood Av. *M40* 1B **42**
Eastwood Av. *Droy* 2A **74**
Eastwood Av. *Urm* 2D **93**
Eastwood Rd. *M40* 1A **42**
Eaton Clo. *Swin* 4B **14**
Eaton Rd. *M8* 1B **36**
Eaves La. *Chad* 1C **27**
Ebberstone St. *M14* 2C **101**
Ebden St. *M1* 3D **69** (3E **11**)
Ebenezer St. *M15* 1B **84** (5B **10**)
Ebnall Wlk. *M14* 2B **118**
Ebor Ho. *Stret* 3D **97**
Ebsworth St. *M40* 2D **39**
Eccles 1B **62**
Eccles Clo. *M11* 3C **73**
Eccles Crematorium. *Eccl* 3A **60**
Eccleshall Clo. *M15* 2C **85**
Eccleshall St. *M11* 2C **73**
(in three parts)
Eccles New Rd. *Eccl & Salf* . . . 1C **63**
Eccles Recreation Cen. 2B **62**
Eccles Rd. *Swin* 1B **46**
Eccleston Av. *M14* 3D **101**
Eccleston Av. *Swin* 3D **29**
Eccleston Pl. *Salf* 2D **35**
Eccleston St. *Fail* 2C **43**
Echo St. *M1* 3D **69** (3E **11**)

Eckford St. *M8* 1D **53**
Edale Av. *M40* 2A **40**
Edale Av. *Stoc* 3C **107**
Edale Av. *Urm* 3B **92**
Edale Rd. *Stret* 1D **95**
Edale St. *Salf* 2B **50**
Edbrook Wlk. *M13* 3B **86**
Eddie Colman Clo. *M40* 2B **56**
Eddie Colman Ct. *Salf* 4A **50**
(off Belvedere Rd.)
Eddisbury Av. *M20* 1B **116**
Eddystone Clo. *Salf* 2A **66**
Edenbridge Rd. *M40* 3B **56**
Eden Clo. *M15* 3C **85**
Eden Ct. *M19* 4A **104**
Edenfield Av. *M21* 4D **115**
Edenfield La. *Wors* 3A **44**
Edenfield Rd. *P'wich* 3A **20**
Edenhall Av. *M19* 4D **103**
Edenham Wlk. *M40* 4D **25**
Eden Pl. *Sale* 4D **111**
Edgbaston Dri. *M16* 1A **98**
Edgedale Av. *M19* 4C **119**
Edgefield Av. *M9* 2C **23**
Edgehill Clo. *Salf* 1D **65**
Edgehill Ct. *Stret* 2C **97**
Edgehill Rd. *Salf* 4A **48**
Edgehill St. *M4* 1C **69** (4D **7**)
Edge La. *Droy & M11* 1D **73**
Edge La. *Stret & M21* 3B **96**
Edgeley Rd. *Urm* 4A **92**
Edge St. *M4* 1C **69** (4D **7**)
Edge, The 4D **27**
Edgeview Wlk. *M13* 1D **85** (5F **11**)
Edgeware Av. *P'wich* 2B **20**
Edgeware Rd. *Chad* 3A **26**
Edgeware Rd. *Eccl* 3A **44**
Edgewater. *Salf* 1B **64**
Edgeworth Dri. *M14* 2C **119**
Edgware Rd. *M40* 3B **56**
Edilom Rd. *M8* 4A **20**
Edinburgh. *Eccl* 1A **62**
(off Monton St.)
Edinburgh Ho. *Salf* 2D **67** (5D **5**)
(off Rocket St.)
Edinburgh Sq. *M40* 3B **54**
Edison Rd. *Eccl* 2C **61**
Edison St. *M11* 4A **74**
Edith Av. *M14* 1C **101**
Edith Cavell Clo. *Open* 2C **73**
Edith Cliff Wlk. *M40* 1B **42**
Edlin Clo. *M12* 3C **87**
Edlington Wlk. *M40* 1C **57**
Edmonton Rd. *M40* 3D **57**
Edmund St. *Droy* 2C **75**
Edmund St. *Fail* 3B **42**
Edmund St. *Salf* (M3) . . . 1A **68** (4E **5**)
Edmund St. *Salf* (M6) 4C **49**
Edson Rd. *M8* 3B **20**

Edward Av. *M21* 1D **113**
Edward Av. *Salf* 4A **48**
Edward Charlton Rd. *M16* 2A **98**
Edward Grant Ct. *M9* *1C* **39**
     (off Hemsley St. S.)
Edward Onyon Ct. *Salf* 4C **49**
Edward Rd. *M9* 1B **22**
Edward St. *M9* 2C **39**
Edward St. *Droy* 3C **75**
Edward St. *P'wich* 1A **18**
Edward St. *Salf* 3A **52** (1F **5**)
Edward Sutcliffe Clo. *M14* 2C **101**
Edwin Rd. *M11* 1C **71**
Edzell Wlk. *Open* 2C **73**
Eeasbrook. *Urm* 3D **93**
Egbert St. *M40* 3A **40**
Egerton Ct. *M14* 4A **86**
     (off Up. Park Rd.)
Egerton Ct. *M21* 4D **97**
Egerton Ct. *Wors* 2A **28**
Egerton Cres. *M20* 2D **117**
Egerton Dri. *Sale* 4D **111**
Egerton M. *M14* 1B **118**
Egerton M. *Droy* 3C **75**
Egerton Park 3B **28**
Egerton Pk. *Wors* 3B **28**
Egerton Rd. *M14* 1B **118**
Egerton Rd. *Eccl* 3D **45**
Egerton Rd. N. *M16 & M21* 2C **99**
Egerton Rd. N. *Stoc* 4C **121**
Egerton Rd. S. *M21* 4C **99**
Egerton Rd. S. *Stoc* 4C **121**
Egerton St. *M15* 4D **67** (3D **9**)
Egerton St. *Droy* 2D **75**
Egerton St. *Eccl* 1B **60**
Egerton St. *P'wich* 2C **19**
Egerton St. *Salf* 2D **67** (5D **5**)
Egerton Ter. *M14* 2B **118**
Eggington St. *M40* 2A **54**
Egmont St. *M8* 2C **37**
Egmont St. *Salf* 1C **49**
Egremont Av. *M20* 2C **117**
Egremont Ct. *Salf* 2C **35**
Eighth St. *Traf P.* 2B **80**
     (in two parts)
Eighth St. W. *Traf P* 2A **80**
Eileen Gro. *M14* 2A **102**
Eileen Gro. W. *M14* 2D **101**
Elaine Av. *M9* 4B **24**
Elbain Wlk. *M40* 2C **57**
Elberton Wlk. *M8* *3B* **36**
     (off Chantry Wlk.)
Elbe St. *M12* 3A **70**
Elbow St. *M19* 3A **104**
Elbow St. Trad. Est. *M19* 3B **104**
Elcot Clo. *M40* 2A **54**
Elder Gro. *M40* 4B **26**
Elder Mt. Rd. *M9* 4B **22**
Elder Wlk. *Sale* 3C **109**

Eldon Pl. *Eccl* 2C **61**
Eldridge Dri. *M40* 2A **56**
Eleanor Rd. *M21* 1D **113**
Electo St. *M11* 1A **90**
Elevator Rd. *Traf P.* 2C **81**
Eleventh St. *Traf P* 2A **80**
Elford Gro. *M18* 4C **91**
Elgar St. *M12* 4A **88**
Eliot Rd. *Eccl* 2D **61**
Eli St. *Chad* 3C **27**
Elitex Ho. *Salf* 3A **52**
Eliza Ann St. *M40* 3A **54**
Eliza Ann St. *Eccl* 2C **61**
Elizabeth Av. *Chad* 3C **27**
Elizabeth Clo. *Stret* 2B **96**
Elizabeth Ct. *M14* 2B **118**
Elizabeth Ct. *M15* 2A **84**
     (off Ribston St.)
Elizabeth Slinger Rd.
  M20 . . . . 4A **116**
Elizabeth St. *M8* 1B **52**
Elizabeth St. *P'wich* 2C **19**
Elizabeth St. *Swin* 1B **30**
Elizabeth Yarwood Ct.
  M13 . . . . 5F **11**
Eliza St. *M15* 2A **84** (5E **9**)
Eliza St. *Sale* 4D **111**
Elkanagh Gdns. *Salf* 4D **49**
Ella Dene Pk. *M21* 1C **115**
Ellanby Clo. *M14* 1D **101**
Ellaston Dri. *Urm* 2D **93**
Ellastone Rd. *Salf* 3A **48**
Ellbourne Rd. *M9* 3C **21**
Ellenbrook Clo. *M12* 2B **88**
Ellenbrook St. *M12* 2B **88**
Ellen Gro. *Kear* 1C **13**
Ellenhall Clo. *M9* 2B **38**
Ellen St. *Droy* 3D **75**
Ellen Wilkinson Cres.
  M12 . . . . 3A **88**
Elleray Rd. *Midd* 1D **23**
Elleray Rd. *Salf* 2B **48**
Ellerby Av. *Swin* 3C **15**
Ellesmere Av. *Eccl* 1A **62**
Ellesmere Circ. *Urm* 1D **77**
Ellesmere Park 3B **46**
Ellesmere Pl. *M15* 2D **83**
Ellesmere Rd. *M21* 3C **99**
Ellesmere Rd. *Eccl* 3A **46**
Ellesmere Rd. N. *Stoc* 4C **121**
Ellesmere Rd. S. *M21* 4C **99**
Ellesmere St. *M15* 1D **83** (5C **8**)
Ellesmere St. *Eccl* 2D **61**
     (in two parts)
Ellesmere St. *Fail* 2B **42**
Ellesmere St. *Swin* 1C **31**
     (Bolton Rd.)
Ellesmere St. *Swin* 3D **29**
     (Moorside Rd.)

Ellesmere Ter. *M14*. 2B **118**
Ellingham Clo. *M11*. 2D **71**
Ellisbank Wlk. *M13* 1D **85** (5F **11**)
    (off Hanworth Clo.)
Ellis Dri. *M8*. 1D **37**
Ellishaw Row. *Salf*. 2D **65**
Ellisland Wlk. *M40*. 4A **40**
Ellis St. *M15*. 2A **84**
Ellis St. *Salf*. 3A **52**
Elliston Sq. *M12*. 2A **88**
Ellon Wlk. *Open*. 2C **73**
Ellor St. *Salf*. 4D **49**
Elmbridge Wlk. *M40*. 3A **40**
Elm Cres. *Wors*. 3A **28**
Elmdale Wlk. *M15*. 1C **85** (5C **10**)
Elm Dri. *Stret*. 3D **95**
Elmfield St. *M8*. 1C **53**
Elmgate Gro. *M19*. 3A **104**
Elm Gro. *Droy*. 1D **73**
Elm Gro. *Sale*. 3D **111**
Elm Gro. *Swin*. 4B **12**
Elm Gro. *Urm*. 2A **94**
Elmham Wlk. *M40*. 3A **54**
Elmhurst Dri. *M19*. 4D **119**
Elm Rd. *Kear*. 1A **12**
Elmscott Wlk. *M13*. 3B **86**
Elmsdale Av. *M9*. 1B **22**
Elmsleigh Ct. *Eccl*. 4B **46**
Elms Rd. *Stoc*. 4B **120**
Elmstead Av. *M20*. 3C **117**
Elm St. *Eccl*. 2D **61**
Elm St. *Fail*. 2B **42**
Elm St. *Swin*. 1A **30**
Elmswood Av. *M14*. 2B **100**
Elmsworth Av. *M19*. 3B **104**
Elmton Rd. *M9*. 3C **23**
Elm Tree Clo. *Fail*. 3D **43**
Elmwood. *Sale*. 4C **109**
Elmwood. *Wors*. 2A **44**
Elmwood Ct. *Stret*. 4A **96**
Elmwood Gro. *M9*. 3D **39**
Elrick Wlk. *Open*. 2B **72**
Elsa Rd. *M19*. 3C **105**
Elsdon Dri. *M18*. 2D **89**
Elsdon Rd. *M13*. 2D **103**
Elsham Gdns. *M18*. 4B **88**
Elsie St. *M9*. 2C **39**
Elsinore Bus. Cen. *M16*. 4A **82**
Elsinore Clo. *Fail*. 3D **43**
Elsinore Rd. *M16*. 4A **82**
Elsinor Ter. *Urm*. 2B **94**
Elsma Rd. *M40*. 3A **58**
Elsmore Rd. *M14*. 3C **101**
Elstead Wlk. *M9*. 3C **21**
Elstree Av. *M40*. 3B **56**
Elstree Ct. *Urm*. 2D **93**
Elswick Av. *M21*. 4D **115**
Elsworth St. *M3*. 4C **53** (1C **6**)
Eltham Dri. *Urm*. 4C **77**

Eltham St. *M19*. 2A **104**
Elton Av. *M19*. 1A **120**
Elton St. *Salf*. 4D **51** (1D **5**)
Elton St. *Stret*. 3D **81**
Eltons Yd. *Salf*. 1D **5**
Elvate Cres. *M8*. 2B **52**
Elverdon Clo. *M15*. 3A **84**
Elvey St. *M40*. 2D **55**
Elvira Clo. *Fail*. 3D **43**
Elwick Clo. *M16*. 1B **100**
Ely Av. *Stret*. 1B **94**
Ely Cres. *Fail*. 2B **58**
Ely Gdns. *Urm*. 2A **94**
Elysian St. *Open*. 3C **73**
Ely St. *Chad*. 1D **27**
Embassy Wlk. *M18*. 4D **89**
Ember St. *M11*. 1D **73**
Embleton Wlk. *M18*. 2C **89**
Emerson Av. *Eccl*. 4C **47**
Emerson Ho. *Eccl*. 1B **62**
Emerson St. *Salf*. 1B **64**
Emery Av. *M21*. 3C **115**
Emery Clo. *Stoc*. 4A **120**
Emily Beavan Clo. *M11*. 2B **72**
Emily Pl. *Droy*. 2B **74**
Emley St. *M19*. 3B **104**
Emlyn St. *Swin*. 2D **29**
Emmaus Wlk. *Salf*. 4D **49**
Emmeline Grange. *Salf*. 1C **65**
Emmerson St. *Swin*. 1B **30**
Emmett St. E. *M40*. 2C **55**
Empire St. *M3*. 3B **52** (1C **6**)
Empress Bus. Pk. *M16*. 2C **83**
Empress Ct. *M15*. 2C **83**
Empress Dri. *Stoc*. 4D **121**
Empress St. *M8*. 2B **36**
Empress St. *Old T*. 2C **83**
Enbridge St. *Salf*. 3A **66**
Encombe Pl. *Salf*. 1D **67** (4C **4**)
Endcott Clo. *M18*. 2B **88**
Enderby Rd. *M40*. 1C **41**
Endon Dri. *M21*. 1B **116**
Endsleigh Rd. *M20*. 3A **118**
Energy St. *M40*. 4C **55**
Enfield Av. *M19*. 3A **120**
Enfield Clo. *Eccl*. 4C **47**
Enfield Clo. *M11*. 1C **73**
Enfield Ho. *Eccl*. 3D **61**
Enfield Rd. *Eccl*. 3D **45**
Enfield Rd. *Swin*. 1A **46**
Engell Clo. *M18*. 3D **89**
Engels Ho. *Eccl*. 3D **61**
    (off Trafford Rd.)
Engine St. *Chad*. 2D **27**
Englefield Gro. *M18*. 4D **89**
Enid Clo. *Salf*. 2A **52**
Ennerdale Av. *M21*. 4D **115**
Ennerdale Av. *Swin*. 4B **30**
Ennerdale Dri. *Sale*. 4A **110**

Ennerdale Rd. *Stret* 1A **96**
Ennismore Av. *Eccl.* 1C **63**
Enoch St. *M3.* 3C **55**
Enstone Dri. *M40.* 1D **41**
Enterprise Ho. *Salf.* 1D **81**
Enterprise Trad. Est. *Traf P.* . . 3C **63**
Entwisle Av. *Urm* 4B **76**
Entwisle St. *Swin.* 1D **29**
Enver Rd. *M8.* 2D **37**
Enville Rd. *M40.* 1B **40**
Enville Rd. *Salf.* 1C **49**
Enville St. *M9.* 3B **22**
Enys Wlk. *Salf* 2A **50**
Epping Dri. *Sale.* 3C **109**
Epping Rd. *Dent.* 2D **107**
Epping St. *M15* 2B **84** (5B **10**)
Epping Wlk. *M15* 3C **85**
(off Eden Clo.)
Eppleworth Ri. *Swin.* 3C **15**
Epsley Clo. *M15.* 2C **85**
Epsom Av. *M19.* 3D **119**
Epsom M. *Salf.* 4D **35**
Epworth St. *M1.* 2A **70**
Ercall Av. *M12.* 2C **87**
Erica Clo. *Stoc.* 4B **106**
Eric Brook Clo. *M14.* 1C **101**
Eric St. *Salf.* 2D **65**
Erindale Wlk. *M40.* 1B **54**
Erin St. *M11.* 4A **74**
Erith Clo. *Stoc.* 3D **123**
Erley Rd. *Swin.* 3A **32**
Erlington Av. *M16.* 1B **98**
Ermen Rd. *Eccl.* 3C **61**
Ermington Dri. *M8.* 4B **36**
Erneley Clo. *M12.* 1B **104**
Ernest St. *P'wich.* 2D **17**
Ernocroft Gro. *M18.* 2A **90**
Errington Dri. *Salf.* 3D **51** (1C **4**)
Errol Av. *M9.* 1C **21**
Errwood Cres. *M19.* 1A **120**
Errwood Pk. Works. *Stoc.* . . . 3B **120**
Errwood Rd. *M19.* 4D **119**
Erskine Rd. *M9.* 1C **23**
Erskine St. *M15.* 2D **83**
Erwin St. *M40.* 1B **56**
Escott St. *M16.* 1B **100**
Esk Clo. *Urm.* 4A **76**
Eskdale Av. *M20.* 2C **117**
Eskdale Ho. *M13.* 4C **87**
Eskrigge Clo. *M7.* 2B **36**
Esmond Rd. *M8.* 3C **37**
Essex Av. *Droy.* 4C **59**
Essex Clo. *Fail.* 2B **58**
Essex Pl. *Swin.* 4B **14**
Essex Rd. *M18.* 3C **89**
Essex St. *M2.* 2B **68** (1B **10**)
Essex Wlk. *M15.* 3D **83**
Essex Way. *M15.* 3D **83**
Essoldo Clo. *M18.* 3C **89**

Estonfield Dri. *Urm.* 2B **94**
Eston St. *M13.* 4B **86**
Eswick St. *M11.* 2C **73**
Etchell St. *M40.* 2A **54**
Ethel Av. *M9.* 1B **22**
Ethel Av. *Swin.* 2D **31**
Ethel Ter. *M19.* 3A **104**
Etherow Gro. *M40.* 4B **26**
Etherstone St. *M8.* 2A **38**
Eton Clo. *M16.* 3D **83**
Eton Ct. *M16.* 3D **83**
Etruria Clo. *M13.* 3B **86**
Ettrick Clo. *Open.* 4D **73**
Euclid Clo. *M11.* 2C **71**
Europa Circ. *Traf P.* 3B **80**
(in two parts)
Europa Ga. *Traf P.* 3B **80**
Europa Way. *Traf P.* 3B **80**
Euston Av. *M9.* 3A **24**
Evans Rd. *Eccl.* 2A **60**
Evans St. *Salf* 4A **52** (2F **5**)
Evan St. *M40.* 2C **55**
Evanton Wlk. *M9* 3C **39**
(off Nethervale Dri.)
Eva St. *M14.* 1A **102**
Evelyn St. *M14.* 4B **102**
Evening St. *Fail.* 2B **42**
Evenley Clo. *M11.* 2D **89**
Everard St. *Salf.* 4C **67** (4B **8**)
Everett Ct. *M20.* 3D **117**
Everett Rd. *M20.* 3C **117**
Evergreen Wlk. *Sale.* 3C **109**
Everleigh Dri. *M7.* 4B **36**
Eversden Ct. *Salf.* 3A **52** (1E **5**)
Everton Rd. *Stoc.* 2B **106**
Everton St. *Swin.* 2A **30**
Every St. *M4.* 2B **70**
Evesham Clo. *Midd.* 1B **24**
Evesham Gdns. *Midd.* 1A **24**
Evesham Gro. *Sale.* 4C **113**
Evesham Rd. *M9.* 4A **24**
Evesham Rd. *Midd.* 1A **24**
Evesham Wlk. *Midd.* 1B **24**
Evington Av. *Open.* 1C **91**
Ewan St. *M18.* 2D **89**
Ewart Av. *Salf.* 2A **66**
Ewhurst Av. *Swin.* 4D **29**
Ewing Clo. *M8.* 1C **37**
Ewood Ho. *Eccl.* 1B **62**
Exbridge Wlk. *M40.* 3D **57**
Exbury St. *M14.* 2B **118**
Exchange Quay. *Salf.* 2A **82**
Exchange Sq. *M4* 1B **68** (4B **6**)
Exchange St. *M2.* . . . 2B **68** (5B **6**)
Exeter Av. *Eccl.* 3C **47**
Exeter Rd. *Stoc.* 4D **123**
Exeter Rd. *Urm.* 4D **77**
Exford Clo. *M40.* 4B **54**
Exford Clo. *Stoc.* 3B **122**

Exford Wlk. *M40* 4B **54**
Exmouth Av. *Stoc.* 4D **123**
Exmouth Rd. *Sale.* 4D **109**
Eynford Av. *Stoc* 3D **123**
Eyre St. *M15.* 3C **85**

F

Faber St. *M4.* 4C **53** (1D **7**)
Factory La. *M9.* 1A **38**
Factory La. *Salf.* 2D **67** (5C **4**)
Failsworth **3B 42**
Failsworth Ind. Est. *Fail* 4C **41**
Failsworth Rd. *Fail.* 3D **43**
Failsworth Shop. Precinct.
    Fail. 3B **42**
Failsworth Sports Cen. 3C **43**
Fairbank. *Droy.* 3B **74**
Fairbank Av. *M14.* 4D **85**
Fairbottom Wlk. *Droy.* 3C **75**
Fairbourne Rd. *M19.* 3C **105**
Fairbrook Dri. *Salf.* 1C **65**
Fairbrother St. *Salf.* 1C **83** (5A **8**)
Fairburn Clo. *Urm.* 4A **76**
Fairclough St. *M11.* 1A **72**
Fairfax Av. *M20.* 4D **117**
Fairfax Rd. *P'wich.* 1A **18**
Fairfield. **3C 75**
Fairfield Av. *Droy.* 3C **75**
Fairfield Ct. *M13.* 4B **86**
Fairfield Ct. *Droy.* 3B **74**
Fairfield Ho. *Droy.* 2C **75**
                            (off Manchester Rd.)
Fairfield Rd. *M11.* 4A **74**
Fairfield Rd. *Droy.* 3A **74**
Fairfield Sq. *Droy.* . . . .
                            (in two parts)
Fairfield St.
    M1 & M12. . . . . 3D **69** (2E **11**)
Fairfield St. *Salf.* 2B **48**
Fairfield Vw. *Aud.* 4C **75**
Fairford Clo. *Stoc.* 4B **122**
Fairford Way. *Stoc.* 4B **122**
Fairham Wlk. *M4.* 2B **70**
Fairhaven *M21.* 1B **114**
Fairhaven St. *M12.* 2D **87**
Fairholme Av. *Urm.* 3C **93**
Fairholme Cvn. Pk. *M8.* 3D **53**
Fairholme Rd. *M20.* 3A **118**
Fairhope Av. *Salf.* 3D **47**
Fairisle Clo. *M11.* 2D **71**
Fairlawn Clo. *M14.* 4C **85**
Fairlee Av. *Aud.* 2D **75**
Fairleigh Av. *Salf.* 4A **48**
Fairless Rd. *Eccl.* 2D **61**
Fairman St. *M16.* 1B **100**
Fairmount Rd. *Swin.* 1B **44**
Fair Oak Rd. *M19.* 4D **119**

Fairstead Wlk. *Open.* 4B **74**
Fair St. *M1.* 2A **70**
Fair St. *Swin.* 1C **31**
Fairview Av. *M19.* 2D **103**
Fairview Av. *Dent.* 3C **107**
Fairview Rd. *Dent.* 2C **107**
Fairway. *Droy.* 3C **75**
Fairway. *P'wich.* 4D **19**
Fairway. *Swin.* 3A **32**
Fairway Ct. *Dent.* 4D **91**
Fairway, The. *M40.* 3C **41**
Fairy La. *M8.* 2A **52**
Falcon Av. *Urm.* 2A **94**
Falcon Clo. *Salf.* 2A **64**
Falcon Ct. *M15.* 3A **84**
Falcon Ct. *Salf.* (M7) 1D **35**
Falcon Ct. *Salf.* (M50) 3B **64**
Falcon Cres. *Swin.* 4D **15**
Falkland Av. *M40.* 3C **55**
Falkland Ho. *M14.* 3A **102**
Fall Bank. *Stoc.* 3D **121**
Fallons Rd. *Wors.* 1C **29**
Fallowfield **4A 102**
Fallowfield Av. *Salf.* 3B **66**
Fallow Fields Dri. *Stoc.* 3C **107**
Fallowfield Shop. Cen.
    M14. . . . . 3C **103**
Falmer Clo. *M18.* 2B **90**
Falmouth Av. *Sale.* 4D **109**
Falmouth Cres. *Stoc.* 4D **123**
Falmouth St. *M40.* 3D **55**
Falsgrave Clo. *M40.* 2A **56**
Falside Wlk. *M40.* 2C **57**
Falston Av. *M40.* 4D **25**
Fane Wlk. *M9.* 3D **21**
Faraday Av. *M8.* 1C **53**
Faraday Av. *Swin.* 4B **16**
Faraday St. *M1.* 1D **69** (4E **7**)
Fareham Ct. *M16.* 3D **83**
Fargner St. *M11.* 2D **73**
Far La. *M18.* 4D **89**
Farm Av. *M18.* 4C **91**
Farley Way. *Stoc.* 3A **106**
Farm Av. *Stret.* 4C **79**
Farm Clo. *Stoc.* 3C **121**
Farmfield. *Sale.* 3A **110**
Farm La. *Wors.* 2A **44**
Farmside Pl. *M19.* 3A **104**
Farmstead Clo. *Fail.* 4D **43**
Farm St. *Fail.* 1D **57**
Farm Yd. *M19.* 3A **104**
Farm Av. *Redd.* 2A **106**
Farnborough Rd. *M40.* 4B **54**
Farndale Wlk. *M9.* 2C **39**
                            (off Up. Conran St.)
Farndon Rd. *Stoc.* 2A **106**
Farnsworth St. *M11.* 4D **73**
Farnworth Dri. *M14.* 2A **102**

Farrand Rd. *Oldh* 4D **27**
Farrand Rd. *M12*. 4A **88**
Farrar Rd. *Droy* 3B **74**
Farrell St. *Salf* 4A **52** (1E **5**)
Farrer Rd. *M13* 1D **103**
Farringdon St. *Salf*. 4C **49**
Farrington Av. *M20*. 2C **117**
Farwood Clo. *M16* 3C **83**
Fastnet St. *M11*. 3A **72**
Faulkner Rd. *Stret* 2C **97**
Faulkner St. *M1*. 3C **69** (2C **10**)
Faversham St. *M40* 3B **40**
Fay Av. *M9*. 4B **24**
Federation St. *M4* 1C **69** (3C **6**)
Federation St. *P'wich* 1D **17**
Fellbrigg Clo. *M18* 1C **105**
Felling Wlk. *M14* 1D **101**
(off Seaham Wlk.)
Felltop Dri. *Stoc*. 4C **107**
Feltham St. *M12*. 2A **88**
Felthorpe Dri. *M8*. 4B **36**
Fencegate Av. *Stoc*. 4D **121**
Fenchurch Av. *M40*. 3C **57**
Fencot Dri. *M12*. 4A **88**
Fenella St. *M13*. 4C **87**
Fenham Clo. *M40*. 2A **54**
Fenmore Av. *M18*. 1B **104**
Fennel St. *M4* 1B **68** (3B **6**)
Fenney St. *Salf*. 2D **51**
Fenney St. E. *Salf*. 1A **52**
Fenn St. *M15*. 2A **84**
Fenstock Wlk. *M40*. 3D **57**
Fenton St. *M12*. 3A **88**
Fenwick St. *M15*. 2C **85**
Ferdinand St. *M40*. 3B **54**
Ferguson Ct. *M19*. 1D **119**
Fernacre. *Sale* 4A **112**
Fern Av. *Urm* 2A **92**
Fernbrook Clo. *M13*. 3B **86**
Fernbrook Wlk. *M8*. 3B **36**
(off Hillbrow Wlk.)
Fernclough Rd. *M9*. 3B **38**
Ferndale Gdns. *M19*. 3C **119**
Ferndene Gdns. *M20*. 4D **117**
Ferndene Rd. *M20*. 4D **117**
Ferngate Dri. *M20*. 3D **117**
Fernhill Dri. *M18*. 4B **88**
Fernhurst Rd. *M20*. 4A **118**
Fernie St. *M4*. 4C **53** (1C **6**)
Fernlea. *Stoc* 4C **121**
Fernlea Cres. *Swin* 3A **30**
Fernleaf St. *M14*. 4C **85**
Fernleigh Av. *M19* 3C **105**
Fernleigh Dri. *M16* 3C **83**
Fernside Av. *M20*. 4B **118**
Fern St. *M8*. 3C **53** (1C **6**)
Fernwood Av. *M18*. 1D **105**
Ferris St. *M11*. 3D **73**
Ferry St. *M11*. 3C **71**

Festival Village. *Urm*. 3A **78**
(off Trafford Cen., The)
Fettler Clo. *Swin*. 4A **30**
Fiddick Ct. *Salf*. 1D **65**
(off Milford St.)
Fld. Bank Gro. *M19*. 3C **105**
Fielden Av. *M21*. 3B **98**
Fielden Rd. *M20*. 4B **116**
Fielders Way. *Swin*. 2A **14**
Fieldfare Av. *M40*. 3B **56**
Fielding St. *Eccl*. 2C **61**
Field Rd. *Sale*. 3A **110**
Fields New Rd. *Chad* 2C **27**
Field St. *M18*. 2A **90**
Field St. *Droy*. 3B **74**
Field St. *Fail*. 3A **42**
Field St. *Salf*. 1D **65**
Fld. Vale Dri. *Stoc*. 3C **107**
Fld. View Wlk. *M16*. 3B **100**
Fife Av. *Chad* 2B **26**
Fifth Av. *Traf P*. 3A **80**
Fifth Av. *M11*. 1C **73**
Fifth St. *Traf P*. 3A **80**
(in two parts)
Filby Wlk. *M40*. 3C **55**
Filey Av. *M16*. 2D **99**
Filey Av. *Urm*. 4A **76**
Filey Dri. *Salf*. 1B **48**
Filey Rd. *M14*. 1B **118**
Filton Wlk. *M9*. 4A **38**
(off Westmere Dri.)
Finborough Clo. *M16*. 4A **84**
Finchley Av. *M40*. 3C **57**
Finchley Gro. *M40*. 1A **40**
Finchley Rd. *M14*. 1D **117**
Findlay Wlk. *M9*. 3B **38**
Finghall Rd. *Urm*. 2B **92**
Finishing Wlk. *M4*. 2A **70**
Finney Dri. *M21*. 2A **114**
Finningley Rd. *M9*. 1D **21**
Finny Bank Rd. *Sale*. 3C **111**
Finsbury Av. *M40*. 3C **57**
Finsbury Rd. *Stoc*. 4A **106**
Finstock Clo. *Eccl*. 2B **60**
Fintry Gro. *Eccl*. 2D **61**
Firbank. *P'wich*. 2C **19**
Firbeck Dri. *M4*. 1B **70**
Firdale Av. *M40*. 1A **42**
Firdon Wlk. *M9*. 3C **39**
(off Nethervale Dri.)
Firefly Clo. *Salf* 2D **67** (5C **4**)
Fire Sta. Sq. *Salf* 1B **66** (4A **4**)
Firethorn Av. *M19*. 3D **119**
Firethorn Wlk. *Sale*. 4C **109**
(in two parts)
Fir Gro. *M19* 3A **104**
Fir Rd. *Swin*. 1A **46**
Firs Av. *M16*. 2B **98**
Firs Av. *Fail*. 3A **42**

Firsby St. *M19* 3A **104**
First Av. *M11* 1D **73**
First Av. *Swin.* 2D **45**
First Av. *Traf P* 3B **80**
Fir St. *M16* 4C **83**
Fir St. *M40* 3B **54**
Fir St. *Eccl.* 2D **61**
Fir St. *Fail* 3A **42**
Fir St. *Salf.* 1D **65**
Firsway. *Sale* 4D **109**
Firswood 1A **98**
Firswood Dri. *Swin.* 4A **30**
Firth Clo. *Salf.* 1D **51**
Firth Rd. *M20.* 4A **118**
Firtree Av. *Sale.* 4C **109**
Firwood Av. *Urm* 2C **95**
(in two parts)
Firwood Ct. *Eccl.* 4A **46**
Fiscall Way. *Fail* 3A **42**
Fishbourne Sq. *M14.* 1A **102**
Fitness First Club. 3C 25
Fitton Av. *M21* 3B **114**
Fitton Cres. *Swin.* 3B **14**
Fitzgeorge St. *M40.* 2A **54**
Fitzgerald Clo. *P'wich* 4D **17**
Fitzgerald Way. *Salf.* 4A **50**
Fitzroy St. *Droy.* 3D **75**
Fitzwarren Ct. *Salf.* 1D **65**
Fitzwarren St. *Salf.* 4D **49**
Fitzwilliam St. *Salf.* 3D **51** (1D **5**)
Fiveways. *Droy.* 1C **75**
Flagship Av. *Salf.* 3B **66**
Flamborough Wlk. *M14.* 4D **85**
Flamingo Clo. *M12.* 2A **88**
Flashfields. *P'wich* 1D **33**
Flash St. *M40.* 1C **57**
Flatley Clo. *M15.* 2C **85**
Flavian Wlk. Open *3B 72*
(off Herne St.)
Flaxpool Clo. *M16* 4A **84**
(in two parts)
Flax St. *Salf.* 4D **51** (2D **5**)
Fleeson St. *M14.* 1A **102**
Fleet St. *M18.* 2B **90**
Fletcher Av. *Swin.* 3C **15**
Fletcher Sq. *M1.* 2A **70**
Fletcher St. *M40.* 2D **55**
Flexbury Wlk. *M40.* 3D **57**
Flint Clo. *M11.* 1B **72**
Flint St. *Droy.* 1D **75**
Flixton Rd. *Urm.* 2A **92**
(in two parts)
Flixton Wlk. *M13.* 3B **86**
Flora Dri. *Salf.* 3D **51** (1D **5**)
Floral Ct. *Salf.* 4D **35**
Flora St. *M9.* 3A **22**
Florence St. *Droy.* 3D **75**
Florence St. *Eccl.* 2B **60**
Florence St. *Fail.* 2B **42**

Florence St. *Sale* 3D **111**
Florin Gdns. *Salf.* 4D **49**
Floyd Av. *M21* 3C **115**
Floyer Rd. *M9* 1C **23**
Flynn Ct. *Salf.* 3C **49**
Fold Av. *Droy.* 1D **75**
Fold St. *M40* 2A **40**
Fold, The. *M9.* 3B **22**
Fold, The. *Urm.* 1A **92**
Foleshill Av. *M9* 3B **38**
Foliage Cres. *Stoc* 4D **123**
Foliage Gdns. *Stoc.* 4D **123**
Foliage Rd. *Stoc.* 4D **123**
Folkestone Rd. *M11.* 1D **73**
Folkestone Rd. E. *M11.* 1D **73**
Folkestone Rd. W. *M11* 4C **57**
Follows St. *M18.* 2D **89**
Folly La. *Swin.* 2D **45**
Fontwell Clo. *M16* 1C **99**
Fontwell Wlk. *M40.* 4D **25**
Forber Cres. *M18.* 1D **105**
Fordel Wlk. *Salf.* 3A **52**
Ford La. *Salf.* 3A **50**
Ford St. *M12.* 1B **86**
Ford St. *Salf.* (M3) 1D **67** (4D **5**)
Ford St. *Salf.* (M7) 2C **51**
Foreland Clo. *M40.* 2B **54**
Forest Bank. *Swin.* 2C **33**
Forest Range. *M19.* 3A **104**
Forest St. *Eccl.* 3A **44**
Formby Av. *M21* 2D **115**
Formby Rd. *Salf.* 1C **49**
Forrester Ho. M12 . . . . *2A 88*
(off Blackwin St.)
Forrester St. *Wors* 2A **28**
Forshaw Av. *M18.* 2B **90**
Forston Wlk. *M8* 1D **53**
Fortson Clo. *Salf.* 2A **66**
Fort Rd. *P'wich* 4D **19**
Fortrose Av. *M9.* 3D **21**
Fortuna Gro. *M19* 4D **103**
Forum Gro. *Salf.* 2A **52**
Foster St. *Salf.* 1B **64**
Fotherby Dri. *M9* 3B **22**
Foundry La. *M4.* 1D **69** (4E **7**)
Fountain Sq. *Swin.* 2B **30**
Fountains Rd. *Stret* 1B **94**
Fountain St. *M2.* 2C **69** (1C **10**)
Fountain St. *Eccl.* 3D **61**
Fountains Wlk. *Chad* 1C **27**
Fourth Av. *M11* 4C **57**
Fourth Av. *Chad.* 1C **27**
Fourth Av. *Swin.* 2D **45**
Fourth Av. *Traf P* 3A **80**
Fourways. *Traf P* 2C **79**
Fourways Wlk. *M40.* 4B **24**
Four Yards. *M2.* 2B **68** (1B **10**)
Fovant Cres. *Stoc.* 3A **106**
Fowler Av. *M18* 1B **90**

Fowler St. *Oldh* 3D **27**
Foxbank St. *M13* 4C **87**
Foxbench Wlk. *M21* 3D **115**
Foxdale St. *M11* 2C **73**
Foxdenton Dri. *Urm* 1B **94**
Foxdenton La. *Midd & Chad* 1B **26**
Foxfield Dri. *Oldh* 1D **43**
Foxham Wlk. *Salf* 1A **52**
Foxhill Rd. *Eccl* 2A **60**
Foxley Clo. *Droy* 3A **74**
Foxley Wlk. *M12* 3A **88**
Fox Pk. Rd. *Oldh* 4D **27**
Fox St. *Eccl* 1B **62**
Foxwell Wlk. *M8* 1D **53**
Foxwood Gdns. *M19* 4C **119**
Foynes Clo. *M40* 2B **54**
Framley Rd. *M21* 2B **116**
Fram St. *M9* 2D **39**
Fram St. *Salf* 1C **65**
Francesca Wlk. *M18*. 2C **89**
Frances St. *M13*. 2D **85**
Francis Av. *Eccl* 1A **62**
Francis Av. *Wors* 4A **12**
Francis Rd. *M20*. 4A **118**
Francis St. *M3*. 4B **52** (1A **6**)
Francis St. *Eccl* 4D **45**
Francis St. *Fail* 3B **42**
Frandley Wlk. *M13*. 4D **69** (4F **11**)
Frankby Clo. *Swin* 3A **32**
Frank Cowin Ct. *Salf* 3D **51** (1D **5**)
Frank Hulme Ho. *Stret* 3C **97**
Frankland Clo. *M11* 1B **72**
Franklin Av. *Droy* 2C **75**
Franklin St. *Eccl*. 1D **61**
Franklyn Clo. *Dent* 2C **107**
Franklyn Rd. *M18*. 2A **90**
Frank St. *Fail* 3A **42**
Frank St. *Salf*. 3A **50**
Frank Swift Wlk. *M14*. 1C **101**
Franton Rd. *M11* 1B **72**
Fraser Pl. *Traf P* 3B **80**
Fraser Rd. *Crum*. 1B **36**
Fraser St. *Swin* 1C **31**
Fraternitas Ter. *Droy*. 4A **58**
Freda Wlk. *M11* 2D **71**
Frederick Rd.
　　Salf & M7 . . . . 4B **50** (1A **4**)
Frederick St. *Salf* 1A **68** (4E **5**)
Fred Tilson Clo. *M14* 1C **101**
Freeland Wlk. *Open* 3C **73**
Freeman Sq. *M15*. 2C **85**
Freetown Clo. *M14*. 4C **85**
Free Trade Hall 2A **10**
Fremantle Av. *M18*. 1D **105**
French Barn La. *M9* 3A **22**
Freshfield Clo. *Fail* 4C **43**
Freshfield Wlk. *M11* 1C **73**
Freshville St. M1 . . . . . . 2D **69** (1F **11**)
　　　　　　(off Leycroft St.)

Freshwater St. *M18* 2A **90**
Frew Clo. *M40* 4B **24**
Freya Gro. *Salf*. 3C **67** (3A **8**)
Friar's Ct. *Salf* 1D **63**
Friar's Rd. *Sale*. 4D **111**
Friendship Av. *M18* 4A **90**
Frinton Av. *M40*. 3D **25**
Frobisher Clo. *M13* 3B **86**
Frodesley Wlk. *M12*. 2D **87**
Frodsham St. *M14*. 1D **101**
Frome Av. *Urm*. 3B **92**
Frome Dri. *M8* 3D **37**
Frostlands St. *M16*. 1A **100**
Frost St. *M4*. 2B **70**
Froxmer St. *M18* 2C **89**
Fuchsia Gro. *Salf* 4D **35**
Fulbeck Wlk. *M8* 2A **52**
Fulford St. *M16* 4C **83**
Fulham Av. *M40* 2B **56**
Fulmead Wlk. M8. . . . . *1B 52*
　　　　(off Kilmington Dri.)
Fulmer Dri. *M4*. 1A **70**
Fulmere Ct. *Swin* 4D **29**
Fulneck Sq. *Droy* 3C **75**
Fulshaw Wlk. *M13* 1D **85** (5F **11**)
Fulton Ct. *M15*. 3C **85**
Fulwood Av. *M9* 2D **23**
Furness Quay. *Salf* 4A **66**
Furness Rd. *M14* 3A **102**
Furness Rd. *Urm* 1D **93**
Furnival Clo. *Dent*. 2C **107**
Furnival Rd. *M18* 2C **89**
Furnival St. *Stoc*. 2B **106**
Furrow Dri. *Eccl* 3B **44**
Fyfield Wlk. *M8* 1D **53**
Fylde Ct. *Stret* 4A **96**

G

Gables, The. *Sale* 4A **112**
Gable St. *M11* 3D **71**
Gainford Gdns. *M40*. 1B **40**
Gainford Rd. *Stoc* 3B **106**
Gainsborough Av. *M20*. 4A **118**
Gainsborough Av. *Stret* 1D **97**
Gainsborough St. *Salf* 3A **36**
Gairlock Av. *Stret*. 2D **95**
Gair Rd. *Stoc* 4B **122**
Gaitskell Clo. *M12* 2C **71**
Galbraith St. *M1* 3C **69** (3C **10**)
Gale Rd. *P'wich* 3D **17**
Galgate Clo. *M15* 1A **84** (5E **9**)
Galleria Apartments. *Salf* 1D **81**
Galloway Dri. *Swin*. 2B **14**
Galloway Rd. *Swin*. 1D **45**
Galston St. *M11* 3A **72**
Galsworthy Av. *M8*. 1C **53**

Galvin Rd. *M9*	3D	**21**
Gamma Wlk. *M11*	1B	**72**
Gan Eden. *Salf*	2A	**36**
Gantock Wlk. *M14*	1A	**102**
Garbo Ct. *Salf*	3C	**49**
Garbrook Av. *M9*	1A	**22**
Garden Av. *Droy*	1D	**75**
Garden Av. *Stret*	1B	**96**
Gardenfold Ho. *Droy*	1D	**75**
(off Fold Av.)		
Garden La. *M3*	5A	**6**
Garden La. *Salf*	1A **68** (3F **5**)	
(in two parts)		
Gardens, The. *M2*	1B **68** (4B **6**)	
Gardens, The. *Eccl*	3C	**47**
Garden St. *M4*	1C **69** (4C **6**)	
Garden St. *Eccl*	2A	**62**
Garden Vw. *Sale*	3D	**111**
Garden Wall Clo.		
Salf	3C **67** (3A **8**)	
Gardner Ho. *Eccl*	1A	**62**
Gardner Rd. *P'wich*	2D	**17**
Gardner St. *M12*	2B	**88**
Gardner St. *Salf*	4A	**50**
Garfield Av. *M19*	3B	**104**
Garfield St. *Salf*	2A	**82**
Garforth Av. *M4*	1A	**70**
Garforth Cres. *Droy*	4D	**59**
Gargrave St. *Salf*	2D	**33**
Garlick St. *M18*	3D	**89**
Garnant Clo. *M9*	2D	**39**
Garner Dri. *Eccl*	4C	**45**
Garner Dri. *Salf*	4B	**48**
Garratt Way. *M18*	3C	**89**
Garrowmore Wlk. *M9*	3C	**23**
Garstang Ho. *M15*	3D	**85**
Garswood Rd. *M14*	2B	**100**
Garthorne Clo. *M16*	4D	**83**
Garth, The. *Salf*	1B	**64**
Gartland Wlk. *M8*	2A	**38**
Gartside St. *M3*	2A **68** (1F **9**)	
Garwood St. *M15*	1B **84** (5A **10**)	
Gascoyne St. *M14*	1D	**101**
Gaskell Rd. *Eccl*	2D	**61**
Gaskell St. *M40*	2C	**57**
Gaskell St. *Swin*	4B	**14**
Gaston Wlk. *M9*	1B	**22**
(off Eastlands Rd.)		
Gatcombe Sq. *M14*	1A	**102**
Gate Rd. *Stret*	4C	**79**
Gateshead Clo. *M14*	4D	**85**
Gateside Wlk. *M9*	1C	**23**
(off Brockford Dri.)		
Gate St. *M11*	3C	**73**
Gateway Cres. *Chad*	1D	**25**
Gateway Ind. Est.		
M1	2D **69** (1F **11**)	
Gateway Rd. *M18*	2C	**89**
Gateways, The. *Swin*	1B	**30**
Gathurst St. *M18*	2A	**90**
Gatley Av. *M14*	3C	**101**
Gatling Av. *M12*	2B	**104**
Gavin Av. *Salf*	2A	**66**
Gawsworth Ct. *M9*	1C	**21**
(off Deanswood Dri.)		
Gaydon Rd. *Sale*	4D	**109**
Gayford Wlk. *M9*	1C	**23**
(off Brockford Dri.)		
Gaythorn	4B **68** (4B **10**)	
Gaythorn St. *Salf*	2C **67** (5B **4**)	
Gayton Wlk. *M40*	4D	**25**
Gaywood Wlk. *M40*	1A	**54**
Gee La. *Eccl*	4B	**44**
Gee La. *Oldh*	4D	**27**
Gemini Rd. *Salf*	3C	**51**
Geneva Wlk. *M8*	1D	**53**
Genista Gro. *Salf*	4D	**35**
Geoff Bent Wlk. *M40*	2B	**56**
George H. Carnall		
Leisure Cen.	4A	**78**
George Leigh St. *M4*	1D **69** (4F **7**)	
George Parr Rd. *M15*	2B	**84**
George St. *M1*	3B **68** (2B **10**)	
(in two parts)		
George St. *Eccl*	2C	**61**
George St. *Fail*	2B	**42**
George St. *P'wich*	1B	**34**
George St. *Urm*	2A	**94**
George St. N. *M7*	2B	**36**
George St. S. *M7*	2A	**36**
George Ter. *Eccl*	1D	**61**
George Thomas Ct. *M9*	2B	**38**
Georgette Dri. *Salf*	4A **52** (2F **5**)	
Gerald Av. *M8*	2C	**37**
Gerald Rd. *Salf*	2A	**50**
Gerrard St. *Salf*	4B	**50**
Gertrude Clo. *Salf*	3A	**66**
Gervis Clo. *M40*	2B	**54**
Gibbon Av. *M18*	1B	**90**
Gibb Rd. *Wors*	3B	**28**
Gibbs St. *Salf*	2D **67** (5C **4**)	
(in two parts)		
Gibson Av. *M18*	1B	**90**
Gibson Pl. *M3*	4C **53** (1C **6**)	
Gidlow St. *M18*	1C	**90**
Gifford Av. *M9*	2D	**23**
Gilbert St. *M15*	4A **68** (4F **9**)	
Gilbert St. *Eccl*	3B	**60**
Gilbert St. *Salf*	2D	**65**
Gilda Brook Rd. *Eccl*	2C	**63**
(in three parts)		
Gilda Cres. Rd. *Eccl*	2C	**47**
Gildenhall. *Fail*	3C	**43**
Gilden Wlk. *M9*	1C	**23**
Gildridge Rd. *M16*	3A	**100**
Gilesgate. *M14*	1A	**102**
(off Grelley Wlk.)		
Giles St. *M12*	4A	**88**

Gillford Av. *M9* 1D **39**
Gillingham Rd. *Eccl* 1B **60**
Gillingham Sq. *M11* *2D* **71**
(off Jobling St.)
Gill St. *M9* 2D **39**
Gilman Clo. *M9* 4A **22**
Gilman St. *M9* 4A **22**
Gilmerton Dri. *M40* 2C **57**
Gilmore Dri. *P'wich* 1B **18**
Gilmour Ter. *M9* 1D **39**
(in two parts)
Gilpin Rd. *Urm* 3B **94**
Giltbrook Av. *M40* 3B **54**
Girton St. *Salf* 3A **52** (1E **5**)
Girton Wlk. *M40* 1D **41**
Girvan Av. *M40* 4D **25**
Gisborne Dri. *Salf* 2A **50**
Gisburne Av. *M40* 4D **25**
Gissing Wlk. *M9* 4B **38**
Givendale Dri. *M8* 4C **21**
Glade Wood Dri. *Fail* 2D **43**
Gladstone Clo. *M15* 4A **84**
Gladstone Rd. *Eccl* 1A **62**
Gladstone Rd. *Urm* 2A **94**
Gladstone St. *Swin* 2C **31**
Gladys St. *M16* 4C **83**
Glamis Av. *M11* 4B **56**
Glamis Av. *Stret* 2C **95**
Glamorgan Pl. *Oldh* 1D **27**
Glanford Av. *M9* 3C **21**
Glanton Wlk. *M40* 1D **41**
Glasshouse St. *M4* 4A **54**
Glastonbury Rd. *Stret* 1B **94**
Glaswen Gro. *Stoc* 4B **122**
Gleaves Rd. *Eccl* 2A **62**
Gleave St. *Sale* 3D **111**
Glebelands Rd. *P'wich* 1A **18**
Glebelands Rd. *Sale* 3B **110**
Glebelands Rd. E. *P'wich* 1B **18**
Glebe Rd. *Urm* 2D **93**
Glebe St. *Chad* 3C **27**
Gleden St. *M40* 1C **71**
(in two parts)
Gledhill Av. *Salf* 1A **82**
Gledhill St. *M20* 2D **117**
Glemsford Clo. *M40* 1B **56**
Glenacre Gdns. *M18* 1A **106**
Glenart. *Eccl* 4A **46**
Glen Av. *M9* 1C **39**
Glen Av. *Sale* 3C **111**
Glen Av. *Swin* 2D **29**
Glen Av. *Wors* 2A **28**
Glenbarry Clo. *M13* 2D **85**
Glenbarry St. *M12* 3B **70**
Glenbrook Rd. *M9* 1C **21**
Glencar Dri. *M40* 4D **25**
Glencastle Rd. *M18* 3C **89**
Glencross Av. *M21* 2A **98**
Glendale. *Swin* 4D **15**

Glendale Av. *M19* 3D **119**
Glendale Rd. *Eccl* 4C **47**
Glendinning St. *Salf* 1C **65**
Glendore. *Salf* 1A **64**
Glendower Dri. *M40* 2A **54**
Gleneagles Av. *M11* 1C **73**
Glenfyne Rd. *Salf* 2B **48**
Glenhaven Av. *Urm* 2C **93**
Glenhurst Rd. *M19* 4C **119**
Glenmay Ct. *Stret* 2A **96**
Glen Maye. *Sale* 4A **112**
Glenmore Dri. *M8* 3D **37**
Glenmore Dri. *Fail* 2D **43**
Glenolden St. *M11* 1D **73**
Glenpark Wlk. *M9* *3C* **39**
(off Craigend Dri.)
Glenroy Wlk. *M9* 1C **23**
Glensdale Dri. *M40* 1A **42**
Glenside Av. *M18* 1D **105**
Glenside Gdns. *Fail* 3C **43**
Glen St. *Salf* 4A **66**
Glenville Ter. *Droy* *4A* **58**
(off Greenside La.)
Glenwood Dri. *M9* 3C **39**
Glenwyn Av. *M9* 2C **23**
Globe Clo. *M16* 3D **83**
Glossop Ter. *M40* 3D **25**
Gloucester Av. *M19* 4B **104**
Gloucester Ho. *Salf* 4D **35**
Gloucester Pl. *Salf* 4A **50**
Gloucester Rd. *Dent* 2C **107**
Gloucester Rd. *Droy* 4C **59**
Gloucester Rd. *Salf* 3A **48**
Gloucester Rd. *Urm* 2D **93**
Gloucester St. *M1* 4B **68** (4B **10**)
Gloucester St.
   Salf (M5) 3A **8**
Gloucester St.
   Salf (M6) 3A **50**
Gloucester St. S.
   Oldh 1D **27**
Glover Av. *M8* 4D **37**
Glover Ct. *M7* 2B **36**
Glover Fld. *Salf* *4D* **35**
(off Devonshire St.)
Glyneath Clo. *M11* 3D **71**
Glynrene Dri. *Swin* 1C **29**
G-MEX Cen. 3B **68** (3A **10**)
Goadsby St. *M4* 1C **69** (3D **7**)
Godbert Av. *M21* 4C **115**
Godfrey Av. *Droy* 4D **57**
Godfrey Range. *M18* 4B **90**
Godfrey Rd. *Salf* 2A **48**
Godlee Dri. *Swin* 3A **30**
Godley Clo. *Open* 3C **73**
Godwin St. *M18* 2A **90**
Golborne Av. *M20* 2B **116**
Goldenhill Av. *M11* 4C **57**

Golden Sq. *Eccl* 2D **61**
(off Golden St.)
Golden St. *Eccl* 2D **61**
Goldsmith Av. *Salf* 1B **64**
Goldsmith Rd. *Stoc* 3D **105**
Gold St. *M1* 2C **69** (1D **11**)
Golf Rd. *Sale* 4D **113**
Golfview Dri. *Eccl* 3D **45**
Gomer Wlk. *M8* 1A **54**
Goodiers Dri. *Salf* 3A **66**
Goodier St. *M40* 2D **55**
Goodman St. *M9* 2C **39**
Goodwill Clo. *Swin* 3B **30**
Goodwin Ct. *Chad* 2D **27**
Goodwood Ct. *Salf* 4D **35**
(off Bury New Rd.)
Goodwood Dri. *Swin* 3D **31**
Goodworth Wlk. *M40* 3A **40**
(off Hanson Rd.)
Goole St. *M11* 3A **72**
Goostrey Av. *M20* 1C **117**
Gordon Av. *M19* 3B **104**
Gordon Av. *Chad* 3C **27**
Gordon Av. *Sale* 3D **111**
Gordon Pl. *M20* 4D **117**
Gordon Rd. *Eccl* 4D **45**
Gordon Rd. *Swin* 4C **29**
Gordon St. *Abb H.* 2A **90**
Gordon St. *Chad* 2B **26**
Gordon St. *Old T.* 3D **83**
Gordon St. *Salf* 3D **51**
Gordon Ter. *M9* 2C **39**
Gore Av. *Fail* 2D **43**
Gore Av. *Salf* 1B **64**
Gorebrook Ct. *M12* 4A **88**
Gore Cres. *Salf* 4B **48**
Goredale Av. *M18* 1A **106**
Gore Dri. *Salf* 4B **48**
Gorelan Rd. *M18* 3D **89**
Gore St. *M1* 2D **69** (1E **11**)
Gore St. *Salf* (M3) 1A **68** (5E **5**)
Gore St. *Salf* (M6) 4A **50**
Goring Av. *M18* 2D **89**
Gorse Av. *Droy* 1D **75**
Gorse Av. *Stret* 1D **97**
Gorse Cres. *Stret* 1D **97**
Gorse Dri. *Stret* 1D **97**
Gorsefield Dri. *Swin* 3B **30**
Gorse Hill. 4C **81**
Gorse La. *Stret* 1D **97**
Gorse Rd. *Swin* 1A **46**
Gorse St. *Chad* 2B **26**
Gorse St. *Stret* 1C **97**
Gorseway. *Stoc* 4D **123**
Gorsey Brow. *Urm* 2B **94**
Gorseyfields. *Droy* 3C **75**
Gorton. 4D **89**
Gorton Cross Cen. *M18* 3D **89**
Gorton Ind. Est. *M18* 2C **89**

Gorton La. *M12 & M18* 1A **88**
Gorton Mkt. *M18* 3D **89**
Gorton Pk. *M18* 2C **89**
Gorton Rd. *M11 & M12* 4D **71**
Gorton Rd. *Stoc* 1B **122**
Gorton St. *Eccl* 2A **60**
Gorton St. *Salf* 1B **68** (3A **6**)
Gortonvilla Wlk. *M12* 2D **87**
Gosport Sq. *Salf* 2D **51**
Gosport Wlk. *M8* 1A **54**
(off Smeaton St.)
Gotha Wlk. *M13* 2A **86**
Goulden Rd. *M20* 3C **117**
Goulden St. *M4* 1D **69** (3E **7**)
Goulden St. *Salf* 1C **65**
Goulder Rd. *M18* 1A **106**
Gould St. *M4* 4D **53** (1D **7**)
Gowan Rd. *M16* 3A **100**
Gower Rd. *Stoc* 4D **121**
Gower St. *Swin* 1C **31**
Grace Wlk. *M4*. 2B **70**
Grafton Av. *Eccl* 3C **47**
Grafton Ct. *M15* 3D **83**
Grafton St. *M13* 3D **85**
Grafton St. *Fail* 2C **43**
Graham Rd. *Salf* 3A **48**
Graham St. *M11* 3A **72**
Grainger Av. *M12* 1A **104**
Grain Vw. *Salf* 3A **66**
Grammar School Rd.
Oldh. 4D **27**
Grampian Clo. *Chad* 1C **27**
Granada M. *M16* 3A **100**
Granada Rd. *Dent* 1B **106**
Granary La. *Wors* 2A **44**
Granby Ho. *M1* 3C **69** (3D **11**)
Granby Rd. *Stret* 3B **96**
Granby Rd. *Swin* 3C **29**
Granby Row. *M1* 3C **69** (3D **11**)
(in two parts)
Granby St. *Chad*. 3C **27**
Grandale St. *M14*. 1A **102**
Grand Union Way. *Eccl*. 3D **61**
Grange Av. *Eccl* 3D **45**
Grange Av. *Lev*. 4D **103**
Grange Av. *Stoc* 4D **121**
Grange Av. *Stret*. 2B **96**
Grange Av. *Swin* 4D **13**
Grange Cres. *Urm* 3C **93**
Grange Dri. *M9* 3D **23**
Grange Dri. *Eccl*. 3D **45**
Grangeforth Rd. *M8*. 2B **36**
Grange Mill Wlk. *M40*. 3B **40**
Grange Pk. Rd. *M9* 3D **23**
Grange Rd. *M21*. 2A **98**
Grange Rd. *Eccl*. 3A **44**
Grange Rd. *Sale*. 4B **110**
Grange Rd. *Urm*. 3C **93**
Grange St. *Fail*. 4D **41**

Grange St. *Salf* 1C **65**
Grange, The. *M14* 1A **102**
Grangethorpe Dri. *M19* 2C **119**
Grangethorpe Rd. *M14* 2A **102**
Grangethorpe Rd. *Urm* 3C **93**
Grangewood Dri. *M9* 3B **38**
Gransden Dri. *M8* 1A **54**
Granshaw St. *M40* 4C **55**
Gransmoor Av. *M11* 4B **74**
Gransmoor Rd. *M11* 4B **74**
Grant Clo. *M9* 4B **22**
Grantham St. *M14* 1C **101**
Granville Av. *M16* 2C **99**
Granville Av. *Salf* 2A **36**
Granville Ct. *M16* 1C **99**
Granville Rd. *M14* 1A **118**
Granville Rd. *Aud* 2D **75**
Granville Rd. *Urm* 1A **94**
Granville St. *Eccl* 4D **45**
Granville St. *Swin* 2B **30**
Grasdene Av. *M9* 3C **23**
Grasmere Av. *Stoc* 3A **122**
Grasmere Av. *Swin* 4C **13**
Grasmere Cres. *Eccl* 4B **44**
Grasmere Rd. *Stret* 1B **96**
Grasmere Rd. *Swin* 4B **30**
Grasmere St. *M12* 1B **104**
Grasscroft Clo. *M14* 2B **100**
Grassfield Av. *Salf* 1C **51**
Grassingham Gdns. *Salf* 4D **49**
Grassington Av. *M40* 1A **40**
Gratrix Av. *Salf* 1B **82** (5A **8**)
Gratrix St. *M18* 4A **90**
Gravel La. *Salf* 1A **68** (4F **5**)
(in two parts)
Gravenmoor Dri. *Salf* 1A **52**
Graver La. *M40* 2D **57**
(in three parts)
Grayrigg Wlk. *M9* 3B **38**
Graythorpe Wlk. *Salf* 2A **66**
Graythorp Wlk. *M14* 1D **101**
Greame St *M16 & M14* 1B **100**
Gt. Ancoats St. *M4* 1D **69** (4E **7**)
Gt. Bridgewater St. *M1* 3A **68** (3F **9**)
Gt. Cheetham St. E. *Salf* 1A **52**
Gt. Cheetham St. W. *Salf* 2C **51**
Gt. Clowes St.
   Salf & M3 . . . . 2D **51** (1D **5**)
(Cheetham)
Gt. Clowes St. *Salf* 4C **35**
(Higher Broughton)
Gt. Ducie St. *M3* 4B **52** (1A **6**)
Greater Manchester
   Police Mus. 5E **7**
Gt. George St. *Salf* 1D **67** (4C **4**)
Great Horrocks **3D 53**
Gt. Jackson St. *M15* 4A **68** (4E **9**)
Gt. John St. *M3* 3A **68** (2E **9**)
Gt. Jones St. *M12* 2A **88**

Gt. Marlborough St. *M1* . . 4C **69** (4C **10**)
Gt. Newton St. *M40* 2C **57**
Great Northern **3B 68** (2A **10**)
Gt. Northern. *M3* 3B **68**
Gt. Southern St. *M14* 1D **101**
Gt. Stone Rd. *Stret & M16* . . . 4D **81**
Gt. Western St.
   M16 & M14 . . . . 1A **100**
Greaves Av. *Fail* 1D **57**
Grecian St. *Salf* 2C **51**
Grecian St. N. *Salf* 1C **51**
Grecian Ter. *Salf* 2C **51**
Gredle Clo. *Urm* 2B **94**
Greek St. *M1* 4D **69** (5E **11**)
Green Av. *Swin* 3B **30**
Green Bank. *Stoc* 2D **121**
Greenbank Av. *Swin* 4D **29**
Greenbank Rd. *Sale* 4A **110**
Greenbank Rd. *Salf* 4C **49**
Greencroft Rd. *Eccl* 3B **44**
Greendale Dri. *M9* 3C **23**
Green Dri. *M19* 3D **103**
Green End **4D 119**
Green End Rd. *M19* 4C **119**
Greenfield Av. *Eccl* 3A **60**
Greenfield Av. *Urm* 2D **93**
Green Fold. *M18* 2B **90**
Greenford Rd. *M8* 3C **37**
Greengate. *M24 & Midd* 3C **25**
Greengate. *Salf* 4B **52** (2A **6**)
Greengate E. *M40* 3C **25**
Greengate Ind. Est. *Midd* 1C **25**
Greengate La. *P'wich* 2A **18**
Greengate W. *Salf* 4A **52** (2E **5**)
Greenhalgh St. *Fail* 4C **41**
Greenhalgh Wlk. *M4* 1A **70**
(off Jackroom Dri.)
Greenheys **3C 85**
Greenheys. *Droy* 1C **75**
Greenheys Bus. Cen. *M15* . . . 3C **85**
Greenheys Cen. *M14* 4C **85**
Greenheys La. *M15* 3B **84**
Greenheys La. W. *M15* 3A **84**
Green Hill. *P'wich* 2A **18**
Greenhill Av. *Sale* 3C **111**
Greenhill Rd. *M8* 3C **37**
Greenholme Clo. *M40* 1D **41**
Greenhow St. *Droy* 3B **74**
Greening Rd. *M19* 2B **104**
Greenland St. *M8* 3B **36**
Greenland St. *Salf* 1C **65**
Green La. *M18* 2D **89**
Green La. *Eccl* 1C **61**
Green La. *Fail* 3A **58**
Green La. *Sale* 3A **110**
Greenlaw Ct. *M16* 3C **83**
Greenlea Av. *M18* 1D **105**
Greenleach La. *Wors* 2A **28**
Green Room Theatre **4B 10**

Greenside 1B 74
Greenside. *Wors* 2A 44
Greenside Ct. *Eccl* 4D 45
Greenside Cres. *Droy* 1B 74
Greenside La. *Droy* 4A 58
Greenside St. *M11* 3B 72
Greenside Trad. Cen. *Droy* . . 2C 75
Greenside Way. *Midd* 1C 25
Greenstead Av. *M8* 2C 37
Greenstone Dri. *Salf* 2D 49
Green St. *M14* 2B 118
Green St. *Eccl* 3B 60
Green St. *Stret* 4A 96
Green, The. *Swin* 4D 15
Green, The. *Wors* 2A 44
Greenthorne Av. *Stoc* 2D 121
Greenthorn Wlk. *M15* 3B 84
(off Botham Clo.)
Green Wlk. *M16* 1C 99
Green Wlk. *Stret* 2D 95
Green Walks. *P'wich* 3C 19
Greenwatch Clo. *Eccl* 2C 61
Greenway. *Midd* 1D 23
Greenway Av. *M19* 4B 104
Greenways. *M40* 1D 41
Greenwich Clo. *M40* 3D 57
Greenwood Av. *Swin* 1D 31
Greenwood Bus. Cen. *Salf* . . 2A 66
Greenwood St. *Salf* 3D 49
Greer St. *Open* 3C 73
Greetland Dri. *M9* 2D 23
Gregory St. *M12* 2D 87
Gregory St. *Oldh* 3D 27
Gregory Way. *Stoc* 3B 122
Gregson Rd. *Stoc* 3A 122
Greg St. *Stoc* 4A 122
Greg St. Ind. Est. *Stoc* 4A 122
Grelley Wlk. *M14* 1D 101
Grendale Dri. *M16* 3C 83
Grendon Wlk. *M12* 2A 88
Grenham Av. *M15* 2D 83
Gresford Clo. *M21* 1A 114
Greton Clo. *M13* 4C 87
Greville St. *M13* 4C 87
Grey Friar Ct. *Salf* 4A 52 (2E 5)
Greyhound Dri. *Salf* 2B 50
Greylands Clo. *Sale* 4B 110
Grey Mare La. *M11* 2D 71
Greysham Ct. *M16* 2A 100
Greystoke Av. *M19* 3C 105
Greystoke La. *Fail* 4D 41
Greystone Av. *M21* 1B 116
Greystone Wlk. *Stoc* 2D 121
Grey St. *M12* 2C 87
Grey St. *P'wich* 2C 19
Greyswood Av. *M8* 3B 36
Greytown Clo. *Salf* 2D 49
Grierson St. *M16* 1A 84
Griffin Ct. *Salf* 1A 68 (4E 5)

Griffin Gro. *M19* 1A 120
Griffin Rd. *Fail* 3D 41
Griffin St. *Salf* 1C 51
Griffiths Clo. *Salf* 3D 51 (1D 5)
Griffiths St. *M40* 2C 57
Grimscott Clo. *M9* 1D 39
Grimshaw Av. *Fail* 2C 43
Grimshaw La. *M40* 2D 55
Grimshaw St. *Fail* 2A 42
Grindall Av. *M40* 4B 24
Grindleford Wlk. *M21* 4D 115
Grindle Grn. *Eccl* 3C 61
Grindley Av. *M21* 4D 115
Grindlow St. *M13* 3C 87
Grindon Av. *Salf* 3A 34
Grindon Av. *M13* 2C 103
Grisedale Ct. *M9* 2A 24
Grizebeck Clo. *M18* 2C 89
Groby Rd. *M21* 4B 98
Groom St. *M1* 4D 69 (4E 11)
Grosvenor Ct. *M16* 1A 100
Grosvenor Ct. *Sale* 4B 110
Grosvenor Ct. *Salf* 2D 35
Grosvenor Gdns. *Salf* 3D 51
Grosvenor Ho. *M16* 3A 100
(off Arnold Rd.)
Grosvenor Ho. M. *Crum* 4B 20
Grosvenor Rd. *M16* 2D 99
Grosvenor Rd. *Eccl* 4A 44
Grosvenor Rd. *Sale* 4B 110
Grosvenor Rd. *Swin* 3D 31
Grosvenor Rd. *Urm* 2C 93
Grosvenor Sq. *M15* 1C 85 (5D 11)
Grosvenor Sq. *Salf* 3D 51
Grosvenor St.
   M13 & M1 . . . . . . 1C 85 (5D 11)
Grosvenor St. *P'wich* 2C 19
Grosvenor St. *Stret* 2B 96
Grosvenor St. *Swin* 4B 14
Grove Av. *Fail* 2A 58
Grove Clo. *M14* 1A 102
Grove Ho. *M15* 3D 85
Grovehurst. *Swin* 1B 44
Grove St. *Droy* 3B 74
Grove St. *Salf* 2A 52
Grove, The. *Eccl* 2B 62
Grove, The. *Urm* 3A 92
Grundy Av. *P'wich* 4D 17
Guardian Ct. *Sale* 4C 111
Guernsey Clo. *M19* 3A 120
Guide Post Sq. *M13* 2B 86
Guide St. *Salf* 2A 64
Guido St. *Fail* 3A 42
Guildford Rd. *M19* 2B 104
Guildford Rd. *Salf* 3D 47
Guildford Rd. *Urm* 4A 78
Guildhall Clo. *Man S* 3C 85
Guilford Rd. *Eccl* 2B 60
Guinness Circ. *Traf P* 3C 63

Guinness Rd. *Traf P* 3B **62**
Guinness Rd. Trad. Est.
  Traf P 3B **62**
Gullane Clo. *M40* 3C **41**
Gunson Ct. *M40* 4A **54**
Gunson St. *M40* 4A **54**
Gun St. *M4* 1D **69** (4F **7**)
Gurner Av. *Salf* 1B **82** (5A **8**)
Gurney St. *M4* 2B **70**
Guy Fawkes St. *Salf* 1B **82**
Guy St. *Salf* 3B **36**
Gwelo St. *M11* 1A **72**
Gwendor Av. *M8* 3B **20**
Gwynant Pl. *M20* 2A **118**

H

Hacking St. *P'wich* 2A **18**
Hacking St. *Salf* 1A **52**
Hackle St. *M11* 1C **73**
Hackleton Clo. *M4* 2B **70**
Hackness Rd. *M21* 4D **97**
Hackney Av. *M40* 3C **57**
Hackwood Wlk. M8 . . . . *3B* **36**
     (off Levenhurst Rd.)
Haddington Dri. *M9* 3C **23**
Haddon Av. *M40* 1B **42**
Haddon Gro. *Stoc* 2A **122**
Haddon Hall Rd. *Droy* 1A **74**
Haddon Ho. *Salf* 4B **48**
Haddon Rd. *M21* 4D **115**
Haddon Rd. *Eccl* 3B **60**
Haddon Rd. *Wors* 1C **45**
Haddon St. *Salf* 2B **50**
Haddon St. *Stret* 4B **80**
Hadfield Av. *Chad* 1D **27**
Hadfield St. *M16* 2C **83** (5B **8**)
Hadfield St. *Salf* 4A **36**
Hadley Av. *M13* 2C **103**
Hadley St. *Salf* 2B **50**
Hadlow Grn. *Stoc* 3D **123**
Hadlow Wlk. *M40* 4C **55**
Hafton Rd. *Salf* 1B **50**
Hagley Rd. *Salf* 2A **82**
Hague Ct. *M20* 4C **117**
Hague Rd. *M20* 4C **117**
Hague St. *M40* 2D **55**
Haigh Av. *Stoc* 4A **122**
Haigh Pk. *Stoc* 4A **122**
Haig Rd. *Stret* 1B **96**
Haldene Wlk. *M8* 4B **36**
Haldon Rd. *M20* 4B **118**
Hale Bank Av. *M20* 2B **116**
Hale La. *Fail* 2A **42**
Hales Clo. *Droy* 4B **58**
Halesden Rd. *Stoc* 4D **121**
Halesworth Wlk. *M40* 3A **54**
Haley Clo. *Stoc* 1B **122**

Haley St. *M8* 3C **37**
Half Edge La. *Eccl* 4A **46**
Half Moon St. *M2* 2B **68** (5B **6**)
Halford Dri. *M40* 2B **40**
Halfst St. *Salf* 4A **52** (2F **5**)
Hallam Rd. *M40* 2B **56**
Hall Av. *M14* 1B **102**
Hall Av. *Sale* 3A **110**
Hall Bank. *Eccl* 1C **61**
Halle Mall. M4 . . . . 1C **69** (4C **6**)
    (off Arndale Shop. Cen.)
Halle Sq. M4 . . . . 1C **69** (4C **6**)
    (off Arndale Shop. Cen.)
Hall Farm Av. *Urm* 1B **92**
Hall Gro. *M14* 1B **102**
Halliday Rd. *M40* 3B **56**
Halliford Rd. *M40* 4A **40**
Halliwell La. *M8* 3B **36**
Halliwell Rd. *P'wich* 1D **33**
Halliwell St. *Chad* 1C **43**
Halliwell St. W. *M8* 3B **36**
Halliwell Wlk. *P'wich* 1D **33**
Hallkirk Wlk. *M40* 4D **25**
Hall Moss Rd. *M9* 3A **24**
Hall Rd. *M14* 1B **102**
Hall St. *M2* 3B **68** (2B **10**)
Hall St. *Fail* 4D **41**
Hall St. *Swin* 4B **14**
Hallsville Rd. *M19* 3C **105**
Hallsworth Rd. *Eccl* 2A **60**
Hallwood Av. *Salf* 2A **48**
Hallworth Av. *Aud* 2D **75**
Hallworth Rd. *M8* 2D **37**
Halmore Rd. *M40* 1B **70**
Halsbury Clo. *M12* 2C **87**
Halsey Clo. *Chad* 4A **26**
Halsey Wlk. *M8* 3B **36**
Halsmere Dri. *M9* 3C **23**
Halstead Av. *M21* 2A **114**
Halstead Av. *Salf* 2C **49**
Halstock Wlk. M40 . . . . *2B* **54**
    (off Carslake Rd.)
Halston St. *M15* 2A **84**
Halton Bank. *Salf* 3D **49**
Halton Ho. *Salf* 2D **65**
Halton Rd. *M11* 1C **73**
Halvis Gro. *M16* 1B **98**
Hambleton Dri. *Sale* 4D **109**
Hambridge Clo. *M8* 3C **37**
Hamer Dri. *M16* 3D **83**
Hamer Hill. *M9* 3A **22**
Hamerton Rd. *M40* 3A **54**
Hamilcar Av. *Eccl* 1A **62**
Hamilton Av. *Eccl* 2A **62**
Hamilton Clo. *P'wich* 3A **18**
Hamilton Gro. *M16* 3D **83**
Hamilton Lodge. *M14* 1A **102**
Hamilton M. *Eccl* 4B **44**
Hamilton M. *P'wich* 3A **18**

Hamilton Rd. *M13* 1D **103**
Hamilton Rd. *P'wich.* 3A **18**
Hamilton St. *Eccl.* 4B **44**
Hamilton St. *Old T.* 3D **83**
Hamilton St. *Salf.* 3D **35**
Hamilton St. *Swin.* 1D **29**
Hamlet Dri. *Sale.* 3A **110**
Hammerstone Rd. *M18* 2C **89**
Hammett Rd. *M21* 1A **114**
Hammond Av. *Stoc.* 4A **122**
Hamnett St. *M11* 2D **73**
Hampden Ct. *Eccl.* 1D **61**
Hampden Cres. *M18* 3C **89**
Hampden Gro. *Eccl.* 1D **61**
Hampden Rd. *P'wich.* 2B **18**
Hampshire Rd. *Chad.* 1D **27**
Hampshire Rd. *Droy.* 4C **59**
Hampshire St. *Salf.* 3A **36**
Hampshire Wlk. *M8.* 1D **53**
Hampson Clo. *Eccl.* 2B **60**
Hampson Rd. *Stret.* 2A **96**
Hampson St. *M40.* 3B **54**
Hampson St. *Droy.* 1C **75**
Hampson St. *Eccl.* 2B **60**
Hampson St. *Salf.* 2C **67** (1B **8**)
Hampson St. *Swin.* 1C **31**
Hampson St. Trad. Est.
  Salf. 2D **67** (1C **8**)
Hampton Rd. *M21.* 3D **97**
Hampton Rd. *Fail.* 2C **43**
Hampton Rd. *Urm.* 3D **93**
Hamsell Rd. *M13.* 1A **86**
Hancock Clo. *M14.* 1D **101**
Hancock St. *Stret.* 4B **96**
Handel Av. *Urm.* 2A **92**
Handford Ho. *Urm.* 1A **94**
Handforth Gro. *M13.* 2C **103**
Handforth Rd. *Stoc.* 4B **122**
Handley Av. *M14.* 3D **101**
Handsworth St. *M12* 4B **70**
Hanging Bri. M3 . . . . 1B **68** (4B **6**)
  (off Cateaton St.)
Hani Ct. *M8.* 1B **36**
Hani Wells Bus. Pk. *M19* 2B **120**
Hankinson Way. *Salf.* 4A **50**
Hanlith M. *M19.* 1D **119**
Hanlon St. *M8.* 1B **36**
Hannah Baldwin Clo. *M11.* 3D **71**
Hannah St. *M12.* 2A **104**
Hanover Ct. *Salf.* 3D **35**
Hanover Ct. *Wors.* 1B **44**
Hanover Cres. *M14.* 4B **86**
Hanover Gdns. *Salf.* 2A **36**
Hanover St. *M4.* 1C **69** (3C **6**)
Hansdon Clo. *M8.* 4C **37**
Hanslope Wlk. M9 . . . . 2C **39**
  (off Swainsthorpe Dri.)
Hanson Rd. *M40* 3A **40**

Hanworth Clo. *M13.* 1D **85** (5F **11**)
Hapsford Wlk. *M40.* 2A **56**
Hapton Av. *Stret.* 3B **96**
Hapton St. *M19.* 2A **104**
Harbern Clo. *Eccl.* 3D **45**
Harboro Rd. *Sale.* 4A **110**
Harcombe Rd. *M20.* 3A **118**
Harcourt Av. *Urm.* 3B **94**
Harcourt Clo. *Urm.* 3B **94**
Harcourt Rd. *Sale.* 3C **111**
Harcourt St. *Stoc.* 1B **122**
Harcourt St. *Stret.* 1C **97**
Hardcastle Av. *M21.* 3C **115**
Hardfield Rd. *Midd.* 1A **24**
Hardicker St. *M19.* 2B **120**
Harding St. *M4.* 2B **70**
Harding St. *Salf.* (M3) 1B **68** (3A **6**)
Harding St. *Salf.* (M6) 3A **50**
Hardman Av. *P'wich.* 4D **19**
Hardman La. *Fail.* 2A **42**
Hardman Rd. *Stoc.* 1B **122**
Hardman St. *M3.* 2A **68** (1F **9**)
Hardman St. *Chad.* 3D **27**
Hardman St. *Fail.* 3D **41**
Hardon Gro. *M13.* 2D **103**
Hardrush Fold. *Fail.* 4C **43**
Hardshaw Clo. *M13.* 2D **85** (5F **11**)
Hardwood Clo. *M8.* 3C **37**
Hardy Av. *M21.* 1A **114**
Hardy Gro. *Swin.* 2D **45**
Hardy La. *M21.* 3B **114**
Hardy St. *Eccl.* 3B **60**
Harecastle Av. *Eccl.* 3A **62**
Haredale Dri. *M8.* 4D **37**
Hereford Wlk. M9. . . . . 4A **38**
  (off Westmere Dri.)
Harehill Clo. *M13.* 4D **69** (4F **11**)
Hare St. *M4.* 1C **69** (4D **7**)
Harewood Ct. M9. . . . . 1C **21**
  (off Deanswood Dri.)
Harewood Gro. *Stoc.* 4A **106**
Harewood Way. *Swin.* 4B **14**
Hargreaves St. *M4.* 4C **53** (1D **7**)
Harkerside Clo. *M21.* 1C **115**
Harkness St. *M12* 1A **86**
Harland Dri. *M8.* 3D **37**
Harley Av. *M14.* 1C **103**
Harley Rd. *Sale.* 4D **111**
Harley St. *M11.* 3D **73**
Harlow Dri. *M18* 1D **105**
Harmer Clo. *M40.* 2A **56**
Harmsworth Dri. *Stoc.* 4B **120**
Harmsworth St. *Salf.* 1C **65**
Harold Av. *M18* 4B **90**
Harold Priestnall Clo.
  M40. . . . . 1B **56**
Harold St. *M16* 2C **83**
Harold St. *Fail.* 3A **42**
Harold St. *P'wich.* 2D **17**

Harper Ho. *M19*. 3D **103**
    (off Park Lodge)
Harp Rd. *Traf P*. 3C **63**
Harp St. *M11*. 4A **74**
Harp Trad. Est. *Traf P*. 3C **63**
Harpurhey. 3C **39**
Harpurhey District Cen. *M9* . . . 2C **39**
Harpurhey Rd. *M8 & M9*. 2A **38**
Harpurhey Swimming Pools. . . . 2C **39**
Harriet St. *M4*. 1A **70**
Harringay Rd. *M40*. 2B **56**
Harrington St. *M18*. 3A **90**
Harris Av. *Dent*. 1D **107**
Harris Av. *Urm*. 3D **77**
Harris Clo. *Dent*. 1D **107**
Harrison Av. *M19*. 2B **104**
Harrison St. *M4*. 2B **70**
Harrison St. *Eccl*. 3B **60**
Harrison St. *Salf*. 3D **51** (1D **5**)
Harris St. *M8*. 3A **52** (1F **5**)
Harrogate Av. *P'wich*. 4D **19**
Harrogate Clo. *Open*. 1A **90**
Harrogate Dri. *Stoc*. 4A **106**
Harrogate Rd. *Stoc*. 4A **106**
Harroll Ga. *Swin*. 3C **31**
Harrop St. *M18*. 2B **90**
Harrow Av. *M19*. 3A **120**
Harrowby Dri. *M40*. 2B **54**
Harrowby Rd. *Swin*. 3A **30**
Harrowdene Wlk. *M9*. 2B **38**
Harrow St. *M8*. 1D **37**
Harry Hall Gdns.
    Salf 3C **51** (1B **4**)
Harry Rd. *Stoc*. 1B **122**
Harry Thorneycroft Wlk.
    M11. . . . . 3C **71**
Hart Av. *Droy*. 2D **75**
Harter St. *M1* 3C **69** (2C **10**)
Hartfield Clo. *M13*. . . 2A **86** (5F **11**)
Hartford Av. *Stoc*. 3D **121**
Hartford Rd. *Urm*. 4A **78**
Hart Hill Dri. *Salf*. 4B **48**
Harthill St. *M8*. 2B **52**
Hartington Clo. *Urm*. 2A **94**
Hartington Dri. *M11*. 4B **56**
Hartington Rd. *M21*. 1B **114**
Hartington Rd. *Eccl*. 4A **44**
Hartington St. *M14*. 1B **100**
Hartis Av. *Salf*. 4A **36**
Hartland Av. *Urm*. 2C **95**
Hartlepool Clo. *M14*. 1D **101**
Hartley Av. *P'wich*. 3C **19**
Hartley Hall Gdns. *M16*. 3A **100**
Hartley Rd. *M21*. 3A **98**
Hartley St. *M40*. 2D **39**
Harton Av. *M18*. 1C **105**
Hart Rd. *M14*. 2C **101**
Hartshead Clo. *M11*. 4C **75**
Hartshead Cres. *Fail*. 4D **43**

Hartspring Av. *Swin*. 3C **31**
Hart St. *M1*. 3C **69** (2C **10**)
    (in two parts)
Hart St. *Droy*. 1C **75**
Hartswood Rd. *M20*. 3B **118**
Hartwell Clo. *M11*. 3D **71**
Harty Ho. *Eccl*. 1A **62**
Harvest Clo. *Salf*. 2C **49**
Harvey Clo. *M11*. 3D **71**
Harwich Clo. *M19*. 3B **104**
Harwood Ct. *Salf*. 3B **50**
Harwood Rd. *M19*. 3C **119**
Haslam Ct. *Salf*. 1D **35**
Haslemere Rd. *M20*. 3B **118**
Haslemere Rd. *Urm*. 3B **92**
Hasper Av. *M20*. 2C **117**
Hassall Av. *M20*. 1B **116**
Hassop Av. *Salf*. 3A **34**
Hassop Clo. *M11*. 2C **71**
Hassop Rd. *Stoc*. 3C **107**
Hastings Av. *M21*. 4A **98**
Hastings Rd. *Eccl*. 3A **44**
Hastings Rd. *P'wich*. 1C **19**
Haston Clo. *Stoc*. 4B **122**
Hateley Rd. *M16*. 2A **98**
Hatfield Av. *M19*. 3D **119**
Hatherley Rd. *M20*. 3B **118**
Hatherop Clo. *Eccl*. 2B **60**
Hathersage Av. *Salf*. 4B **48**
Hathersage Rd. *M13*. 4A **86**
Hatro Ct. *Urm*. 3C **95**
Hatter St. *M4*. 1D **69** (3E **7**)
Hatton Av. *Salf*. 4D **51** (1C **4**)
Hattons Clo. *Stret*. 1A **96**
Hattons Rd. *Traf P*. 2D **79**
Hatton St. *M12*. 1A **104**
Havana Clo. *M11*. 2D **71**
    (in two parts)
Havelock Dri. *Salf*. 3D **51** (1C **4**)
Haven Dri. *Droy*. 1A **74**
Havenscroft Av. *Eccl*. 3D **61**
Haven St. *Salf*. 2C **65**
Haverfield Rd. *M9*. 3C **23**
Haverford St. *M12*. 2D **87**
Haversham Rd. *M8*. 4A **20**
Haverthwaite Rd. *M18*. 3A **90**
Hawarden Av. *M16*. 2C **99**
Hawes Av. *M14*. 2C **119**
Hawes Av. *Swin*. 3B **30**
Haweswater Clo. *Dent*. 2C **107**
Hawkeshead Rd. *M8*. 1D **53**
    (in two parts)
Hawkhurst Rd. *M13*. 1D **103**
Hawkshaw Ct. *Salf*. 2A **66**
Hawksley Clo. *Oldh*. 3D **27**
Hawksley Ind. Est. *Oldh*. 3D **27**
Hawksley St. *Oldh*. 3D **27**
Hawkstone Av. *Droy*. 4A **58**
Hawley St. *M19*. 1B **120**

Haworth Dri. *Stret* 1B **94**
Haworth Rd. *M18.* 4C **89**
Hawsworth Clo. *M15.* 3D **85**
Hawthorn Av. *Eccl.* 4D **45**
Hawthorn Av. *Urm.* 3B **94**
Hawthorn Dri. *M19.* 2D **119**
Hawthorn Dri. *Salf.* 3D **47**
Hawthorn Dri. *Swin.* 3A **32**
Hawthorne Dri. *Wors.* 3A **28**
Hawthorn La. *M21.* 1D **113**
Hawthorn La. *Sale.* 3D **109**
Hawthorn Rd. *M40.* 1A **42**
Hawthorn Rd. *Dent.* 1D **107**
Hawthorn Rd. *Droy.* 1D **75**
(in two parts)
Hawthorn Rd. *Kear.* 1B **12**
Hawthorn Rd. *Oldh.* 4D **27**
Hawthorn Rd. *Sale.* 4B **96**
Hawthorn Rd. S. *Droy.* 1D **75**
Hawthorn St. *M18.* 2D **89**
Haxby Rd. *M18.* 1D **105**
Hayden Ct. *M40.* *2B **54***
(off Sedgeford Rd.)
Haydn Av. *M14.* 4D **85**
Haydock M. Salf. *4D **35***
(off Epsom M.)
Hayeswater Circ. *Urm.* 1C **93**
Hayeswater Rd. *Urm* 1C **93**
Hayfield Clo. *M12.* 1C **87**
Hayfield Rd. *Salf.* 3D **47**
Hayfield St. *Sale.* 4D **111**
Haygrove Wlk. *M9.* 2B **38**
Hayley St. *M13.* 4C **87**
Hayling Rd. *Sale.* 4A **110**
Haymans Wlk. *M13.* . . . 1D **85** (5F **11**)
(in two parts)
Haymarket Clo. *M13.* 3A **86**
Haymond Clo. *Salf.* 1A **50**
Hazel Av. *M16.* 2D **99**
Hazel Av. *Swin.* 3C **31**
Hazelbank Av. *M20.* 2D **117**
Hazelbottom Rd. *M8.* 3D **37**
Hazel Clo. *Droy.* 1D **75**
Hazeldene Rd. *M40.* 1A **42**
Hazelfields. *Wors.* 3B **28**
Hazel Gro. *Salf.* 1A **64**
Hazel Gro. *Urm.* 2A **94**
Hazelhurst **3C 29**
Hazelhurst Fold. *Wors.* 3C **29**
Hazelhurst M. *Chad.* 3B **26**
Hazelhurst Rd. *Wors.* 3B **28**
Hazelmere Av. *Eccl.* 3B **44**
Hazel Ter. *M9.* 2B **22**
Hazelwood Ct. *Urm.* 1D **93**
Headingley Dri. *M16.* 1A **98**
Headingley Rd. *M14.* 2B **118**
Headlands Dri. *P'wich* 1A **34**
Heald Av. *M14.* 1D **101**
Heald Gro. *M14.* 4D **85**

Heald Pl. *M14.* 4D **85**
(in two parts)
Healey Clo. *Salf.* 2C **35**
Heath Av. *Salf.* 3C **51** (1B **4**)
Heath Av. *Urm.* 1A **94**
Heathbank Rd. *M9.* 1A **22**
Heathcliffe Wlk. *M13.* 3A **86**
Heathcote Rd. *M18.* 4C **89**
Heather Ct. *Stoc.* 4D **121**
Heatherdale Dri. *M8.* 1C **53**
Heather Gro. *Droy.* 3D **75**
Heathersett Dri. *M9.* 3B **38**
Heatherside. *Stoc.* 3C **107**
Heather St. *M11.* 1B **72**
Heatherway. *M14.* 4D **85**
Heatherway. *Sale.* 4D **109**
Heathfield. *Wors.* 2A **44**
Heathfield Av. *Stoc.* 4C **121**
Heathfield Dri. *Swin.* 3C **31**
Heathfield St. *M40.* 2C **57**
Heathland Rd. *Salf.* 2B **34**
Heathlands Dri. *P'wich.* 1A **34**
Heathside Rd. *M20.* 4A **118**
Heath St. *M8.* 3B **36**
Heath Vw. *Salf.* 1A **34**
Heathway Av. *M11.* 1D **73**
Heathwood Rd. *M19.* 4C **119**
Heatley Clo. *Dent.* 2D **107**
Heaton Chapel. **4C 121**
Heaton Ct. *M9.* 3C **21**
Heaton Ct. *P'wich.* 3C **19**
Heaton Hall 1A **20**
(Museum)
Heaton Moor Rd. *Stoc.* 4B **120**
Heaton Pk. 1D **19**
Heaton Park **2C 19**
Heaton Pk. Farm Cen. 1A **20**
Heaton Pk. Rd. *M9.* 1C **21**
Heaton Pk. Tramway 1A **20**
Heaton Pk. Tramway Mus. 1B **20**
Heaton Rd. *M20.* 2A **118**
Heaton St. *P'wich.* 2B **18**
Heaton St. *Salf.* 3A **36**
Hebburn Wlk. *M14.* 4D **85**
Hebden Av. *Salf.* 4A **48**
Hebden Wlk. *M15.* *3B **84***
(off Arnott Cres.)
Hector Rd. *M13.* 1D **103**
Heddon Wlk. *M8.* 1A **54**
(off Smedley Rd.)
Hedgehog Ho. *Salf.* 3D **65**
Hedgelands Wlk. *Sale.* 4C **109**
Hedges St. *Fail.* 2C **43**
Hedley Wlk. *M8.* *3B **36***
(off Halliwell La.)
Helena St. *Salf.* 2A **48**
Helen St. *Eccl.* 3B **60**
Helen St. *Salf.* 2C **51**
Helensville Av. *Salf.* 2D **49**

Helga St. *M40* 3B **54**
Hellidon Clo. *M12* 2B **86**
Helmet St. *M1* 3A **70**
Helmshore Wlk.
  M13 . . . . 1D **85** (5F **11**)
Helrose St. *M40* 2C **57**
Helsby Wlk. *M12* 3C **71**
Hembury Av. *M19* 3D **119**
Hemming Dri. *Eccl.* 2A **62**
Hemmington Dri. *M9* 3B **38**
Hemmons Rd. *M12* 2B **104**
Hemsley St. *M9* 1C **39**
Hemsley St. S. *M9* 2C **39**
Hemswell Clo. *Salf.* 3C **49**
Hemsworth Rd. *M18* 1D **105**
Henbury St. *M14* 1C **101**
Henderson Av. *Swin.* 1B **30**
Henderson St. *M19* 1B **120**
Hendham Va. *M9* 3A **38**
      (in two parts)
Hendon Rd. *M9* 2A **22**
Hengist St. *M18* 4D **89**
Henley Av. *M16* 1B **98**
Henley Pl. *M19* 3A **120**
Henley St. *Chad.* 3C **27**
Henlow Wlk. *M40* 4D **25**
Henniker St. *Swin* 4A **30**
Henrietta St. *M16* 4C **83**
Henry St. *M4.* 1D **69** (4E **7**)
      (in two parts)
Henry St. *Droy.* 2C **75**
Henry St. *Eccl.* 2C **61**
Henry St. *Fail.* 3B **42**
Henry St. *Old T.* 3C **83**
Henry St. *P'wich.* 1C **19**
Henshaw Ct. *M16.* 4B **82**
Henshaw La. *Chad.* 4B **26**
Henshaw St. *Stret.* 2B **96**
Henshaw Wlk. *M13* 1D **85** (5F **11**)
Henton Wlk. *M40.* 3A **54**
Henwood Rd. *M20* 4A **118**
Hepburn Ct. *Salf.* 3C **49**
Heppleton Rd. *M40* 4D **25**
Heptonstall Wlk. *M18.* 3C **89**
Heraldic Ct. *Salf.* 2A **50**
Herbert St. *M8.* 2B **52**
Herbert St. *Droy.* 2B **74**
Herbert St. *P'wich.* 2D **17**
Herbert St. *Stret.* 2B **96**
Hereford Dri. *P'wich.* 3C **19**
Hereford Dri. *Swin.* 4B **30**
Hereford Gro. *Urm.* 2C **93**
Hereford Rd. *Eccl.* 2C **47**
Hereford Rd. *Stoc.* 4D **123**
Hereford St. *Oldh.* 1D **27**
Hereford St. *Sale.* 4D **111**
      (in two parts)
Hermitage Rd. *M8.* 1C **37**
Herne St. *M11* 3A **72**

Heron Ct. *Salf.* 4D **47**
Herondale Clo. *M40.* 2B **56**
Heron St. *M15.* 3A **84**
Heron St. *Oldh.* 2D **27**
Heron St. *Swin.* 1C **31**
Herristone Rd. *M8.* 4C **21**
Herrod Av. *Stoc.* 4A **122**
Hersalls St. *Salf.* 4A **52** (1E **5**)
Herschel St. *M40.* 2A **40**
Hersey St. *Salf.* 1C **65**
Hersham Wlk. *M9* 1C **39**
      (off Huncote Dri.)
Hertford Rd. *M9.* 1B **38**
Hesford Av. *M9* 3D **39**
Hessel St. *Salf.* 2B **64**
Hester Wlk. *M15* 2C **85**
Heston Av. *M13* 2C **103**
Heston Dri. *Urm.* 1C **93**
Heswall Av. *M20* 2D **117**
Heswall Rd. *Stoc.* 3B **106**
Hetherington Wlk. *M12* 4A **88**
Hethorn St. *M40.* 2C **57**
Hetton Av. *M13.* 2C **103**
Heversham Wlk. *M18.* 2C **89**
      (off Grizebeck Clo.)
Hever Wlk. *M4.* 1B **70**
      (off Saltford Av.)
Hewart Clo. *M40.* 3A **54**
Hewitt Av. *Dent.* 1B **106**
Hewitt St. *M15.* 4A **68** (4F **9**)
Hewlett Rd. *M21.* 3A **98**
Hexham Rd. *M18.* 1C **105**
Hexon Clo. *Salf.* 4C **49**
Heybury Clo. *M11.* 3D **71**
Heyford Av. *M40.* 4D **25**
Heyrod St. *M1.* 3A **70**
Heyrose Wlk. *M15.* 2D **83**
Heys Av. *Swin.* 4C **13**
Heys Clo. N. *Swin* 4C **13**
Heyscroft Rd. *M20.* 3A **118**
Heysham Av. *M20.* 2B **116**
Heys Rd. *P'wich.* 1B **18**
Heys, The. *P'wich.* 1B **18**
Heys, The. *Stoc.* 3C **107**
Heys Vw. *P'wich* 2B **18**
Heywood Av. *Swin.* 4D **15**
Heywood Gdns. *P'wich.* 2B **18**
Heywood Gro. *Sale.* 3C **111**
Heywood Ho. *Salf.* 4A **48**
Heywood M. *P'wich.* 2B **18**
Heywood Rd. *P'wich.* 3B **18**
Heywood St. *M8.* 3C **37**
Heywood St. *Fail.* 3D **41**
Heywood St. *Swin.* 2A **30**
Heywood Way. *Salf.* 4D **49**
Heyworth St. *Salf.* 2C **65**
Hibbert Cres. *Fail.* 3C **43**
Hibbert St. *M14.* 1A **102**
Hibbert St. *Stoc.* 4A **122**

Holmwood Ct. *M20* 4D **117**
Holmwood Rd. *M20* 4D **117**
Holroyd St. *M11*. 3A **72**
Holst Av. *M8* 1C **53**
Holtby St. *M9*. 1C **39**
Holt La. *Fail* 4C **43**
Holt Lane End 3D **43**
Holt La. M. *Fail* 3D **43**
Holtown Ind. Est. *M40* 1C **71**
Holts La. *Fail* 3D **43**
Holt St. *M40* 2D **55**
Holt St. *Eccl*. 3C **61**
Holt St. *Swin* 4B **14**
Holt Town 1C **71**
Holt Town. *M40* 1C **71**
Holt Town Ind. Est. *M40*. 1C **71**
Holway Wlk. *M9*. 3A **38**
       (off Hendham Va.)
Holwood Dri. *M16* 4A **100**
Holyoake St. *Droy*. 1D **75**
Holyoak St. *M40* 1C **57**
Holyrood Dri. *Swin* 3D **29**
Holyrood Rd. *P'wich* 1C **19**
Holyrood St. *M40* 3A **58**
Holywood St. *M14* 1D **101**
Homebury Dri. *M11*. 1B **72**
Home Front Mus. 4A **112**
      (Sale Leisure Cen.)
Homelands Wlk. *M9*. 3B **38**
Homerton Rd. *M40* 3B **56**
Homestead, The. *Sale*. 4B **110**
Honey St. *M8* 3D **53** (1D **7**)
Honeysuckle Wlk. *Sale*. 4D **109**
Honister Rd. *M9* 3D **39**
Honiton Ho. *Salf* 4C **47**
Honor St. *M13*. 1D **103**
Hood St. *M4*. 4F **7**
Hooper St. *M12*. 3B **70**
Hooton St. *M40* 4D **55**
Hope Av. *Stret* 1D **95**
Hopecourt Clo. *Salf* 3A **48**
Hope Cres. *Salf* 4A **48**
Hopedale Clo. *M11* 2D **71**
Hopedale Rd. *Stoc* 3B **122**
Hopelea St. *M20* 2D **117**
Hope Pk. Clo. *P'wich* 3B **18**
Hope Pk. Rd. *P'wich* 3B **18**
Hope Rd. *M14* 4B **86**
Hope Rd. *P'wich* 4A **18**
Hope Rd. *Sale* 4D **111**
Hope St. *M1* 2C **69** (1D **11**)
Hope St. *Eccl*. 1B **62**
Hope St. *Salf* (M5) 2C **67** (5A **4**)
Hope St. *Salf* (M7) 3D **35**
Hope St. *Swin* 3D **29**
       (Arthur St.)
Hope St. *Swin* 2C **31**
       (Bridge St.)
Hopgarth Wlk. *M40* 2D **57**

Hopkinson Rd. *M9* 1B **22**
Hopkins St. *M12* 1A **104**
Hoppet La. *Droy*. 1D **75**
Hopton Ct. *M15*. 2C **85**
Hopwood Av. *Eccl* 4D **45**
Hopwood St. *M40* 1B **56**
Hopwood St. *Salf* 1A **68** (3F **5**)
Hopwood St. *Swin* 2C **31**
Horace Barnes Clo. *M14*. 1C **101**
Horatio St. *M18*. 2B **90**
Horbury Av. *M18* 1D **105**
Horlock Ct. *Salf*. 4B **50** (2A **4**)
Hornbeam Clo. *Sale* 4C **109**
Hornbeam Ct. *Salf* 4A **50**
Hornbeam Rd. *M19* 2B **104**
Hornby Av. *M9*. 1C **23**
Hornby Rd. *Stret* 4D **81**
Hornby St. *M8*. 3B **52** (1A **6**)
Horncastle Rd. *M40*. 4B **24**
Hornchurch Ct. *M15*. 5B **10**
Hornchurch St. *M15*. 2A **84**
Horne Dri. *M4* 1A **70**
Hornsea Wlk. *M11* 2A **72**
Horsefield Clo. *M21* 2A **116**
Horsham St. *Salf* 1C **65**
Horstead Wlk. *M19* 2A **104**
Horton Rd. *M14*. 2C **101**
Hortree Rd. *Stret* 2C **97**
Horwood Cres. *M20*. 4B **118**
Hoscar Dri. *M19* 2D **119**
Hoskins Clo. *M12*. 3A **88**
Hospital Av. *Eccl* 1A **62**
Hospital Rd. *Swin* 3D **31**
Hothersall Rd. *Stoc* 2B **122**
Hothersall St. *Salf* 4A **52** (1E **5**)
Hotspur Clo. *M14*. 4C **101**
Houghend Av. *M21*. 3C **115**
Hough End Cen. *M21* 2A **116**
Houghend Cres. *M21* 1A **116**
Hough Hall Rd. *M40* 2D **39**
Hough Rd. *M20* 2C **117**
Hough St. *M40* 2C **55**
Houghton La. *Swin* 2D **45**
Houghton Rd. *M8* 1C **37**
Houghton St. *Swin*. 3D **29**
Hough Wlk. *Salf* 4C **51** (1B **4**)
Houldsworth Mill Ind. Est.
   Stoc 4A **106**
Houldsworth Sq. *Stoc* 2A **122**
Houldsworth St. *M1* . . . 1D **69** (4E **7**)
Houldsworth St. *Stoc*. 2A **122**
Houseley Av. *Chad* 3C **27**
Houston Pk. *Salf* 2D **65**
Hoveden St. *M8*. 3B **52**
Hove Dri. *M14* 2C **119**
Hovey Clo. *M8* 3B **36**
Hovington Gdns. *M19* 3C **119**
Hovis St. *M11* 3C **73**
Howard Av. *Eccl*. 4D **45**

Howard Av. *Stoc* 3C **121**
Howard Spring Wlk. *M8* 2B **36**
Howard St. *M8* 3B **52**
Howard St. *Salf* 3A **66**
Howard St. *Stret* 2B **96**
Howarth Av. *Wors* 3C **29**
Howarth Clo. *M11* 2A **72**
Howarth St. *M16* 4C **83**
Howbrook Wlk. *M15* 2B **84**
Howden Clo. *Stoc* 2A **106**
(in two parts)
Howden Rd. *M9* 1A **22**
Howells Av. *Sale* 4D **111**
Howe St. *Salf* 3C **35**
Howgill St. *M11* 2D **73**
Howton Clo. *M12* 4A **88**
Hoy Dri. *Urm* 3D **77**
Hoylake Clo. *M40* 2D **41**
Hoyland Clo. *M12* 2D **87**
Hoyle St. *M12* 3A **70**
Hoyle St. Ind. Est. M12 . . . . . **4A 70**
(off Hoyle St.)
Hoyle Wlk. *M13* 2A **86**
Huddart Clo. *Salf* . . 3B **66** (2A **8**)
Hudson Ct. *M9* 3D **21**
Hudson St. *Oldh* 4C **27**
Hughes Clo. *Fail* 2A **42**
Hughes St. *M11* 3C **71**
Hughes Way. *Eccl* 3A **60**
Hugh Oldham Dri. *Salf* 4C **35**
Hugo St. *M40* 3A **40**
Hull Sq. *Salf* 1D **67** (3C **4**)
Hulme 2B **84**
Hulme Ct. *M15* 1A **84** (5D **9**)
Hulme Hall La. *M40 & M11* . . . 3C **55**
Hulme Hall Rd. *M15* . . . 4D **67** (4C **8**)
Hulme High St. *M15* 4B **84**
Hulme Mkt. Hall. *M15* 3B **84**
Hulme Pl. *Salf* 2C **67** (5A **4**)
Hulme Rd. *Dent* 1D **107**
Hulme Rd. *Stoc* 4D **121**
Hulmes Rd. *M40 & Fail* 2A **58**
(in two parts)
Hulme St. *M15 & M1* . . 1B **84** (5B **10**)
(Cambridge St.)
Hulme St. *M15* 1A **84** (5F **9**)
(Jackson Cres.)
Hulme St. *Salf* 2C **67** (5B **4**)
Hulme Wlk. *M15* 2B **84**
Hulton St. *M16* 4A **84**
Hulton St. *Fail* 3D **41**
Hulton St. *Salf* 4A **66**
Humberstone Av. *M15* . . 2B **84** (5F **9**)
Humber St. *M8* 3C **37**
Humber St. *Salf* 2B **64**
Hume St. *M19* 1B **120**
Humphrey Booth Gdns. *Salf* . . 4C **49**
Humphrey Cres. *Urm* 2B **94**
Humphrey La. *Urm* 2C **95**

Humphrey Pk. *Urm* 2C **95**
Humphrey Rd. *M16* 3B **82**
Humphrey St. *M8* 2B **36**
Humphries Ct. M40 . . . . **3A 54**
(off Whitley Rd.)
Huncoat Av. *Stoc* 4D **121**
Huncote Dri. *M9* 1C **39**
Hunmanby Av. *M15* . . 1B **84** (5A **10**)
Hunters M. *Sale* 4C **111**
Hunterston Av. *Eccl* 1C **63**
Huntingdon Av. *Chad* 1D **27**
Huntington Av. *M20* 2C **117**
Huntley Rd. *M8* 4A **20**
Hunt's Bank. *M3* 1B **68** (3A **5**)
Huntsman Rd. *M9* 2D **39**
Hunts Rd. *Salf* 2B **48**
Hunt St. *M9* 1B **38**
Huntsworth Wlk. *M13* 3B **86**
Hurdlow Av. *Salf* 3A **34**
Hurdlow Wlk. *M9* 3B **38**
Hurford Av. *M18* 2D **89**
Hurstbourne Av. *M11* 4B **56**
Hurstbrook Dri. *Urm* 2B **94**
Hurstfield Ind. Est. Stoc 3A **122**
Hursthead Wlk. *M13* . . . 1D **85** (5F **11**)
Hurst St. *Stoc* 2A **122**
Hurstville Rd. *M21* 3B **114**
Hurstway Dri. *M9* 3C **23**
Hus St. *Droy* 3B **74**
Hutton Wlk. M13 . . . . **2A 86**
(off Copeman Clo.)
Huxley Av. *M8* 1C **53**
Hyde Fold Clo. *M19* 3D **119**
Hyde Gro. *M13* 3A **86**
Hyde Ho. *Stoc* 4C **121**
Hyde Pl. *M13* 3A **86**
Hyde Rd. *M12 & M18* 3B **86**
Hyde's Cross. *M4* 1C **69** (3B **6**)
Hyde St. *M15* 3D **83**
(in two parts)
Hydrangea Clo. *Sale* 4C **109**
Hyman Goldstone Wlk. *M8* . . . 3B **36**
Hyndman Ct. *Salf* 2B **64**
Hythe Clo. *M14* 1A **102**

I

*I*bberton Wlk. *M9* 1D **39**
(off Carnaby St.)
Iceland St. *Salf* 1D **65**
Ifco Cen. *M14* 1A **102**
Ilex Gro. *Salf* 4D **35**
Ilford St. *M11* 1B **72**
Ilfracombe St. *M40* 1D **57**
Ilkeston Wlk. M40 . . . . **3A 40**
(off Halliford Rd.)
Ilkley Cres. *Stoc* 4A **106**
Ilkley Dri. *Urm* 4A **76**

Ilkley St. *M40* 1A **40**
Ilk St. *M11* 1B **72**
Illona Dri. *Salf* 2A **34**
Ilminster Wlk. *M9* *1C* **23**
(off Crossmead Dri.)
Ilthorpe Wlk. *M40* 4A **40**
Imex Bus. Pk. *M13* 1D **103**
Imogen Ct. *Salf* 3C *67* (3B 8)
Imperial Ter. *Sale* 3C **111**
Imperial War Mus. North 1C **81**
Ince Clo. *M20* 2D **117**
Inchcape Dri. *M9* 2D **21**
Inchfield Rd. *M40* 1A **40**
Inchley Rd. *M13* 1D **85** (5E 11)
Incline Rd. *Oldh* 4D **27**
Indigo St. *Salf* 2D **49**
Indigo Wlk. *Salf* 2D **49**
Indoor Tennis Cen. 1D **71**
Industry St. *Chad* 2C **27**
Infant St. *P'wich* 2C **19**
Ingham St. *M40* 3A **58**
Inghamwood Clo. *Salf* 3B **36**
Ingleby Av. *M9* 2C **23**
Ingleby St. *Stret* 3C **97**
Ingledene Av. *Salf* 1A **36**
Ingledene Ct. *Salf* 1A **36**
Ingleton Av. *M8* 4D **21**
Inglewood Wlk. *M13* *2A* **86**
(off Brunswick St.)
Ingoldsby Av. *M13* 4B **86**
Inkerman St. *M40* 1B **54**
(off Topley St.)
Innes St. *M12* 1B **104**
Innis Av. *M40* 2C **57**
Instow Clo. *M13* 2B **86**
Invar Rd. *Swin* 1D **29**
Invergarry Wlk. *M11* 2C **73**
Inverness Av. *M9* 2A **24**
Inver Wlk. *M40* 4D **25**
Inwood Wlk. *M8* 1A **54**
Inworth Wlk. *M8* *3B* **36**
(off Highshore Dri.)
Iona Way. *Urm* 3D **77**
Ionian Gdns. *Salf* 2C **51**
Ipswich Wlk. *M12* *3C* **87**
(off Martindale Cres.)
Iqbal Clo. *M12* 3A **88**
Iredine St. *M11* 2C **73**
Iris Av. *Open* 3D **73**
Irkdale St. *M8* 1A **54**
Irk St. *M4* 4C **53** (1D 7)
Irlam Av. *Eccl* 2D **61**
Irlam Rd. *Sale* 4A **112**
Irlams o' th' Height 1B **48**
Irlam Sq. *Salf* 2B **48**
Irlam St. *M40* 2C **55**
Irmass Ind. Est. *Traf P* 2B **80**
Iron St. *M40* 4C **55**
Irving St. *Oldh* 4D **27**

Irvin St. *M40* 4C **41**
Irwell Av. *Eccl* 2B **62**
(in two parts)
Irwell Gro. *Eccl* 2B **62**
Irwell Pk. Way. *Eccl* 2B **62**
Irwell Pl. *Eccl* 2B **62**
Irwell Pl. *Salf* 1C **67** (4A 4)
Irwell St. *M8* 3A **52** (1F 5)
Irwell St. *Salf* (M3) 2A **68** (5F 5)
Irwell St. *Salf* (M6) 1A **50**
Isaac Clo. *Salf* 3A **66**
Isabella Clo. *M16* 4C **83**
Isca St. *M11* 2D **71**
Isherwood Rd. *C'ton* 4A **108**
Isis Clo. *Salf* 2D **33**
Islington Way. *Salf* 2D **67** (5C 4)
Isobel Bailey Lodge. *M16* 3D **83**
Isobel Clo. *M16* 4B **84**
Isobel Clo. *Eccl* 2B **60**
Iver Ho. *Salf* 2D **65**
(off Amersham St.)
Ivory St. *M4* 3D **53** (1F 7)
Ivybridge Clo. *M13* 3B **86**
Ivy Clo. *Droy* 4B **58**
Ivy Ct. *M21* 2B **114**
Ivygreen Rd. *M21* 1D **113**
Ivy Leaf Sq. *Salf* 1A **52**
Ivylea Rd. *M19* 4C **119**
Ivy St. *M40* 2A **40**
Ivy St. *Eccl* 2D **61**

J

Jackie Brown Wlk. *M40* 2B **54**
Jack La. *Droy* 1D **75**
(in two parts)
Jack La. *Urm* 2A **94**
(in two parts)
Jackroom Dri. *M4* 2A **70**
Jackson Ct. *M21* 3D **97**
Jackson Ct. *Urm* 2A **92**
Jackson Cres. *M15* 2A **84** (5E 9)
Jackson's Row. *M2* 2B **68** (1A 10)
Jackson St. *Fail* 4D **41**
Jackson St. *Sale* 4B **112**
Jackson St. *Stret* 3A **96**
Jacobite Clo. *Salf* 1C **35**
James Bentley Wlk. *M40* 2C **57**
James Brindley Basin. *M1* 2A **70**
James Corbett Rd. *Salf* 2A **64**
James Henry Av. *Salf* 3B **66**
James Leigh St. *M1* 3C **69** (3C 10)
James Nasmyth Way. *Eccl* 1C **61**
James St. *M40* 4B **54**
James St. *Droy* 1D **75**
James St. *Fail* 2C **43**
James St. *P'wich* 1A **18**
(in two parts)

James St. *Salf* 2D **67** (5C **4**)
Japan St. *M8* 2B **36**
Jardine Way. *Chad* 2B **26**
Jasmine Av. *Droy* 1D **75**
Jean Clo. *M19* 2A **104**
Jehlum Clo. *M8* 3D **37**
Jenkinson St. *M13* 2C **85**
Jenkinson St. *M15* . . . 2C **85** (5D **11**)
Jenkyn Wlk. *M11* 2D **71**
Jennings Av. *Salf* 3A **66**
Jennings Clo. *Salf* 3A **66**
Jennison Clo. *M18* 2B **88**
Jenny St. *Oldh* 4D **27**
Jersey Clo. *M19* 2D **119**
Jersey St. *M4* 1D **69** (4F **7**)
Jerusalem Pl. *M2* 3B **68** (2A **10**)
Jesmond Av. *P'wich* 4B **18**
Jesmond Wlk. M9 . . . . *1B 22*
(off Claygate Dri.)
Jessamine Av. *Salf* . . . 3D **51** (1C **4**)
Jessel Clo. *M13* 2A **86**
Jessie St. *M40* 1A **56**
Jessup St. *M18* 3D **89**
Jetson St. *M18* 2B **90**
Jevington Wlk. M13 . . . . *2A 86*
(off Dilston Clo.)
Jimmy McMullen Wlk.
  M14 . . . . 1C **101**
Jinnah Clo. *Open* 3C **73**
JJB Soccer Dome 2B **76**
JJB Sports Health Club 2B **76**
J. J. Thomson M. *M14* 2B **118**
Joan St. *M40* 3A **40**
Jobling St. *M11* 3D **71**
Jocelyn St. *M40* 1C **55**
Joddrell St. *M3* 2A **68** (1F **9**)
John Atkinson Ct. *Salf* 1B **64**
John Beeley Av. *M11* 3D **73**
John Clynes Av. *M40* 4A **54**
John Dalton St. *M2* . . . 2B **68** (1A **10**)
John Dalton St. *Salf* 1D **67** (4C **4**)
John Derby Ho. *M16* 4A **82**
John Foran Clo. *M40* 1B **56**
John Gilbert Way. *Traf P* 3B **80**
John Heywood St. *M11* 1B **72**
John Lester Ct. Salf *4A 50*
(off Belvedere Rd.)
Johnny King Clo. *M40* 2B **54**
John Paine Ct. Swin *4B 14*
(off Pott St.)
John Robinson Wlk. *M40* 3A **40**
John Rylands Library . . . 2B **68** (1A **10**)
Johns Clo. *M21* 4B **98**
John Smeaton Ct. *M1* 2A **70**
Johnson's Sq. *M40* 3B **54**
Johnson St. *M15* 2D **83**
Johnson St. *Salf* 1A **68** (4F **5**)
Johnson Av. *Swin* 4B **32**
John Stone Ct. *Stret* 1C **95**

John St. *M4* 1C **69** (4D **7**)
John St. *Droy* 2B **74**
John St. *Eccl* 2B **60**
John St. *Fail* 1B **42**
John St. *Sale* 4D **111**
John St. *Salf* 3D **51**
  (Lower Broughton, in two parts)
John St. *Salf* 1A **68** (3F **5**)
  (Salford)
John St. *Swin* 2C **31**
John William St. *M11* 2C **73**
John William St. *Eccl* 1B **62**
Joiner St. *M4* 2C **69** (5D **7**)
Joiner St. *Salf* 2C **67** (5B **4**)
Join Rd. *Sale* 4B **112**
Jonas St. *Salf* 4A **52** (1E **5**)
Jones St. *M9* 2C **39**
Jones St. *Salf* 4D **49**
Jordan St. *M15* 4A **68** (4F **9**)
Joseph Dean Ct. *M40* 3A **40**
Josephine Dri. *Swin* 3C **31**
Joseph Mamlock Ho. *M8* 1A **36**
Joseph St. *Eccl* 2B **60**
Joseph St. *Fail* 2B **42**
Josslyn Rd. *Salf* 4B **48**
Jo St. *Salf* 2A **66**
Joule Clo. *Salf* 3A **66**
Joule St. *M9* 1C **39**
Joyce St. *M40* 3B **40**
Joynson Av. *Salf* 3D **51**
Joynson St. *Sale* 4D **111**
Jubilee Clo. *Eccl* 4D **45**
Jubilee Ct. *M16* 4B **82**
Jubilee Ct. *Stoc* 2B **106**
Jubilee St. *Salf* 1D **65**
Judson Av. *M21* 3C **115**
Judy St. *M9* 2D **39**
Julia St. *M3* 4B **52** (1A **6**)
Julius St. *M19* 1B **120**
Juniper Bank. *Stoc* 4C **107**
Juniper Clo. *Sale* 3B **110**
Juniper Cres. *Droy* 3B **74**
Jupiter Wlk. *M40* 2A **56**
Jura Dri. *Urm* 3A **78**
Jurby Av. *M9* 2A **22**
Jury St. *M8* 3B **52**
Justin Clo. *M13* 1D **85** (5E **11**)
Jutland St. *M1* 2D **69** (1F **11**)

K

Kale St. *M13* 4D **69** (5F **11**)
Kalima Gro. *Salf* 1D **51**
Kansas Av. *Salf* 3C **65**
Kara St. *Salf* 1C **65**
Katherine St. *M16* 3C **83**
Kathkin Av. *M8* 4D **21**
Kathleen Gro. *M14* 2A **102**

Kays Gdns. *Salf*. 1D **67** (4D **5**)
Kay St. *M11*. 4D **71**
Kay St. *Salf*. 4D **33**
Keadby Clo. *Eccl* 3D **61**
Kean Pl. *Eccl* 2D **61**
Kearsley Av. *M8*. 4C **21**
Kearsley St. *Eccl* 1B **60**
Kearton Dri. *Eccl* 2C **63**
Keary Clo. *M18* 2D **89**
Keaton Clo. *Salf*. 3C **49**
Keats Av. *Droy*. 1C **75**
Keats Ho. *Stoc*. 4D **105**
Keats Rd. *Eccl*. 2D **61**
Kedington Clo. *M40*. 2A **54**
Kedleston Av. *M14*. 4C **87**
Keele Clo. *M40*. 4A **54**
Keeley Clo. *M40*. 3C **57**
Keighley Av. *Droy*. 4C **59**
Keith Wlk. *M40* 4B **54**
Kelbrook Rd. *M11* 3B **72**
Kelday Wlk. M8 . . . . *1A* **54**
          (off Smedley Rd.)
Keld Wlk. *M18*. 3C **89**
Kelham Wlk. *M40*. 1C **41**
Kellbrook Cres. *Salf* 1B **34**
          (in two parts)
Kellett Wlk. *M11*. 1B **72**
Kelling Wlk. *M15*. 1D **83** (5D **9**)
Kelmarsh Clo. *M11*. 4A **74**
Kelmscott Lodge. Urm *1B* **92**
          (off Cornhill Rd.)
Kelsall Dri. *Droy*. 4B **58**
Kelsall St. *M12* 2D **87**
Kelsey Wlk. *M9*. 1D **21**
Kelstern Av. *M13* 1C **103**
Kelstern Sq. *M13* 1C **103**
Kelvin Gro. *M8*. 1C **53**
Kelvington Dri. *M9*. 4B **38**
Kelvin St. *M4* 1C **69** (4D **7**)
Kemball. *Eccl*. 1B **62**
Kemnay Wlk. *M11*. 2C **73**
Kempley Clo. *M12*. 2D **87**
Kempsey Wlk. *M40*. 1D **41**
Kempster St. *Salf*. 3D **51**
Kempton Ho. *Salf*. 1C **51**
Kempton Rd. *M19* 1A **120**
Kemsing Wlk. *Salf* 2A **66**
Kenchester Av. *M11*. 3D **73**
Kendal Ct. *Eccl*. 2B **60**
Kendall Rd. *M8* 3B **20**
Kendal Rd. *Salf*. 2A **48**
Kendal Rd. *Stret*. 1B **96**
Kendrew Wlk. *M9*. 1C **39**
Kenford Wlk. *M8*. 1B **52**
Kenilworth Av. *M20*. 4B **116**
Kenilworth Av. *Swin*. 3D **15**
Kenilworth Rd. *Sale* 4A **110**
Kenley Wlk. M8 . . . . *1A* **54**
          (off Smedley Rd.)

Kenmere Gro. *M40*. 1B **40**
Kennard Clo. *M9* 1D **39**
Kennedy Rd. *Salf*. 1A **64**
Kennedy St. *M2*. 2B **68** (1B **10**)
Kennington Av. *M40*. 3B **56**
Kenside Rd. *M16*. 1B **100**
Kensington Av. *M14*. 4B **86**
Kensington Ct. *Dent*. 4D **91**
Kensington Ct. *Salf*. 2C **35**
Kensington Dri. *Salf*. 4B **48**
Kensington Gro. *Dent*. 4D **91**
Kensington Rd. *M21* 2A **98**
Kensington Rd. *Fail*. 2D **43**
Kensington St. *M14*. 1C **101**
Kenslow Av. *M8*. 4B **20**
Kent Av. *Droy*. 2A **74**
Kentford Dri. *M40*. 3A **54**
Kent Gro. *Fail*. 1A **58**
Kentmere Ct. *M9*. 2A **24**
Kenton Av. *M18*. 4C **89**
Kent Rd. *Dent* 2C **107**
Kent Rd. E. *M14*. 1B **102**
Kent Rd. W. *M14* 1A **102**
          (in three parts)
Kent St. *M2*. 2B **68** (5B **6**)
Kent St. *Salf*. 3D **51**
Kent St. *Swin*. 4B **14**
Kenwick Dri. *M40*. 4A **26**
Kenwood Av. *M19* 3D **119**
Kenwood Clo. *Stret*. 2C **97**
Kenwood Ct. *Stret* 3C **97**
Kenwood Rd. *Stoc*. 2A **106**
Kenwood Rd. *Stret*. 3C **97**
Kenwright St. *M4* 1C **69** (3D **7**)
Kenwyn St. *M40*. 4C **55**
Kenyon La. *M40*. 2A **40**
Kenyon La. *P'wich* 2A **20**
Kenyon St. *M18*. 2A **90**
Keppel Rd. *M21*. 2B **98**
Kerfield Wlk. *M13* 1D **85** (5F **11**)
Kerrera Dri. *Salf*. 2B **64**
Kerridge Wlk. M16. . . . . 1B **100**
          (off Chattock St.)
Kerrier Clo. *Eccl*. 1C **63**
Kerr St. *M9* 3B **22**
Kersal 2A **34**
Kersal Av. *Swin* 2A **32**
Kersal Bank. *Salf* 2C **35**
Kersal Bar. *Salf* 1C **35**
Kersal Cell. *Salf*. 2D **33**
Kersal Clo. *P'wich* 1A **34**
Kersal Clo. *Salf* 1C **35**
Kersal Crag. *Salf* 1C **35**
Kersal Dale 2C **35**
Kersal Gdns. *Salf* 1C **35**
Kersal Hill Av. *Salf* 2A **34**
Kersal Rd. *P'wich & Salf* 1A **34**
Kersal Va. Ct. *Salf* 2A **34**

Kersal Va. Rd. *Salf* 1D 33
Kersal Way. *Salf.* 3B 34
Kersh Av. *M19* 4B 104
Kershaw Av. *P'wich* 4D 17
　(in two parts)
Kershaw Dri. *Chad* 3D 25
Kershaw Gro. *Aud* 3D 75
Kershaw La. *Aud* 3D 75
Kershaw Rd. *Fail* 3B 42
Kershaw St. *Droy* 2B 74
Kershaw Wlk. *M12.* 2B 86
Kershope Gro. *Salf.* 3A 66
Kerswell Wlk. *M40* 1A 56
Kerwin Wlk. *Open* 3A 72
Kesteven Rd. *M9* 3B 38
Keston Av. *M9* 3A 24
Keston Av. *Droy* 2A 74
Keston Cres. *Stoc* 3D 123
Kestral Ct. *Salf.* 3B 64
Kestrel Av. *Swin* 4D 15
Kestrel Rd. *Traf P.* 3B 62
Kestrel Wlk. *M12* 2A 88
Keswick Clo. *M13* 3B 86
Keswick Gro. *Salf.* 4D 49
Keswick Rd. *Stoc.* 2D 121
Keswick Rd. *Stret.* 1A 96
Kettering Rd. *M19* 2B 104
Kettlewell Wlk. *M18* 3C 89
Ketton Clo. *M11* 4A 74
Kevin St. *M19* 4B 104
Kew Dri. *Urm* 4A 76
Kew Gdns. *M40* 1A 40
Kew Rd. *Fail.* 2C 43
Keyhaven Wlk. *M40* 2A 54
　(Dalbury Dri.)
Keyhaven Wlk. *M40* 1A 54
　(Reedshaw Rd.)
Keymer St. *M11.* 1C 71
Keynsham Rd. *M11* 4B 56
Keystone Clo. *Salf* 3C 49
Key West Clo. *M11* 2D 71
Keyworth Wlk. *M40* 3C 55
Khartoum St. *M11* 1D 73
Khartoum St. *M16* 4D 83
Kibworth Wlk. M9 . . . . 1C 23
　(off Crossmead Dri.)
Kidacre Wlk. *M40.* 3A 40
Kidwall Wlk. *M9.* 1D 39
Kiel Clo. *Eccl* 3A 62
Kielder Sq. *Salf* 2D 65
Kildare Rd. *M21.* 4D 99
Kildare Rd. *Swin* 3A 30
Kilmarsh Wlk. *M8* 3B 36
Kilmington Dri. *M8.* 1B 52
Kilner Wlk. *M40.* 3A 54
Kilnsey Wlk. *M18.* 3C 89
Kilnside Dri. *M9.* 3B 38
Kilnwick Clo. *M18* 1B 104
Kilrush Av. *Eccl* 3D 61

Kilsby Wlk. *M40.* 3B 54
Kilton Wlk. *M40.* 3A 54
Kilvert Dri. *Sale* 4B 110
Kimberley St. *Salf* 3A 36
Kimberley Wlk. *M15.* 5D 9
Kimbolton Clo. *M12* 1A 88
Kinbury Wlk. *M40* 3A 54
Kincardine Rd. *M13* . . . 1D 85 (5E 11)
Kincraig Clo. *M11* 2B 72
Kinder Ho. *Salf.* 4B 48
Kinderton Av. *M20.* 2D 117
Kineton Wlk. *M13* 2A 86
　(off Lauderdale Cres.)
Kingcombe Wlk. *M9.* 2C 39
King Edward St. *M19.* 3B 104
King Edward St. *Eccl* 1C 61
King Edward St. *Salf* . . . 3B 66 (3A 8)
Kingfisher Clo. *M12* 3C 87
Kingfisher Ct. *Salf* 3B 64
Kingham Dri. *M4* 1A 70
Kings Av. *M8* 2C 37
Kingsbridge Clo. *M9* 3A 38
Kingsbridge Rd. *M9.* 3A 38
Kingsbrook Rd. *M16* 4A 100
Kingsbury Rd. *M11* 1C 73
Kingscliffe St. *M9.* 2C 39
King's Clo. *M18* 2B 90
Kings Clo. *P'wich* 1C 19
King's Ct. Salf 3A 50
　(off Union St.)
King's Cres. *M16* 1B 98
Kingsdale Rd. *M18.* 4C 91
Kingsdown Wlk. *Stoc* 4D 123
Kingsfold Av. *M40* 3A 54
Kingsford St. *Salf.* 1B 64
Kings Gro. *Stret.* 1D 97
Kingsheath Av. *M11.* 4B 56
Kingshill Rd. *M21* 1A 114
Kingsland Clo. *M40* 4B 54
Kings La. *Stret.* 1D 97
Kingslea Rd. *M20.* 4A 118
Kingsleigh Rd. *Stoc* 4D 119
Kingsley Av. *M9.* 3D 39
Kingsley Av. *Salf* 3A 34
Kingsley Av. *Stoc* 4A 122
Kingsley Av. *Stret.* 1D 97
Kingsley Av. *Urm* 2C 93
Kingsley Clo. *Salf.* 2A 66
Kingsley Gro. *Aud* 3D 75
Kingsley Rd. *Swin* 1D 29
Kingsmead M. *M9* 1A 22
Kingsmere Av. *M19* 3D 103
Kingsmill Av. *M19* 1B 120
Kings Pk. *Traf P.* 4D 79
King's Rd. *Aud.* 3C 91
Kings Rd. *Chad* 3A 26
Kings Rd. *Chor H.* 4D 99
King's Rd. *P'wich.* 4C 19
Kings Rd. *Sale* 4B 110

King's Rd. *Stret & M16* 3C **97**
Kings Ter. *Stret* 1D **97**
Kingston Av. *Chad* 2C **27**
Kingston Clo. *Salf* 2D **35**
Kingston Dri. *Sale* 4B **112**
Kingston Dri. *Urm* 1B **108**
Kingston Gro. *M9* 2D **23**
Kingston M. *Fail.* 3D **43**
Kingston Rd. *Fail* 3D **43**
King St. *M2* 2B **68** (5A **6**)
           (in two parts)
King St. *Droy.* 3C **75**
           (in two parts)
King St. *Eccl* 2B **62**
King St. *Fail.* 4D **41**
King St. *Salf* (M3) 1A **68** (3F **5**)
King St. *Salf* (M6) 2B **48**
King St. *Salf* (M7) 3A **36**
King St. *Stret.* 3B **96**
King St. W. *M3* 2B **68** (5A **6**)
Kings Wlk. *Droy.* 3C **75**
Kingsway. *M20 & M19.* 4C **119**
Kingsway. *Stret* 3A **96**
Kingsway. *Swin* 4A **32**
Kingsway. *Urm.* 4A **78**
Kingsway Av. *M19* 3D **103**
Kingsway Bldgs. *M19.* 4C **119**
Kingsway Cres. *M19* 4C **119**
Kingsway Pk. *Urm* 4C **77**
Kingswood Gro. *Stoc* 3B **106**
Kingswood Rd. *M14.* 1B **118**
Kingswood Rd. *Eccl* 3B **44**
Kingswood Rd. *P'wich.* 1D **17**
King William Enterprise Pk.
   Salf 3A **66**
King William St. *Eccl* 4A **44**
King William St. *Salf* 3A **66**
Kinlett Wlk. *M40* 4D **25**
Kinley Clo. *M12.* 2D **87**
Kinloch St. *M11.* 1A **72**
Kinmel Av. *Stoc* 4D **123**
Kinmount Wlk. *M9.* *4B* **38**
        (off Lathbury Rd.)
Kinnaird Rd. *M20.* 4A **118**
Kinross. *Eccl* 1B *62*
        (off Peel St.)
Kinross Rd. *M14* 1C **103**
Kintore Wlk. *M40.* 2A **54**
       (off Keyhaven Wlk.)
Kintyre Av. *Salf* 2B **64**
Kintyre Clo. *M11.* 2D **73**
Kinver Rd. *M40.* 4C **25**
Kipling Av. *Droy.* 4C **59**
Kipling St. *Salf.* 4D **35**
Kippax St. *M14.* 1D **101**
Kirby Av. *Chad.* 3D **25**
Kirby Av. *Swin.* 2D **45**
Kirby Wlk. *M4* 1A **70**
Kirkby Av. *M40* 3B **40**

Kirkdale Av. *M40* 4D **25**
Kirkgate Clo. *M40* 4A **54**
Kirkham Av. *M18* 2D **89**
Kirkham St. *Salf.* 2C **65**
Kirkhaven Sq. *M40.* 3C **55**
Kirkhill Wlk. *M40.* 4D **25**
Kirkholt Wlk. *M9* 3C **23**
Kirklinton Dri. *M9.* 4B **38**
Kirkman Av. *Eccl* 3C **61**
Kirkman Clo. *M18* 4D **89**
Kirkmanshulme La. *M12* 4D **87**
Kirk Rd. *M19* 2B **120**
Kirkstall Rd. *Urm* 1A **94**
Kirkstall Sq. *M13* 2A **86**
Kirkstead Clo. *M11.* 3A **72**
Kirkstile Pl. *Swin* 2A **14**
Kirkstone Rd. *M40.* 4C **25**
Kirk St. *M18* 3D **89**
Kirktown Wlk. *Open* 3C **73**
Kirkway. *M9.* 2A **24**
Kirkwood Dri. *M40.* 3A **54**
Kirtley Av. *Eccl.* 4D **45**
Kirton Lodge. *P'wich.* 2C **19**
        (in two parts)
Kirton Wlk. *M9.* 1A **22**
Kitepool St. *Eccl.* 3A **44**
Kitty Wheeldon Gdns. *Sale* 4C **111**
Kiwi St. *Salf.* 1A **66**
Knaresborough Clo. *Stoc* 3A **106**
Knightley Wlk. *M40* 2B **54**
Knightsbridge. M4. . . . . 1C *69* (4C *6*)
      (off Arndale Shop. Cen.)
Knightsbridge Clo. *Salf.* 2D **35**
Knightsbridge M. *M20* 4D **117**
Knights Clo. *P'wich* 1B **18**
Knight's Ct. *Salf.* 1C **63**
Kniveton Clo. *M12.* 2D **87**
Kniveton Rd. *M12* 2D **87**
Knoll St. *Salf.* 3D **35**
Knoll St. Ind. Pk. *Salf.* 3D **35**
Knott Mill 4A **68** (4F **9**)
Knott St. *Salf.* 2B **64**
Knowl Clo. *Dent.* 2C **107**
Knowldale Way. *M12* 3C **87**
Knowle Dri. *P'wich* 4A **18**
Knowles Ct. *Salf.* 4C **47**
Knowles Pl. *M15* 2C **85** (5B **10**)
Knowls, The. *Oldh* 1D **43**
Knowl St. *Oldh.* 4D **27**
Knowsley Av. *Salf.* 3B **66**
Knowsley Av. *Urm* 4C **77**
Knowsley Dri. *Swin* 1D **45**
Knowsley Grn. Salf. *3B* **66**
      (off Knowsley Av.)
Knowsley St. *M8.* 3B **52** (1C **6**)
Knutsford Av. *M16.* 4D **83**
Knutsford Av. *Stoc.* 2D **121**
Knutsford Rd. *M18* 3C **89**
Knutsford St. *Salf.* 1C **65**

L

Labrador Quay. *Salf* 4A 66
Labtec St. *Swin* 1D 31
Laburnum Av. *Aud* 2D 75
Laburnum Av. *Eccl* 3A 60
Laburnum Av. *Fail* 1B 58
Laburnum Av. *Swin* 1A 46
Laburnum Rd. *M18* 4D 89
Laburnum Rd. *Dent* 1B 106
Laburnum Rd. *Urm* 4B 76
Laburnum St. *Salf* 1D 65
Laburnum Vs. Urm *2A 94*
   (off Cavendish Rd.)
Laburnum Wlk. *Sale* 4C 109
Lackford Dri. *M40* 3A 54
Lacy Gro. *Stret*. 3B 96
Lacy St. *Stret*. 3B 96
Lacy Wlk. *M12*. 3C 71
Ladybarn 2B 118
Ladybarn Cres. *M14*. 2B 118
Ladybarn Ho. *M14*. 4B 102
Ladybarn La. *M14*. 4B 102
Ladybarn Rd. *M14*. 4B 102
Lady in Leisure Health &
   Fitness Cen. 5A 6
Ladylands Av. *M11*. 1C 73
Ladyshore Clo. *Salf* 2D 65
Ladythorne Av. *P'wich* 4A 18
Ladythorne Ct. *P'wich* 4A 18
Ladythorne Dri. *P'wich* 4A 18
Ladywell Trad. Est. *Salf* 1D 63
Lagos Clo. *M14* 4C 85
Laindon Rd. *M14* 4C 87
Lake Rd. *Traf P* 4A 64
Lakeside Clo. *M18* 2B 90
Lakeside Ct. *Salf* 1D 35
Lake Vw. *M9* 4A 24
Lakin St. *M40* 3A 40
Lamb Clo. *M12* 3D 87
Lamb Ct. *Salf*. 1A **68** (4E 5)
Lambert Dri. *Sale*. 3D 109
Lambeth Av. *Fail* 2D 43
Lambeth Rd. *M40* 3C 57
Lambeth Rd. *Stoc* 1B 122
Lamb La. *Salf* 1A **68** (4E 5)
Lambrook Wlk. *M40* 3D 57
Lambs Fold. *Stoc*. 4D 121
Lambton Rd. *M21* 4D 99
Lambton Rd. *Wors*. 4C 29
Lambton St. *Eccl* 3B 44
Lamburn Av. *M40* 4D 25
Lamorna Clo. *Salf* 2B 34
Lamplight Way. *Swin* 3C 33
Lamport Clo. *M1*. 4D **69** (4E 11)
Lamport Ct. M1. . . . . . 4D **69** (4E 11)
   (off Lamport Clo.)
Lampson St. *M8* 3A 52

Lamsholme Clo. *M19*. 2A 104
Lanbury Dri. *M8*. 3B 36
Lancashire County
   Cricket Club Mus. 4A 82
Lancashire County
   Cricket Ground 4A 82
Lancashire St. *M40* 2D 55
Lancaster. *M1* 3C 69
Lancaster Av. *Fail*. 3A 42
Lancaster Av. *Urm* 1A 94
Lancaster Ct. *M19*. 4D 103
Lancaster Ct. *M40*. 3C 57
Lancaster Dri. *P'wich* 4C 19
Lancaster Lodge. Salf *1D 47*
   (off Lancaster Rd.)
Lancaster Rd. *Droy* 4B 58
Lancaster Rd. *Salf*. 1D 47
Lancaster St. *Chad*. 2C 27
Lancastrian Ho. *P'wich* 1C 35
Lanchester St. *M40* 4C 55
Landcross Rd. *M14* 3A 102
Landells Wlk. *M40* 2A 56
Lander Gro. *M9* 3D 23
Landfield Dri. *M8* 3B 36
Landor Ct. *Dent* 1B 106
Landos Ct. *M40* 4A 54
Landos Rd. *M40* 4A 54
Landsberg Rd. *Fail*. 2D 43
Landsberg Ter. *Fail*. 2D 43
Landstead Dri. *M40* 1C 71
Lane End. *Eccl* 2B 62
Lane End Clo. *Fail* 4C 43
Lanesfield Wlk. M8. . . . . *2A 38*
   (off Crescent Rd.)
Langcliffe Wlk. *M18*. 3C 89
Langcroft Dri. *M40*. 2C 57
Langdale Av. *M19*. 4B 104
Langdale Ct. *M8*. 4D 37
Langdale Rd. *M14* 4B 86
Langdale Rd. *Stoc* 3C 121
Langdale Rd. *Stret* 1A 96
Langfield Av. *M14* 1D 99
Langfield Wlk. *Salf*. 1D 65
Langford Rd. *M20* 3C 117
Langford Rd. *Stoc* 4C 121
Langham Ct. *Stret* 4C 79
Langham Rd. *Salf* 1D 65
Langholme Clo. *M15* 5D 9
Langholme Pl. *Eccl* 1B 60
   (in two parts)
Langland Clo. *M9*. 2C 23
Langland Clo. *Lev* 3D 105
Langland Dri. *Eccl* 4C 61
Langley Av. *P'wich* 1B 18
Langley Clo. *Urm* 2A 94
Langley Ct. *Salf*. 1A 36
Langley Rd. *M14* 3A 102
Langley Rd. *P'wich* 1A 18
Langley Rd. *Swin & Salf* 2D 33

Langley Rd. S. *Salf* 1D **49**
Langness St. *M11* 2C **73**
Lango St. *M16* 4C **83**
Langport Av. *M12* 2C **87**
Langroyd Wlk. *M8* *3B* **36**
(off Highshore Dri.)
Langsett Av. *Salf* 4A **48**
Langshaw St. *M16* 4C **83**
Langshaw St. *Salf* 2D **65**
Langside Av. *M9* 2C **23**
Langston St. *M3* 4B **52** (1A **6**)
Langthorne St. *M19* 1B **120**
Langton Clo. *Fail* 2D **43**
Langton St. *Salf* 1C **65**
Langworthy Rd. *M40* 3A **40**
Langworthy Rd. *Salf* 3C **49**
Lanhill Dri. *M8* 1A **54**
Lankro Way. *Eccl* 2B **62**
Lanreath Wlk. *M8* *1D* **53**
(off Moordown Clo.)
Lansbury Ho. *M16* 1D **99**
Lansdale Gdns. *M19* 4C **119**
Lansdale St. *Eccl* 3A **60**
Lansdowne Av. *Aud* 2D **75**
Lansdowne Rd. *M8* 1C **37**
Lansdowne Rd. *Eccl* 4D **45**
Lansdowne Rd. *Sale* 3C **111**
Lapwing Ct. *M20* 4C **117**
Lapwing La. *M20* 4C **117**
Lapwing La. *Stoc* 2D **123**
Larch Av. *Stret* 3B **96**
Larch Av. *Swin* 4C **29**
Larch Clo. *Fail* 1B **58**
Larch Gro. *Swin* 4B **12**
Larch Rd. *Eccl* 3A **44**
Larchwood Av. *M9* 3D **39**
Larchwood Clo. *Sale* 4C **109**
Larden Wlk. *M8* 4B **36**
Larkhill Wlk. *M8* 1D **53**
Larmuth Av. *M21* 3C **115**
Larne Av. *Stret* 2A **96**
Larne St. *M11* 3A **72**
Lascar Av. *Salf* 3A **66**
Lashbrook Clo. *M40* 3B **54**
Lassell St. *M11* 4B **74**
(in two parts)
Lastingham St. *M40* 1C **57**
Latchmere Rd. *M14* 1A **118**
Lathbury Rd. *M9 & M40* 4B **38**
Lathom Rd. *M20* 2B **118**
Latrobe St. *Droy* 3C **75**
Lauderdale Cres. *M13* 2A **86**
Laundry St. *Salf* 3D **49**
Laurel Av. *M14* 2C **101**
Laurel Bank Gdns. *M9* 3B **22**
Laurel Ct. *Stoc* 4B **120**
Laurel Gro. *M20* 3D **117**
Laurel Gro. *Salf* 1A **64**

Laurel Ho. *Salf* 3D **47**
Laurel Rd. *Stoc* 4B **120**
Laurence Clo. *M12* 2B **88**
Laurence Lowry Ct. *Swin* 1B **30**
Lausanne Rd. *M20* 2D **117**
Lavender Clo. *Sale* 4C **109**
Lavenham Av. *M11* 2D **73**
Lavington Gro. *M18* 4D **89**
Lavinia St. *Eccl* 1B **60**
Lawefield Cres. *Swin* 1D **13**
Lawler Av. *Salf* 2B **82**
Lawn Dri. *Swin* 3A **30**
Lawngreen Av. *M21* 2A **114**
Lawnside M. *M20* 4C **117**
Lawnswood Dri. *Swin* 4C **31**
Lawnswood Pk. Rd. *Swin* 4C **31**
Lawnswood Wlk. *M12* 3C **87**
Lawson Clo. *Wors* 3C **29**
Lawson Gro. *Sale* 3C **111**
Lawson St. *M9* 4A **22**
Lawton Rd. *Stoc* 4C **121**
Lawton St. *Droy* 1D **75**
Lawton St. *Open* 1D **89**
Laxey St. *M40* 3B **40**
Laycock Cres. *Fail* 3B **42**
Laycock Gro. *Fail* 3B **42**
Laystall St. *M1* 2D **69** (5F **7**)
Layton St. *M40* 1B **70**
Lazenby Wlk. *M13* 4D **87**
Leabank St. *M19* 2A **104**
Leabrook Dri. *M40* 2A **42**
Leach M. *P'wich* 2D **17**
Leach St. *M18* 2B **88**
Leach St. *P'wich* 2D **17**
Lea Ct. *Fail* 3A **42**
Lea Ct. *Stoc* 4B **120**
Leacroft Rd. *M21* 4D **115**
Lea Dri. *M9* 3D **23**
Leaf St. *Hulme* 2B **84** (5A **10**)
Leaf St. *Stoc* 2A **122**
Leagate. *Urm* 3A **94**
Leaholm Clo. *M40* 2D **57**
Leak St. *M16* 2C **83**
Leamington Av. *M20* 4B **116**
Leamington Ct. *Stoc* 2A **122**
Leamington Rd. *Eccl* 4B **44**
Leamington Rd. *Stoc* 2A **122**
(in two parts)
Leamington Rd. *Urm* 1B **92**
Leamington St. *Open* 4D **73**
Leamore Wlk. *M9* *3C* **23**
(off White Moss Rd.)
Leander Clo. *M9* 4C **23**
Leaside Dri. *M20* 4B **118**
Leaway Clo. *M13* 4B **86**
Le Bas Ho. *M20* 3B **116**
Lecester Rd. *M8* 1D **53**
Leconfield Dri. *M9* 3C **23**
Leconfield Rd. *Eccl* 3A **44**

Ledbrooke Clo. *Salf* 3B **66**
Ledburn Clo. *M15* 2D **83** (5D **9**)
Ledburn Ct. *M15* 5D **9**
Ledbury Av. *Urm* 1C **93**
Ledbury Rd. *Fail.* 3A **58**
Ledbury Wlk. *M9* 3A **22**
Ledsham Av. *M9* 1C **21**
Lee Cres. *Stret.* 1C **97**
Leedale St. *M12* 2A **104**
Leegate Dri. *M9* 2D **23**
Leegate Rd. *Stoc* 4D **119**
                (in two parts)
Leegrange Rd. *M9* 1C **39**
Lee Rd. *M9* 2B **38**
Lees Hall Cres. *M14* 1B **118**
Lees Pk. Av. *Droy.* 1D **75**
Lees Pk. Way. *Droy.* 1D **75**
Lees St. *Droy.* 1D **75**
Lees St. *Open & M18.* 4D **73**
Lees St. *Swin.* 1B **30**
Lees St. Enterprise Trad. Est.
    Abb H. 2A **90**
Leeswood Av. *M21.* 3C **115**
Leewood. *Swin.* 2D **13**
Left Bank. *Salf* 2A **68** (5F **5**)
Legh Dri. *Aud* 2D **75**
Leghorn Wlk. M11 . . . . *2D **71***
          (off Seabright Wlk.)
Legh Rd. *Salf.* 2D **35**
Legh St. *Eccl.* 2C **61**
Legh St. *Salf.* 3D **35**
Legion Gro. *Salf.* 1A **52**
Legwood Ct. *Urm.* 2C **93**
Leicester Av. *Droy.* 4B **58**
Leicester Av. *Salf.* 2B **36**
Leicester Ct. *Salf.* 1A **36**
Leicester Rd. *Fail.* 2C **59**
Leicester Rd. *Sale* 4D **111**
Leicester Rd. *Salf.* 4A **36**
Leicester St. *Stoc.* 2B **106**
Leicester Wlk. *Salf.* 4A **36**
Leigh Av. *Swin.* 2D **45**
Leighbrook Rd. *M14* 1D **117**
Leighton Rd. *M16* 4C **83**
Leighton St. *M40.* 2A **40**
Leinster Rd. *Swin.* 3A **30**
Leith Av. *Sale.* 4C **113**
Leith Rd. *Sale* 4C **113**
Lena St. *M1.* 2D **69** (1E **11**)
Len Cox Wlk. *M4* 1D **69** (4D **7**)
Leng Rd. *M40* 2D **57**
Lenham Av. *Eccl.* 1B **60**
Lenham Clo. *Stoc* 3D **123**
Lenham Towers. *Stoc.* 3D **123**
Lennie Rd. *Urm* 4D **61**
Lenthall Wlk. M8 . . . . *3B **36***
          (off Lanbury Dri.)
Lentmead Dri. *M40* 1A **40**
Leopold Av. *M20* 4C **117**

Leopold St. *Salf.* 2B **64**
Lepton Wlk. *M9* 2C **23**
Leroy Dri. *M9.* 4B **22**
Lesley Rd. *Stret.* 3C **95**
Leslie Av. *Chad* 3D **27**
Leslie Hough Way.
    Salf 3B **50** (1A **4**)
Leslie St. *M14.* 1D **101**
Lester St. *Stret.* 2B **96**
Letchworth St. *M14* 1D **101**
Levedale Rd. *M9* 2C **23**
Levenhurst Rd. *M8* 3B **36**
Levenshulme. **3C 105**
Levenshulme Rd. *M18* 4D **89**
Levenshulme Swimming
   Pool 3B **104**
Levenshulme Ter. M19 . . . . *3A **104***
          (off Yew Tree Av.)
Levenshulme Trad. Est.
    M19 . . . . 2C **105**
Levens St. *M40* 3A **40**
Levens St. *Salf.* 2B **50**
Levens Wlk. *Chad* 1C **27**
Lever Av. *Swin.* 4D **15**
Lever St. *M1.* 2C **69** (5D **7**)
Lewis Av. *M9.* 1C **39**
Lewis Av. *Urm.* 3D **77**
Lewisham Av. *M40.* 3B **56**
Lewis Rd. *Droy* 1A **74**
Lewis Rd. *Stoc.* 3B **106**
Lewis St. *M40* 4B **54**
                (in two parts)
Lewis St. *Eccl.* 2D **61**
Lewtas St. *Eccl.* 2A **62**
Lexton Av. *M8* 4D **21**
Leybourne Av. *M19* 2B **104**
Leybourne M. *Salf* 1A **52**
Leyburn Av. *Stret.* 1A **96**
Leyburn Av. *Urm.* 3A **92**
Leyburn Ho. *M13.* 4B **86**
Leyburn Rd. *M40.* 4C **25**
Leycroft St. *M1.* 2D **69** (2F **11**)
                (in two parts)
Leyton Av. *M40* 3B **40**
Leywell Rd. *M9* 2D **39**
Library Theatre, The . . 3B **68** (2B **10**)
Library Wlk. *M2.* 2B **68** (1B **10**)
Lichfield Av. *Stoc* 2A **122**
Lichfield Dri. *M8* 3D **37**
Lichfield Dri. *P'wich.* 4C **19**
Lichfield Dri. *Swin.* 4B **30**
Lichfield Rd. *Eccl.* 3B **46**
Lichfield Rd. *Urm.* 4D **77**
Lichfield St. *Salf.* 2A **50**
Lidbrook Wlk. *M12* 2C **87**
Lidiard St. *M8* 1C **37**
Lieutenant Wlk. Salf. 3B **66** (3A **8**)
          (off Belfort Dri.)
Lifton Av. *M40.* 3C **55**

Lightborne Rd. *Sale* 4D **109**
Lightbourne Av. *Swin* 3B **30**
Lightbourne Green 3B **30**
Lightbowne Rd. *M40* 4A **40**
Lightfoot Wlk. *M11* 2D **71**
Light Oaks Rd. *Salf* 3D **47**
Lilac Av. *Swin* 2C **31**
Lilac Ct. *Salf* 1A **66**
Lilac Gro. *M40* 1A **40**
Lila St. *M9* 3D **39**
Lilford Clo. *M12* 2A **88**
Lilian St. *M16* 4C **83**
Lillian Gro. *Stoc* 4B **106**
Lilmore Av. *M40* 4C **41**
Lilstock Wlk. *M9* 3C **23**
Lily La. *M9* 3D **39**
Lily St. *Eccl* 2B **60**
Lily Thomas Ct. *M11* 4D **73**
Lime Av. *Swin* 4C **29**
Lime Av. *Urm* 2B **92**
Lime Bank St. *M12* 3B **70**
Limebrook Clo. *Open* 1A **90**
Lime Clo. *Salf* 4A **50**
Lime Ct. *Salf* 4A **50**
Lime Cres. *M16* 4B **82**
Lime Ditch Rd. *Fail* 1C **43**
Limefield Ct. *Salf* 1D **35**
Limefield Rd. *Salf* 1D **35**
Limefield Ter. *M19* 3A **104**
Lime Gate 1D **43**
Lime Gro. *M15* 3D **85**
Lime Gro. *M16* 4B **82**
Limehurst Av. *M20* 4B **100**
Limekiln La. *M12* 3B **70**
Lime La. *Fail* 3D **43**
Lime La. *Oldh* 1D **43**
(in two parts)
Lime Rd. *Stret* 3B **96**
Limerston Dri. *M40* 2D **55**
Limeside Rd. *Oldh* 4D **27**
Limestead Av. *M8* 2C **37**
Lime St. *Eccl* 2D **61**
Lime Tree Clo. *Urm* 3A **94**
Lime Tree Gro. *Fail* 3D **43**
Limetree Wlk. *M11* 2D **71**
Limley Gro. *M21* 2C **115**
Linby St. *M15* 1A **84** (5E **9**)
Lincoln Av. *M19* 3B **104**
Lincoln Av. *Droy* 4C **59**
Lincoln Av. *Stret* 1B **94**
Lincoln Ct. *M40* 3B **56**
Lincoln Ct. *Salf* 1A **36**
Lincoln Dri. *P'wich* 4C **19**
Lincoln Grn. *Stoc* 3D **123**
Lincoln Gro. *M13* 3A **86**
Lincoln Gro. *Sale* 4C **113**
Lincoln Rd. *Fail* 1C **59**
Lincoln Rd. *Midd* 1C **25**
Lincoln Rd. *Swin* 3A **30**

Lincoln Sq. *M2* 2B **68** (1A **10**)
(off Brazennose St.)
Lincoln St. *M13* 4D **87**
Lincoln St. *Eccl* 2C **61**
Lincoln St. *Oldh* 1D **27**
Lindale Av. *M40* 4D **25**
Lindale Av. *Urm* 1A **92**
Linden Av. *Salf* 1C **49**
Linden Av. *Swin* 3D **29**
Linden Dri. *Salf* 3A **66**
Linden Gro. *M14* 1B **118**
Linden Pk. *M19* 1D **119**
Linden Way. *Droy* 3A **74**
Lindeth Av. *M18* 4D **89**
Lindfield Rd. *Stoc* 3B **106**
Lindinis Av. *Salf* 1A **66**
Lindley Wood Rd. *M14* 1C **119**
Lindow Rd. *M16* 1C **99**
Lindrick Clo. *M40* 3C **41**
Lindsay Av. *M19* 3D **103**
Lindsay Av. *Swin* 3A **30**
Lindsay Rd. *M19* 1D **119**
Lindside Wlk. *M9* 3C **23**
Lind St. *M40* 1C **71**
Lindum Av. *M16* 4C **83**
Lindum St. *M14* 1D **101**
Lindy Av. *Swin* 3B **14**
Linear Walkway. *Eccl* 4D **45**
Linen Ct. *Salf* 4D **51** (2C **4**)
Lines Rd. *Droy* 2D **75**
Linfield St. *M11* 2B **72**
Linford Av. *M40* 4C **25**
Lingard Clo. *Aud* 3D **75**
Lingard St. *Stoc* 1B **122**
Lingard Ter. *Aud* 3D **75**
Lingcrest Clo. *M19* 2C **121**
Lingdale Wlk. *M40* 3A **40**
Lingfield Rd. *M11* 1C **73**
Lingmell Clo. *Urm* 4A **76**
Lingmoor Wlk. *M15* 2B **84**
Link Av. *Urm* 3C **95**
Links Av. *Fail* 2B **58**
Links Cres. *P'wich* 4A **20**
Links Dri. *M13* 1D **85** (5E **11**)
Links Ri. *Urm* 4A **76**
Links, The. *M40* 3C **41**
Links Vw. *P'wich* 1A **34**
Linksway. *P'wich* 4D **19**
Linksway. *Swin* 4C **31**
Linksway Clo. *Stoc* 4A **120**
Link, The. *Stoc* 3D **123**
Linley Rd. *Sale* 4D **111**
Linnett Clo. *M12* 4D **87**
Linn St. *M8* 1C **37**
Linnyshaw 3A **12**
Linslade Ho. *Salf* 2D **65**
(off Amersham St.)
Linslade Wlk. *M9* 3B **38**
(off Foleshill Av.)

Linsley St. *Salf* 1A **68** (3F **5**)
Linstead Dri. *M8* 4B **36**
Linton Av. *Dent* 1C **107**
Linton Clo. *M4* 3B **70**
Linton Rd. *Sale* 3A **112**
Linton Wlk. *Salf* 2D **33**
(in two parts)
Linwood Gro. *M12* 2A **104**
Linwood St. *Fail* 4C **41**
Lion Brow. *M9* 4B **22**
Lion Fold La. *M9* 3B **22**
Lions Dri. *Swin* 3B **30**
Lion St. *M9* 4B **22**
Lisburn Av. *M21* 3C **99**
Lisburn Rd. *M40* 2A **40**
Liscard Av. *M14* 3D **101**
Lismore Way. *Urm* 3D **77**
Lissadel Science Pk.
Salf 4B **50** (1A **4**)
Lissadel St. *Salf* 3A **50**
Litcham Clo. *M1* 4D **69** (4E **11**)
Litchfield Gro. *Wors* 3A **28**
Lit. Ancoats St. *M1* 1D **69** (4E **7**)
Little Bolton 1D **63**
Lit. David St. *M1* 3C **69** (2D **11**)
Lit. Ees La. *Sale* 3B **110**
(in two parts)
Littlegreen Gdns. *Salf* 4D **49**
Littleham Wlk. *M18* 3C **89**
Littlehaven Clo. *M12* 3C **87**
Lit. Holme St. *M4* 2B **70**
Lit. John St. *M3* 2A **68** (5A **5**)
Little La. *M9* 2D **21**
Lit. Lever St. *M1* 2D **69** (5E **7**)
(in two parts)
Lit. Moss La. *Swin* 4B **14**
Littlemoss Rd. *Droy* 4D **59**
Lit. Peter St. *M15* 4A **68** (4F **9**)
Lit. Pitt St. *M1* 2D **69** (5F **7**)
Lit. Quay St. *M3* 3A **68** (1A **10**)
Littler Av. *M21* 4C **115**
Littlers Point. *Traf P* 3B **80**
Littleton Rd. *Salf & M6* 2A **34**
Littlewood St. *Salf* 1C **65**
Liverpool Clo. *Stoc* 2A **122**
Liverpool Rd. *Eccl* 4A **60**
Liverpool Rd. *M3* . . . 3D **67** (2D **9**)
Liverpool Rd. Steam Railway . . . 2D **9**
Liverpool St.
Salf & M6 (M5) 1B **64**
Liverpool St.
Salf & M5 (M6) 1D **65** (5A **4**)
Liverpool St. *Stoc* 2A **122**
Liverstudd Av. *Stoc* 1B **122**
Liverton Ct. *M9* 1D **21**
Liverton Dri. *M9* 1D **21**
Livesey St. *M4* 4A **54** (1F **7**)
Livesey St. *Lev* 1B **120**
Livingstone Pl. *M16* 3B **82**

Living Well Premier
Manchester 1F **9**
(Gymnasium)
Lizard St. *M1* 2D **69** (5E **7**)
Lizmar Ter. *M9* 2D **39**
Lloyd Ct. M12 . . . . 2D **87**
(off Frodesley Wlk.)
Lloyd Rd. *M19* 2B **120**
Lloyd St. *M2* 2B **68** (1A **10**)
(in two parts)
Lloyd St. *Droy* 2B **74**
Lloyd St. N. *M14 & M15* 4C **85**
Lloyd St. S. *M14* 3C **101**
Lockett Gdns. *Salf* 1D **67** (3D **5**)
Lockett St. *M8* 3A **52**
Lockett St. *Salf* 2A **50**
Lockhart Clo. *M12* 3A **88**
Lockton Clo. *M1* 4D **69** (4F **11**)
Lockton Clo. *Stoc* 3A **122**
Lockton Ct. *M1* 4D **69** (4E **11**)
Lockwood St. *M12* 1B **104**
Loddon Wlk. *M9* 2C **39**
Lodge Av. *Urm* 2A **94**
Lodge Fold. *Droy* 1D **75**
Lodgeside Clo. *Droy* 1D **75**
Lodges, The. *Wors* 2A **28**
Lodge St. *M40* 2C **55**
Lodge Vw. *Droy* 1D **75**
Loganberry Av. *Salf* 4A **50**
Lok Fu Gdns. *M8* 2A **52**
Lomas St. *Fail* 1C **43**
Lomax St. *M1* 2A **70** (5F **7**)
Lombard Gro. *M14* 1A **118**
Lombardy Ct. *Salf* 4A **50**
Lomond Av. *Stret* 1B **96**
Lomond Lodge. *M8* 4B **20**
London Rd. *M1* 2D **69** (1E **11**)
London St. *Salf* 3B **50**
Longacre St. *M1* 2A **70**
Longbow St. *Salf* 2D **51**
Longbridge Rd. *Traf P* 2C **79**
Longcrag Wlk. M15 . . . . 3C **85**
(off Botham Clo.)
Longcroft Gro. *Aud* 3D **75**
Longdell Wlk. M9 . . . . 2C **39**
(off Moston La.)
Longden Rd. *M12* 2A **104**
Longfellow St. *Salf* 3C **51**
Longfield. *P'wich* 1A **18**
Longfield Av. *Urm* 3C **93**
Longfield Cotts. Urm 2B **92**
(off Stamford Rd.)
Longfield Dri. *Urm* 2B **92**
Longfield Shop. Cen. *P'wich* . . 1A **18**
Longford Av. *Stret* 2C **97**
Longford Clo. *Stret* 1C **97**
Longford Cotts. Stret 2D **97**
Longford Ho. *M21* 3D **97**
Longford Pl. *M14* 4C **87**

Longford Rd. *M21* 3A **98**	Lostock Gro. *Stret* 1D **95**
Longford Rd. *Stoc* 3B **106**	Lostock Rd. *Salf* 1C **65**
Longford Rd. *Stret* 1B **96**	Lostock Rd. *Urm* 4C **77**
Longford Rd. W.	Lostock St. *M40* 4B **54**
M19 & Stoc 3D **105**	Lothian Av. *Eccl* 4B **44**
Longford St. *M18* 2D **89**	Lottie St. *Swin* 2C **31**
Longford Trad. Est. *Stret* 1B **96**	Loughfield. *Urm* 2A **92**
Longford Wharf. *Stret* 2C **97**	Louisa St. *M11* 3C **73**
Longham Clo. *M11* 2C **71**	Louvaine Clo. *M18* 2A **90**
Longhill Wlk. *M40* 4A **40**	Lovell Ct. *M8* 4B **20**
Longhurst Rd. *M9* 2D **21**	Lowcock St. *Salf* 3A **52** (1E **5**)
Long La. *Chad* 3B **26**	Lowcross Rd. *M40* 1A **56**
Longley Dri. *Wors* 4B **28**	Lwr. Albion St. *M1* 3D **69** (3E **11**)
Longmead Rd. *Salf* 2B **48**	Lwr. Brooklands Pde. *M8* 4A **20**
Long Millgate. *M3* 1B **68** (3B **6**)	Lwr. Brook La. *Wors* 2A **44**
Longport Av. *M20* 2B **116**	Lwr. Brook St. *M1* 2E **11**
Longshaw Av. *Swin* 1B **30**	**Lower Broughton** 3D **51** (1D **5**)
Longsight 4D **87**	Lwr. Broughton Rd.
Longsight Ind. Est. *Long* 4D **87**	*Salf* 2C **51** (1B **4**)
Longsight Rd. *M18* 1B **104**	Lwr. Byrom St. *M3* 3A **68** (2E **9**)
Longsight Shop. Cen. *M12* 4D **87**	Lwr. Chatham St. *M1* 4C **69** (4C **10**)
Long St. *M18* 2A **90**	Lwr. Chatham St.
Long St. *Swin* 3B **30**	*M15* 1C **85** (5C **10**)
Longton Av. *M20* 4C **117**	**Lower Crumpsall** 2A **38**
Longton Rd. *M9* 1A **22**	Lower Grn. *Midd* 1D **23**
Longton Rd. *Salf* 2A **48**	Lwr. Hardman St. *M3* 2A **68** (1E **9**)
Longview Dri. *Swin* 1C **29**	**Lower Kersal** 4B **34**
Long Wood Rd. *Traf P* 2D **79**	Lwr. Lime Rd. *Oldh* 2D **43**
Long Wood Rd. Est. *Traf P* 2D **79**	Lwr. Monton Rd. *Eccl*. 1A **62**
Longworth St. *M3* 3A **68** (2F **9**)	Lwr. Mosley St. *M2* 3B **68** (3A **10**)
Lonsdale Av. *Stoc* 1B **106**	Lwr. Moss La. *M15* 1D **83** (5D **9**)
Lonsdale Av. *Swin* 2D **45**	Lwr. Ormond St. *M1* 4C **69** (4C **10**)
Lonsdale Av. *Urm* 4B **76**	Lwr. Ormond St.
Lonsdale Rd. *M19* 2B **104**	*M15* 1C **85** (5C **10**)
Lonsdale Rd. *Oldh* 4D **27**	Lwr. Park Rd. *M14* 4A **86**
Lonsdale St. *M40* 4C **41**	Lwr. Seedley Rd. *Salf* 4C **49**
Loom St. *M4* 1D **69** (4F **7**)	Lwr. Sutherland St. *Swin* 2A **30**
Lord Byron Sq. *Salf* 2D **65**	Lwr. Vickers St. *M40* 4B **54**
Lord Kitchener Ct. *Sale* 3D **111**	Lowestead Rd. *M11* 1C **73**
Lord La. *Droy*. 3A **58**	Lowestoft St. *M14* 2D **101**
Lord La. *Fail*. 3B **42**	Lowfell Wlk. *M18* 1D **105**
Lord Napier Dri. *Salf* 1B **82**	Lowfield Av. *Droy*. 4B **58**
Lord North St. *M40* 3C **55**	*Lowfield Wlk. M9*. *3C* **23**
Lord's Av. *Salf* 1B **64**	*(off Normanton Dri.)*
Lordship Clo. *M9*. 1D **39**	Lowgill Wlk. *M18*. 3D **89**
Lordsmead St. *M15* 2D **83** (5D **9**)	Lowlands Clo. *Midd* 1B **24**
Lord St. *M3 & M4* 3B **52** (1B **6**)	*Lowndes Wlk. M13* *2A* **86**
Lord St. *Dent* 4C **91**	*(off Copeman Clo.)*
Lord St. *Salf* 3C **51**	Lowood Av. *Urm* 4A **76**
Loretto Rd. *Urm*. 3B **94**	*Lowrey Wlk. M9*. *3C* **39**
Loring St. *M40*. 2C **57**	*(off Craigend Dri.)*
Lorne Gro. *Urm* 2A **94**	Lowry Dri. *Swin*. 1B **30**
Lorne Rd. *M14* 1A **118**	Lowry Galleria. *Salf* 1D **81**
Lorne St. *M13* 3A **86**	Lowry Ho. *Eccl*. 1A **62**
Lorne St. *Eccl* 3B **60**	Lowry Lodge. *M16*. 3D **83**
Lostock Av. *M19* 3B **104**	Lowry, The 1C **81**
Lostock Av. *Urm* 1B **92**	Lowry, The. *M14* 1A **118**
Lostock Circ. *Urm* 4B **78**	Lowther Av. *M18* 1B **104**
Lostock Ct. *Stret* 4B **78**	Lowther Clo. *P'wich* 3A **18**

Lowther Ct. *P'wich*	3D 17
Lowther Rd. *M8*	1C 37
Lowther Rd. *P'wich*	3D 17
Lowthorpe St. *M14*	2C 101
Lowton Av. *M9*	3D 39
Low Wood Rd. *Dent*	4C 91
Loxford Ct. *M15*	2B 84 (5B 10)
Loxford St. *M15*	2B 84 (5B 10)
Loxley Wlk. *M40*	3C 55
Lubeck St. *M9*	2C 39
Lucas Wlk. *M11*	3D 71
Lucien Clo. *M12*	3C 87
Lucy St. *M15*	2D 83
Lucy St. *Salf*	2D 51
Ludgate Hill. *M4*	4D 53 (2E 7)
Ludgate Rd. *M40*	3C 57
Ludgate St. *M4*	4C 53 (2D 7)
Ludlow Av. *Swin*	4C 15
Ludwell Wlk. *M8*	1C 53
Luke Kirby Ct. *Swin*	1B 30
Luke Rd. *Droy*	2D 75
Luke Wlk. *M8*	1D 53
Lullington Rd. *Salf*	3B 48
Lulworth Cres. *Fail*	2D 43
Lulworth Rd. *Eccl*	4C 45
Lumb La. *Aud*	2D 75
	(in two parts)
Lumb La. *Droy*	4D 59
	(in three parts)
Lumley Clo. *M14*	4D 85
Lumn's La. *Swin*	4A 16
Luna St. *M4*	1D 69 (4E 7)
Lundale Wlk. *M40*	4A 40
Lund St. *M16*	2C 83
Lundy Av. *M21*	4C 115
Lune Wlk. *Droy*	3D 75
Lune Way. *Stoc*	4B 122
Lunn Av. *M18*	2B 90
Lupton St. *Salf*	1D 67 (4D 5)
Lurden Wlk. *Chad*	2D 27
Luton Rd. *Stoc*	1B 122
Luxhall Wlk. *M40*	3B 56
Luxor Gro. *Dent*	1B 106
Lyceum Pl. *M15*	1C 85 (5C 10)
Lydden Av. *M11*	4D 57
Lydford St. *Salf*	2B 50
Lydford Wlk. *M13*	3A 86
	(off Torquay Clo.)
Lydgate Rd. *Droy*	4A 58
Lyme Gro. *Droy*	2B 74
Lymington Clo. *Midd*	1B 24
Lyndale Av. *Stoc*	1B 106
Lyndale Av. *Swin*	4D 29
Lyndene Av. *Wors*	2A 28
Lyndhurst Av. *Chad*	1B 26
Lyndhurst Av. *P'wich*	3A 20
Lyndhurst Av. *Urm*	4C 77
Lyndhurst Rd. *M20*	4C 117
	(in two parts)

Lyndhurst Rd. *Stoc*	2A 106
Lyndhurst Rd. *Stret*	1D 95
Lyndhurst St. *Salf*	1C 65
Lyneham Wlk. *M9*	1C 23
Lyneham Wlk. *Salf*	4B 36
Lynmouth Av. *M20*	3C 117
Lynmouth Av. *Stoc*	2A 122
Lynmouth Av. *Urm*	4B 92
Lynmouth Ct. *P'wich*	3D 17
Lynmouth Gro. *P'wich*	3D 17
Lynn Av. *Sale*	3B 112
Lynn Dri. *Droy*	1A 74
Lynn St. *Oldh*	2D 27
Lynthorpe Rd. *M40*	3D 25
Lynton Av. *Oldh*	4D 27
Lynton Av. *Swin*	1B 30
Lynton Dri. *M19*	2D 119
Lynton Rd. *M21*	3A 98
Lynton Rd. *Stoc*	4B 120
Lynton Rd. *Swin*	1B 30
Lynton St. *M14*	2D 101
Lyn Town Trad. Est. *Eccl*	1D 61
Lynway Dri. *M20*	4D 117
Lynwell Rd. *Eccl*	1D 61
Lynwood Av. *M16*	2C 99
Lynwood Av. *Eccl*	1D 61
Lynwood Ct. *M8*	4B 20
Lynwood Gro. *Aud*	2D 75
Lynwood Gro. *Sale*	4A 112
Lynwood Gro. *Stoc*	3C 121
Lyon Gro. *Wors*	2A 28
Lyon's Fold. *Sale*	3D 111
Lyons Rd. *Traf P*	1C 79
Lyon St. *Swin*	3A 30
Lyon Way. *Stoc*	3A 122
Lysander Clo. *M14*	4D 101
Lytham Av. *M21*	2C 115
Lytham Rd. *M14 & M19*	3C 103
Lyth St. *M14*	2B 118
Lytton Av. *M8*	1C 53
Lytton Rd. *Droy*	1C 75

M

Mabel Av. *Wors*	3A 28
Mabel Rd. *Fail*	1C 43
Mabel St. *M40*	2D 57
Mabfield Rd. *M14*	3A 102
Macauley Rd. *M16*	2B 98
Macauley Rd. *Stoc*	3D 105
McCall Wlk. *M11*	1B 72
McConnell Rd. *M40*	3A 40
McCready Dri. *Salf*	3B 66
McDougall Sports Cen.	3C 85
McDowall Wlk. *M8*	4D 21
Macefin Av. *M21*	4D 115
Macfarren St. *M12*	1A 104
Mackenzie Rd. *Salf*	1B 50

Mackenzie St. *M12* 1A **104**
McLaren Ct. *M21* 3A **98**
Maclaren Dri. *M8* 1A **36**
Maddison Rd. *Droy* 3B **74**
Madeira Pl. *Eccl* 1B **60**
Madison Apartments.
   M16 . . . . 3B **82**
Madison Gdns. *Fail* 3A **42**
Madison St. *M18* 2A **90**
Magna Carta Ct. *Salf* 1D **47**
Magnolia Clo. *Sale* 3C **109**
Magnolia Ct. Sale *4C 109*
   (off Magnolia Clo.)
Magnolia Ct. *Salf* 1A **66**
Magnolia Dri. *M8* 4C **37**
Magpie Wlk. *M11* 2D **71**
Maher Gdns. *M15* 4A **84**
Mahogany Wlk. *Sale* 4C **109**
Maida St. *M12* 2B **104**
Maiden M. *Swin* 3B **30**
Maidford Clo. *M4* 2B **70**
Maidford Clo. *Stret* 2C **97**
Maidstone Av. *M21* 3A **98**
Maidstone M. *M21* 3A **98**
Main Av. *M19* 2D **119**
Maine Rd. *M14* 4C **85**
   (in two parts)
Mainhill Wlk. *M40* 2C **57**
Main Pde. *Swin* 2B **30**
Mainprice Clo. *Salf* 3D **49**
Main Rd. *Swin* 3B **16**
Main St. *Fail* 2B **42**
Mainwood Sq. *M13* 1D **85** (5E **11**)
Maitland Av. *M21* 4C **115**
Major St. *M1* 3C **69** (2C **10**)
Major Wlk. Salf *3B 66*
   (off Robert Hall St.)
Makepeace Wlk. *M8* 4A **20**
Makin St. *M1* 3C **69** (3C **10**)
Makkah Clo. *M40* 2A **56**
Malbrook Wlk. M13 . . . . *2A 86*
   (off Jessel Clo.)
Malcolm Av. *Swin* 3C **15**
Malcolm Dri. *Swin* 4C **15**
Maldon Cres. *Swin* 4B **30**
Maldon Dri. *Eccl* 3A **46**
Maldwyn Av. *M8* 4C **21**
Maleham Bourne. *Salf* 4A **36**
Malford Dri. *M8* 4B **36**
Malimson Bourne. Salf *1D 51*
   (off Gt. Cheetham St. W.)
Mallaig Wlk. *Open* 3C **73**
Mallard Ct. *Salf* 3B **64**
Mallard Clo. *M1* 4C **69** (4C **10**)
Malley Wlk. M9 . . . . *3C 23*
   (off Greendale Dri.)
Mallow St. *M15* 2A **84**
Mall, The. *Eccl* 1B **62**
Mall, The. *Sale* 4D **111**

Mallus Ct. *Salf* 4A **50**
Malpas St. *M12* 2A **88**
Malpas Wlk. *M16* 3D **83**
Malta St. *M4* 2B **70**
Malton Av. *M21* 1B **114**
Malt St. *M15* 1D **83** (5C **8**)
Malvern Av. *Urm* 1B **92**
Malvern Clo. *P'wich* 1C **19**
Malvern Clo. *Swin* 1B **48**
Malvern Dri. *Swin* 4B **32**
Malvern Gro. *M20* 3C **117**
Malvern Gro. *Salf* 4A **48**
Malvern Rd. *Midd* 1D **23**
Malvern Row *M15* 2D **83**
Malvern St. *M15* 2D **83**
Mamucium Roman Fort
   . . . . 3E **9**
Manby Rd. *M18* 4B **88**
Manby Sq. *M18* 4B **88**
Mancentral Trad. Est.
   Salf 2D **67** (1D **9**)
Manchester 2C **69** (5C **6**)
Manchester Aquatics Cen.
   . . . . 1C **85** (5D **11**)
Manchester Cathedral
   . . . . 1B **68** (4B **6**)
Manchester Cathedral
   Vis. Cen. 1B **68** (4B **6**)
Manchester City
   Art Gallery 2C **69** (1C **10**)
Manchester City
   Football Club. 1D **71**
Manchester College of Arts &
   Technology. 5E **5**
Manchester Crematorium.
   M21 . . . . 3C **115**
Manchester Ind. Cen.
   M3 . . . . 3D **67** (2D **9**)
Manchester Jewish Mus.
   . . . . 3C **53**
Manchester Metropolitan University.
   . . . . 4A **86**
   (Elizabeth Gaskell Campus)
Manchester Metropolitan University.
   . . . . 1C **85** (5C **10**)
   (Faculty of Humanities &
               Social Science)
Manchester Metropolitan University.
   . . . . 3D **69** (2E **11**)
   (Faculty of Management & Business)
Manchester Metropolitan University.
   . . . . 4C **69** (4C **10**)
   (Faculty of Science & Engineering)
Manchester Metropolitan University.
   . . . . 2B **102**
   (Hollings Campus)
Manchester Mus., The 2D **85**
Manchester New Rd. *Midd* 1C **23**
   (in two parts)

Manchester Rd. *M21* 3B **98**
    (Barlow Moor Rd.)
Manchester Rd. *M21* 4A **98**
    (Wilbraham Rd.)
Manchester Rd. *Aud & Ash L* . . . 4C **75**
Manchester Rd. *Dent* 4C **91**
Manchester Rd. *Droy* 2A **74**
Manchester Rd. *Kear & Swin* 1C **13**
Manchester Rd. *Oldh & Chad* . . . 4D **27**
Manchester Rd. *Stoc* 4C **121**
Manchester Rd. *Swin* 3C **31**
Manchester Rd. *Wors* 4A **12**
Manchester Science Pk. *M15* . . . 3C **85**
Manchester St Ann's
    Church 2B **68** (5B **6**)
Manchester St. *M16* 3C **83**
Manchester Town
    Hall 2B **68** (1B **10**)
Manchester United
    Football Club 3D **81**
    (Old Trafford)
Manchester United
    Mus. & Tour 3D **81**
    (North Stand)
Manchester Vis.
    Info. Cen. 2B **68** (1B **10**)
Mancroft Wlk. *M1* 4D **69** (4E **11**)
Mancunian Way.
    M15 & M12 . . . . 1A **84** (5E **9**)
    (in two parts)
Mandarin Wlk. *Salf.* 4A **50**
Mandeville St. *M19* 1B **120**
Mandley Av. *M40* 4D **25**
Mandley Pk. Av. *Salf.* 3A **36**
Manet Clo. *Salf* 2B **34**
Mangle St. *M1* 2D **69** (5E **7**)
Mango Pl. *Salf.* 1A **66**
Manifold St. *Salf.* 2B **50**
Manilla Wlk. *M11* 2D **71**
Manipur St. *M11* 3D **71**
Manley Av. *Swin.* 2A **14**
Manley Park 2C **99**
Manley Rd. *M21 & M16* 3C **99**
Manley St. *Salf.* 1D **51**
Mannington Dri. *M9* 3A **38**
Manor Av. *M16* 2D **99**
Manor Av. *Sale.* 4D **109**
Manor Av. *Urm* 3D **93**
Manor Ct. *Sale.* 4D **109**
Manor Ct. *Stret* 3D **95**
Manordale Wlk. *M40* 1A **54**
Manor Dri. *M21* 4D **115**
Manor Heath. *Salf* 2C **35**
Manor Ind. Est. *Stret* 4A **96**
Manor Lodge. *Swin* 2B **32**
Manor Pk. *Urm* 3D **93**
Manor Rd. *Aud* 4D **75**
Manor Rd. *Droy.* 2A **74**
Manor Rd. *Lev.* 2B **104**

Manor Rd. *Sale* 4D **111**
Manor Rd. *Salf.* 3B **48**
Manor Rd. *Stoc* 4D **123**
Manor Rd. *Stret.* 3D **95**
Manor Rd. *Swin.* 1B **46**
Manor St. *M12* 4A **70** (4F **11**)
    (in two parts)
Manor St. *Kear.* 1B **12**
Mansfield Av. *M9* 2B **22**
Mansfield Dri. *M9* 2C **23**
Mansfield Rd. *M9.* 2B **22**
Mansfield Rd. *Urm.* 3B **92**
Mansford Dri. *M40* 2D **55**
Manshaw Cres. *Aud* 4C **75**
Manshaw Rd. *M11.* 4C **75**
Manson Av. *M15* 1D **83** (5C **8**)
Manstead Wlk. *M40.* 1C **71**
Manswood Dri. *M8* 3C **37**
Mantell Wlk. *M40.* 2A **56**
Manthorpe Av. *Wors.* 3A **28**
Manton Av. *M9* 4B **24**
Manton Av. *Dent* 1C **107**
Manton Clo. *Salf.* 4B **36**
Manton Ho. *Stoc* 4D **123**
Manwaring St. *Fail.* 2A **42**
Maple Av. *M21.* 4B **98**
Maple Av. *Dent* 2D **75**
Maple Av. *Eccl.* 3A **44**
Maple Av. *Stret* 3B **96**
Maple Clo. *Kear.* 1A **12**
Maple Clo. *Salf.* 4D **49**
Maple Ct. *M16.* 4B **82**
Maple Ct. *Stoc.* 4C **121**
Mapledon Rd. *M9.* 2D **39**
Maple Gro. *M40.* 4B **26**
Maple Gro. *Fail.* 2A **58**
Maple Rd. *Swin* 1A **46**
Maple St. *Oldh.* 3D **27**
Maplin Clo. *M13* 1A **86** (5F **11**)
Marble St. *M2.* 2C **69** (5C **6**)
    (in two parts)
Marbury Av. *M14.* 3D **101**
Marbury Rd. *Stoc* 3D **121**
Marcer Rd. *M40.* 1B **70**
Marchers M. *Eccl.* 2B **60**
Marchioness St. *M18.* 2B **90**
Marchmont Clo. *M13.* 2B **86**
Marchwood Av. *M21.* 3D **99**
Marcliffe Dri. *M19.* 3C **105**
Marcus Garvey Ct. *M16.* 2A **100**
Marcus Gro. *M14.* 2A **102**
Mardale Av. *M20.* 4A **118**
Mardale Av. *Swin.* 4C **13**
Mardale Av. *Urm.* 1A **92**
Mardale Rd. *Swin.* 4D **29**
Margaret Ashton Clo. *M9.* 3D **39**
Margaret Rd. *Droy.* 1A **74**
Margaret St. *Oldh.* 4D **27**
Margaret St. *Stoc.* 2A **122**

Margate Av. *M40* 2B **56**
Margate Rd. *Stoc* 2B **122**
Margrove Clo. *Fail* 3D **43**
Margrove Rd. *Salf* 3A **48**
Marguerita Rd. *M40* 3D **57**
(in two parts)
Marham Clo. *M21* 2A **116**
Marie St. *Salf* 3A **36**
Mariman Dri. *M8* 4C **21**
Marina Cres. *M11* 4B **56**
Marina Rd. *Droy* 1D **75**
Marjorie Clo. *M18* 2B **88**
Mark Av. *Salf* 3B **50**
Markendale St. *Salf* 2A **82**
Market Brow. *M9* 4B **22**
Market Cen., The.
M2 . . . . 2C **69** (5C **6**)
Market Pl. *Droy* 2C **75**
Market Pl. *Swin* 1C **31**
Market St. *M1* 1B **68** (4B **6**)
(in three parts)
Market St. *Droy* 3C **75**
Market St. *Swin* 1C **31**
Market Wlk. *Sale* 4D **111**
Market Way. M4 . . . . *1C* ***69*** *(4C* ***6****)*
(off Arndale Shop. Cen.)
Market Way. *Salf* 4D **49**
Markfield Av. *M13* 3B **86**
Markham Clo. *M12* 3B **70**
Markington St. *M14* 1C **101**
Mark Jones Wlk. *M40* 2B **56**
Mark La. M4 . . . . *1C* ***69*** *(4C* ***6****)*
(off Withy Gro.)
Marland Cres. *Stoc* 1B **122**
Marland St. *Chad* 3C **27**
Marlborough Av. *M16* 2C **99**
Marlborough Ct. *M8* 1B **20**
Marlborough Dri. *Fail* 4A **42**
Marlborough Dri. *Stoc* 4D **121**
Marlborough Gro. *Droy* 1D **75**
Marlborough Rd. *Eccl* 3C **47**
Marlborough Rd. *Sale* 4D **111**
Marlborough Rd. *Salf* 4B **36**
(in two parts)
Marlborough Rd. *Stret* 1A **96**
Marley Dri. *Sale* 3C **111**
Marleyer St. *M40* 3C **41**
Marley Rd. *M19* 1B **120**
Marlfield St. *M9* 1C **39**
Marlinford Dri. *M40* 2C **57**
Marlow Clo. *Urm* 4B **76**
(in four parts)
Marlow Dri. *Swin* 1A **46**
Marlowe Pl. M11 . . . . *3C* ***71***
(off Bellew St.)
Marlow Ho. Salf *2D* ***65***
(off Amersham St.)
Marlow Rd. *M9* 1D **39**

Marlton Wlk. *M9* *3C* ***23***
(off Leconfield Dri.)
Marmion Dri. *M21* 1A **114**
Marple Gro. *Stret* 1A **96**
Marple St. *M15* 3D **83**
Marquis St. *M19* 3D **105**
Marriott's Ct. *M2* 2C **69** (5C **6**)
Marriott St. *M20* 3D **117**
Marryat Ct. M12 . . . . *2D* ***87***
(off Gregory St.)
Marsden Ct. M4 . . . . *1C* ***69*** *(4C* ***6****)*
(off Arndale Shop. Cen.)
Marsden St. *M2* 2B **68** (5B **6**)
Marsden St. *Eccl* 4C **45**
Marsden St. *Wors* 4B **12**
Marsden Way. M4 . . . . . . *1C* ***69*** *(4C* ***6****)*
(off Arndale Shop. Cen.)
Marshall Rd. *M19* 3A **104**
Marshall Stevens Way. *Traf P* 2D **79**
Marshall St. *M4* 1D **69** (3E **7**)
Marshall St. *M12* 2A **86**
Marsham Clo. *M13* 3C **87**
Marshbrook Rd. *Urm* 1C **93**
Marshfield Wlk. M13 . . . . *2A* ***86***
(off Lauderdale Cres.)
Marsland Clo. *Dent* 1D **107**
Marsland St. N. *Salf* 3B **36**
Marsland St. S. *Salf* 3B **36**
Marston Clo. *Fail* 4D **43**
Marston Ho. Salf *2D* ***65***
(off Cypress Clo.)
Marston Rd. *Salf* 2A **36**
Marston Rd. *Stret* 2D **97**
Marsworth Dri. *M4* 1A **70**
Martindale Cres. *M12* 2C **87**
Martin Ho. *M14* 1B **102**
Martin Rd. *Swin* 4D **15**
Martin St. *Salf* 1B **64**
Martlesham Wlk. M4 . . . . . 1C **69** (4D **7**)
Martlet Clo. *M14* 3D **101**
Marton Grange. *P'wich* 3D **19**
Marton Gro. *Stoc* 3A **122**
Marvic Ct. *M13* 1C **103**
Maryfield Ct. *M16* 4A **100**
Mary France St. *M15* 2A **84** (5E **9**)
Mary St. *M3* 4B **52** (1F **5**)
Mary St. *Droy* 2D **75**
Masboro St. *M8* 3B **36**
Masefield Av. *P'wich* 3D **17**
Masefield Cres. *Droy* 2C **75**
Masefield Gro. *Stoc* 3A **106**
Masefield Rd. *Droy* 2C **75**
Mason St. *M4* 1D **69** (3E **7**)
Mason St. *Salf* 1D **67** (4D **5**)
Massey Av. *Fail* 2D **43**
Massey St. *Salf* 2C **67** (5B **4**)
Matham Wlk. M15 . . . . . 2C **85** (5C **10**)
(off Chevril Clo.)

Mather Av. *Eccl* 1A 62
Mather Av. *P'wich* 1C 35
Mather Rd. *Eccl* 1A 62
Mather St. *Fail* 3D 41
Mather Way. *Salf* 4A 50
Matisse Way. *Salf* 2B 34
Matlock Av. *M20* 3B 116
Matlock Av. *Sale* 3A 34
Matlock Av. *Urm* 1B 108
Matlock Rd. *Stoc* 3C 107
Matlock Rd. *Stret* 1C 95
Matlock St. *Eccl* 3C 61
Matt Busby Clo. *Swin* 3D 31
Matthews La. *M19* 2A 104
Matthew's St. *M12* 1D 87
Matthias Ct. *Salf* 4D 51 (2C 4)
Mattison St. *M11* 1A 90
Mauldeth Rd. *M19 & Stoc* . . . 4D 119
Mauldeth Rd. *M20 & M14* . . . 2A 118
Mauldeth Rd. W. *M21 & M20* . 3C 115
Maureen Av. *M8* 2C 37
Maurice Dri. *Salf* 3D 49
Maurice Pariser Wlk. *M8* 3B 36
Maurice St. *Salf* 3D 49
Mawdsley Dri. *M8* 2A 38
Max Woosnam Wlk. *M14* 1C 101
Mayan Av. *Salf* 1D 67 (3D 5)
Mayberth Av. *M8* 4C 21
Maybrook Wlk. *M9* 2B 38
Maybury St. *M18* 2A 90
Maycroft. *Stoc* 3D 123
Maycroft Av. *M20* 4A 118
May Dri. *M19* 3D 119
Mayes Ct. M14 . . . . 2B 118
(off Sheringham Rd.)
Mayes Gdns. *M4* 2B 70
Mayes St. *M4* 1C 69 (3C 6)
(in two parts)
Mayfair. *Salf* 1C 35
Mayfair Av. *Salf* 4D 47
Mayfair Av. *Urm* 2B 92
Mayfair Ct. *M14* 4A 102
Mayfair Cres. *Fail* 2D 43
Mayfield Av. *Stoc* 4B 122
Mayfield Av. *Stret* 3D 95
Mayfield Av. *Swin* 4C 29
Mayfield Gro. *M18* 4B 90
Mayfield Gro. *Stoc* 4B 122
Mayfield Mans. *M16* 1A 100
Mayfield Rd. *M16* 1A 100
Mayfield Rd. *Salf* 1B 34
Mayflower Av. *Salf* 3A 66
Mayford Rd. *M19* 2A 104
May Gro. *M19* 1B 120
Mayhill Dri. *Salf* 3C 47
Mayhill Dri. *Wors* 2A 28
Mayorlowe Av. *Stoc* 4D 123
Mayo St. *M12* 3B 70

Maypool Dri. *Stoc* 3B 122
May Rd. *M16* 1D 99
May Rd. *Swin* 4D 31
Maysmith M. *Salf* 4D 35
May St. *M40* 2C 57
(in two parts)
May St. *Eccl* 3C 45
May St. *Oldh* 2D 27
Mayton St. *M11* 3A 72
Mayville Dri. *M20* 4D 117
Meachin Av. *M21* 4C 115
Meade Clo. *Urm* 2C 93
Meade Gro. *M13* 1D 103
Meade Hill Rd. *P'wich* 3A 20
Meade, The. *M21* 2B 114
Meadfoot Av. *P'wich* 3C 19
Meadfoot Rd. *M18* 2D 89
Meadon Av. *Swin* 1D 31
Meadow Bank. *M21* 2A 114
Meadowbank Clo. *Fail* 4C 43
Mdw. Bank Ct. *Stret* 3C 95
Meadowburn Nook. *Eccl* 3B 44
Meadow Clo. *Stret* 3C 97
Meadow Ct. *M21* 4D 97
Meadow Ct. *Salf* 4D 47
Meadowgate. *Salf* 1A 64
Meadowgate. *Urm* 3D 93
Meadowgate. *Wors* 2A 28
Meadowgate Rd. *Salf* 4D 47
Meadow La. *Wors* 2A 44
Meadow Rd. *Salf* . . . 4C 51 (1B 4)
Meadow Rd. *Urm* 3D 93
Meadows Rd. *Sale* 3A 112
Meadows Rd. *Stoc* 3C 121
(in two parts)
Meadows, The. *P'wich* 2B 18
Meadow Way. *M40* 1A 40
Mead, The. *Salf* 1B 64
Meadway. *Chad* 4A 26
Medlock Leisure Cen. 1D 75
Medlock Rd. *Fail* 3B 58
Medlock St. *M15* . . . 4B 68 (4A 10)
Medlock St. *Droy* 1C 75
Medlock Vale 3C 59
Medway Clo. *Salf* 4B 48
Medway Dri. *Kear* 1B 12
Medway Wlk. *M40* 4B 54
Meech St. *M11* 3C 73
Mee's Sq. *Eccl* 3C 61
Melanie Dri. *Stoc* 4B 106
Melba St. *Open* 3A 74
Melbourne Av. *Stret* 2B 96
Melbourne M. *Salf* 2A 52
Melbourne St. *M9* 2C 39
Melbourne St. *M15* . . . 1A 84 (4E 9)
Melbourne St. *Salf* 2D 51
Melbourne St. *Stoc* 4B 106

Melbourne St. *Swin* 2D **31**
Meldon Rd. *M13* 2C **103**
Meldreth Dri. *M12* 4D **87**
Melford Av. *M40* 1A **42**
Melfort Av. *Stret* 3C **97**
Melksham Clo. *Salf* 1B **66**
Melland Av. *M21* 4C **115**
Melland Rd. *M18* 1C **105**
Melland Sports Cen. 1C **105**
Meller Rd. *M13* 2D **103**
Melling Av. *Stoc* 3A **122**
Melling St. *M12* 4A **88**
Mellors Rd. *Traf P* 1D **79**
Mellor St. M12. . . . . *3A **70***
(off N. Western St.)
Mellor St. *M40.* 4B **54**
Mellor St. *Droy.* 2B **74**
Mellor St. *Eccl.* 2D **61**
Mellor St. *Fail.* 4D **41**
Mellor St. *P'wich* 2D **17**
Mellor St. *Stret* 4C **81**
Mellor Way. *Chad.* 2D **27**
Mellowstone Dri. *M21* 4B **100**
Melloy Pl. *M8.* 3C **53**
Melmerby Ct. *Salf* 2D **65**
Melon Pl. *Salf* 1B **66**
Melrose Apartments. M14 . . . . *4A **86***
(off Hathersage Rd.)
Melrose Av. *Eccl.* 3A **44**
Melrose St. *Chad.* 2C **27**
Melrose St. *M40* 2C **57**
Meltham Av. *M20.* 3C **117**
Melton Av. *Dent.* 1C **107**
Melton Rd. *M8.* 1A **36**
Melton St. *M9* 1D **39**
Melverley Rd. *M9.* 1C **21**
Melville Clo. *M11.* 1A **90**
Melville Rd. *Stret.* 1D **95**
Melville St. *Salf.* 1D **67** (4D **5**)
M.E.N. Arena 4B **52** (2B **6**)
(Manchester Evening News Arena)
Mendip Clo. *Chad.* 1C **27**
Menston Av. *M40.* 1A **42**
Mentor Ct. *M13.* 1D **103**
Menzies Ct. *M21* 3B **98**
Mercer Rd. *M18.* 3D **89**
Mercer St. *M19* 3B **104**
Mercer St. *Droy.* 1D **75**
Merchants Quay. *Salf.* 2D **81**
Merchants Quay Ct. *Eccl.* 4C **45**
Mercury Bus. Pk. *Urm* 2B **78**
Mercury Way. *Urm.* 3B **78**
Mere Av. *Droy.* 3A **74**
Mere Av. *Salf.* 1C **65**
Mere Clo. *Dent.* 2D **107**
Meredew Av. Swin 1A **46**
Meredith Ct. M15. . . . . *2C **85***
(off Epsley Clo.)

Meredith St. *M14.* 2B **118**
Mere Dri. *Swin.* 4C **15**
Mereside Wlk. *M15* 2D **83**
Meriton Wlk. *M18* 4B **88**
Merlewood Av. *M19* 2C **121**
Merlewood Av. *Dent.* 2D **75**
Merlewood Dri. *Swin* 4C **29**
Merlin Dri. *Swin.* 4D **15**
Merlyn Av. *Sale* 3A **112**
Merridge Wlk. *M8* 4B **36**
Merrill St. *M4.* 2B **70**
Merriman St. *M16.* 4A **84**
Merrow Wlk. M1 . . . . . 4D **69** (4E **11**)
(off Grosvenor St.)
Merry Bower Rd. *Salf.* 2A **36**
Merrydale Av. *Eccl* 3A **46**
Merseybank Av. *M21* 4D **115**
Mersey Rd. *Sale.* 3D **111**
Mersey Rd. Ind. Est. *Fail* 1D **43**
Mersey Rd. N. *Fail.* 1C **43**
Mersey St. *Open* 3A **74**
(in two parts)
Mersey Valley Vis. Cen. 4D **113**
Mersey Valley Vis. Cen.
Nature Reserve 3D **113**
Mersy Ct. *Sale* 4C **113**
Merton Dri. *Droy* 2A **74**
Merton Gro. *Chad.* 3D **25**
Merton Rd. *P'wich* 1C **19**
Merton Rd. *Sale.* 4C **111**
Merton Wlk. M9. . . . . *3C **39***
(off Nethervale Dri.)
Merville Av. *M40* 1D **39**
Mervyn Rd. *Salf.* 4A **34**
Merwood Gro. *M14.* 4C **87**
Mesnefield Rd. *Salf* 2A **34**
Metfield Wlk. *M40.* 4D **25**
Methuen St. *M12.* 1B **104**
Metroplex Bus. Pk. *Salf.* 3C **65**
Mews, The. *M40.* 4D **55**
Mews, The. *P'wich.* 3B **18**
Meyrick Rd. *Salf.* 4A **50**
Michigan Av. *Salf.* 3D **65**
Mickleby Wlk. *M40.* 4B **54**
Middlebourne St. *Salf.* 1C **65**
Middlegate. *M40.* 3D **25**
Middleham St. *M14.* 2C **101**
Middlesex Rd. *M9* 4B **22**
Middlesex Rd. *Stoc.* 3D **123**
Middlestone Dri. *M9.* 3B **38**
Middleton Av. *Fail.* 3B **42**
Middleton Old Rd. *M9* 3B **22**
Middleton Rd. *M8 & Midd* 1B **36**
(in two parts)
Middleton Rd. *Stoc.* 2B **106**
Middlewich Wlk. *M18.* 3C **89**
Middlewood St. *Salf* . . . 2C **67** (1B **8**)
Middlewood Wlk. *M9.* 3B **38**

National Squash Cen. 1D **71**
Naunton Wlk. *M9.* 2C **39**
Naval St. *M4.* 1A **70** (3F **7**)
Nave Ct. *Salf* 3D **49**
Navenby Av. *M16.* 4C **83**
Naylor Ct. *M40.* 4A **54**
Naylor St. *M40.* 4B **54**
Naze Wlk. *Stoc.* 3D **123**
Neale Rd. *M21.* 2A **114**
Neary Way. *Urm.* 3C **77**
Neden Clo. *M11.* 3B **72**
Needham Av. *M21.* 4B **98**
Needwood Clo. *M40.* 2B **54**
Needwood St. *M40.* 1B **54**
Neenton Sq. *M12.* 1A **88**
Neill St. *Salf.* 3A **52**
Neilston Av. *M40.* 3B **40**
Nell La. *M21 & M20.* 2C **115**
Nelson Av. *Eccl* 4D **45**
Nelson Clo. *M15.* 4A **84**
Nelson Ct. *M40.* 3B **54**
Nelson Dri. *Droy.* 1D **73**
Nelson Fold. *Swin* 1C **31**
Nelson Mandela Ct. M16 . . . . *1A* **100**
(off Range Rd.)
Nelson Rd. *M9.* 1B **22**
Nelson St. *M4.* 4C **53** (2D **7**)
Nelson St. *M13.* 3D **85**
Nelson St. *Eccl* 1D **61**
Nelson St. *Mile P.* 3B **54**
Nelson St. *Salf* (M5) 2C **65**
Nelson St. *Salf* (M7) 2D **51**
Nelson St. *Stret* 3B **96**
Nelson Way. *Chad* 2D **27**
Nelstrop Cres. *Stoc* 3D **121**
Nelstrop Rd. *Stoc.* 3D **121**
Nelstrop Rd. N. *Stoc & Man.* . . 2C **121**
Nelstrop Wlk. *Stoc.* 3C **121**
Nepaul Rd. *M9.* 1C **39**
Neptune Gdns. *Salf* 2C **51**
Neston Av. *M20.* 3C **117**
Neston St. *M11.* 1B **90**
Netherbury Clo. *M18* 1C **105**
Nether St. *M12.* 3A **70** (3F **11**)
Netherton Rd. *M14.* 3C **101**
Nethervale Dri. *M9.* 3C **39**
Netherwood. *Fail.* 2D **43**
Nettleford Rd. *M16.* 1A **116**
Nettleton Gro. *M9.* 1D **39**
Nevile Ct. *Salf.* 2B **34**
Nevile Rd. *Salf.* 2B **34**
Neville Cardus Wlk. M14 . . . . . *2A* **102**
(off Taylor St.)
Nevin Clo. *Oldh* 4D **27**
Nevin Rd. *M40.* 1D **41**
New Allen St. *M40.* 4A **54**
Newark Av. *M14.* 1D **101**
Newark Rd. *Stoc* 4B **122**

Newark Rd. *Swin* 4D **15**
New Bailey St. *Salf.* 2A **68** (4E **5**)
New Bank St. *M12.* 2C **87**
Newbank Tower. *Salf* 4A **52** (1E **5**)
New Barns Av. *M21.* 3C **115**
New Barton St. *Salf.* 2A **48**
Newbeck St. *M4.* 1C **69** (3D **7**)
Newbold Wlk. Man. *2B* **84**
(off Clarendon St.)
New Bri. St. *Salf.* 4B **52** (2A **6**)
Newburn Av. *M9.* 2D **23**
Newbury Dri. *Eccl* 4B **44**
Newbury Dri. *Urm.* 3C **77**
Newbury Pl. *Salf.* 3D **35**
Newbury Wlk. M9 . . . . *4B* **38**
(off Ravelston Dri.)
Newcastle St. *M15.* 1B **84** (5B **10**)
(in two parts)
New Cathedral St. *M3* 1B **68** (4B **6**)
New Century Ho. *Dent* 2D **107**
Newchurch St. *M11.* 3D **71**
Newcliffe Rd. *M9.* 2D **23**
Newcombe Clo. *M11.* 2D **71**
Newcombe Ct. *Sale* 4B **110**
Newcombe St. *M3.* 4B **52** (1B **6**)
Newcroft. *Fail.* 4D **43**
Newcroft Cres. *Urm.* 3B **94**
Newcroft Dri. *Urm.* 3C **95**
Newcroft Rd. *Urm.* 3B **94**
New Cross. *M4.* 1D **69** (4E **7**)
New Cross St. *Salf.* 1A **64**
New Cross St. *Swin* 3C **31**
Newdale Rd. *M19.* 2B **104**
New Elizabeth St. *M8.* 2C **53**
New Elm Rd. *M3.* 3D **67** (2D **9**)
Newgate St. *M4.* 1C **69** (3D **7**)
New Hall Av. *Eccl.* 4A **60**
New Hall Av. *Salf.* 2D **35**
New Hall Rd. *Salf.* 2D **35**
Newhall Rd. *Stoc.* 2C **107**
Newham Av. *M11.* 1B **72**
Newhaven Av. *M11.* 1B **90**
Newhaven Bus. Pk. *Eccl.* 2A **62**
New Herbert St. *Salf.* 2A **48**
Newholme Ct. *Stret* 2C **97**
Newholme Rd. *M20.* 4B **116**
Newick Wlk. M9. . . . . *3C* **23**
(off Leconfield Dri.)
Newington Av. *M8.* 3B **20**
New Islington. *M4.* 1A **70**
New Kings Head Yd.
Salf. 1B **68** (3A **6**)
(off Chapel St.)
Newlands. *Fail.* 3A **58**
Newlands Av. *Eccl.* 3A **60**
Newlands Dri. *P'wich* 1A **18**
Newlands Dri. *Swin* 4A **32**
Newland St. *M8.* 1D **37**

New La. *Eccl* 2B **60**
New Lawns. *Stoc* 3C **107**
Newlyn St. *M14* 2D **101**
New Market. *M2* 2B **68** (5B **6**)
New Mkt. La. *M2* 2C **69** (5C **6**)
Newmarket M. *Salf* 1D **51**
Newmill Wlk. *M8* *4B 36*
(off Alderford Pde.)
New Moston **1A 42**
New Mount St. *M4* 4C **53** (2D **7**)
New Oak Clo. *Fail* 2D **43**
New Park Rd. *Salf* 1B **82**
. . . . 1C **53**
Newpark Wlk. *M8* *1C 53*
(off Magnolia Dri.)
Newport Av. *Stoc* 2A **122**
Newport Rd. *M21* 3A **98**
Newport St. *M14* 1D **101**
Newport St. *Salf.* 1C **65**
Newquay Av. *Stoc* 2A **122**
New Quay St. *Salf* 2A **68** (1E **9**)
Newry Rd. *Eccl* 3A **62**
Newry Wlk. *M9* 3D **21**
Newsham Wlk. *M12* 1B **104**
Newsholme St. *M8* 3B **36**
New Smithfield Mkt. *M11* 1C **89**
Newstead Av. *M20* 4B **118**
Newstead Rd. *Urm* 1A **94**
New St. *M40* 3C **55**
New St. *Droy* 3C **75**
New St. *Eccl* 2C **61**
New St. *Swin* 1C **31**
New Thomas St. *Salf* 3A **50**
Newton Av. *Long* 4D **87**
Newton Av. *Wthtn* 3C **117**
Newton Heath **2B 56**
Newtonmore Wlk. *Open* 2B **72**
Newton Rd. *Fail* 3A **58**
Newton Rd. *Urm* 2C **93**
Newton St. *M1* 2D **69** (5E **7**)
Newton St. *M40* 1C **57**
Newton St. *Droy* 4D **59**
Newton St. *Fail.* 4C **41**
Newton St. *Stret.* 3B **96**
Newtown **3D 53**
(Manchester)
Newtown **4A 14**
(Swinton)
Newtown Clo. *M11.* 3B **72**
Newtown Clo. *Swin* 4B **14**
Newtown Ct. *M40* 3A **54** (1F **7**)
Newtown Ct. *P'wich* 2C **19**
Newtown M. *P'wich* 2C **19**
Newtown St. *P'wich* 2C **19**
New Union St. *M4* 1A **70**
New Viaduct St. *M11* 1C **71**
Nevville Dri. *M20.* 4B **118**
New Vine St. *M15* 2B **84** (5A **10**)
New Wakefield St. *M1* . . . 4C **69** (4C **10**)

New Welcome St. *M15.* . . . 2B **84** (5F **9**)
New Windsor **1B 66** (5A **4**)
Nicholas Cft. *M4* 1C **69** (4D **7**)
Nicholas Owen Clo. *M11* 3C **73**
Nicholas St. *M1.* 2C **69** (1C **10**)
Nicholls St. *M12* 2B **86**
Nicholls St. *Salf.* 4B **50**
Nico Ditch. *M18* 2C **105**
Nicolas Rd. *M21* 3A **98**
Nigel Rd. *M9* 3D **39**
Nightingale St. *M3.* 4B **52** (2A **6**)
Nile Ter. *Salf* 2D **51**
Nimble Nook. **1C 27**
Nimble Nook. *Chad* 1C **27**
Nina Dri. *M40* 3C **25**
Nine Acre Ct. *Salf.* 1B **82**
Nine Acre Dri. *Salf* 1B **82**
Niven St. *M12* 4A **70**
Nixon St. *Fail.* 3A **42**
Nolan St. *M9* 3C **39**
Nona St. *Salf* 1C **65**
Nook, The. *Eccl* 4A **44**
Nook, The. *Urm* 3D **93**
Nook, The. *Wors* 2A **28**
Norbet Wlk. *M9* 3C **39**
Norbreck Av. *M21* 2B **114**
Norburn Rd. *M13.* 2D **103**
Norbury Av. *Salf.* 2B **48**
Norbury Clo. *M40* 3C **55**
Norbury Gro. *Swin* 1B **30**
Norbury St. *Salf.* 1A **52**
Norcliffe Wlk. *M18* 4B **88**
Norcot Wlk. *M15* 2D **83**
Norden Av. *M20.* 3C **117**
Noreen Av. *P'wich* 1C **19**
Norfolk Av. *M18.* 4C **89**
Norfolk Av. *Dent.* 1B **106**
Norfolk Av. *Droy.* 4B **58**
Norfolk Av. *Stoc.* 3C **121**
Norfolk Cres. *Fail.* 4A **42**
Norfolk Ho. *Salf.* 1A **36**
Norfolk Rd. *M18* 4C **89**
Norfolk St. *M2.* 2B **68** (5B **6**)
Norfolk St. *Oldh.* 2D **27**
(in two parts)
Norfolk St. *Salf* 2A **50**
Norland Wlk. *M40* 2D **55**
Norley Av. *Stret* 1D **97**
Norley Dri. *M19* 2C **105**
Normanby Gro. *Swin* 1A **30**
Normanby St. *M14.* 4C **85**
Normanby St. *Swin* 1A **30**
Norman Gro. *M12* 4D **87**
Norman Gro. *Stoc* 2A **122**
Norman Rd. *M14.* 2B **102**
Norman Rd. *Salf* 3A **36**
Norman Rd. W. *M9* 3D **39**
Norman St. *M12* 3B **88**

Norman St. *Fail* 1C 43
Normanton Av. *Salf* 4A 48
Normanton Dri. *M9* 3C 23
Northallerton Rd. *Salf*. 4B 34
Northampton Rd. *M40* 1D 55
North Av. *M19* 2D 119
Northavon Clo. Eccl 2C 63
         (off Kearton Dri.)
Northbank Gdns. *M19* 3C 119
Northbank Ho. *Wors* 2A 44
N. Blackfield La. *Salf* 2C 35
Northbourne St. *Salf* 1C 65
Northbrook Av. *M8* 2B 20
N. Broughton St. *Salf*. . . . 1A 68 (4E 5)
N. Clifden La. *Salf* 4A 36
North Cres. *M11* 4D 57
Northdale Rd. *M9* 1D 21
N. Dean St. *Swin* 1C 31
Northdown Av. *M15*. 2D 83
North Dri. *Aud*. 2D 75
North Dri. *Swin* 3D 31
Northenden Rd. *Sale* 4D 111
Northen Gro. *M20* 4B 116
Northerly Cres. *M40*. 3D 25
Northern Av. *Swin* 3A 16
Northern Tennis Club 4C 117
Northfield Av. *M40*. 4B 26
Northfield Rd. *M40* 4B 26
Northfleet Rd. *Eccl*. 2A 60
N. George St. *Salf* 4D 51 (2C 4)
North Gro. *M13* 3B 86
North Gro. *Urm* 3C 93
N. Hill St. *Salf* 4D 51 (2D 5)
Northland Rd. *M9* 3A 24
Northleigh Dri. *P'wich* 3D 19
Northleigh Ho. *M16* 2B 98
Northleigh Rd. *M16* 1B 98
N. Lonsdale St. *Stret* 1C 97
N. Manchester Bus. Pk. *M40* . . 4C 39
North Meade. *M21* 2B 114
Northmoor Rd. *M12*. 4A 88
Northolme Gdns. *M19* 4C 119
Northolt Ct. *M11* 1D 73
North Pde. *M3*. 2B 68 (5A 6)
N. Phoebe St. *Salf* 3A 66
North Reddish 3A 106
North Rd. *M11*. 1B 72
North Rd. *C'ton* 4A 108
North Rd. *P'wich*. 1D 17
North Rd. *Stret* 4C 79
North Stage. *Salf* 3D 65
N. Star Dri. *Salf*. 2D 67 (5C 4)
North St. *M8* 2C 53
Northumberland Clo. *M16* 3C 83
Northumberland Cres. *M16*. . . . 3C 83
Northumberland Rd. *M16*. 4C 83
Northumberland Rd. *Stoc*. 2D 123
Northumberland St. *Salf*. 3D 35

Northurst Dri. *M8*. 3B 20
Northway. *Droy* 3C 75
Northway. *Eccl*. 1B 62
North Way. *Stoc*. 3D 123
N. Western St. *M1 & M12* 3A 70
         (in two parts)
N. Western St. *Lev*. 4A 104
Northwold Dri. *M9* 3B 24
Norton Av. *M12*. 1B 104
Norton Av. *Dent*. 1C 107
Norton Av. *Sale* 3D 109
Norton Av. *Urm* 4D 77
Norton Grange. *P'wich* 3D 19
Norton St. *M1* 2A 70
Norton St. *Mile P*. 3C 55
Norton St. *Old T*. 4C 83
Norton St. *Salf* (M3). . . . 1B 68 (3A 6)
Norton St. *Salf* (M7). 3A 36
Norville Av. *M40* 3D 25
Norway St. *M11*. 3C 71
Norway St. *Salf* 1C 65
Norway St. *Stret* 1C 97
Norwich Rd. *Stret* 1B 94
Norwood. *P'wich* 4B 18
Norwood Av. *Salf*. 2B 34
Norwood Ct. *Stret* 3C 97
Norwood Dri. *Swin*. 3C 29
Norwood Lodge. *Salf* 2B 34
Norwood Rd. *Stret*. 3C 97
Nottingham Av. *Stoc*. 3D 123
Nottingham Clo. *Stoc*. 4D 123
Nottingham Dri. *Fail*. 2C 59
Nottingham Ter. *Stoc*. 3D 123
Nuneaton Dri. *M40*. 4B 54
Nuneham Av. *M20* 2A 118
Nunfield Clo. *M40* 4B 24
Nunthorpe Dri. *M8*. 2A 38
Nursery Clo. *Sale* 4B 112
Nursery Rd. *Fail*. 3C 43
Nursery Rd. *P'wich*. 1A 18
Nursery Rd. *Urm* 4A 76
Nursery St. *M16*. 1B 100
Nursery St. *Salf*. 4D 49
Nuthurst Rd. *M40* 1C 41
Nutsford Vale 4B 88
Nutsford Va. *M18*. 4B 88
Nuttall St. *M11*. 4A 72
Nuttall St. *M16*. 3C 83

O

Oadby Clo. *M12* 3A 88
Oak Av. *M21* 4B 98
Oak Bank. *M9* 2B 38
Oak Bank. *P'wich*. 1D 33
Oak Bank Av. *M9*. 1D 39
Oakdene. *Swin*. 1B 44

Oakdene Av. *Stoc*. 4D **121**
Oakdene St. *M9*. 2D **39**
Oak Dri. *M14*. 3B **102**
Oak Dri. *Dent*. 4C **91**
Oaker Av. *M20*. 4A **116**
Oakfield. *P'wich*. 3D **19**
Oakfield. *Sale*. 4C **111**
Oakfield Av. *Droy*. 2B **74**
Oakfield Av. *Firs*. 1A **98**
Oakfield Av. *Whal R*. 1D **99**
Oakfield Gro. *M18*. 4D **89**
Oakfield M. *Sale*. 4C **111**
Oakfield St. *M8*. 1C **53**
Oakford Av. *M40*. 4A **54**
Oak Gro. *Eccl*. 2B **60**
Oak Gro. *Urm*. 2A **94**
Oakham M. *Salf*. 1C **35**
Oakhill Ct. *Salf*. 3B **36**
Oakhill Way. *M8*. 3B **36**
Oakhouse Dri. *M21*. 2B **114**
Oakington Av. *M14*. 1D **101**
Oakland Av. *M16*. 4A **82**
Oakland Av. *M19*. 4C **119**
Oakland Av. *Salf*. 3C **47**
Oakland Ho. *M16*. 4A **82**
Oaklands Dri. *P'wich*. 2B **18**
Oaklands Dri. *Sale*. 4C **111**
Oaklands Ho. *M14*. 3A **102**
Oaklands Rd. *Salf*. 3A **34**
Oaklands Rd. *Swin*. 1D **45**
Oaklea Rd. *Sale*. 4A **110**
Oakleigh Av. *M19*. 2D **119**
Oakley Clo. *M20*. 2C **57**
Oakley St. *Salf*. 2B **64**
Oakmere Av. *Eccl*. 3C **45**
Oakmoor Dri. *Salf*. 2A **34**
Oakridge Wlk. *M9*. 3B **38**
Oak Rd. *M20*. 4D **117**
Oak Rd. *Fail*. 1B **58**
Oak Rd. *Sale*. 4B **112**
Oak Rd. *Salf*. 1C **51**
Oak St. *M4*. 1C **69** (4D **7**)
  (in two parts)
Oak St. *Eccl*. 2D **61**
Oak St. *Swin*. 1C **31**
Oakville Dri. *Salf*. 3C **47**
Oakville Ter. *M40*. 1D **39**
Oakwell Dri. *Salf*. 1A **36**
Oakwell Mans. *Salf*. 1A **36**
Oakwood. *Sale*. 4C **109**
Oakwood Av. *M40*. 1D **41**
Oakwood Av. *Swin*. 2A **14**
Oakwood Av. *Wors*. 4A **12**
Oakwood Dri. *Salf*. 2D **47**
Oakwood Dri. *Wors*. 4A **12**
Oakwood Est. *Salf*. 2B **64**
Oakwood Ho. *M21*. 1C **115**
Oakworth St. *M9*. 4A **22**

Oats Wlk. *M13*. 4A **86**
Oban Av. *M40*. 3B **56**
Oberon Clo. *Eccl*. 1D **61**
Ocean Wlk. *M15*. 3B **84**
Ockenden Dri. *M9*. 3C **39**
Octavia Dri. *M40*. 3C **57**
Odell St. *M11*. 4B **72**
Odessa Av. *Salf*. 3D **47**
Odette St. *M18*. 4C **89**
Ogbourne Wlk. M13. . . . . 2A 86
  (off Lauderdale Cres.)
Ogden La. *M11*. 1D **89**
Ogden Rd. *Fail*. 1B **58**
Ogden St. *P'wich*. 2C **19**
Ogden St. *Swin*. 3B **30**
Ogmore Wlk. *M40*. 4C **25**
Ogwen Dri. *P'wich*. 1B **18**
Ohio Av. *Salf*. 3D **65**
O'Kane Ho. *Eccl*. 2D **61**
Okehampton Cres. *Sale*. 4D **109**
Okeover Rd. *Salf*. 2D **35**
Old Bank St. *M2*. 2B **68** (5B **6**)
Old Barton Rd. *Urm*. 4D **61**
  (in two parts)
Old Birley St. *M15*. 3B **84**
Old Broadway. *M20*. 4D **117**
Oldbury Clo. *M40*. 4B **54**
Oldcastle Av. *M20*. 1C **117**
Old Church St. *M40*. 1B **56**
Old Clough La. *Wors*. 2A **28**
  (in two parts)
Old Ct. Ho., The. *Salf*. . . 1D **67** (4C **4**)
Old Crofts Bank. *Urm*. 4C **77**
Old Elm St. *M13*. 2A **86**
Oldershaw Dri. *M9*. 4B **38**
Old Farm Cres. *Droy*. 3B **74**
Oldfield Gro. *Sale*. 4A **112**
Oldfield Rd. *Sale*. 4A **112**
Oldfield Rd. *Salf*. 3C **67** (4A **8**)
Oldfield St. *M11*. 2B **72**
Old Fold. *Eccl*. 3C **45**
Oldgate Wlk. *M15*. 2D **83**
Old Hall Dri. *M18*. 4D **89**
Old Hall La. *M14 & M13*. 3B **102**
Old Hall La. *W'fld*. 1A **16**
  (in two parts)
Old Hall Rd. *M40*. 3B **40**
Old Hall Rd. *Sale*. 4C **113**
Old Hall Rd. *Salf*. 1D **35**
Old Hall Rd. *Stret*. 4B **78**
Old Hall St. *M11*. 4A **74**
Oldham B'way. Bus. Pk. *Chad*. . . 2A **26**
Oldham Ct. *M40*. 4A **54**
Oldham Rd. *M4 & M40*. . . 1D **69** (3F **7**)
Oldham Rd. *Fail*. 4D **41**
Oldham St. *M1*. 2C **69** (5D **7**)
Oldham St. *Droy*. 1D **75**
Oldham St. *Salf*. 2D **67** (1C **8**)

Oldham St. *Stoc* 2A **122**
Old La. *M11* 3D **73**
Old La. *Chad* 2D **27**
Old Lansdowne Rd. *M20* 4B **116**
Old Mkt. St. *M9* 4A **22**
Old Medlock St. *M3* 3D **67** (2D **9**)
Old Mill Clo. *Swin* 2D **31**
Old Mill St. *M4* 2A **70**
Old Moat La. *M20* 2C **117**
Old Mount St. *M4* 4C **53** (2D **7**)
Old Pk. La. *Urm* 2C **77**
Old Parrin La. *Eccl* 4B **44**
Old Rd. *M9* 4B **22**
Old Rd. *Fail* 3A **42**
Old School Ct. *M9* 4A **22**
Old School Ct. *Eccl* 3D **45**
Old School Dri. *M9* 4A **22**
Old Shaw St. *Salf* 3B **66**
Old Station St. *Eccl* 2C **61**
Oldstead Wlk. *M9* 4B **38**
      (off Kelvington Dri.)
Old Trafford 3C **83**
Old Trafford
   Cricket Ground 4A **82**
      (Lancashire C.C.C.)
Old Trafford
   Football Ground 3D **81**
     (Manchester United F.C.)
Oldway Wlk. *M40* 2B **56**
Old Wellington Rd. *Eccl* 1D **61**
Old York St. *M15* 2A **84**
Oliver St. *M13* 2C **85**
Olive St. *Fail* 2A **42**
Olive Wlk. *Sale* 3C **109**
Olivia Ct. *Salf* 3C **67** (2B **8**)
Olivia Gro. *M14* 1B **102**
Ollerenshaw Hall. *M14* 4B **86**
Ollerton Av. *M16* 1C **99**
Ollerton Av. *Sale* 3D **109**
Ollerton Dri. *Fail* 1B **58**
Ollier Av. *M12* 2A **104**
Olney St. *M13* 4B **86**
Olwen Av. *M12* 3A **88**
Olwen Cres. *Stoc* 4B **106**
Olympia Trad. Est. *M15* . . 4A **68** (4F **9**)
Olympic Ct. *Salf* 3D **65**
Omer Av. *M13* 2D **103**
Omer Dri. *M19* 2C **119**
Ongar Wlk. *M9* 3D **21**
Onslow Av. *M40* 1A **42**
Ontario Ho. *Salf* 4A **66**
Opal Ct. *M14* 4B **102**
Opal Gdns. *M14* 4B **86**
Opal St. *M19* 1B **120**
Openshaw 3D **73**
Openshaw Ct. *Swin* 4C **15**
Openshaw Wlk. *Open* 3C **73**
Opera House 1F **9**

Orama Av. *Salf* 3C **47**
Orange Hill Rd. *P'wich* 1C **19**
Orchard Gro. *M20* 4B **116**
Orchard Ind. Est. *Salf* 2A **50**
Orchard Pl. *Sale* 4D **111**
Orchard Rd. *Fail* 3B **42**
Orchard St. *M20* 4B **116**
Orchard St. *Salf* 2A **50**
         (in two parts)
Orchard Trad. Est. *Salf* 2D **49**
Orchid St. *M9* 3B **38**
Ordell Wlk. *M9* 3C **23**
Ordnance St. *Eccl* 1D **61**
Ordsall 4B **66**
Ordsall District Cen. *Salf* 3B **66**
Ordsall Dri. *Salf* 1B **82** (5A **8**)
Ordsall Hall 2B **82**
         (Museum)
Ordsall La. *Salf* 2A **82** (5A **8**)
Ordsall Recreation Cen. 1A **82**
Oregon Clo. *M13* 2A **86**
Orford Rd. *M40* 2C **57**
Orford Rd. *P'wich* 1B **18**
Oriel Clo. *Chad* 1C **27**
Oriel Ct. *Sale* 4D **111**
Orient Ho. *M1* 3C **69** (3D **11**)
Orient Rd. *Salf* 3C **47**
Orient Sq. *M1* 3C **69** (3D **11**)
       (off Granby Row)
Orient St. *Salf* 3B **36**
Orient, The. *Urm* 2D **77**
     (off Trafford Cen., The)
Orion Pl. *Salf* 3C **51** (1B **4**)
Orion Trad. Est. *Traf P* 3C **63**
Orkney Dri. *Urm* 3D **77**
Orlanda Av. *Salf* 3C **47**
Orlanda Dri. *Salf* 1B **52**
Orme Av. *Salf* 2D **47**
Orme Clo. *M11* 2C **71**
Orme Clo. *Urm* 2B **94**
Ormerod St. *M40* 4A **58**
Ormeston Lodge. *Urm* 3D **93**
Orme St. *M11* 2C **71**
Ormonde Av. *Salf* 3D **47**
Ormsby Av. *M18* 4B **88**
Ormsgill Clo. *M15* 2B **84**
Ormskirk Av. *M20* 3B **116**
Ormskirk Rd. *Stoc* 3B **122**
Ornsay Wlk. *Open* 2C **73**
Oronsay Gro. *Salf* 2B **64**
Orpington Rd. *M9* 3C **39**
Orrell St. *M11* 3D **73**
Orrel St. *Salf* 1C **65**
Orsett Clo. *M40* 4A **54**
Orthes Gro. *Stoc* 4D **121**
Orvietto Av. *Salf* 3C **47**
Orville Dri. *M19* 2D **119**
Orwell Av. *Dent* 1C **107**

Osborne Dri. *Swin* 3A **32**
Osborne Ho. *Eccl.* 1C **61**
(off Police St.)
Osborne Rd. *M9.* 3C **39**
Osborne Rd. *M19.* 3D **103**
Osborne Rd. *Salf.* 1C **63**
Osborne St. *Col.* 3A **54**
Osborne St. *Salf.* 4D **49**
Oscar St. *M40.* 3A **40**
(in two parts)
Oscroft Clo. *M8.* 4B **36**
Oscroft Wlk. *M14.* 2B **118**
(off Lyth St.)
Osprey Clo. *M15.* 3A **84**
Osprey Ct. *M15.* 3A **84**
(off Osprey Clo.)
Osprey Ct. *Salf.* 3B **64**
Osprey Wlk. *M13.* 2A **86**
Ossory St. *M14.* 1D **101**
Osterley Rd. *M9.* 3D **23**
Ostrich La. *P'wich.* 3C **19**
Oswald Clo. *Salf.* 2A **50**
Oswald La. *M21.* 3B **98**
Oswald Rd. *Chor H.* 3A **98**
Oswald St. *M4.* 2B **70**
(Every St.)
Oswald St. *M4.* 4C **53** (2C **6**)
(Miller St.)
Oswald St. *Stoc.* 1B **106**
Othello Dri. *Eccl.* 1D **61**
Otley Av. *Salf.* 4A **48**
Otranto Av. *Salf.* 3D **47**
Otterburn Ho. *Eccl.* 4A **46**
Otter Dri. *M8.* 2A **52**
Otterham Wlk. *M40.* 2D **57**
Oulton Av. *Sale.* 4C **113**
Oulton Wlk. *M40.* 4B **54**
Oundle Clo. *M14.* 1A **102**
Ouse St. *Salf.* 2A **64**
Outram Ho. *M1.* 2A **70**
(off Millbank St.)
Outram Sq. *Droy.* 3C **75**
Outrington Dri. *Open.* 3A **72**
Outwood Av. *Swin.* 2D **13**
Overbridge Rd. *Salf.* 3A **52** (1F **5**)
Overbrook Av. *M40.* 2B **54**
Overbrook Dri. *P'wich.* 3B **18**
Overcombe Wlk. *M40.* 1A **54**
(off Westmount Clo.)
Overdale. *Swin.* 4C **31**
Overdale Ho. *Salf.* 3D **47**
Overlea Dri. *M19.* 4C **119**
Overlinks Dri. *Salf.* 2D **47**
Overstone Dri. *M8.* 3B **36**
Ovington Wlk. *M40.* 2A **54**
Owens Pk. *M14.* 3B **102**
Owen St. *Eccl.* 2B **60**
Owen St. *Salf.* 2A **50**

Owler La. *Chad.* 3D **25**
Oxendon Av. *M11.* 4B **56**
Oxenholme Wlk. *M18.* 2C **89**
Oxford Av. *Droy.* 4B **58**
Oxford Ct. *M2.* 3B **68** (2B **10**)
Oxford Ct. *M15.* 2C **85** (5B **10**)
Oxford Ct. *Old T.* 3D **83**
(off Globe Clo.)
Oxford Pl. *M14.* 4A **86**
Oxford Rd. *M1 & M13.* . . . 4C **69** (4C **10**)
(in three parts)
Oxford Rd. *Salf.* 3C **47**
Oxford St. *M1.* 3B **68** (2B **10**)
Oxford St. *M16.* 3D **83**
Oxford St. *Eccl.* 1A **62**
Oxford St. *Oldh.* 1D **27**
Oxhill Wlk. *M40.* 4D **25**
Oxney Rd. *M14.* 4A **86**
Oxted Wlk. *M8.* 1C **53**
Oxton St. *M11.* 1B **90**
Ozanam Ct. *Salf.* 3D **35**

P

Pacific Quays. 3B **64**
Pacific Way. *Salf.* 3A **64**
Padbury Ho. *Salf.* 2D **65**
(off Cypress Clo.)
Padbury Wlk. *M40.* 2D **55**
Paddington Av. *M40.* 2B **56**
Paddington Clo. *Salf.* 1A **66**
Paddison St. *Swin.* 3A **30**
Paddock Ct. *Fail.* 2B **58**
Paddock Fld. *Salf.* 3B **66**
Paddock La. *Fail.* 2B **58**
Paddock St. *M12.* 4A **70**
Padstow St. *M40.* 4C **55**
Paget St. *M40.* 2B **54**
Pagnall Ct. *Chad.* 1D **27**
Paignton Av. *M19.* 1D **119**
Paignton Dri. *Sale.* 4D **109**
Paignton Gro. *Stoc.* 2A **122**
Palace Rd. *Sale.* 4C **111**
Palace Theatre 3C **69** (3C **10**)
Palatine Av. *M20.* 3D **117**
Palatine Cres. *M20.* 4D **117**
Palatine M. *M20.* 3D **117**
Palfrey Pl. *M12.* 1A **86**
Palgrave Av. *M40.* 2B **54**
Palladium, The 2D **61**
Pall Mall. *M2.* 2B **68** (5B **6**)
(Marsden St.)
Pall Mall. *M2.* 2B **68** (1B **10**)
(Tib La.)
Pall Mall Ct. *M2.* 2B **68** (5B **6**)
Palm Clo. *Sale.* 4C **109**
Palmer Clo. *M8.* 4D **21**

Palmerston Av. *M16*. 2D **99**
Palmerston Clo. *Dent* 1D **107**
Palmerston Rd. *Dent* 1D **107**
Palmerston St. *M12* 3B **70**
Palmer St. *Salf* 2C **51**
(in two parts)
Palm St. *M13* 1D **103**
Palm St. *Droy* 1D **73**
Pandora St. *M20* 4C **117**
Pangbourne Av. *Urm* 1A **94**
Pankhurst Cen. 3D **85**
(Museum)
Pankhurst Wlk. *M14* 1D **101**
Paradise Wharf. *M1*. . 2D **69** (1F **11**)
Parbold Av. *M20* 3C **117**
Parbrook Clo. *M40* 2B **54**
Pardoner's Ct. *Salf* 1D **63**
Parham Wlk. *M9* 3C **23**
Paris Av. *Salf* 1B **82**
Parish Vw. *Salf* 3B **66**
Park Av. *Fail*. 2D **41**
Park Av. *Lev*. 3A **104**
Park Av. *Old T* 3C **83**
Park Av. *P'wich* 2B **18**
Park Av. *Sale* 3C **111**
Park Av. *Salf* 2B **36**
Park Av. *Swin*. 3C **31**
Park Av. *Urm* 2C **93**
Park Bank. *Salf* 1B **64**
Parkbridge Wlk. *M13* . . . 2D **85** (5F **11**)
Pk. Brow Clo. *M21*. 1C **115**
Park Ct. *Sale* 4C **111**
Park Cres. *M14* 1A **102**
Parkdale Av. *M18*. 3C **89**
Park Dri. *M16* 2C **99**
Park Dri. *Eccl*. 3D **45**
Parker Arc. *M1*. 1D **11**
Parker St. *M1* 2C **69** (1D **11**)
Parkfield. *Salf*. 1B **64**
Parkfield Av. *M14*. 1D **101**
Parkfield Av. *Oldh* 4D **27**
Parkfield Av. *P'wich* 3D **19**
Parkfield Av. *Urm* 3B **92**
Parkfield Est. *Swin* 4C **31**
Parkfield Rd. N. *M40* 4A **26**
Parkfield St. *M14* 1D **101**
(Claremont Rd.)
Parkfield St. *M14* 4D **85**
(Moss La. E.)
Park Ga. Av. *M20* 3D **117**
Parkgate Dri. *Swin* 3C **31**
Park Gro. *M19* 2A **104**
Park Gro. *Stoc*. 4B **120**
Park Hill. *P'wich*. 1D **35**
Parkhill Av. *M8* 4D **21**
Park Ho. *Droy* 3C **75**
Pk. House Bri. Est. *Salf* 3D **33**
Pk. House Bri. Rd. *Salf*. 4D **33**

Parkhouse St. *M11* 3B **72**
Parkhouse St. Ind. Est.
M11. . . . . 3B **72**
Parkhurst Av. *M40* 1A **42**
Parkin St. *M12*. 1A **104**
Pk. Lake Av. *Salf* 2A **36**
Parklands. *Sale* 4A **112**
Parklands, The. *Stoc* 4A **122**
Park La. *Salf* (M6). 2A **48**
Park La. *Salf* (M7). 2D **35**
Park La. *Swin*. 3B **32**
Park La. Ct. *Salf*. 2D **35**
Park La. W. *Swin* 3B **32**
Pk. Lea Ct. *Salf* 1A **36**
Parkleigh Dri. *M40*. 4A **26**
Park Lodge. *M19* 3D **103**
Park Lodge. *Salf* 2D **35**
Park M. *M16* 2C **99**
Parkmount Rd. *M9*. 1C **39**
Park Pl. *M4*. 4C **53** (1C **6**)
Park Pl. *P'wich*. 1C **19**
Park Pl. *Salf*. 4C **47**
Park Range. *M14*. 1B **102**
Park Rd. *Eccl*. 3D **45**
Park Rd. *Eccl & Salf*. 3C **47**
Park Rd. *P'wich* 3D **19**
Park Rd. *Sale*. 3C **111**
Park Rd. *Stoc*. 4B **120**
Park Rd. *Stret* 1A **96**
Park Rd. N. *Urm* 1C **93**
Park Rd. S. *Urm*. 2C **93**
Parkside Av. *Eccl* 2C **61**
Parkside Av. *Fail*. 2A **58**
Parkside Av. *Salf* 2A **36**
Parkside Bowling &
Tennis Club. 3C **111**
Parkside Rd. *M14* 2B **100**
Park Sq. *M16*. 2A **98**
Parkstead Dri. *M9* 4B **38**
Parkstone Av. *M18*. 2B **90**
Parkstone Dri. *Swin* 1D **47**
Parkstone La. *Wors* 3A **44**
Park St. *M3*. 4B **52** (1B **6**)
(Manchester)
Park St. *M3*. 2D **67** (5C **4**)
(Salford)
Park St. *Droy*. 1D **75**
Park St. *P'wich* 2C **19**
Park St. *Salf* 2D **35**
Park St. *Swin*. 3C **31**
Parksway. *P'wich*. 4C **19**
Parksway. *Swin* 4A **32**
Park Vw. *M9* 1A **54**
Park Vw. *Fail*. 2C **119**
Park Vw. *Salf*. 4B **66** (4A **8**)
Pk. View Clo. *M32*. 3D **97**
Pk. View Ct. *P'wich* 3A **18**
Parkview Ct. *Stret* 3D **97**

Pk. View Rd. *P'wich* 3B **18**
Parkville Rd. *M20* 4A **118**
Park Way. *Urm & Traf P* 4B **78**
Parkway Bus. Cen. *M14* 2B **100**
Parkway Circ. *Traf P* 2C **79**
Parkway Four Ind. Est.
   Traf P 2C **79**
Parkway Ind. Est. *Traf P* 2C **79**
Parkway Trad. Est. *Stret* 3C **79**
Parlane St. *M4* 4D **53** (1E **7**)
Parrfield Rd. *Wors* 3A **28**
Parrin La. *Eccl* 4B **44**
Parrot St. *M11* 2C **73**
Parr St. *M11* 4A **74**
Parr St. *Eccl* 2D **61**
Parrs Wood Rd. *M20* 4B **118**
Parry Rd. *M12* 4A **88**
Parslow Av. *M8* 2C **37**
Parsonage Clo. *Salf* . . . 3C **67** (3A **8**)
Parsonage Ct. *M20* 3D **117**
Parsonage Gdns. *M3* . . . 2B **68** (5A **6**)
Parsonage La. *Salf* 1B **68** (4A **6**)
Parsonage Rd. *M20* 3D **117**
Parsonage St. *M8* 1B **36**
Parsonage St. *M15* 3A **84**
Parsons Fld. *Salf* 1A **50**
Partington La. *Swin* 3A **30**
Partington Pl. *Sale* 4D **111**
Partington St. *M40* 2D **55**
Partington St. *Fail* 3B **42**
Partington St. *Wors* 3C **29**
Partridge Rd. *Fail* 1D **59**
Partridge St. *Stret* 3D **81**
Parvet Av. *Droy* 4B **58**
Pascal St. *M19* 4A **104**
Patchett St. *M12* 2D **87**
Patey St. *M12* 1A **104**
Pathfield Wlk. *M9* 2B **38**
        (off Smallfield Dri.)
Paton St. *M1* 2D **69** (1E **11**)
Patrick Roddy Ct. *M18* 3C **89**
Patricroft Bri. *Eccl* 2C **61**
Patricroft Rd. *Eccl* 1C **61**
Patten St. *M20* 3D **117**
Patterdale Av. *Urm* 4B **76**
Patterson Av. *M21* 3A **98**
Pattishall Clo. *M4* 2B **70**
Patton Ct. *Salf* 3C **51**
Paulden Dri. *Fail* 3C **43**
Paulhan Rd. *M20* 4B **118**
Pavilion Lodge. *M16* 1A **98**
Pavilions, The. *M21* 3C **99**
Peacehaven Av. *M11* 1C **73**
Peace St. *Fail* 1C **43**
Peaceville Rd. *M19* 3D **103**
Peach St. *P'wich* 1C **19**
Peach Tree Clo. *Salf* 1B **52**

Peach Tree Ct. *Salf* 1A **66**
Peacock Av. *Salf* 2B **48**
Peacock Clo. *M18* 2C **89**
Peacock Gro. *M18* 4D **89**
Peakdale Av. *Crum* 2D **37**
Peakdale Rd. *Droy* 4A **58**
Peaknaze Clo. *Swin* 2D **31**
Peak St. *M1* 2D **69** (1F **11**)
Pearl Av. *Salf* 1A **36**
Pearn Av. *M19* 4D **119**
Pearn Rd. *M19* 4D **119**
Pearson Ho. *Eccl* 3D **61**
Pear St. *P'wich* 1C **19**
Pear Tree Clo. *Salf* 1A **66**
Pear Tree Ct. *Salf* 1A **66**
Pear Tree Wlk. *Sale* 4C **109**
Peary St. *M4* 4D **53** (1F **7**)
Peatfield Av. *Swin* 4A **14**
Peatfield Wlk. *M15* 3B **84**
Pebworth Clo. *Midd* 1D **23**
Peckford Dri. *M40* 2A **56**
Pedley Wlk. *M13* 4D **69** (4F **11**)
Peebles Dri. *M40* 3D **57**
Peel Av. *Urm* 2D **77**
       (off Trafford Cen., The)
Peel Circ. *Urm* 2A **78**
Peel Cross Rd. *Salf* 2A **66**
Peel Green 3B **60**
Peel Grn. Rd. *Eccl* 3B **60**
Peel Grn. Trad. Est.
   Eccl 3B **60**
Peel Gro. *M12* 4A **88**
Peel Ho. *Eccl* 1B **62**
Peel La. *M8* 3C **53**
Peel Moat Ct. *Stoc* 4B **120**
Peel Moat Rd. *Stoc* 4B **120**
Peel Moat Sports Cen. 4B **120**
Peel Mt. *Salf* 4B **50** (1A **4**)
Peel Sq. *M18* 3D **89**
Peel St. *Droy* 3B **74**
Peel St. *Eccl* 1B **62**
Peel St. *Fail* 4D **41**
Pegasus Ct. *Sale* 4B **112**
       (off Kingston Dri.)
Pegasus Sq. *Salf* 4C **51** (1B **4**)
Pegwell Dri. *Salf* 2A **52**
Pelham Pl. *M8* 4D **21**
Pelton Av. *Swin* 4D **13**
Pelton Wlk. *M40* 2B **54**
       (off Pitsford Rd.)
Pemberton St. *M16* 4C **83**
Pembridge Rd. *M9* 2D **23**
Pembroke Av. *Eccl* 1D **61**
Pembroke Av. *Sale* 4B **110**
Pembroke Clo. *M13* 2B **86**
Pembroke Ct. *Swin* 2D **31**
Pembroke St. *Salf* 4A **36**
       (Hightown)

Pembroke St. *Salf* 2C **65**
                    (Weaste)
Pembry Clo. *Stoc*. 4D **123**
Pencombe Clo. *M12*. 3A **88**
Pencroft Way. *Man S* 3C **85**
Pender Wlk. *M18*. 3D **89**
Pendlebury 2D **31**
Pendlebury Clo. *P'wich* 4D **17**
Pendlebury Ho. Swin *1C* **31**
       (off Pendlebury Rd.)
Pendlebury Recreation Cen. . . . 1A **30**
Pendlebury Rd. *Swin* 2B **30**
Pendlecroft Av. *Swin* 2A **32**
Pendlegreen Clo. *M11* 3D **71**
Pendleton 4D **49**
Pendleton Grn. Salf *4D* **49**
         (off Nursery St.)
Pendleton Ho. Salf 3A **50**
       (off Broughton Rd.)
Pendleton Way. *Salf*. 4D **49**
Pendle Wlk. *M40* 4B **54**
Pendle Wlk. *Stoc* 4C **123**
Pendleway. *Swin* 1C **31**
Pendragon Pl. *Fail* 3C **43**
Pendrell Wlk. M9 . . . . *3C* **23**
      (off Sanderstead Dri.)
Penelope Rd. *Salf* 2B **48**
Penerley Dri. *M9* 4B **38**
Penfair Clo. *M11* 2A **72**
Penfield Clo. *M1* 4D **69** (4E **11**)
Penfold Wlk. *M12* 2D **87**
Penhall Wlk. M40. . . . . *2D* **55**
       (off Mansford Dri.)
Peninsula Building. *Salf* 3B **34**
Penistone Av. *M9*. 3A **24**
Penistone Av. *Salf* 4A **48**
Penketh Av. *M18* 4B **88**
Pennant Dri. *P'wich* 1A **18**
Pennell St. *M11* 2D **73**
Pennine Av. *Chad* 1C **27**
Pennine Clo. *M9* 2D **23**
Pennine Ct. *Swin* 1C **31**
Pennington St. *M12* 2A **104**
Pennington St. *Chad* 3D **27**
Penn St. *M40*. 2D **39**
Penny Black Chambers.
   Wors 2A **44**
Penny Bri. La. Urm 3A **92**
        (in two parts)
Penrhyn Dri. *P'wich* 2B **18**
Penrith Av. *M11*. 4B **56**
Penrith Av. *Stoc*. 3B **106**
Penrod Pl. *Salf*. 3B **50**
Penroyson Clo. *M12*. 2D **87**
Penruddock Wlk. M13. . . . . . . *4D* **87**
        (off Bates St.)
Penryn Ct. *Salf*. 1D **35**
Pensarn Av. *M14* 1C **119**

Pensarn Gro. *Stoc* 4B **122**
Pensby Clo. *Swin*. 3A **32**
Pensby Wlk. *M40*. 2B **54**
Penshurst Rd. *Stoc* 3D **123**
Pentland Av. *M40*. 4C **25**
Pentlands Av. *Salf* 1D **51**
Penzance St. *M40* 4C **55**
People's History Mus. 5E **5**
Pepperhill Rd. *M16* 4B **84**
Perch Wlk. M4 . . . . *2A* **70**
        (off Winder Dri.)
Percival Clo. *M8*. 1B **52**
Percival Rd. *Droy*. 2D **75**
Percy Dri. *Salf* 1B **82**
Percy St. *M15* 2D **83**
Peregrine St. *M15* 3B **84**
Periton Wlk. M9. . . . . *3C* **23**
      (off Leconfield Dri.)
Perkins Av. *Salf* 2A **52**
Perrygate Av. *M20* 3C **117**
Perth. Eccl *1A* **62**
       (off Monton La.)
Perth Av. *Chad* 2C **27**
Perth St. *Swin* 3D **29**
Peru St. *Salf* 1D **67** (3C **6**)
Peterborough St. *M18* 2B **90**
Peterchurch Wlk. *Open*. 3C **73**
Peterhead Wlk. *Salf* 2A **66**
Peterloo Ct. Salf. *1C* **65**
       (off St Luke's Rd.)
Peter Moss Way. *M19* 3C **105**
Peter St. *M2* 3B **68** (2A **10**)
Peter St. *Eccl*. 2D **61**
Peter Wood Gdns.
   Stret. 3C **95**
Petrie Ct. *Salf*. 3B **50**
Petrock Wlk. *M40* 2C **57**
Pevensey Ct. *M9* 4A **24**
Pevensey Rd. *Salf* 2C **49**
Peveril Cres. *M21*. 2A **98**
Peveril Rd. *Salf* 1B **64**
Pheasant Dri. *M21*. 2D **115**
Phelan Clo. *M40*. 2A **54**
Philips Park 4A **56**
Philips Pk. Rd. *M11* 1C **71**
Philips Pk. Rd. W. *W'fld* 1A **16**
Philip St. *Eccl* 2D **61**
Phoebe St. *Salf* 3A **66**
Phoenix Ind. Est. *Fail* 2C **43**
Phoenix St. *M2* 2C **69** (5C **6**)
Phoenix Way. *M15* 3B **84**
Phoenix Way. *Urm* 2A **78**
Piccadilly. *M1* 2C **69** (5D **7**)
        (in two parts)
Piccadilly Pl. *M1* 5D **7**
Piccadilly Plaza. *M1*. . . 2C **69** (1D **11**)
Piccadilly Trad. Est. *M1* 3A **70**
Piccadilly Village 2A **70** (1F **11**)

Piccard Clo. *M40* 2B **54**
Pickering Clo. *Urm* 2B **92**
Pickford Clo. *M15* 3A **84**
Pickford St. *M4* 1D **69** (4F **7**)
Pickmere Av. *M20* 1D **117**
Pickmere Clo. *Droy* 2D **75**
Picton Clo. *Salf* 1A **68** (3E **5**)
Picton St. *Salf* 4D **51** (1D **5**)
Picton Wlk. *M16* 1B **100**
(off Bedwell St.)
Piercy Av. *Salf* 3D **51**
Piercy St. *M4* 2B **70**
Piercy St. *Fail* 3A **42**
Pigeon St. *M1* 2D **69** (5F **7**)
Pike Av. *Fail* 1D **59**
Pike Fold La. *M9* 3A **22**
Pilgrim Dri. *M11* 2D **71**
Pilkington Rd. *M9* 4A **24**
Pilling St. *M40* 2D **55**
Pimblett St. *M3* 4B **52** (1B **6**)
Pimlico Clo. *Salf* 1D **51**
Pimlott Gro. *P'wich* 4D **17**
Pincher Wlk. *Open* 2C **73**
Pinder Wlk. *M15* 2B **84**
Pine Ct. *M20* 4C **117**
Pine Gro. *M14* 4C **87**
Pine Gro. *Eccl* 3D **45**
Pine Gro. *Sale* 3D **109**
Pine Gro. *Swin* 3D **29**
Pinehurst Rd. *M40* 2C **55**
Pine St. *M1* 2C **69** (1C **10**)
Pinetop Clo. *M21* 2D **115**
Pinetree St. *M18* 3C **89**
Pinewood. *Sale* 4D **109**
Pinewood Ct. *Sale* 4B **112**
Pinewood Rd. *M21* 2A **114**
Pinfield Ct. *Stret* 3A **96**
(off Kingsway)
Pinfold Av. *M9* 4A **24**
Pink Bank La. *M12* 4A **88**
(in two parts)
Pin Mill Brow. *M12* 3B **70**
Pinner Pl. *M19* 3A **120**
Pinnington La. *Stret* 3B **96**
Pinnington Rd. *M18* 2D **89**
Pioneer Rd. *Swin* 4B **16**
Pioneer St. *M11* 4B **56**
Pipewell Av. *M18* 3C **89**
Pirie Wlk. *M40* 1C **57**
Pitcairn Ho. *Eccl* 2D **61**
Pitman Clo. *M11* 3A **72**
Pitmore Wlk. *M40* 4D **25**
Pitsford Rd. *M40* 2C **55**
Pit St. *Chad* 2D **27**
Pittbrook St. *M12* 4B **70**
Plane Ct. *Salf* 1A **66**
Plane Rd. *Fail* 2B **58**
Plantagenet Wlk. *M40* 3D **57**

Plantation St. *M18* 3A **90**
Plant Clo. *Sale* 4C **111**
Plant Hill Rd. *M9* 1A **22**
Plant St. *M1* 2D **69** (1E **11**)
Plasman Ind. Cen.
M19 . . . . 3D **105**
Plattbrook Clo. *M14* 3D **101**
Platt Ct. *M14* 2A **102**
Platt Hall (Art Galley & Mus.)
(Gallery of Costume) 2A **102**
Platt La. *M14* 3C **101**
Plattwood Wlk. *M15* 2D **83**
Playfair St. *M14* 4D **85**
Pleasant Rd. *Eccl* 2A **62**
Pleasant St. *M9* 3B **38**
Pleasant Vw. *M9* 2D **21**
Pleasington Dri. *M40* 4C **25**
Ploughbank Dri. *M21* 2D **115**
Plover Ter. *M21* 2D **115**
Plumbley Dri. *M16* 1C **99**
Plumbley St. *M11* 1A **90**
Plummer Av. *M21* 3B **114**
Plumpton Wlk. *M13* 4D **87**
Plumtree Clo. *Eccl* 1A **62**
Plum Tree Ct. *Salf* 1A **66**
Pluto Clo. *Salf* 3C **51**
Plymouth Av. *M13* 3C **87**
Plymouth Gro. *M13* 3A **86**
Plymouth Gro. W. *M13* 3C **87**
Plymouth Rd. *Sale* 4D **109**
Plymouth Vw. *M13* 2A **86**
Plymtree Clo. *M8* 4A **20**
Pochin St. *M40* 4C **55**
Poland St. *M4* 1A **70** (3F **7**)
Poland St. Ind. Est.
M4 . . . . 1A **70**
Polden Wlk. *M9* 1D **39**
Polebrook Av. *M12* 2B **86**
Polefield Rd. *M9* 4B **22**
Pole La. *Fail* 2B **42**
Polesworth Clo. *M12* 2A **88**
Police St. *M2* 2B **68** (5A **6**)
Police St. *Eccl* 1C **61**
Pollard St. *M4* 2A **70**
Pollard St. E. *M40* 1B **70**
Pollitt Clo. *M12* 2D **87**
Pollitts Clo. *Eccl* 1B **60**
Polruan Rd. *M21* 2A **98**
Polworth Rd. *M9* 1C **39**
Polygon Av. *M13* 2A **86**
Polygon Rd. *M8* 1B **36**
Polygon St. *M13* 1A **86**
Polygon, The. *Eccl* 1C **63**
Polygon, The. *Salf* 1C **51**
Pomfret St. *M12* 2A **88**
Pomfret St. *Salf* 2A **48**
Pomona Cres. *Salf* 1B **82**
(in three parts)

Pomona Docks.
  M15 . . . . 2C **83** (5A **8**)
Pomona Strand.
  M16 & M15 . . . . . . 3A **82** (5A **8**)
    (in three parts)
Ponds Clo. *M21* 3B **98**
Ponsford Av. *M9* 3A **24**
Ponsonby Rd. *Stret* 1B **96**
Pontefract Clo. *Swin* 3D **31**
Pool Fold. *Fail* 4C **43**
Poolton Rd. *M9* 2D **21**
Poplar Av. *M19* 1B **120**
Poplar Ct. *M14* 3B **102**
Poplar Dri. *P'wich* 4A **18**
Poplar Gro. *M18* 4D **89**
Poplar Gro. *Urm* 2A **94**
Poplar Rd. *Eccl* 3A **46**
Poplar Rd. *Stret* 4D **95**
Poplar Rd. *Swin* 3D **29**
Poplar St. *M11* 3C **71**
Poplar St. *Fail* 4D **41**
Poplin Dri. *Salf* 4A **52**
Poppythorn La. *P'wich* 1A **18**
    (in two parts)
Porchfield Sq. *M3* . . . 3A **68** (2F **9**)
Porlock Av. *Aud* 3D **75**
Porlock Rd. *Urm* 4A **92**
Portal Wlk. M9 . . . . 2B **38**
    (off Alderside Rd.)
Porter Dri. *M40* 1B **54**
Portfield Wlk. M40 . . . . 1A **56**
    (off Harmer Clo.)
Portgate Wlk. *M13* 2B **86**
Portico Library Gallery,
  The 2C **69** (1C **10**)
Portland Arc. *M1* 1D **11**
Portland Cres. *M13* 3B **86**
Portland Gro. *Stoc* 4B **120**
Portland Ho. *Salf* 4C **47**
Portland Rd. *M13* 1D **103**
Portland Rd. *Eccl* 4B **46**
Portland Rd. *Stret* 4C **81**
Portland Rd. *Swin* 3C **31**
Portland St. *M1* 3C **69** (2C **10**)
Portland, The. *M14* 1B **118**
Portman Rd. *M16* 1A **100**
Portree Clo. *Eccl* 1B **60**
Portsmouth Clo. *Salf* 2D **51**
Portsmouth St. *M13* 2D **85**
    (in two parts)
Port Soderick Av. *Salf* 2A **66**
Portstone Clo. *M16* 4A **84**
Port St. *M1* 2D **69** (5E **7**)
Portugal Rd. *P'wich* 4B **18**
Portugal St. *M4* 1A **70** (3F **7**)
    (in two parts)
Portugal St. E. *M1* 3A **70**
Portville Rd. *M19* 2A **104**

Portwood Wlk. *M9* 3B **38**
Postal St. *M1* 2D **69** (5E **7**)
Postbridge Clo. *M13* 2A **86**
Potato Wharf. *M3* . . . 3D **67** (3D **9**)
Potter's La. *M9* 3C **39**
Pottery La. *M12 & M11* 3D **87**
Pottery Row. *M11* 1C **71**
Pottery Wlk. *M40* 4D **25**
Pott St. *M40* 2D **57**
Pott St. *Swin* 4B **14**
Poulton St. *M11* 4A **74**
Powell St. *Clay* 1D **73**
Powell St. *Old T* 4C **83**
Powerleague Soccer Cen. 4B **70**
Pownall Av. *M20* 1C **117**
Poynter St. *M40* 1C **41**
Poynton St. *M15* 2B **84**
Praed Rd. *Traf P* 3A **80**
Pratt Wlk. M11 . . . . 2D **71**
    (off Turnpike Wlk.)
Precinct Cen. *M13* 2C **85**
Premier Rd. *M8* 3B **52**
Premier St. *M16* 4D **83**
Prentice Wlk. *M11* 2A **72**
Prenton St. *Open* 3A **74**
Prescot Rd. *M9* 3B **38**
Press St. *M11* 4D **73**
Presswood Ct. *Salf* 1A **48**
Prestage St. *Long* 2B **104**
Prestage St. *Old T* 3C **83**
    (in four parts)
Prestbury Av. *M14* 3B **100**
Preston Av. *Eccl* 4C **47**
Preston Clo. *Eccl* 4C **47**
Preston Rd. *M19* 4A **104**
Preston St. *M18* 2C **89**
Prestwich 1A **18**
Prestwich Hills. *P'wich* 3A **18**
Prestwich Park 3A **18**
Prestwich Pk. Rd. S.
  P'wich 3A **18**
Prestwick Wlk. *M40* 4C **25**
Prestwood Rd. *Salf* 3A **48**
Price St. *M4* 2B **70**
Pridmouth Rd. *M20* 3A **118**
Priestley Rd. *Wors* 2C **29**
Primley Wlk. M9 . . . . 2C **39**
    (off Edward St.)
Primrose Av. *Urm* 2D **93**
Primrose Clo. *Salf* 1D **65**
Primrose St. *M4* 1D **69** (3F **7**)
Prince Albert Av. *M19* 2A **104**
Princedom St. *M9* 2C **39**
Prince's Bri. *M3* 3D **67** (2D **9**)
Princes Ct. *Eccl* 4D **45**
Princes Rd. *Stoc* 4A **120**
Princess Av. *P'wich* 4C **19**
Princess Ct. *M15* 2D **83**

Princess Ct. *P'wich* 3B **18**
Princess Pde. *M14* 3B **100**
Princess Rd.
  M15 & M14 . . . . . . 2B **84** (5A **10**)
  (in three parts)
Princess Rd. *M21 & M20* 4A **116**
Princess Rd. *Chad* 3A **26**
Princess Rd. *P'wich* 2C **19**
Princess Rd. *Urm* 1B **92**
Princess St.
  M2 & M1 . . . . 2B **68** (1B **10**)
Princess St. *M15* 2C **83** (5B **8**)
Princess St. *Chad* 1C **27**
Princess St. *Eccl* 1C **61**
Princess St. *Fail* 3A **42**
Princess St. *Salf* 3A **50**
Princess St. *Swin* 3C **31**
Princeton Clo. *Salf* 4A **48**
Printer St. *M11* 3D **73**
Printon Av. *M9* 2D **71**
Printworks La. *M19* 3C **105**
Printworks, The 1C **69** (3C **6**)
Priory Av. *M21* 4B **98**
Priory Av. *Salf* 4C **35**
Priory Clo. *Sale* 3B **112**
Priory Ct. *Eccl* 1A **62**
Priory Ct. *Stoc* 1A **122**
Priory Gro. *Chad* 2C **27**
Priory Gro. *Salf* 4C **35**
Priory La. *Stoc* 1A **122**
Priory Pl. *Salf* 4C **35**
Priory Rd. *Sale* 4A **112**
Priory Rd. *Swin* 1A **30**
Priory, The. *Salf* 4C **35**
Pritchard St. *M1* 3C **69** (3D **11**)
Pritchard St. *Stret* 2B **96**
Progress Way. *Dent* 2D **107**
Propps Hall Dri. *Fail* 1D **57**
Prospect Dri. *Fail* 2B **58**
Prospect Ho. M9 . . . . *3C **39***
  (off Church La.)
Prospect Pl. *Swin* 3C **31**
Prospect Vw. *Swin* 3C **31**
Prospect Vs. *M9* 1D **39**
Prout St. *M12* 1A **104**
Providence St. *M4* 2B **70**
Provident Av. *M19* 3C **105**
Provis Rd. *M21* 2B **114**
Pryme St. *M15* 4A **68** (4E **9**)
Pugin Wlk. M9 . . . . *4B **38***
  (off Oldershaw Dri.)
Pulford Av. *M21* 4D **115**
Pullman Clo. *M19* 4B **104**
Pullman Dri. *Urm* 2B **94**
Pump St. *M40* 1C **71**
Pump St. *Oldh* 4D **27**
Pump Yd. *M4* 1C **69** (3C **6**)
Purcell St. *M12* 1A **104**

Puritan Wlk. *M40* 2A **54**
  (off Ribblesdale Dri.)
Purslow Clo. *M12* 2C **71**
Purton Wlk. *M9* *3C **39***
  (off Broadwell Dri.)
Pym St. *M40* 2D **39**
Pym St. *Eccl* 1D **61**
Pyramid Ct. *Salf* 4D **35**
Pytha Fold Rd. *M20* 4A **118**

Q

Quadrant, The. *M9* 3A **24**
Quadrant, The. *Droy* 2B **74**
Quainton Ho. Salf *2D **65***
  (off Amersham St.)
Quantock St. *M16* 4A **84**
Quarmby Rd. *M18* 4B **90**
Quarry Wlk. M11 . . . . 2D **71**
  (off Pilgrim Dri.)
Quays, The. *Salf* 1D **81**
Quay St. *M3* 2A **68** (1E **9**)
  (Manchester)
Quay St. *M3*. 1A **68** (4F **5**)
  (Salford)
Quayview. *Salf* 3A **66**
Quay W. *Traf P.* 2C **81**
Queen Alexandra Clo.
  Salf 3C **67** (3A **8**)
Queens Av. *M18* 3B **88**
Queensbury Ct. *M40* 4B **54**
Queensbury Pde. *M40* 4C **55**
Queen's Ct. *M20* 4C **117**
Queens Ct. *M40* 2B **54**
Queenscroft. *Eccl* 4B **46**
Queen's Dri. *P'wich* 4C **19**
Queensferry St. *M40* 1C **57**
Queen's Gro. *M12* 4A **88**
Queensland Rd. *M18* 3B **88**
Queen's Rd. *M8 & M9* 2C **53**
Queen's Rd. *M40* 1B **54**
Queens Rd. *Sale* 4B **110**
Queen's Rd. *Urm* 3D **93**
Queenston Rd. *M20* 4C **117**
Queensway. *Swin* 4C **15**
Queensway. *Urm* 4A **78**
Queen Victoria St. *Eccl* 1C **61**
Queen St. *M2* 2B **68** (1A **10**)
Queen St. *Fail* 3A **42**
Queen St. *Salf* 2B **48**
  (Irlams o' th' Height)
Queen St. *Salf* 1A **68** (3F **5**)
  (Salford)
Queen St. W. *M20* 2D **117**
Quenby St. *M15* 1D **83** (5D **9**)
Quendon Av. *Salf* 3A **52**

Quilter Gro. *M9* 4A **22**
Quinney Cres. *M16* 4A **84**
Quinn St. *M11* 2A **72**
Quinton Wlk. *M13* 2D **85** (5F **11**)

R

Raby St. *M14*. 4B **84**
Raby St. *M16*. 4A **84**
Rachel Rosing Wlk. *M8* 2B **36**
Rachel St. *M12* 3A **70**
Radbourne Clo. *M12* 2A **88**
Radcliffe Pk. Cres. *Salf*. 2A **48**
Radcliffe Pk. Rd. *Salf*. 2D **47**
Radcliffe Vw. Salf. *1B **82***
  (off Ordsall Dri.)
Radford Dri. *M9*. 2C **39**
Radford St. *Salf*. 2C **35**
Radium St. *M4* 1A **70** (3F **7**)
Radlett Wlk. M13. . . . . *3A **86***
  (off Plymouth Gro.)
Radley St. *M16* 1B **100**
Radley St. *Fail*. 3A **74**
Radley Wlk. *M16* 1B **100**
  (off Radley St.)
Radnor Av. *Dent*. 1D **107**
Radnor St. *Gort*. 4C **89**
Radnor St. *Hulme* 3B **84**
Radnor St. *Stret*. 2B **96**
Radstock Clo. *M14*. 3D **101**
Radstock Rd. *Stret*. 2A **96**
Raglan Av. *Swin*. 4D **15**
Raglan Clo. *M11* 2D **71**
Raglan Rd. *Stret* 1D **95**
Raglan Wlk. *M15* 2B **84**
Railside Ter. *Eccl* 1B **62**
Railton Av. *M16*. 1D **99**
Railton Ter. *M9* 3D **39**
Railway Rd. *Chad*. 4C **27**
Railway Rd. *Stret*. 3C **81**
Railway Rd. *Urm* 2D **93**
Railway St. *M18*. 2C **89**
Railway St. Ind. Est. *M18*. . . . 2C **89**
Railway Ter. *M21* 2B **98**
Railway Vw. *Stoc* 2A **106**
Rainbow Clo. *M21* 2B **114**
Raincliff Av. *M13* 2D **103**
Rainford Av. *M20* 1C **117**
Rainforth St. *M13* 1D **103**
Rainham Dri. *M8* 3C **37**
Rainham Way. *Stoc* 3D **123**
Rainhill Wlk. *M40* 3D **57**
Rainow Av. *Droy* 2A **74**
Rainsough 1A **34**
Rainsough Av. *P'wich* 1A **34**
Rainsough Brow. *P'wich* 1D **33**
Rainsough Clo. *P'wich* 1A **34**

Rainsough Hill. *P'wich* 1D **33**
Rainton Wlk. *M40* 4D **25**
Raja Clo. *M8* 3D **37**
Rakehead Wlk. M15 . . . . *3C **85***
  (off Botham Clo.)
Rake La. *Swin* 3C **15**
Raleigh Clo. *M20* 4C **117**
Raleigh St. *Stret*. 2B **96**
Ralli Courts. *Salf* 2A **68** (5E **5**)
Ralli Quays. *Salf* 2A **68** (5E **5**)
Ralph Grn. St. *Chad* 3D **27**
Ralph St. *M11*. 2D **73**
Ralston Clo. *M7*. 2A **36**
Ramage Wlk. *M12* 2C **71**
Ramsbottom Row. *P'wich* . . . 2A **18**
Ramsbury Dri. *M40* 4D **25**
Ramsden Fold. *Swin* 4B **14**
Ramsey Av. *M19* 3D **105**
Ramsey St. *M40* 3B **40**
Ramsey St. *Chad* 1D **27**
Ramsgate Rd. *M40* 3C **57**
Ramsgate Rd. *Stoc* 2B **122**
Ramsgate St. *Salf* 2A **52**
Ranby Av. *M9* 2D **23**
Randall Wlk. *M11* 2D **71**
  (off Turnpike Wlk.)
Randerson St. *M12* 4A **70**
Randlesham St. *P'wich*. 2C **19**
Randolph St. *M19* 2B **104**
Ranelagh Rd. *Swin*. 3A **32**
Ranelagh St. *M11* 1B **72**
Ranford Rd. *M19* 1A **120**
Range Rd. *M16* 1A **100**
Range St. *M11*. 3C **73**
Rankin Clo. *M15* 3A **84**
Ranmore Av. *Open* 3A **74**
Ransfield Rd. *M21* 2B **98**
Ranulph Ct. *Salf*. 2B **48**
Ranworth Clo. *M11* 3D **71**
Rastell Wlk. M9 . . . . *3C **23***
  (off Ravenswood Dri.)
Ratcliffe St. *M19* 3B **104**
Rathan Rd. *Urm*. 4C **77**
Rathbourne Av. *M9* 2B **22**
Rathen Rd. *M20*. 4D **117**
Rathmore Av. *M40* 2C **55**
Rath Wlk. *M40*. 2C **57**
Rattenbury Ct. *Salf*. 2A **48**
Raveley Av. *M14* 1B **118**
Ravelston Dri. *M9* 4B **38**
Raven Av. *Chad* 1C **27**
Raven Ct. *M15*. 3A **84**
Ravenhead Clo. *M14* 1B **118**
Ravenhurst. *Salf*. 1A **36**
Ravenoak Av. *M19* 4C **105**
Ravenoak Dri. *Fail* 2C **43**
Ravensbury St. *M11*. 1B **72**
Ravens Clo. *M9* 4A **20**

Ravensdale Gdns. *Eccl*	4A **46**
Ravensdale St. *M14*	1A **102**
Ravenside Pk. *Chad*	1C **27**
Ravens Pl. *P'wich*	4A **20**
Ravenstone Dri. *Sale*	4C **113**
Raven St. *M12*	3A **70**
Ravensway. *P'wich*	4D **19**
Ravenswood Dri. *M9*	3C **23**
Ravenswood Rd. *Stret*	3D **81**
Raven Way. *Salf*	4A **50**
Ravine Av. *M9*	3C **39**
Rawcliffe St. *M14*	1D **101**
Rawdon Clo. *M19*	3B **104**
Rayburn Way. *M8*	2C **53**
Raycroft Av. *M9*	4A **24**
Raydon Av. *M40*	2B **54**
Rayleigh Av. *Open*	1B **90**
Raymond Av. *Chad*	2D **27**
Raymond St. *Swin*	1B **30**
Raysonhill Dri. *M9*	4A **22**
Reabrook Av. *M12*	2D **87**
Reading Clo. *M11*	3C **73**
Reading St. *Salf*	2B **50**
Readitt Wlk. *M11*	1B **72**
Reaney Wlk. *M12*	2A **88**
Rear Grn. *Swin*	4D **15**
Reather Wlk. *M40*	4A **54**
Rebecca St. *M8*	2C **37**
Recreation Rd. *Fail*	1D **43**
Recreation St. *P'wich*	2C **19**
Rectory Av. *M8*	1C **37**
Rectory Av. *P'wich*	2B **18**
Rectory Gdns. *P'wich*	2B **18**
Rectory Grn. *P'wich*	2A **18**
Rectory Gro. *P'wich*	3B **18**
Rectory La. *P'wich*	1A **18**
Rectory Rd. *M8*	1B **36**
Redacre Rd. *M18*	2A **90**
Red Bank. *M4 & M8*	4C **53** (1C **6**)
Redbridge Gro. *M21*	1A **114**
Redbrook Av. *M40*	2C **55**
Redby St. *M11*	4B **72**
Redcar Av. *M20*	3D **117**
Redcar Av. *Urm*	4A **76**
Redcar Lodge. Swin	*3A **32***
	(off Redcar Rd.)
Redcar Rd. *Swin*	3A **32**
Redclyffe Av. *M14*	1A **102**
Redclyffe Circ. *Urm*	2C **77**
Redclyffe Rd. *M20*	4C **117**
Redclyffe Rd. *Urm*	3D **61**
Redcote St. *M40*	2A **40**
Redcourt Av. *M20*	4D **117**
Redcroft Gdns. *M19*	4C **119**
Redcroft Rd. *Sale*	3A **110**
Reddaway Clo. *Salf*	2A **50**
Reddish	**2B 122**
Reddish Green	**2D 121**
Reddish La. *M18*	4A **90**
Reddish Rd. *Stoc*	2B **122**
Reddish Sports Cen.	**2A 122**
Reddish Swimming Pool	**4B 106**
Reddish Vale	**2C 123**
Reddish Vale Country Pk.	**2C 123**
Reddish Vale	
Nature Reserve	**1D 123**
Reddish Va. Rd. *Stoc*	2B **122**
Reddish Vale Sports Cen.	**2C 123**
Reddish Vale Vis. Cen.	**2C 123**
Redesmere Clo. *Droy*	2D **75**
Redesmere Pk. *Urm*	1B **108**
Redfern St. *M4*	1C **69** (3C **6**)
Redfield Clo. *M11*	2D **71**
Redford Rd. *M8*	2B **20**
Redgate La. *M12*	2D **87**
	(in two parts)
Redgates Wlk. M21	*3B **98***
	(off Manchester Rd.)
Redgrave Wlk. *M19*	3C **105**
Redhill St. *M4*	1D **69** (5F **7**)
Redland Av. *Stoc*	4B **122**
Redland Cres. *M21*	3B **114**
Red Lion St. *M4*	1C **69** (4D **7**)
Redlynch Wlk. *M8*	3C **37**
Redmere Gro. *M14*	4A **102**
Redmires Ct. *Salf*	2A **66**
Redmoor Sq. *M13*	4D **69** (4F **11**)
Redrose Cres. *M19*	2C **121**
Red Rose Gdns. *Sale*	3D **111**
Red Rose Retail Cen.	
Salf	2B **66** (1A **8**)
Redruth St. *M14*	2D **101**
Redshaw Clo. *M14*	3B **102**
Redthorn Av. *M19*	2D **119**
Redvale Dri. *Salf*	1A **52**
Redvale Wlk. *Salf*	1A **52**
Redvers St. *M11*	3C **71**
Redwing Cen. *Traf P.*	2A **80**
Redwood. *Sale*	4C **109**
Redwood Dri. *M8*	2D **53**
Redwood St. *Salf*	3A **50**
Reedham Wlk. M40	*3C **55***
	(off Lifton Av.)
Reedham Wlk. *Oldh*	2D **27**
Reedshaw Rd. *M9*	1A **54**
Reed St. *M18*	2D **89**
Reeve's Ct. *Salf*	1C **63**
Reeves Rd. *M21*	2B **114**
Reform Wlk. *Open*	3B **72**
Regal Ind. Est. *M12*	1A **88**
Regal Wlk. *M40*	1C **57**
Regan Av. *M21*	2D **115**
Regatta Clo. *Chad*	3C **27**
Regatta St. *Salf*	4D **33**
Regency Clo. *M40*	2B **54**

Regency Lodge. *P'wich* 2A **18**
Regent Av. *M14* 2C **101**
Regent Cvn. Pk. *Salf* 3D **49**
Regent Ct. *Salf* 1D **35**
Regent Ct. *Stoc* 4C **121**
Regent Cres. *Fail* 4A **42**
Regent Ho. *M14* 1B **102**
Regent Pl. *M14* 4A **86**
Regent Rd. *Salf* 3B **66** (2A **8**)
Regent Rd. Ind. Area.
  Salf 3D **67** (3C **8**)
Regents Ct. *M15* 2A **84**
  (off Stretford Rd.)
Regents Cres. *Urm* 2D **77**
  (off Trafford Cen., The)
Regents Pl. *Salf* 2B **66**
Regent Sq. *Salf* 3B **66** (2A **8**)
  (in two parts)
Regents Retail Pk.
  Salf 3C **67** (2C **8**)
Regent St. *M40* 2D **57**
Regent St. *Eccl* 1B **62**
Regent Trad. Est. *Salf* . 2D **67** (5C **4**)
Regina Ct. *Salf* 4C **47**
Reginald Latham Ct.
  M40 . . . . 4B **54**
Reginald St. *Eccl* 3A **60**
Reginald St. *Open* 4B **74**
Reginald St. *Swin* 1D **29**
Reilly St. *M15* 2B **84** (5A **10**)
Reliance St. *M40* 3C **41**
Reliance St. Enterprise Pk.
  M40 . . . . 4B **40**
Reliance Trad. Est. *M40* 4C **41**
Rendel Clo. *Stret* 2B **96**
Rennie Clo. *Stret* 2C **97**
Renshaw Av. *Eccl* 2D **61**
Renshaw Sq. *Eccl* 2C **61**
Renshaw St. *Eccl* 2D **61**
Renton Rd. *Stret* 2C **97**
Repton Av. *M40* 1A **42**
Repton Av. *Dent* 1C **107**
Repton Av. *Droy* 4D **57**
Reservoir St. *Salf* 1D **65**
  (Pendleton)
Reservoir St. *Salf* 4A **52** (2F **5**)
  (Salford)
Reynard Ct. *M13* 4C **87**
Reynard Rd. *M21* 2B **114**
Reynell Rd. *M13* 2D **103**
Reyner St. *M1* 3C **69** (2C **10**)
Reynolds Dri. *M18* 2D **89**
Reynolds Rd. *M16* 4C **83**
Rhine Dri. *M8* 2A **52**
Rhos Av. *M14* 1C **119**
Rial Pl. *M15* 2C **85**
Rialto Gdns. *Salf* 1A **52**
Ribble Dri. *Kear* 1A **12**

Ribblesdale Dri. *M40* 2A **54**
Ribble Wlk. *Droy* 3C **75**
Ribston St. *M15* 2A **84**
Rice St. *M3* 3A **68** (2E **9**)
Richardson Rd. *Eccl* 1A **62**
Richardson St. *M11* 1A **90**
Richard St. *Fail* 3B **42**
Richborough Clo. *Salf* 2A **52**
Richmond Av. *Chad* 2C **27**
Richmond Av. *P'wich* 1C **35**
Richmond Av. *Urm* 2A **94**
Richmond Ct. *M9* 1C **21**
  (off Deanswood Dri.)
Richmond Ct. *M13* 4B **86**
Richmond Dri. *Wors* 2C **29**
Richmond Gro. *M12* 3C **87**
Richmond Gro. *M13* 4B **86**
Richmond Gro. *Eccl* 4A **46**
Richmond Ho. *Swin* 4B **14**
  (off Berry St.)
Richmond Rd. *M14* 1B **118**
Richmond Rd. *Dent* 1C **107**
Richmond Rd. *Fail* 2C **43**
Richmond Rd. *Traf P* 4C **63**
Richmond St. *M1* 3C **69** (2D **11**)
Richmond St. *Droy* 1D **75**
Richmond St. *Salf* 4A **52** (2E **5**)
Riddell Ct. *Salf* 1A **64**
Ridgefield. *M2* 2B **68** (1A **10**)
Ridgefield St. *Fail* 3D **41**
  (in two parts)
Ridge Wlk. *M9* 3B **22**
Ridgeway. *Swin* 4D **15**
Ridgewood Av. *M40* 2B **54**
Ridgway St. *M40* 1B **70**
Ridgway St. E. *M4* 1B **70**
Ridingfold La. *Wors* 2A **44**
Ridings St. *M11* 3B **72**
Ridings St. *M40* 2D **55**
Riding St. *Salf* 1A **68** (4E **5**)
Ridley Wlk. *M15* 3C **85**
  (off Wellhead Clo.)
Ridsdale Av. *M20* 3C **117**
Ridsdale Wlk. *Salf* 2A **50**
Rifle Rd. *Sale* 4D **113**
Riga Rd. *M14* 3A **102**
Riga St. *M4* 1C **69** (3D **7**)
Rigby Ct. *Salf* 3D **35**
Rigby St. *Salf* 3D **35**
  (in two parts)
Rigby Wlk. *Salf* 4A **36**
Rigel Pl. *Salf* 1B **4**
Rigel St. *M4* 4A **54**
Righton Gallery 5D **11**
Rigton Clo. *M12* 3A **88**
Rimmer Clo. *M11* 2C **71**
Rimmington Clo. *M9* 4A **24**
Rimworth Dri. *M40* 3A **54**

Ringcroft Gdns. *M40* 1B **40**
Ringford Wlk. *M40*. 2C **55**
Ringley St. *M9*. 2B **38**
Ringlow Av. *Swin*. 3C **29**
Ringlow Pk. Rd. *Swin*. 4C **29**
Rings Clo. *Fail*. 1B **58**
Ringstead Dri. *M40*. 3A **54**
Ringstone Clo. *P'wich*. 3A **18**
Ringwood Av. *M12*. 2B **104**
Ringwood Av. *Aud*. 2D **75**
Rink St. *M14*. 2B **118**
Ripley Clo. *M4*. 3B **70**
Ripley Cres. *Urm*. 3A **76**
Ripon Cres. *Stret*. 1B **94**
Ripon Gro. *Sale*. 3B **110**
Ripon Rd. *Stret*. 1B **94**
Ripon St. *M15*. 3C **85**
Rippenden Av. *M21*. 2A **98**
Rippingham Rd. *M20*. 2D **117**
Ripton Wlk. M9 . . . . *2D* **21**
(off Selston Rd.)
Risbury Wlk. *M40*. 1C **57**
Rishworth Dri. *M40*. 2A **42**
Risley Av. *M9*. 2B **38**
Rita Av. *M14*. 1D **101**
Ritson Clo. *M18*. 2B **88**
Riverbank Lawns.
  Salf 4A **52** (1E **5**)
Riverbank Tower.
  Salf 4A **52** (2E **5**)
Riverdale Ct. *M9*. 3D **21**
Riverdale Rd. *M9*. 3C **21**
Riverpark Rd. *M40*. 4A **56**
River Pl. *M15*. 4A **68** (4F **9**)
Riversdale Ct. *P'wich*. 2A **18**
(in two parts)
Rivershill. *Sale*. 3C **111**
Riverside. *Salf*. 4C **51** (2B **4**)
Riverside Dri. *Urm*. 4B **92**
Rivers La. *Urm*. 3B **76**
River St. *M12*. 3A **70**
River St. *M15* 1B **84** (5A **10**)
River Tame Path. *Stoc* 3D **123**
  (Northumberland Rd.)
River Tame Path. *Stoc* 4D **123**
  (Tiviot Way, in two parts)
River Vw. *Stoc*. 2C **123**
River Vw. Clo. *P'wich*. 4D **17**
River Vw. Ct. *Salf*. 2C **35**
Rivington. *Salf*. 3A **48**
Rivington Av. *Swin*. 2A **32**
Rivington Cres. *Swin*. 2A **32**
Rivington Gro. *Aud*. 3D **75**
Rivington Rd. *Salf*. 3A **48**
Rivington Wlk. *M12*. 3D **87**
Rixton Ct. *M16*. 1B **98**
Roach Ct. M40. . . . . 3A **54**
(off Hamerton Rd.)

Robert Hall St. *Salf* 3B **66** (3A **8**)
Robert Lawrence Ct. *Urm*. 3A **92**
Robert Malcolm Clo. *M40*. . . . 2B **54**
Robert Owen St. *Droy*. 1D **75**
Roberts Av. *M14*. 4D **85**
Robertshaw Av. *M21*. 3B **114**
Robertson Clo. *M18*. 3C **89**
Roberts St. *Eccl*. 2D **61**
Robert St. *M3*. 4B **52** (1B **6**)
Robert St. *M40*. 2D **55**
Robert St. *Fail*. 1C **43**
Robert St. *Oldh*. 3D **27**
Robert St. *P'wich*. 2C **19**
Robe Wlk. *M18*. 2D **89**
Robin Hood St. *M8*. 2B **36**
Robson Av. *Urm*. 4A **62**
Roby Rd. *Eccl*. 3C **61**
Roby St. *M1* 2D **69** (1E **11**)
Rochdale Rd.
  M4 & M40. . . . . . . 1D **69** (3E **7**)
Rochdale Rd. *M9*. 2B **38**
Rochester Av. *P'wich*. 4C **19**
Rochester Rd. *Urm*. 4D **77**
Rochford Rd. *Eccl*. 3A **60**
Rockall Wlk. *M11*. 2D **71**
Rockdove Av. *M15*. 1B **84** (5A **10**)
Rocket St. *Salf* 2D **67** (5D **5**)
Rockfield Dri. *M9*. 2C **39**
Rockhampton St. *M18*. 3D **89**
Rockhouse Clo. *Eccl*. 3C **61**
Rockingham Clo. *M12*. 2B **86**
Rockland Wlk. *M40*. 4C **25**
Rockley Gdns. *Salf*. 3B **50**
Rocklyn Av. *M40*. 4C **25**
Rockmead Dri. *M9*. 3C **23**
Rock Rd. *Urm*. 2B **94**
Rock St. *M11*. 3A **74**
Rock St. *Salf*. 1D **51**
Rocky La. *Eccl*. 2D **45**
Roda St. *M9*. 3D **39**
Rodenhurst Dri. *M40*. 3A **40**
Rodmell Av. *M40*. 2B **54**
Rodmill Ct. *M14*. 3A **102**
Rodney Ct. *M4*. 4A **54**
Rodney St. *M4*. 1A **70**
Rodney St. *Salf*. 2D **67** (5D **5**)
Roe Green 2A **28**
Roe Grn. *Wors*. 2A **28**
Roe Grn. Av. *Wors*. 2A **28**
Roe St. *M4* 4A **54**
Roger Byrne Clo. *M40*. 2B **56**
Roger St. *M4* 4C **53** (1D **7**)
Rokeby Av. *Stret*. 3B **96**
Roker Av. *M13*. 2D **103**
Roland Rd. *Stoc*. 2B **122**
Role Row. *P'wich*. 1B **34**
Rolla St. *Salf* 1A **68** (3F **5**)
Rolleston Av. *M40* 1B **70**

Rolls Cres. *M15* 2A **84**
Rollswood Dri. *M40* 4A **40**
Roman Amphitheatre 2A **10**
Roman Ct. *Salf* 2D **51**
Roman Rd. *Fail & Oldh.* 2C **43**
Roman Rd. *P'wich* 1A **34**
Roman St. *M4.* 1C **69** (4D **7**)
Romer Av. *M40* 1A **42**
Rome Rd. *M40* 4A **54**
Romford Rd. *Sale* 3A **110**
Romford Wlk. *M9* 3C **21**
Romiley St. *Salf* 2B **48**
Romley Rd. *Urm* 4D **77**
Romney St. *M40* 2A **40**
Romney St. *Salf* 2B **50**
Romney Towers. *Stoc* 3D **123**
Romney Way. *Stoc* 4D **123**
Romsley Clo. *M12* 2A **88**
Ronaldsay Gdns. *Salf* 2C **65**
Ronald St. *M11* 2D **73**
Rona Wlk. *M12* 3D **87**
Rondin Rd. *M12 & M11* 3C **71**
Ronton Wlk. *M8.* 2A **38**
Rooden Ct. *P'wich* 2C **19**
Rookery Av. *M18* 2B **90**
Rooke St. *Eccl* 3A **60**
Rookfield. *Sale* 4A **112**
Rookfield Av. *Sale* 4A **112**
Rookley Wlk. *M14* 1A **102**
Rook St. *M15*. 3A **84**
Ropewalk. *Salf*. 4A **52** (2F **5**)
Ropley Wlk. M9 . . . . *1D* **39**
　　　　　(off Oak Bank Av.)
Rosa Gro. *Salf*. 1D **51**
Rosalind Ct. *Salf* 3C **67** (3B **8**)
Rosamond Dri. *Salf* . . . 1D **67** (4D **5**)
Rosamond St. W.
M15. . . . . 2C **85** (5D **11**)
Rose Bank Rd. *M40* 3B **56**
Rosebery St. *M14* 1B **100**
Rose Cottage Rd. *M14*. 1D **117**
Rose Cotts. M14 . . . . *1B* **118**
　　　　　(off Ladybarn La.)
Rosedale Rd. *M14* 2C **101**
Rosedale Rd. *Stoc*. 4D **121**
Rose Hey La. *Fail* 3A **58**
Rose Hill Av. *M40* 3B **56**
Rosehill Clo. *Salf* 1D **65**
Rosehill Ct. *Salf*. 1D **65**
Rosehill M. *Swin* 4B **14**
Rosehill Rd. *Swin*. 4B **14**
　　　　　(in two parts)
Roseland Av. *M20* 4D **117**
Roseleigh Av. *M19* 2D **119**
Rosemary Gro. *Salf* 2C **51**
Rosemead Ct. *Stoc*. 3B **122**
Roseneath Av. *M19* 3C **105**
Roseneath Rd. *Urm* 1C **93**

Rose St. *Chad* 3C **27**
Rosette Wlk. *Swin* 3B **30**
Rosevale Av. *M19*. 4C **119**
Rosewell Clo. *M40*. 3B **54**
Rosewood Av. *Droy* 1D **75**
Rosford Av. *M14* 2D **101**
Rosgill Wlk. *M18* 3C **89**
Rosina St. *M11* 1B **90**
Roslin St. *M11*. 1D **73**
Rossall Av. *Stret*. 1A **96**
Rossall Way. *Salf* 4A **50**
Ross Av. *M19* 3D **103**
Ross Av. *Chad* 3B **26**
Ross Dri. *Swin*. 2A **14**
Rossendale Av. *M9* 1D **39**
Rossett Dri. *Urm* 4A **76**
Ross Gro. *Urm*. 2C **93**
Rosshill Wlk. *M15* 2D **83**
Rossington St. *M40*. 2D **57**
Ross Lave La. *Dent* 4D **107**
Rosslyn Rd. *Most* 1A **40**
Rosslyn Rd. *Old T* 2A **98**
Rostherne Av. *Fall* 3C **101**
Rostherne Av. *Old T*. 1C **99**
Rostherne St. *Salf* 1C **65**
Roston Ct. *Salf*. 2A **36**
Roston Rd. *Salf* 2A **36**
Rostron Av. *M12* 2C **87**
Rostron St. *M19* 3B **104**
Rothay Dri. *Stoc*. 4B **106**
Rotherwood Av. *Stret*. 1C **97**
Rothesay Av. *M8*. 4A **20**
Rothesay Rd. *Swin*. 3A **32**
Rothman Clo. *M40*. 1C **57**
Rothwell St. *M40*. 1C **57**
Rothwell St. *Fail*. 3B **42**
Roughlee Av. *Swin* 2D **29**
Roundham Wlk. *M9*. 2C **39**
Rousden Clo. *M40*. 2B **54**
Routledge Wlk. *M9* 2C **39**
Rowan Av. *M16*. 1D **99**
Rowan Av. *Urm* 1D **93**
Rowan Clo. *Fail* 1B **58**
Rowan Ct. *M14* 2B **118**
Rowanlea. *P'wich* 2C **19**
Rowan Pl. *P'wich* 3B **18**
Rowany Clo. *P'wich* 4A **18**
Rowendale St. *M1* 3B **68** (3A **10**)
Rowland Av. *Urm* 1A **94**
Rowland St. *Salf* 3A **66**
Rowood Av. *M8* 4D **37**
Rowood Av. *Stoc* 2B **106**
Rowsley Av. *M20* 4A **116**
Rowsley Gro. *Stoc* 2A **122**
Rowsley Rd. *Eccl*. 3C **61**
Rowsley Rd. *Stret* 1C **95**
Rowsley St. *M11* 1C **71**
Rowsley St. *Salf*. 2B **50**

Roxburgh St. *M18* 3D **89**
Roxby Wlk. *M40* 4D **25**
Roxton Rd. *Stoc.* 3C **121**
Roxwell Wlk. *M9* 2B **38**
(off Alderside Rd.)
Royal Av. *M21* 1A **114**
Royal Av. *Droy.* 1D **75**
Royal Av. *Urm.* 2D **93**
Royal Exchange. *M2* 2B **68** (5B **6**)
Royal Exchange Arc. *M2* 5B **6**
Royal Exchange Theatre 5B **6**
Royce Ct. *M15* 2D **83**
(off Erskine St.)
Royce Pl. *M15* 2A **84**
Royce Rd. *M15* 2A **84** (5F **9**)
Royce Trad. Est. *Traf P.* 1A **78**
Roydale St. *M40* 4C **55**
Royden Av. *M9* 1B **22**
Royds Clo. *M13* 3B **86**
Roy Grainger Ct. *M16* 1A **100**
Royle-Higginson Ct. *Urm* 3C **93**
Royle St. *M14* 2B **118**
Royle St. *Salf.* 2D **65**
Royston Av. *M16* 1D **99**
Royston Av. *Dent.* 1C **107**
Royston Ct. *M16* 1D **99**
Royston Rd. *M16.* 1B **98**
Royston Rd. *Urm.* 1A **94**
Rozel Sq. *M3.* 3A **68** (2F **9**)
Ruby St. *M15.* 2C **85**
Rudcroft Clo. *M13* 2D **85** (5F **11**)
Rudd St. *M40* 3A **40**
Rudheath Av. *M20* 2C **117**
Rudman Dri. *Salf* 3A **8**
Rudston Av. *M40* 4B **24**
Rudyard Gro. *Stoc.* 3D **121**
Rudyard Rd. *Salf.* 2A **48**
Rudyard St. *Salf.* 4D **35**
Rufford Pl. *M18.* 4B **90**
Rufford Rd. *M16* 1D **99**
Rufus St. *M14* 2C **119**
Rugby Rd. *Salf.* 4C **47**
Rugby St. *Salf* 3A **52**
Rugeley St. *Salf.* 2B **50**
Ruislip Av. *M40* 2C **55**
Rumbold St. *M18.* 2A **90**
Runcorn St. *M15* 5B **8**
Runhall Clo. *M12* 2A **88**
Runnymeade. *Swin & Salf* 1C **47**
Rupert St. *M40* 3A **58**
Rupert St. *Stoc.* 2A **122**
(in two parts)
Rupert Ter. *Stoc.* 2A **122**
Rushbrooke Av. *M11* 4C **57**
Rushcroft Ct. *M9.* 4A **24**
Rushden Rd. *M19* 2B **104**
Rushen St. *M11.* 2C **73**
Rushfield Dri. *M13.* 1D **103**

Rushford Av. *M19* 2A **104**
Rushford Ct. *M19* 2A **104**
(off Rushford Av.)
Rushford Park **2A 104**
Rushford St. *M12* 4A **88**
Rushley Av. *Salf.* 4B **34**
Rushmere Av. *Lev* 3B **104**
Rushmere Wlk. *Old T.* 3D **83**
Rusholme **1A 102**
Rusholme Gdns. *M14.* 2A **102**
(off Wilmslow Rd.)
Rusholme Gro. *M14.* 1A **102**
Rusholme Gro. W. *M14* 1A **102**
Rusholme Pl. *M14* 4A **86**
Rushton Gro. *Open* 1A **90**
Rushwick Av. *M40* 2C **55**
Rushworth Ct. *Stoc* 4C **121**
Ruskin Av. *M14* 4D **85**
Ruskin Av. *Aud* 4D **75**
Ruskin Av. *Chad.* 3B **26**
Ruskin Cres. *P'wich.* 3D **17**
Ruskin Dri. *Sale.* 4C **109**
Ruskington Dri. *M9* 3B **38**
Ruskin Rd. *M16.* 1C **99**
Ruskin Rd. *Droy.* 1C **75**
Ruskin Rd. *P'wich.* 3D **17**
Ruskin Rd. *Stoc.* 3A **106**
Rusland Ct. *M9* 3A **24**
Rusland Ct. *Sale.* 4C **111**
Russell Av. *M16.* 2D **99**
Russell Av. *Sale* 4B **112**
Russell Fox Ct. *Stoc.* 2A **122**
Russell Rd. *M16* 1D **99**
Russell Rd. *Salf.* 2D **47**
Russell St. *M8* 3A **52**
Russell St. *M16* 1B **100**
Russell St. *Eccl* 1B **62**
Russell St. *P'wich* 2B **18**
Russet Rd. *M9.* 1B **38**
Rustons Wlk. *M40* 1A **42**
Ruth Av. *M40.* 1A **42**
Ruthen La. *M16.* 4B **82**
Rutherford Av. *M14* 1D **101**
Rutherglade Clo. *M40* 1A **54**
Rutherglen Wlk. *M40.* 2C **55**
Ruthin Av. *M9* 1A **22**
Ruthin Clo. *Oldh* 4D **27**
Ruthin Clo. *Salf.* 1A **66**
Ruthin Ct. *Salf.* 1A **66**
Ruth St. *M18.* 1D **105**
Rutland Av. *Firs* 1A **98**
Rutland Av. *Swin* 4B **14**
Rutland Av. *Urm.* 2A **94**
Rutland Av. *Wthtn* 3C **117**
Rutland Ct. *M20.* 4D **117**
Rutland Dri. *Salf.* 2C **35**
Rutland La. *Sale.* 4D **113**
(in three parts)

Rutland Rd. *Droy* 1A **74**
Rutland Rd. *Eccl* 3B **46**
Rutland St. *M18* 2A **90**
Rutland St. *Droy* 3D **75**
Rutland St. *Fail* 2B **42**
Rutland St. *Swin* 1A **30**
Ryall Av. *Salf* 3B **66**
Ryall Av. S. *Salf* 3B **66**
Ryan St. *Open* 4A **74**
Rydal Av. *Droy* 2A **74**
Rydal Av. *Eccl* 3B **44**
Rydal Av. *Sale* 3B **110**
Rydal Av. *Urm* 4A **92**
Rydal Clo. *Dent* 2D **107**
Rydal Cres. *Swin* 4B **30**
Rydale Av. *M40* 2C **55**
Rydal Mt. *Stoc* 2B **106**
Rydal Rd. *Stret* 1B **96**
Ryder Brow. 1D **105**
Ryder Brow. *M18*. 4D **89**
Ryderbrow Rd. *M18*. 4D **89**
Ryder St. *M40* 3A **54**
Ryebank M. *Chor H* 3D **97**
Ryebank Rd. *Chor H* 3D **97**
Rye Bank Rd. *Firs* 2A **98**
Ryecroft Av. *Salf* 4A **48**
Ryecroft Clo. *Chad* 3B **26**
　　　　　　　　　　(in two parts)
Ryecroft La. *Wors* 3A **44**
Ryecroft Rd. *Stret* 3A **96**
Ryecroft Vw. *Aud* 3D **75**
Ryefield. *Salf* 1B **48**
Rye Wlk. *M13* 3A **86**
Rygate Wlk. *M8* 4B **36**
Ryhope Wlk. *Salf* 2A **52**
Rylance St. *M11*. 2C **71**
Ryland Clo. *Stoc* 3B **106**
Rylands Ct. *M15* 2D **83**
Rylands St. *M18* 2A **90**
Rylane Wlk. *M40* 2B **54**
Rylatt Ct. *Sale* 4C **111**
Ryther Gro. *M9* 1D **21**
Ryton Av. *M18*. 1C **105**

S

Sabden Clo. *M40* 4C **55**
Sabrina St. *M8* 2A **52**
Sackville St. *M1* 3C **69** (2D **11**)
　　　　　　　　　　(in two parts)
Sackville St. *Salf* 1A **68** (4E **5**)
Saddlecote. *Wors* 3A **44**
Sadie Av. *Stret* 4C **79**
Sadler Clo. *M14* 1C **101**
Sadler Ct. *M15*. 3A **84**
Sagar St. *M8* 3B **52**
Sahal Ct. *Salf* 3D **51**

St Agnes Rd. *M13* 2D **103**
St Agnes St. *Stoc* 1B **106**
St Aidan's Gro. *Salf* 4B **34**
St Albans Av. *M40* 2B **56**
St Alban's Av. *Stoc* 4C **121**
St Alban's Ter. *M8* 2A **52**
St Aldwyn's Rd. *M20* 4D **117**
St Ambrose Gdns. *Salf*. 1D **65**
St Andrew's Av. *Droy* 2A **74**
St Andrews Av. *Eccl* 2A **62**
St Andrews Clo. *Stoc* 4B **120**
St Andrews Av. *Stoc* 4B **120**
St Andrews Rd. *Stret* 2D **95**
St Andrew's Sq. *M1* 3A **70**
St Andrew's St. *M1* 3A **70**
St Anne's Av. *Salf*. 4C **49**
St Annes Ct. *Salf* 3D **49**
St Annes Rd. *M21* 2B **114**
St Ann's Av. *Salf* 2D **55**
St Ann's All. *M2* 2B **68** (5A **6**)
　　　　　　　　　(off St Ann's Pl.)
St Ann's Arc. *M2* 5B **6**
St Ann's Chyd. *M2*. 5B **6**
St Anns Clo. *P'wich* 3A **18**
St Ann's Pl. *M2* 2B **68** (5B **6**)
St Ann's Rd. *P'wich* 3D **17**
St Ann's Sq. *M2* 2B **68** (5B **6**)
St Ann's St. *Swin* 2A **30**
St Ann St. *M2*. 2B **68** (5A **6**)
St Asaph's Dri. *M7*. 2B **36**
St Augustine St. *M40* 2B **54**
St Austell Rd. *M16*. 3A **100**
St Austells Dri. *P'wich* 1B **18**
St Austell's Dri. *Swin* 3A **32**
St Barnabas Sq. *M11* 3B **72**
St Bartholomew's Dri.
　　Salf 3C **67** (2A **8**)
St Bees Clo. *M14* 4C **85**
St Benedict's Av. *M12* 2D **87**
St Bernards Clo. *Salf* 2C **51**
　　　　　　　　　　(in two parts)
St Bernard's Clo. *Salf* 2B **50**
St Bernard's Dri. *Salf* 2C **51**
St Boniface Rd. *Salf* 3C **51**
St Brannock's Rd. *M21*. 3C **99**
St Brelades Dri. *Salf*. 2B **36**
St Brendan's Rd. *M20* 2D **117**
St Brendan's Rd. N. *M20* . . . 2D **117**
St Bride St. *M16* 3D **83**
St Brides Way. *M16* 3D **83**
St Catherine's Rd. *M20* 2D **117**
St Chads Rd. *M20* 2B **118**
St Chad's St. *M8* 3C **53** (1C **6**)
St Christophers Clo. *M20*. . . . 3B **116**
St Clement's Ct. *P'wich* 2C **19**
St Clement's Dri. *Salf*. . . . 4B **66** (4A **8**)
St Clements Fold. *Urm* 2A **94**
St Clement's Rd. *M21* 4A **98**

St Davids Ct. *M8* 2C **53**
St David's Wlk. *Stret* 2C **95**
St Dunstan Wlk. *M40.* 4A **40**
   (off Rollswood Dri.)
St Edmund's Rd. *M40* 1C **55**
St Elizabeth's Way. *Stoc* 2A **122**
St Georges 2D **83** (5D **9**)
St George's Av. *M15* . . 1D **83** (5C **8**)
St Georges Cen. *Salf* 3B **50**
St Georges *M15.* 1D **83** (5D **9**)
   (off Angela St.)
St Georges Ct. *M15* 2A **84**
   (Mallow St.)
St Georges Ct. *Eccl* 2B **62**
St George's Ct. *Stret.* 3A **96**
St George's Cres. *Salf* 4C **47**
St George's Dri. *M40* 3B **40**
St Georges Pl. *Salf.* 2A **50**
St George's Rd. *M14* 2C **119**
St Georges Rd. *Droy* 4B **58**
St Georges Rd. *Stret* 2A **96**
St Georges Sq. *Chad* 3A **26**
St Georges Way. *Salf* 2A **50**
   (in two parts)
St Gregory's Rd. *M12.* 4A **70**
St Helier's Dri. *Salf.* 2B **36**
St Helier Sq. *M19.* 4D **119**
St Hilda's Rd. *Old T* 3C **83**
St Ignatius Wlk. *Salf.* 3B **66**
St Ives Rd. *M14.* 2D **101**
St James Clo. *Salf.* 4D **47**
St James' Ct. *M15* 2A **84**
   (off Old York St.)
St James Ct. *Salf.* 4D **47**
St James Rd. *Stoc* 4B **120**
St James's Rd. *Salf* 4A **36**
St James's Sq. *M2.* . . . 2B **68** (1B **10**)
St James St. *M1* 3C **69** (2B **10**)
St James St. *Eccl.* 1A **62**
St Johns Av. *Droy* 1D **75**
St John's Ct. *Salf* (M6) 1D **65**
   (off Milford St.)
St John's Ct. *Salf* (M7) 4C **35**
St John's Pas. *M3* 2A **68** (2F **9**)
St John's Rd. *Long* 4D **87**
St John's Rd. *Old T* 4C **83**
St John's Rd. *Salf.* 4D **35**
St John St. *M3.* 3A **68** (2F **9**)
St John St. *Droy* 3B **74**
St John St. *Eccl.* 2D **61**
St John St. *Swin* 4B **32**
St Joseph's Dri. *Salf.* 3B **66**
St Kilda's Av. *Droy* 4B **58**
St Kilda's Dri. *Salf.* 2B **36**
St Lawrence Quay. *Salf* 4D **65**
St Leonard's Ct. *Sale* 4B **110**
St Leonards Rd. *Stoc.* 4D **121**
St Luke's Rd. *Salf.* 1B **64**

St Lukes Wlk. *M40.* 4A **40**
St Margaret's Av. *M19* 3D **119**
St Margaret's Gdns. *Oldh* . . . 3D **27**
St Margaret's Rd. *M40.* 3D **25**
St Mark's La. *M8* 3B **36**
St Mark's St. *M19* 2C **105**
St Martin's Clo. *Droy* 4B **58**
St Martin's Dri. *Salf.* 2B **36**
St Martins Rd. *Sale* 3D **109**
St Mary's Clo. *P'wich* 2A **18**
St Mary's Ct. *M8* 1B **36**
St Mary's Ct. *M40* 2B **40**
St Marys Ct. *P'wich* 2A **18**
St Mary's Dri. *Stoc.* 3B **122**
St Mary's Ga. *M1.* 1B **68** (4B **6**)
St Mary's Hall Rd. *M8* 1B **36**
St Mary's Parsonage.
   M3. . . . . 2A **68** (5F **5**)
St Mary's Rd. *M40.* 3B **40**
St Marys Rd. *Eccl* 1B **62**
St Mary's Rd. *P'wich* 2A **18**
St Mary's Rd. *Sale* 4B **110**
St Mary's Rd. *M3* 2B **68** (5A **6**)
St Mary's St. *Hulme* 3A **84**
St Mary St. *Salf* 1D **67** (4D **5**)
St Matthews Ct. *Stret.* 3A **96**
St Michael's Ct. *Eccl.* 3A **60**
St Michaels Clo. *Sale* 3A **110**
St Michael's Pl. *M4* 4C **53** (2D **7**)
   (off Aspin La.)
St Michael's Sq. *M4* 4C **53** (2D **7**)
St Modwen Rd. *Stret* 3B **78**
St Nicholas Rd. *M15* . . . 1A **84** (5E **9**)
St Oswalds Rd. *Lev* 2B **104**
St Paul's Ct. *Salf* 1C **35**
St Paul's Rd. *M20* 3A **118**
St Paul's Rd. *Salf.* 1C **35**
St Peter Quay. *Salf.* 1A **82**
St Peter's Dri. *Stret.* 1C **97**
St Peter's Rd. *Swin* 3A **30**
St Peter's Sq. *M2.* . . . 3B **68** (2B **10**)
St Philip's Pl. *Salf* 1D **67** (4C **4**)
St Philip's Rd. *M18* 4D **89**
St Philip's Sq. *Salf.* 1D **67** (4C **4**)
   (off Bank St.)
St Simon St. *Salf* 4D **51** (1D **5**)
St Stephens Clo. *M13* 3B **86**
St Stephens Ct. *M9* 3B **38**
   (off Shieldborn Dri.)
St Stephen St. *Salf* . . . 1D **67** (4D **5**)
St Stephens Vw. *Droy* 1C **75**
St Teresa's Rd. *M16.* 1A **98**
St Thomas's Pl. *M8* 3C **53**
St Vincent St. *M4.* 1A **70**
St Werburgh's Rd. *M21* 3C **99**
St Wilfrid's St. *M15* . . . 2A **84** (5E **9**)
Salcombe Clo. *Sale* 4A **110**
Salcombe Rd. *M11* 3D **73**

Salcot Wlk. *M40*. 4A **54**
Sale **4D 111**
Sale Leisure Cen. 4A **112**
Sale Water Pk. 3C **113**
Salford . . . . **3B 66 (1A 8)**
Salford App. *Salf*. . . . . 1B **68 (4A 6)**
Salford City Reds Rugby
    League Club 1B **64**
Salford Enterprise Cen. *Salf* 2A **64**
Salford Foyer. *Salf*. 4D **49**
Salford Mus. &
    Art Gallery . . . . 1C **67 (3A 4)**
Salford Quays **1D 81**
Salford R.C.
    Cathedral . . . . 1D **67 (4D 5)**
Salford Shop. City. *Salf* 4A **50**
Salford Tourist Info. Cen. 4A **66**
Salford University Bus. Pk.
    Salf . . . . 4B **50 (1A 4)**
Salisbury Dri. *P'wich* 4C **19**
Salisbury Ho. *M1*. 3D **11**
Salisbury Ho. *Salf*. 3E **5**
Salisbury Rd. *M21*. 3B **98**
Salisbury Rd. *Eccl*. 3B **46**
Salisbury Rd. *Swin*. 3A **30**
Salisbury Rd. *Urm*. 4D **77**
Salisbury St. *M14*. 4C **85**
Salisbury St. *Stoc*. 4B **106**
Salix Ct. *Salf*. 4A **50**
Salmon St. *M4*. . . . . 1C **69 (4D 7)**
Salop St. *Salf*. 3A **50**
Saltburn Wlk. *M9*. 2C **39**
            (off Naunton Wlk.)
Saltergate M. *Salf*. 1A **66**
Salterton Wlk. *M40*. 3A **40**
Salteye Rd. *Eccl*. 2A **60**
Saltford Av. *M4*. 1B **70**
            (in two parts)
Saltford Ct. *M4*. 1B **70**
Saltire Gdns. *Salf*. 2A **36**
Saltney Av. *M20*. 2B **116**
Salutation St. *M15*. 2B **84**
Salvin Wlk. *M9*. 3C **23**
Sam Cowan Clo. *M14*. 1C **101**
Samian Gdns. *Salf*. 2C **51**
Sammy Cookson Clo. *M14*. . . . 1C **101**
            (in two parts)
Samouth Clo. *M40*. 4B **54**
Sampson Sq. *M14*. 4C **85**
Sam Swire St. *M15*. 3B **84**
Samuel Ogden St.
    M1. . . . . 3C **69 (3D 11)**
Samuel St. *M19*. 4B **104**
Samuel St. *Fail*. 2B **42**
Sanby Av. *M18*. 4C **89**
Sanby Rd. *M18*. 4C **89**
Sanctuary Clo. *M15*. 3D **85**
Sanctuary, The. *M15*. 2A **84**

Sandal Ct. *M40* 4C **55**
Sandal St. *M40* 4C **55**
Sandbach Av. *M14*. 4B **100**
Sandbach Rd. *Stoc*. 2A **106**
Sanderson Clo. *Wors* 3A **28**
Sanderson Ct. *M40*. 2C **55**
Sanderson St. *M40*. 2C **55**
Sanderstead Dri. *M9*. 3C **23**
Sandfold. *Stoc*. 2A **106**
Sandfold La. *M19*. 2C **105**
            (in two parts)
Sandford Av. *M18* 2D **89**
Sandford St. *Salf*. . . . . . . 4A **52 (1E 5)**
Sandgate Av. *M11* 1D **73**
Sandgate Dri. *Urm* 4C **77**
Sandheys Gro. *M18* 4A **90**
Sandhurst Av. *M20*. 3C **117**
Sandhutton St. *M9*. 1B **38**
Sandilea Ct. *Salf*. 1B **34**
         (off Kellbrook Cres.)
Sandileigh Av. *M20* 4D **117**
Sandileigh Av. *Stoc*. 4D **123**
Sandimoss Ct. *Sale* 4B **110**
Sandi Way. *P'wich* 3A **18**
Sandiway Rd. *Sale*. 4B **110**
Sandmere Wlk. *M9* 3C **23**
Sandown Av. *Salf*. 1C **65**
Sandown Cres. *M18*. 1D **105**
Sandown Gdns. *Urm* 2A **92**
Sandown St. *M18* 2A **90**
Sandray Gro. *Salf*. 2C **65**
Sandridge Wlk. *M12*. 2C **87**
Sandringham Av. *Dent* 1C **107**
Sandringham Ct. *M9* 1C **21**
        (off Deanswood Dri.)
Sandringham Grange.
    P'wich 3A **20**
Sandringham St. *M18* 4C **89**
Sandsend Clo. *M8* 2A **52**
Sandsend Rd. *Urm*. 1C **93**
Sandstone Way. *M21* 2D **115**
Sand St. *M40*. 3A **54**
Sandwell Dri. *Sale* 3D **111**
Sandwich Rd. *Eccl* 4B **46**
Sandy Bank Rd. *M8* 2B **36**
Sandy Brow. *M9* 4B **22**
Sandy Ga. Clo. *Swin*. 3A **30**
Sandy Gro. *Salf* 4C **49**
Sandy Gro. *Swin* 2B **30**
Sandyhill Ct. *M9*. 3C **21**
Sandyhill Rd. *M9*. 3C **21**
Sandylands Dri. *P'wich*. 1A **34**
Sandy La. *M21*. 1B **114**
Sandy La. *P'wich*. 3D **17**
Sandy La. *Salf* 4C **49**
Sandy La. *Stret* 3D **95**
Sandy Meade. *P'wich*. 3D **17**
Sandywell Clo. *M11*. 4D **73**

Sandywell St. *M11* 3D **73**
Sandywood. *Salf* 4C **49**
Sangster Ct. *Salf* 3A **66**
Sankey Gro. *M9* 3D **21**
Santiago St. *M14* 1D **101**
Santley St. *M12* 1A **104**
Santon Av. *M14* 1C **119**
Sapling Rd. *Swin* 2D **45**
Sarah St. *M11* 3D **71**
Sarah St. *Eccl* 2B **60**
Sardina Ct. *Salf* 3D **35**
Sargent Dri. *M16* 4A **84**
Sark Rd. *M21* 2A **98**
Sarnesfield Clo. *M12* 4A **88**
Satinwood Wlk. *Salf* 2E **5**
Saturn Gro. *Salf* 3C **51**
Saunton Rd. *Open* 3D **73**
Sawley Rd. *M40* 3B **54**
Sawston Wlk. *M40* 3C **25**
Saxby St. *Salf* 2A **48**
Saxelby Dri. *M8* 3D **37**
Saxon Av. *M8* 1C **37**
Saxon Dri. *Droy* 1D **75**
(in two parts)
Saxon Ho. *M16* 1D **99**
Saxon St. *M40* 4C **55**
Saxon St. *Droy* 1D **75**
Saxthorpe Clo. *Sale* 4D **109**
Saxthorpe Wlk. *M12* 3C **87**
Saxwood Av. *M9* 1B **38**
Scale St. *Salf* 2A **66**
Scarborough St. *M40* 2A **40**
Scarcroft Rd. *M12* 3A **88**
Scargill Clo. *M14* 4A **102**
Scarisbrick Rd. *M19* 4D **103**
Scarr Wheel. *Salf* 4C **35**
Scarsdale Rd. *M14* 4C **87**
Scarsdale St. *Salf* 4B **50**
Scawton Wlk. *M9* 1D **21**
Schofield Rd. *Droy* 2D **75**
Schofield Rd. *Eccl* 2A **60**
Schofield St. *M11* 2C **73**
Schofield St. *Fail* 2B **42**
Scholars Dri. *M20* 2C **117**
Scholes Clo. *Salf* 2B **36**
Scholes Dri. *M40* 4A **26**
Scholes La. *P'wich* 3B **18**
Scholes St. *Chad* 2C **27**
Scholes St. *Fail* 1C **43**
Scholes St. *Swin* 2C **31**
Scholes Wlk. *P'wich* 3C **19**
Scholfield Av. *Urm* 3B **94**
School Av. *Stret* 1D **97**
School Brow. *Wors* 1A **44**
School Ct. *M4* 1A **70** (4F **7**)
School Gro. *M20* 3A **118**
School Gro. *P'wich* 4A **18**
School Gro. W. *M20* 3A **118**

School Ho. Flats. *Oldh* 4D **27**
School La. *M9* 4A **22**
School La. *Stoc* 4C **121**
School Rd. *Eccl* 3C **61**
School Rd. *Fail* 3B **42**
School Rd. *Oldh* 4D **27**
School Rd. *Sale* 4D **111**
(in two parts)
School Rd. *Stret* 2A **96**
Schoolside Clo. *M8* 1D **53**
Schools Rd. *M18* 3A **90**
School St. *M4* 4D **53** (2D **7**)
School St. *Eccl* 4B **60**
School St. *Salf* 3A **52** (1E **5**)
School Wlk. *M16* 3D **83**
Score St. *M11* 2A **72**
Scorton Wlk. *M40* 4D **25**
Scotforth Clo. *M15* 1A **84** (5E **9**)
Scotland. *M4* 4C **53** (2C **6**)
Scotland Hall Rd. *M40* 2B **56**
Scotland St. *M40* 2C **57**
Scotta Rd. *Eccl* 3B **60**
Scott Av. *M21* 2B **98**
Scott Av. *Eccl* 4C **45**
Scott Rd. *Droy* 1C **75**
Scott Rd. *P'wich* 3D **17**
Scott St. *Salf* 3C **51**
Scovell St. *Salf* 4D **35**
Scropton St. *M40* 1B **54**
Seabright Wlk. *M11* 2D **71**
Seabrook Cres. *Urm* 4C **77**
Seabrook Rd. *M40* 3C **57**
Seacombe Av. *M14* 3C **101**
Seaford Rd. *Salf* 2B **50**
Seaford Wlk. *M9* 3A **22**
Seaham Wlk. *M14* 1D **101**
Sealand Dri. *Eccl* 3A **60**
Sealand Ho. *P'wich* 1C **19**
Sealey Wlk. *M40* 3C **55**
(off Filby Wlk.)
Searby Rd. *M18* 3C **89**
Seascale Av. *M11* 4B **56**
Seathwaite Wlk. *M18* 3C **89**
Seaton Way. *M14* 4C **85**
Sebastopol Wlk. *M4* 1A **70**
Second Av. *M11* 1C **73**
Second Av. *Swin* 2D **45**
Second Av. *Traf P* 3B **80**
Sedan Clo. *Salf* 2A **66**
Seddon Av. *M18* 2D **89**
Seddon St. *M12* 2B **104**
Sedgeborough Rd. *M16* 4A **84**
Sedge Clo. *Stoc* 4C **107**
Sedgefield Clo. *Salf* 1A **66**
Sedgeford Rd. *M40* 2B **54**
Sedgley Av. *P'wich* 4C **19**
Sedgley Bldgs. *Droy* 3C **75**
Sedgley Park 4C **19**

Sedgley Pk. Rd. *P'wich* 4C **19**
Sedgley Pk. Rd. Trad. Est.
  P'wich 1B **34**
Sedgley Rd. *M8* 2C **37**
Seedley 4C **49**
Seedley Pk. Rd. *Salf* 1C **65**
Seedley Rd. *Salf* 4C **49**
Seedley St. *M14* 1D **101**
Seedley Ter. *Salf* 4C **49**
Seedley Vw. Rd. *Salf* 4C **49**
Sefton Clo. *M13*. 2D **85** (5F **11**)
Sefton Cres. *Sale* 3D **111**
Sefton Dri. *Swin* 1D **45**
Sefton Dri. *Wors* 2A **44**
Sefton Rd. *M21* 4B **98**
Sefton Rd. *Sale* 4D **111**
Sefton Rd. *Swin* 1B **30**
Sefton St. *M8* 2C **37**
Sefton St. *Oldh* 4D **27**
Segal Clo. *Salf* 3D **35**
Selborne Rd. *M21* 3B **98**
Selbourne Clo. *Stoc* 2A **106**
Selby Clo. *Stret* 1C **95**
Selby Dri. *Salf* 4D **47**
Selby Dri. *Urm* 3A **76**
Selby Rd. *Stret*. 1C **95**
Selby St. *M11* 3A **72**
Selby St. *Stoc* 4A **122**
Selham Wlk. *M13*. 1A **86** (5F **11**)
Selhurst Av. *M11* 1C **73**
Selkirk Dri. *M9*. 3D **23**
Selkirk Rd. *Chad* 2B **26**
Sellars Sq. *Droy*. 3C **75**
Sellers Way. *Chad* 3C **27**
Selsby Av. *Eccl*. 1B **60**
Selside Wlk. *M14* 4A **102**
Selston Rd. *M9* 2D **21**
Selwood Wlk. M9. . . . . *3B* **38**
      (off Carisbrook St.)
Selworth Av. *Sale*. 4C **113**
Selworthy Rd. *M16* 4A **84**
Selwyn Av. *M9* 2B **38**
Senior Av. *M14* 2C **119**
Senior Rd. *Eccl* 3A **60**
Senior St. *Salf* 4A **52** (2F **5**)
Sepal Clo. *Stoc*. 3C **107**
Sequoia St. *M9* 2C **39**
Sevenoaks Av. *Stoc* 4A **120**
Sevenoaks Av. *Urm* 4D **77**
Sevenoaks Dri. *Swin* 4C **31**
Sevenoaks Wlk. M13 . . . . *3A* **86**
      (off Lauderdale Cres.)
Severn Rd. *Oldh*. 1D **43**
      (in two parts)
Severnside Trad. Est. *Traf P* . . . 3D **79**
Severn Way. *Stoc*. 4B **122**
Sewerby St. *M16* 4B **84**
Sexa St. *M11*. 3D **73**

Seymour Av. *M11* 1D **73**
Seymour Clo. *M16* 3C **83**
Seymour Ct. *Salf* 2B **36**
Seymour Gro. *M16* 3B **82**
Seymour Gro. Sale. 4D **111**
Seymour Pl. *M16*. 3B **82**
Seymour Rd. *M8* 1B **36**
Seymour Rd. S. *M11* 1D **73**
Seymour St. *M18*. 2D **89**
Shackleton Ct. *M40* 3C **57**
Shackleton St. *Eccl* 4C **45**
      (in two parts)
Shackliffe Rd. *M40*. 4B **24**
Shaftesbury Av. *Eccl*. 3C **61**
Shaftesbury Rd. *M8*. 3C **37**
Shaftesbury Rd. *Swin*. 3B **30**
Shafton Wlk. *M40* 4D **25**
Shakespeare Cres. *Droy* 1C **75**
Shakespeare Cres. *Eccl* 1D **61**
Shakespeare Rd. *Droy* 1C **75**
Shakespeare Rd. *P'wich*. 3D **17**
Shakespeare Rd. *Swin* 2D **29**
Shakespeare Wlk. *M13*. 2A **86**
Shakleton Av. *M9* 3A **24**
Shaldon Dri. *M40*. 3A **58**
Shanklin Clo. *M21* 3A **98**
Shanklin Ho. *M21* 3A **98**
Shanklyn Av. *Urm* 2C **93**
Shapwick Clo. *M9* 2B **38**
Sharcott Clo. *M16* 4B **84**
Shardlow Clo. *M40* 3B **54**
Sharnbrook Wlk. *M8* 4A **20**
Sharnford Sq. *M12* 2A **88**
Sharp St. *M4*. 4D **53** (2E **7**)
Sharp St. *P'wich*. 2A **18**
Sharrow Wlk. M9 . . . . *3C* **39**
      (off Broadwell Dri.)
Shawbrook Rd. *M19* 3D **119**
Shawcross St. *Salf* 2D **65**
Shawe Hall Av. *Urm* 4A **92**
Shawe Hall Cres. *Urm* 4A **92**
Shawe Rd. *Urm* 2A **92**
Shawe Vw. *Urm* 2A **92**
Shawfield Clo. *M14* 4C **101**
Shawford Cres. *M40* 4C **25**
Shawford Rd. *M40*. 4C **25**
Shawgreen Clo. *M15* 2D **83**
Shaw Hall. *M14* 4B **86**
Shawhead Dri. *Fail*. 1B **58**
Shawheath Clo. *M15* 2D **83**
Shawhill Wlk. *M40* 1C **71**
Shawlea Av. *M19*. 3C **119**
Shaw Rd. *Stoc*. 4B **120**
Shaw St. *M3*. 4B **52** (2B **6**)
Sheader Dri. *Salf* 1A **64**
Shearer Way. *Swin* 3B **32**
Shearsby Clo. *M15*. 3A **84**
Shearwater Gdns. *Eccl* 3A **60**

Sheepfoot La. *P'wich* 3D **19**
Sheerness St. *M18* 3D **89**
Sheffield St. *M1* 3D **69** (2E **11**)
Shefford Clo. *M11* 3D **71**
Shelderton Clo. *M40* 3A **40**
Sheldon Av. *Urm* 2B **92**
Sheldon St. *M11* 1B **72**
Shelford Av. *M18* 4B **88**
Shelley Gro. *Droy* 1C **75**
Shelley Rd. *Chad* 3B **26**
Shelley Rd. *P'wich* 3D **17**
Shelley Rd. *Stoc* 3D **105**
Shelley Rd. *Swin* 2D **29**
Shelley St. *M40* 2C **41**
Shelmerdine Gdns. *Salf* 3A **48**
Shelton Av. *Sale* 4D **109**
Shenfield Wlk. *M40* 4B **54**
Shepherd St. *M9* 1C **39**
Shepley St. *M1* 3D **69** (2E **11**)
Shepley St. *Fail* 1C **43**
Shepway Ct. *Eccl* 1B **60**
Sherborne St.
  M3 & M8 . . . . 3A **52** (1F **5**)
    (in two parts)
Sherborne St. Trad. Est. *M8* 2C **53**
Sherborne Ct. W. *Salf* . . . 4A **52** (1F **5**)
Sherbourne Ct. *P'wich* 2A **18**
Sherbourne Rd. *Urm* 1A **94**
Sherbourne St. *P'wich* 2A **18**
Sherdley Ct. *M8* 1C **37**
Sherdley Rd. *M8* 1C **37**
Sheridan Ct. *M40* 2C **55**
Sheringham Dri. *Swin* 1B **46**
Sheringham Rd. *M14* 2B **118**
Sherlock St. *M14* 2B **118**
Sherratt St. *M4* 1D **69** (3F **7**)
Sherrington St. *M12* 1A **104**
Sherwell Rd. *M9* 3D **21**
Sherwood Av. *M14* 4A **102**
Sherwood Av. *Droy* 1D **75**
Sherwood Av. *Sale* 4A **112**
Sherwood Av. *Salf* 3B **34**
Sherwood Clo. *Salf* 4B **48**
Sherwood Dri. *Swin* 3D **31**
Sherwood Rd. *Dent* 1D **107**
Sidmouth St. *M14* 4A **102**
Shetland Circ. *Urm* 3C **77**
Shetland Rd. *M8* 3B **54**
Shetland Way. *Urm* 3C **77**
Shieldborn Dri. *M9* 3B **38**
Shield Dri. *Wors* 2C **29**
Shields Vw. *Salf* 5A **8**
Shilford Dri. *M4* 4A **54** (2F **7**)
Shilton Wlk. *M40* 4D **25**
Shipley Av. *Salf* 4A **48**
Shipley Vw. *Urm* 3A **76**
Shippey St. *M14* 2B **118**
Shiredale Dri. *M9* 3B **38**

Shiregreen Av. *M40* 2A **54**
Shirehills. *P'wich* 3A **18**
Shireoak Rd. *M20* 2B **118**
Shirley Av. *Chad* 4A **26**
Shirley Av. *Dent* 1B **106**
Shirley Av. *Eccl* 3C **61**
Shirley Av. *Salf* 2A **34**
Shirley Av. *Stret* 1D **97**
Shirley Av. *Swin* 3A **32**
Shirley Rd. *M8* 3C **37**
Shoreditch Clo. *Stoc* 4B **120**
Shoreham Clo. *M16* 4A **84**
Shorland St. *Swin* 3C **29**
Short Av. *Droy* 3B **74**
Short St. *M4* 2C **69** (5D **7**)
Short St. *Salf* 4A **52** (1E **5**)
    (in two parts)
Shortwood Clo. *M40* 1A **56**
Shotton Wlk. *M14* 1A **102**
Shrewsbury Ct. *M16* 3D **83**
Shrewsbury Rd. *Droy* 1C **75**
Shrewsbury Rd. *P'wich* 3A **18**
Shrewsbury St. *M16* 3C **83**
Shropshire Av. *Stoc* 3D **123**
Shropshire Rd. *Fail* 1C **59**
Shropshire Sq. *M12* 2D **87**
Shrowbridge Wlk. *M12* 2A **88**
Shude Hill. *M4* 1C **69** (4C **6**)
Shuttle St. *Eccl* 1B **62**
Shuttleworth Clo. *M16* 4A **100**
Siam St. *M11* 3D **71**
Sibley St. *M18* 3D **89**
Sibson Ct. *M21* 3A **98**
Sibson Rd. *M21* 3A **98**
Sibson Rd. *Sale* 4C **111**
Sickle St. *M2* 2C **69** (5C **6**)
Sidbury Rd. *M21* 1C **115**
Siddall St. *M12* 2A **104**
Siddington Av. *M20* 2C **117**
Sidebottom St. *Droy* 2B **74**
Side St. *M11* 2B **72**
Sidings, The. *Wors* 2A **44**
Sidley Av. *M9* 2D **23**
Sidmouth Dri. *M9* 4B **22**
Sidmouth Rd. *Sale* 4D **109**
Sidmouth St. *Oldh* 1D **27**
Sidney Rd. *M9* 1B **38**
Sidney St. *M1* 1C **85** (5D **11**)
Sidwell Wlk. *M4* 2B **70**
Siemens Rd. *M20* 4A **116**
Sighthill Wlk. *M9* 2B **38**
Signal Clo. *Eccl* 1B **60**
Signal Ct. *M40* 1B **54**
Signet Wlk. *M8* 2D **53**
Silbury Wlk. M8 . . . . *2B 52*
    (off Steeple Clo.)
Silchester Dri. *M40* 1B **54**
Silfield Clo. *M11* 2C **71**

Silkin Clo. *M13* 4D **69** (5E **11**)
Silkin Ct. *M13*. 5F **11**
Silk St. *M4*. 1A **70** (3F **7**)
Silk St. *M40*. 1C **57**
Silk St. *Salf*. 4D **51** (2C **4**)
Sillavan Way. *Salf* 1A **68** (4E **5**)
Silsden Av. *M9*. 1D **21**
Silsden Wlk. *Salf* 2D **33**
Silton St. *M9* 3D **39**
Silver Birch Gro. *Swin* 4D **31**
Silverbirch Way. *Fail*. 3B **42**
Silvercroft St. *M15*. 4A **68** (4E **9**)
Silverdale. *Swin* 4C **15**
Silverdale Av. *P'wich* 4A **20**
Silverdale Rd. *M21*. 3C **99**
Silverdale St. *M11* 4B **74**
Silver Jubilee Wlk. *M4* 4E **7**
Silverlea Dri. *M9* 4A **22**
Silverstone Dri. *M40* 3D **57**
Silver St. *M1* 3C **69** (2C **10**)
(Abingdon St.)
Silver St. *M1* 2C **69** (1D **11**)
(Chorlton St., in two parts)
Silverton Ho. Salf 4C **47**
(off Devon Clo.)
Silverwell St. *M40* 2D **57**
Silverwood Av. *M21* 4B **98**
Silvine Wlk. M40 . . . . *3C* **55**
(off Bednal Av.)
Simeon St. *M4* 4D **53** (2E **7**)
Simister Rd. *Fail*. 3B **42**
Simister St. *M9* 2C **39**
Simms Clo. *Salf* 1D **67** (4C **4**)
Simon Freeman Clo. *M19* 2C **121**
Simon Ho. *Stoc* 3C **121**
Simpson Av. *Swin* 4A **16**
Simpson Sq. *Chad* 3D **27**
Simpson St. *M4* 4C **53** (2D **7**)
Simpson St. *Chad* 2D **27**
Sinclair Av. *M8*. 1B **36**
Sindsley Ct. Swin. 1D **29**
(off Moss La.)
Sindsley Rd. *Swin* 4D **13**
Singleton Clo. *Salf* 1C **35**
Singleton Lodge. *Salf*. 1D **35**
Singleton Rd. *Salf* 1C **35**
Singleton Rd. *Stoc* 4B **120**
Sir Charles Groves Hall. M15 . . . . 2C **85**
(off Booth St. W.)
Sirdar St. *M11*. 3B **74**
Sirius Pl. *Salf* 4D **51** (1C **4**)
Sir Matt Busby Way. *M16*. 3D **81**
Sir Robert Thomas Ct. M9 . . . . *2B* **38**
(off Coningsby Dri.)
Sisley Clo. *Salf*. 2B **34**
Sisson St. *Fail* 3B **42**
Sisters St. *Droy* 3C **75**
Sixth St. *Traf P*. 3B **80**

Skaife Rd. *Sale*. 4C **113**
Skarratt Clo. *M12*. 2D **87**
Skelton Gro. *M13*. 2D **103**
Skelton Rd. *Stret* 1B **96**
Skelwith Clo. *Urm* 4A **76**
Skerry Clo. *M13*. 1D **85** (5F **11**)
Skerton Rd. *M16* 4B **82**
Skilgate Wlk. *M40* 1C **57**
Skip Pl. *M3* 4C **53** (1C **6**)
Skipton Av. *M40* 1D **41**
Skipton Clo. *Stoc* 1A **122**
Skipton Dri. *Urm* 3A **76**
Skrigge Clo. *M7* 2B **36**
Skye Rd. *Urm* 3D **77**
Slackey Brow. *Kear* 1C **13**
Slack La. *Swin* 1C **31**
Slack Rd. *M9* 1A **38**
Slade Gro. *M13* 1D **103**
Slade Hall 2A **104**
Slade Hall Rd. *M12* 2A **104**
Slade La. *M19 & M13* 1D **119**
Slade Mt. *M19* 4D **103**
Slaithwaite Dri. *M11*. 1C **73**
Slate Av. *M4*. 2A **70**
Slate La. *Aud*. 3D **75**
Slater St. *Eccl* 1B **60**
Slater St. *Fail* 1B **60**
Slate Wharf. *M15* 3D **67** (4D **9**)
Sleaford Clo. *M40* 4B **54**
Sledmere Clo. *M11* 2A **72**
Slough Ind. Est. *Salf* 3C **67** (3B **8**)
Smalldale Av. *M16* 1B **100**
Smallfield Dri. *M9* 2B **38**
Smallridge Clo. *M40*. 4B **54**
Smallwood St. *M40* 1C **57**
Smart St. *M12* 1A **104**
Smeaton Clo. *Stret* 2C **97**
Smeaton St. *M8*. 1A **54**
Smedley 1D **53**
Smedley Av. *M8*. 4D **37**
Smedley La. *M8*. 4D **37**
(in two parts)
Smedley Rd. *M8 & M40*. 4D **37**
Smedley St. *M8* 1C **53**
Smethurst St. *M9*. 1B **38**
Smith St. *M16* 2C **83**
Smithy La. *M3*. 2B **68** (5A **6**)
Smyrna St. *Salf* 2C **65**
Snell St. *M4*. 2B **70**
Snowden Av. *Urm* 4B **92**
Snowden Wlk. *M40* 4C **25**
Snowdon Rd. *Eccl* 4C **47**
Snowdrop Wlk. *Salf* 4D **35**
Snow Hill Ter. *P'wich* 3B **20**
Soap St. *M4* 1C **69** (4D **7**)
Solent Av. *M8* 4C **21**
Solway Clo. *Swin* 2A **14**
Somerfield Rd. *M9*. 1B **38**

Somerford Av. *M20* 1C **117**
Somerford Rd. *Stoc* 2B **106**
Somerset Pl. *Sale* 3D **111**
Somerset Rd. *Droy* 4B **58**
Somerset Rd. *Eccl* 3C **47**
Somerset Rd. *Fail* 4A **42**
Somers Rd. *Stoc* 3B **106**
Somers Wlk. *M9* 3D **21**
Somerton Ct. *M9* 3A **24**
Somerwood Wlk. *M12* 2D **87**
Sommerville Ct. *Salf* 2D **35**
Sonning Wlk. *M8* 4D **37**
Sopwith Dri. *M14* 3C **101**
Sorrel Bank. *Salf* 3D **49**
Sorrel Bank. *Stoc* 3C **107**
Sorrel St. *M15* 2A **84** (5E **9**)
Sorton St. *M1* 4C **69** (4D **11**)
Southall St. *M3* 4B **52** (1A **6**)
Southampton Clo.
  Salf 2D **51**
Southam St. *M7* 3B **36**
South Av. *M19* 2D **119**
South Av. *Swin* 2D **45**
Southbank Rd. *M19* 4B **118**
Southbourne Av. *Urm* 2B **94**
Southbourne St. *Salf* 1C **65**
Southbrook Av. *M8* 3B **20**
Southchurch Pde. *M40* 3A **54**
Southcliffe Rd. *Stoc* 3B **122**
S. Cliffe St. *M11* 4B **74**
Southcombe Wlk. *M15* 3B **84**
South Cres. *M11* 1D **73**
Southcross Rd. *M18* 1D **105**
S. Croston St. *M16* 4D **83**
Southdown Cres. *M9* 4A **24**
South Dri. *M21* 2A **114**
South Dri. *Urm* 3A **76**
Southend Av. *M15* 2D **83**
Southerly Cres. *M40* 3D **25**
Southern App. *Swin* 4A **16**
Southernby Clo. *M13* 4D **87**
Southern Rd. *Sale* 3C **111**
Southern St. *M3* 3A **68** (3F **9**)
Southern St. *Salf* 1C **65**
South Field Ind. Est.
  Traf P 2A **80**
Southfields Av. *M11* 1C **73**
Southgarth Rd. *Salf* 4C **49**
Southgate. *M3* 2B **68** (5A **6**)
Southgate. *Chor H* 2B **114**
Southgate. *Stoc* 4C **121**
Southgate. *Urm* 1B **108**
Southgate Av. *M40* 3A **56**
Southgate Ct. *Sale* 4A **112**
Southgate M. *Stoc* 4C **121**
Southgate Rd. *Chad* 3A **26**
South Gro. *M13* 3B **86**
S. Hall St. *Salf* 3C **67** (3B **8**)

S. King St. *M2* 2B **68** (5A **6**)
S. King St. *Eccl* 1B **60**
Southlands Av. *Eccl* 3A **60**
S. Langworthy Rd. *Salf* 3C **65**
Southlea Rd. *M20 & M19.* . . . 4B **118**
S. Lonsdale St. *Stret* 1C **97**
South Meade. *M21* 2B **114**
South Meade. *P'wich* 4D **19**
South Meade. *Swin* 4A **30**
Southmere Clo. *M40* 3C **25**
S. Mesnefield Rd. *Salf* 2A **34**
  (in two parts)
Southmill St. *M2* 3B **68** (2A **10**)
  (in two parts)
Southolme Gdns. *M19* 4C **119**
S. Pump St. *M1* 3D **69** (2E **11**)
S. Radford St. *Salf* 3A **34**
South Reddish 4B **122**
South Rd. *Stret* 4C **79**
South Rd. *Swin* 4B **16**
South Row. *P'wich* 1D **33**
Southsea St. *M11* 4D **73**
South Stage. *Salf* 3D **65**
South St. *Long.* 3C **87**
South St. *Oldh.* 4D **27**
South St. *Open* 3B **72**
  (in two parts)
South Vw. *M14* 2A **102**
South Vw. *Stoc* 1B **106**
Southway. *M40* 4B **26**
Southway. *Droy* 3C **75**
Southway. *Eccl.* 1B **62**
Southwell Ct. *Stret.* 3A **96**
Southwell St. *M9* 3C **39**
S. William St. *Salf* 2D **67** (5C **4**)
Southwold Clo. *M19.* 3C **105**
Southworth Ct. *Salf* 1D **67** (4C **4**)
Southyard St. *M19.* 4A **104**
Sovereign Enterprise Pk.
  Salf 4A **66**
Sovereign St. *Salf* 3A **50**
Sowerby Wlk. *M9* 2D **21**
  (off Chapel La.)
Spa Clo. *Stoc.* 4A **106**
Sparkle St. *M1.* 2D **69** (1F **11**)
Sparrow Clo. *Stoc* 2A **106**
Sparta Wlk. *Open* 3A **72**
Sparth Rd. *M40.* 2D **57**
Spa St. *M15* 3D **85**
Spaw St. *Salf.* 1A **68** (4E **5**)
  (in two parts)
Spean Wlk. *M11.* 2C **73**
Spear St. *M1.* 2C **69** (5D **7**)
Spectator St. *M4* 1B **70**
Specton Wlk. *M12* 1B **104**
Spencer Av. *M16* 2C **99**
Spencer St. *Chad.* 2D **27**
Spencer St. *Eccl.* 2C **61**

Spencer St. *Stoc* 4B **106**
Spender Av. *M8* 1C **53**
Spennithorne Rd. *Urm* 2B **92**
Spey Ho. *Stoc* 2B **106**
Spinney, The. *Urm* 2A **92**
Spinningfield. *M3* 2B **68** (1A **10**)
Spinning Jenny Wlk. *M4* 2A **70**
Spire Wlk. *M12* 3C **71**
Spooner Rd. *Eccl* 2C **61**
Sporting Club, The 5D **7**
Spreadbury St. *M40* 3A **40**
Spring Bank. *Salf* 4C **49**
Springbank Ct. *M8* 4B **20**
Spring Bri. Rd. *M16* 2B **100**
Spring Clough. *Swin* 2B **44**
Springfield. *Urm* 2C **93**
Springfield Av. *Stoc* 2A **122**
Springfield Clo. *Fail* 2A **42**
Springfield Ind. Est. *Fail* 2A **42**
Springfield La. *Salf* 4A **52** (1F **5**)
Springfield Rd. *Droy* 1B **74**
Springfield Rd. *Sale* 4D **111**
Springfield Trad. Est.
  Traf P 2B **80**
Spring Gdns. *M2* 2C **69** (5C **6**)
Spring Gdns. *Salf* 4D **49**
Springhead Av. *M20* 2C **117**
Springside. *Heat C* 2D **121**
Springside Wlk. *M15* 2D **83**
Spring St. *M12* 2A **104**
Spring Va. *P'wich* 4A **18**
Springville Av. *M9* 3D **39**
Springwell Clo. *Salf* 1C **65**
Springwood Av. *Swin* 4D **31**
Spruce Ct. *Salf* 1B **66**
Spruce St. *M15* 2A **84**
Spruce Wlk. *Sale* 3C **109**
Spur Wlk. *M8* 3B **36**
Square Fold. *Droy* 1D **75**
Square, The. *Swin* 2A **46**
Squire Rd. *M8* 3B **36**
Squire's Ct. *Salf* 1C **63**
Stable Fold. *Wors* 2A **44**
Stableford Av. *Eccl* 3C **45**
Stables, The. *P'wich* 3C **19**
Stable St. *Chad* 4C **27**
Stable St. *Salf* 1A **68** (4F **5**)
Stafford Rd. *Eccl* 4A **46**
Stafford Rd. *Fail* 2C **59**
Stafford Rd. *Swin* 2B **30**
Stafford St. *Oldh* 2D **27**
Stafford Vw. *Salf* 1B **82** (5A **8**)
Stainburn Rd. *M11* 3B **72**
Stainer St. *M12* 1A **104**
Stainforth St. *M11* 3D **71**
Stainton Av. *M18* 4A **90**
Stakeford Dri. *M8* 2A **38**
Stalham Clo. *M40* 4B **54**

Stalham Wlk. *M40* 4B **54**
Stamford Dri. *Fail* 1D **59**
Stamford Pl. *Sale* 4A **112**
Stamford Rd. *M13* 1C **103**
Stamford Rd. *Salf* 1B **50**
Stamford Rd. *Urm* 2B **92**
Stamford St. *M16* 3C **83**
  (in two parts)
Stamford St. *Sale* 3C **111**
Stamford St. *Swin* 1C **31**
Stanage Av. *M9* 2D **23**
Stanbrook St. *M19* 3C **105**
Stanbury Wlk. *M40* 4B **54**
  (off Berkshire Rd.)
Standall Wlk. *M9* 1C **39**
Standish Rd. *M14* 4B **102**
Standon Wlk. *M40* 4D **25**
Stangate Wlk. *M11* 3D **71**
Stanhope Av. *P'wich* 1A **18**
Stanhope Rd. *Salf* 2C **49**
Stanhope St. *M19* 3B **104**
Stanhope St. *Stoc* 2A **122**
Stanhope Way. *Fail* 2A **42**
Stanhorne Av. *M8* 4C **21**
Stanhurst. *Eccl* 4A **46**
Stanier Av. *Eccl* 4D **45**
Stanier St. *M9* 2C **39**
Stan Jolly Wlk. *M11* 3C **73**
Stanlaw Ho. *Eccl* 2A **62**
Stanley Av. *M14* 1A **102**
Stanley Av. S. *P'wich* 1A **18**
Stanley Clo. *M16* 3C **83**
Stanley Gro. *M12 & M18* 4D **87**
Stanley Gro. *Chor H* 1A **114**
Stanley Gro. *Urm* 2D **93**
Stanley Rd. *Chad* 2D **27**
Stanley Rd. *Dent* 4D **91**
Stanley Rd. *Eccl* 2C **61**
Stanley Rd. *Old T* 3B **82**
Stanley Rd. *Salf* 2A **36**
Stanley Rd. *Swin* 2C **31**
Stanley Rd. *Whal R* 2A **100**
Stanley St. *M8* 3C **53** (1D **7**)
Stanley St. *M40* 2D **55**
Stanley St. *Open* 4A **74**
Stanley St. *P'wich* 1C **19**
Stanley St. *Salf* 2A **68** (1E **9**)
  (in two parts)
Stanlo Ho. *M1* 3D **11**
Stanmore Av. *Stret* 2D **95**
Stannard Rd. *Eccl* 2A **60**
Stansby Gdns. *M12* 2C **87**
Stansfield Rd. *Fail* 2C **43**
Stansfield St. *M11* 3D **73**
Stansfield St. *M40* 3D **57**
Stansfield St. *Chad* 1D **27**
Stanthorne Av. *M20* 1C **117**
Stanton Av. *M20* 4A **116**

Stanton Av. *Salf* 4B **34**
Stanton Ct. *Stret* 4B **80**
Stanton St. *M11* 1C **73**
Stanton St. *Chad* 3D **27**
Stanton St. *Stret* 4B **80**
Stanway St. *M9* 2C **39**
Stanway St. *Stret* 1B **96**
Stanwell Rd. *M40* 1C **41**
Stanwell Rd. *Swin* 3A **30**
Stanwick Av. *M9* 2C **21**
Stanworth Clo. *M16* 1A **100**
Stanyard Ct. *Salf* 3A **66**
Stapleford Clo. *Sale* 4C **113**
Staplehurst Rd. *M40* 3A **56**
Staplers Wlk. *M14* 1A **102**
Stapleton St. *Salf* 2A **48**
Starcross Wlk. *M40* 1B **56**
Star Gro. *Salf* 1A **52**
Starkie St. *Wors* 2A **28**
Starmoor Dri. *M8* 1C **53**
Starmoor Wlk. *M8* 1C **53**
Starry Wlk. *Salf* 3C **51** (1B **4**)
Statham St. *Salf* 4B **50**
Statham Wlk. *M13* 4D **69** (4F **11**)
Station App. *M1* 2D **69** (1E **11**)
  (Oxford Rd. Station)
Station App. *M1* 3C **69** (3C **10**)
  (Piccadilly Station)
Station Bri. *Urm* 2D **93**
Station Rd. *M8* 1C **37**
Station Rd. *Eccl* 2D **61**
Station Rd. *Redd* 2A **106**
Station Rd. *Stret* 1B **96**
Station Rd. *Swin* 2B **30**
Station Rd. *Urm* 2D **93**
Station Vw. *M19* 3A **104**
Station Vw. *Droy* 4C **75**
Staton St. *M11* 3C **73**
Staverton Clo. *M13* 1A **86** (5F **11**)
Staycott St. *M16* 4B **84**
Stedman St. *M11* 2C **71**
Steeple Clo. *M8* 2B **52**
Steeple Dri. *Salf* 3A **66**
Stelfox Av. *M14* 3C **101**
Stelfox St. *Eccl* 3B **60**
Stella St. *M9* 2D **21**
Stelling St. *M18* 3D **89**
Stenbury Clo. *M14* 1A **102**
Stenson Sq. *Open* 4D **73**
Stephen Lowry Wlk. *M9* 3A **40**
Stephenson Av. *Droy* 2C **75**
Stephenson Rd. *Stret* 2C **97**
Stephenson St. *Fail* 1C **43**
Stephens Rd. *M20* 4A **118**
Stephen St. *M3* 3B **52** (1B **6**)
Stephen St. *Urm* 2A **94**
Stern Av. *Salf* 3A **66**
Stevenson Pl. *M1* 2D **69** (5E **7**)

Stevenson Rd. *Swin* 2A **30**
Stevenson Sq. *M1* 2D **69** (5E **7**)
Stevenson St. *Salf* 2D **67** (5C **4**)
Stilton Dri. *M11* 3A **72**
Stirling. Eccl *1B 62*
  (off Monton La.)
Stirling Av. *M20* 1B **116**
Stirling Ct. *Stoc* 4C **121**
Stirling Rd. *Chad* 2B **26**
Stirrup Ga. *Wors* 2A **44**
Stobart Av. *P'wich* 4C **19**
Stockburn Dri. *Fail* 3D **43**
Stockdale Rd. *M9* 2C **23**
Stockholm St. *M11* 1B **72**
Stockland Clo. *M13* 4D **69** (5E **11**)
Stockley Wlk. *M15* 2D **83**
Stockport Rd.
  M12 & M13 . . . . 2A **86**
Stocksfield Dri. *M9* 3C **23**
Stocks Ind. Est. *Eccl* 1C **61**
Stocks St. *M8* 4C **53** (1C **6**)
Stocks St. E. *M8* 4C **53** (1C **6**)
Stockton Rd. *M21* 1A **114**
Stockton St. *M16* 4A **84**
Stockton St. *Swin* 2A **30**
Stockwood Wlk. *M9* 3B **38**
Stokesay Rd. *Sale* 4A **110**
Stokes St. *M11* 1D **73**
Stolford Wlk. M8 . . . . *4B 36*
  (off Ermington Dri.)
Stonall Av. *M15* 2D **83** (5D **9**)
Stoneacre Ct. *Swin* 3B **30**
Stonefield Dri. *M8* 2A **52**
Stonehead St. *M9* 3D **39**
Stonehurst Clo. *M12* 2A **88**
Stoneleigh Av. *Sale* 4D **109**
Stonelow Clo. *M15* 2B **84**
Stone Pl. *M14* 1A **102**
Stonesby Clo. *M16* 4D **83**
Stone St. *M3* 3A **68** (3F **9**)
Stoneyfield Clo. *M16* 2B **100**
Stoneygate Wlk. *Open* 4D **73**
Stoney Knoll. *Salf* 4D **35**
Stoney Nook. *Salf* 4D **35**
Stonyhurst Av. *M3* 2B **68** (1A **10**)
Stonyford Rd. *Sale* 4B **112**
Stopford St. *M11* 4A **74**
Stopley Wlk. *Open* 3A **72**
Stores St. *P'wich* 2C **19**
Store St. *M1* 3D **69** (2F **11**)
Store St. *Open* 4B **72**
Stothard Rd. *Stret* 3D **95**
Stott La. *Salf* 4D **47**
Stott Milne St. *Chad* 1D **27**
Stott Rd. *Chad* 3A **26**
Stott Rd. *Swin* 4D **29**
Stott's La. *M40* 1D **57**
Stott St. *Fail* 1D **57**
Stovell Av. *Long* 2A **104**

Stovell Rd. *M40* 2A **40**
Stowell St. *Salf* 2C **65**
Stowfield Clo. *M9* 2D **21**
Stow Gdns. *M20* 3C **117**
Stracey St. *M40* 4C **55**
(in two parts)
Stradbroke Clo. *M18* 3B **88**
Strain Av. *M9* 2B **22**
Strand Ct. *Stret* 4A **96**
Strangeways 3B **52** (1B **6**)
Stranton Dri. *Wors* 2C **29**
Stratford Av. *M20* 4B **116**
Stratford Av. *Eccl* 3C **61**
Stratford Rd. *Midd* 1B **24**
Strathblane Clo. *M20* 2D **117**
Strathfield Dri. *M11* 1C **73**
Strathmere Av. *Stret* 1B **96**
Strathmore Av. *M16* 2B **98**
Stratton Rd. *M16* 2B **98**
Stratton Rd. *Swin* 1B **30**
Strawberry Bank. *Salf* 4B **50**
Strawberry Hill. *Salf* 4B **50** (1A **4**)
Strawberry Rd. *Salf* 4A **50**
Stray St. *M11* 3A **74**
Street End 2C **43**
Stretford 3B **96**
Stretford Ho. *Stret* 3A **96**
Stretford Leisure Cen. 4D **81**
Stretford Motorway Est.
   Stret. 3C **79**
Stretford Rd.
   M16 & M15 . . . . . . 3C **83** (5B **10**)
Stretford Rd. *Urm* 3D **93**
Stretton Av. *Sale* 4A **110**
Stretton Av. *Stret* 1C **95**
Stretton Clo. *M40* 2B **54**
Stroma Gdns. *Urm* 3C **77**
Strong St. *Salf* 3A **52**
Strontian Wlk. *Open* 2C **73**
Stroud Av. *Eccl* 4B **44**
Stroud Clo. *Midd* 1A **24**
Stuart Ho. *Droy* 3C **75**
Stuart Rd. *Stret* 1B **96**
Stuart St. *M11* 1A **72**
(in two parts)
Stuart St. E. *M11* 1A **72**
Stubbs Clo. *Salf* 2B **34**
Studforth Wlk. M15 . . . . *3C **85***
(off Botham Clo.)
Styal Av. *Stoc*. 3B **122**
Styal Av. *Stret* 1C **95**
Style St. *M4* 4C **53** (2D **7**)
Sudbury Clo. *M16* 3C **83**
Sudell St. *M4 & M40* 4D **53** (2F **7**)
Sudell St. Ind. Est. *M4* 2F **7**
Sue Patterson Wlk. *M40*. 2B **54**
Suffolk Av. *Droy* 4C **59**
Suffolk St. *Oldh* 1D **27**

Suffolk St. *Salf* 2A **50**
Sugden Sports Cen. 1C **85** (5D **11**)
Sulby Av. *Stret* 2C **97**
Sulby St. *M40* 2A **40**
Sullivan St. *M12* 1A **104**
Sulway Clo. *Swin* 3C **31**
Sumac St. *M11* 1D **73**
Sumbland Ho. *Swin* 4D **15**
Summer Av. *Urm* 2A **94**
Summercroft. *Chad* 3D **27**
Summerfield Av. *Droy* 4A **58**
Summerfield Ct. *M32* 3D **97**
Summerfield Dri. *P'wich* 1A **34**
Summerfield Rd. *Wors* 3A **28**
Summer Pl. *M14* 2A **102**
Summerseat Clo. *Salf* 3A **66**
Summerton Ho. Salf *2A **66***
(off Buckingham St.)
Summerville Av. *M9* 3D **39**
Summerville Rd. *Salf* 2C **49**
Sumner Rd. *Salf* 2B **48**
Sumner Way. *Urm* 2C **93**
Sunbeam Wlk. M11 . . . . *2D **71***
(off Hopedale Clo.)
Sunbury Dri. *M40* 3D **57**
Sundance Ct. *Salf* 3C **65**
Sunderton Wlk. *M12* 2C **87**
Sunningdale Av. *M11* 1B **72**
Sunningdale Ct. *Dent* 1D **107**
Sunningdale Dri. *P'wich* 1B **18**
Sunningdale Dri. *Salf* 2C **47**
Sunningdale Rd. *Urm* 3B **92**
Sunnybank Av. *Droy* 2B **74**
Sunnybank Av. *Eccl* 4B **46**
Sunny Bank Rd. *M13* 1C **103**
Sunnybank Rd. *Droy* 2B **74**
Sunny Brow Rd. *M18* 3C **89**
Sunny Dri. *P'wich* 2D **17**
Sunnylea Av. *M19* 4C **119**
Sunnyside. *Droy* 4B **58**
Sunnyside Av. *Droy* 3B **58**
Sunny Side Cotts. *Stret* 2D **97**
Sunnyside Ct. *Droy* 4B **58**
Sunnyside Rd. *Droy* 4B **58**
Sunset Bus. Pk. *Kear* 1C **13**
Surbiton Rd. *M40* 3B **56**
Surrey Av. *Droy* 4B **58**
Surrey Rd. *M9* 4B **22**
Surrey St. *M9* 4A **22**
Surrey St. *Chad* 1D **27**
Surrey Way. *Stoc* 4D **123**
Sussex Clo. *Swin* 4B **14**
Sussex Dri. *Droy* 4C **59**
Sussex St. *M2*. 2B **68** (5B **6**)
Sussex St. *Salf* 4D **51** (1C **4**)
Sutcliffe Av. *M12* 2B **104**
Sutherland Rd. *M16* 1A **98**
Sutherland St. *Eccl*. 4B **44**

Sutherland St. *Swin* 2A **30**
Sutton Dri. *Droy* 4A **58**
Sutton Ho. *Salf* 4D **49**
(off Sutton Dwellings)
Sutton Mnr. *M21* 3A **98**
Sutton Rd. *M18* 1C **105**
Sutton Way. *Salf* 4A **50**
Swainsthorpe Dri. *M9* 2C **39**
Swallow St. *M11* 2D **71**
Swallow St. *M12* 2A **104**
Swanage Rd. *Eccl* 4B **44**
Swanhill Clo. *M18* 2B **90**
Swanley Av. *M40* 2C **55**
Swan St. *M4* 1C **69** (3D **7**)
Swan Ter. *Eccl* 3C **61**
Swanton Wlk. *M8* 1B **52**
(off Kenford Wlk.)
Swarbrick Dri. *P'wich* 4D **17**
Swayfield Av. *M13* 1D **103**
Sweetnam Dri. *M11* 1B **72**
Swiftsure Av. *Salf* 2D **67** (5C **4**)
Swift Wlk. *M40* 1C **57**
Swinbourne Gro. *M20* 2A **118**
Swinburne Av. *Droy* 4C **59**
Swinburne Grn. *Stoc* 3D **105**
Swinburn St. *M9* 1D **39**
Swindell's St. *M11* 4A **74**
Swindon Clo. *M18* 3D **89**
Swinfield Av. *M21* 1D **113**
Swinford Wlk. *M9* 3C **23**
Swinstead Av. *M40* 2C **55**
Swinton **2B 30**
Swinton Ct. *Swin* 3C **31**
(off Park St.)
Swinton Gro. *M13* 3A **86**
Swinton Hall Rd. *Swin* 2B **30**
Swinton Ind. Est. *Swin* 2C **31**
Swinton Leisure Cen. 2B **30**
Swinton Library Art Gallery . . . 2B **30**
Swinton Park **4C 31**
Swinton Pk. Rd. *Salf* 2D **47**
Swinton Shop. Cen.
Swin. 2B **30**
Sycamore Av. *Chad* 3B **26**
Sycamore Clo. *M20* 2A **118**
Sycamore Ct. *M16* 1D **99**
Sycamore Ct. *M40* 4C **55**
Sycamore Ct. *Salf* 4A **50**
Sycamore Gro. *Fail* 3D **43**
Sycamore Rd. *Eccl* 3A **44**
Sydney Av. *Eccl* 1D **61**
Sydney Jones Ct. *M40* 1C **41**
Sydney St. *Fail* 3A **42**
Sydney St. *Salf* (M3) . . 2D **67** (4D **5**)
Sydney St. *Salf* (M6) 1C **65**
Sydney St. *Stret*. 2B **96**
Sydney St. *Swin*. 3D **29**
Sykes St. *Stoc* 1B **122**

Sykes Wlk. *Stoc* 1B **122**
(off Sykes St.)
Sylvan Av. *M16* 1D **99**
Sylvan Av. *Fail*. 2A **58**
Sylvan Av. *Urm* 1D **93**
Sylvandale Av. *M19* 3A **104**
Sylvia Gro. *Stoc*. 2A **122**
Symms St. *Salf* 3B **50**
Symond Rd. *M9*. 1C **23**
Symons Rd. *Sale* 4D **111**
Symons St. *Salf*. 3A **36**
Syndall Av. *M12*. 2B **86**
Syndall St. *M12*. 2B **86**

T

Tabley Av. *M14*. 2D **101**
Tabley Gdns. *Droy* 2D **75**
Tabley Gro. *M13* 2D **103**
Tabley Gro. *Stoc*. 2A **122**
Tabley St. *Salf* 2B **50**
Tackler Clo. *Swin* 3B **30**
Tadlow Wlk. *M40* 4A **54**
Tagge La. *Swin* 4C **33**
Tagore Clo. *M13*. 4C **87**
Tahir Clo. *M8*. 3D **37**
Talavera St. *Salf*. 2D **51**
Talbot Ct. *Stret*. 1C **97**
Talbot Pl. *M16* 3B **82**
Talbot Rd. *Fall* 2C **119**
Talbot Rd. *Stret & M16* 1C **97**
Talbot St. *Eccl* 2A **62**
Talford Gro. *M20* 4C **117**
Talgarth Rd. *M40* 3A **54**
Talland Wlk. *M13* 3B **86**
Tallarn Clo. *M20*. 2A **118**
Tallis St. *M12*. 1A **104**
Tall Trees. *Salf* 1D **35**
Tallyman Way. *Swin* 3C **33**
Talmine Av. *M40* 2C **55**
Tamar Clo. *Kear* 1B **12**
Tamar Ct. *M15*. 2D **83**
Tamarin Clo. *Swin* 1C **29**
Tamerton Dri. *M8*. 1C **53**
Tame St. *M4* 2B **70**
Tamworth Av. *Salf* 3B **66**
Tamworth Av. W. *Salf*. 3A **66**
Tamworth Clo. *M15* 3A **84**
Tamworth Ct. *M15* 3A **84**
Tamworth Ct. *M15*. 4A **84**
Tamworth St. *Oldh* 1D **27**
Tamworth Wlk. *Salf* 3B **66**
Tandis Ct. *Salf* 3C **47**
Tandlewood M. *M40* 2C **57**
Tangmere Clo. *M40* 3C **25**
Tangmere Ct. *M16* 1D **99**
Tannersfield Lodge. *Fail* 4A **42**

Tanners Grn. *Salf.* 4D **49**
        (off Nursery St.)
Tanners St. *M18.* 3A **90**
Tansey Gro. *Salf.* 3B **36**
Tansley Rd. *M8* 4D **21**
Tan Yd. *Brow. M18.* 4A **90**
Tanyard Grn. *Stoc.* 4B **122**
Taplin Dri. *M18* 3C **89**
Taplow Wlk. *M14* 1C **103**
Tarbet Wlk. *M8* 1B **52**
Target Fitness Cen. 4B **120**
        (Peel Moat)
Tariff St. *M1* 2D **69** (5E **7**)
Tarland Wlk. *Open* 2C **73**
Tarleton Ho. *Salf* 3A **48**
Tarleton Wlk. *M13* 2B **86**
Tarnbrook Wlk. *M15.* 3C **85**
     (off Wellhead Clo.)
Tarnside Ho. *M8.* 4B **20**
Tarporley Av. *M14* 4C **101**
Tarrington Clo. *M12* 3A **88**
Tartan St. *M11* 1B **72**
Tarves Wlk. *Open* 2B **72**
Tarvin Av. *M20.* 2C **117**
Tarvin Av. *Stoc.* 2D **121**
Tarvington Clo. *M40.* 1A **54**
Tasle All. *M2* 2B **68** (1B **10**)
Tatchbury Rd. *Fail.* 3C **43**
Tatham Clo. *M13* 1D **103**
Tattenhall Wlk. *M14* 1B **118**
Tatton Ct. *M14.* 1B **118**
Tatton Ct. *Stoc.* 4C **121**
Tatton Gro. *M20.* 3D **117**
Tatton Mere Dri. *Droy.* 2D **75**
Tatton Pl. *M13.* 4C **87**
Tatton Pl. *Sale.* 4D **111**
Tatton Rd. *Sale.* 4D **111**
Tatton Rd. N. *Stoc.* 4C **121**
Tatton Rd. S. *Stoc.* 4C **121**
Tatton St. *M15* 2D **83** (5C **8**)
Tatton St. *Salf.* 3B **66** (3A **8**)
Tatton Vw. *M20.* 3D **117**
Taunton Av. *Eccl.* 4B **44**
Taunton Av. *Stoc.* 4D **123**
Taunton Av. *Urm.* 4B **92**
Taunton St. *M4.* 2B **70**
Tavern Ct. *Fail.* 3D **43**
Tavern Ct. Av. *Fail.* 3C **43**
Tavery Clo. *M4.* 1B **70**
Tavistock Rd. *Sale.* 4D **109**
Tavistock Sq. *M9.* 3B **38**
    (off Grangewood Dri.)
Taylor Rd. *Urm.* 1A **78**
Taylor's La. *M40.* 2C **57**
Taylorson St. *Salf.* 2B **82**
       (in two parts)
Taylorson St. S. *Salf.* 2A **82**
Taylor's Rd. *Stret.* 4B **80**

Taylor St. *M14* 2A **102**
Taylor St. *M18* 2C **89**
Taylor St. *Droy.* 2B **74**
Taylor St. *P'wich* 2C **19**
Teak Dri. *Kear.* 2D **13**
Tealby Av. *M16.* 4C **83**
Tealby Ct. *M21.* 4C **99**
Tealby Rd. *M18* 4B **88**
Teasdale Clo. *Chad.* 3A **26**
Tebbutt St. *M4.* 4D **53** (2F **7**)
Tedburn Wlk. *M40.* 4D **25**
Teddington Rd. *M40.* 1C **41**
Ted Jackson Wlk. *M11.* 3D **71**
    (off Newchurch St.)
Teer St. *M40.* 1B **70**
Teesdale Av. *Urm.* 4A **76**
Teesdale Wlk. *M9.* 3C **23**
Teignmouth Av. *M40.* 3A **54**
Telegraphic Ho. *Salf.* 1A **82**
Telegraph Rd. *Traf P.* 2C **79**
Telfer Av. *M13* 2C **103**
Telfer Rd. *M13.* 2C **103**
Telford St. *M8* 2A **54**
Telford Wlk. *M16* 4D **83**
Tellson Clo. *Salf.* 4B **32**
Tellson Cres. *Salf.* 1B **48**
Telryn Wlk. *M8.* 2A **38**
    (off Stakeford Dri.)
Temperance St. *M12* 3A **70**
Temple Dri. *Swin* 3D **31**
Temple Rd. *Sale.* 4B **112**
Temple Sq. *M8* 1D **53**
Temsbury Wlk. *M40.* 2C **55**
Ten Acres La. *M40.* 2A **56**
Ten Acres Recreation Cen. 2A **56**
Tenax Circ. *Traf P.* 3D **63**
Tenax Rd. *Traf P* 1D **79**
Tenbury Clo. *Salf.* 4D **49**
Tenbury Dri. *Midd.* 1A **24**
Tenby Av. *M20.* 3D **117**
Tenby Av. *Stret.* 4D **81**
Tenby Ct. *M15.* 2C **83**
Tenby Dri. *Salf.* 2B **48**
Tenby Rd. *Oldh.* 4D **27**
Teneriffe St. *Salf.* 2D **51**
Tenham Wlk. *M9.* 3C **23**
    (off Ravenswood Dri.)
Tennis St. *M16.* 4B **82**
Tennyson Gdns. *P'wich* 3D **17**
Tennyson Rd. *Droy.* 1C **75**
Tennyson Rd. *Stoc.* 3D **105**
Tennyson Rd. *Swin* 2D **29**
Tennyson St. *M13* 4A **86**
Tennyson St. *Salf.* 3C **51**
Tenth St. *Traf P* 2B **80**
Terence St. *M40.* 2D **57**
Terrace, The. *P'wich* 3B **18**
Terrington Clo. *M21* 2A **116**

Tetlow Gro. *Eccl* 2C **61**
Tetlow La. *Salf* 2A **36**
Tetlow St. *M40* 2C **57**
Tetsworth Wlk. *M40* 4D **25**
Teviot St. *M13* 4C **87**
Tewkesbury Av. *Droy* 4C **59**
Tewkesbury Av. *Urm* 4D **77**
Tewkesbury Dri. *P'wich* 4C **19**
Tewkesbury Rd. *M40* 4B **54**
Textile St. *M12* 1A **88**
Textilose Rd. *Traf P* 3D **79**
Thackeray Clo. *M8* 4C **37**
Thackeray Gro. *Droy* 1C **75**
Thames Clo. *M11* 3B **72**
Thames Ct. *M15* 2D **83**
Thames Ind. Est. *M12* 4B **70**
Thanet Clo. *Salf* 2A **52**
Thatch Leach **1B 26**
Thatch Leach. *Chad* 1B **26**
Thaxmead Dri. *M40* 3D **57**
Thelwall Av. *M14* 4B **100**
Theta Clo. *M11* 1B **72**
Thetford Dri. *M8* 3C **37**
Third Av. *Clay* 4C **57**
Third Av. *Swin* 2A **46**
Third Av. *Traf P* 3B **80**
                          (in three parts)
Thirkhill Pl. *Eccl* 1B **62**
Thirlmere Av. *Stret* 1A **96**
Thirlmere Av. *Swin* 3C **31**
Thirsfield Dri. *M11* 1C **73**
Thirsk M. *Salf* 4D **35**
Thirsk St. *M12* 4A **70**
Thistle Bank Clo. *M9* 1A **38**
Thistledown Clo. *Eccl* 3C **61**
Thomas Ct. *M15* 5D **9**
Thomas Gibbon Clo. *Stret* . . 3A **96**
Thomas Johnson Clo. *Eccl* . . 2C **61**
Thomas Regan Ct. *M18* 2D **89**
Thomas St. *M4* 1C **69** (4D **7**)
Thomas St. *M8* 2B **36**
Thomas St. *Stret* 1B **96**
Thomas Telford Basin.
M1 . . . . 2A **70** (1F **11**)
Thompson Clo. *Dent* 1D **107**
Thompson Ct. *Dent* 1D **107**
Thompson La. *Chad* 2C **27**
Thompson Rd. *Dent* 1D **107**
Thompson Rd. *Traf P* 3A **62**
Thompson St. *M3* 4B **52** (1A **6**)
Thompson St. *M4* 4D **53** (2E **7**)
Thompson St. *M40* 2D **55**
Thomson Rd. *M18* 4C **89**
Thomson St. *M13* 2A **86**
Thoralby Clo. *M12* 3A **88**
Thoresway Rd. *M13* 1C **103**
Thorgill Wlk. *M40* 3A **40**
Thor Gro. *Salf* 3C **67** (3B **8**)

Thorley Clo. *Chad* 4B **26**
Thorley Dri. *Urm* 2D **93**
Thorley St. *Fail* 2B **42**
Thornaby Wlk. M9 . . . . **4B 38**
                        (off Lathbury Rd.)
Thornage Dri. *M40* 3A **54**
Thorn Av. *Fail* 1A **58**
Thornbank. *Eccl* 4A **46**
Thornbridge Av. *M21* 1B **114**
Thornbury Rd. *Stret* 4C **81**
Thornbury Way. *M18* 3C **89**
Thorncliffe Gro. *M19* 3C **105**
Thorncliffe Ho. *M15* 3D **85**
Thorncombe Rd. *M16* 4A **84**
Thorn Ct. *Salf* 1B **66**
Thorncross. *M15* . . . 1C **83** (5B **8**)
Thornden Rd. *M40* 3B **54**
Thorndyke Wlk. *P'wich* 3B **18**
Thorne Av. *Urm* 1A **92**
Thorne Ho. *M14* 2B **102**
Thorneycroft Av. *M21* 4B **114**
Thornfield Dri. *Swin* 3A **30**
Thornfield Rd. *M19* 4C **119**
Thornfield St. *Salf* 2B **64**
Thornford Wlk. *M40* 4D **25**
Thorngate Rd. *M8* 2C **53**
Thorn Gro. *M14* 1B **118**
Thorn Gro. *Sale* 4D **111**
Thornhill Clo. *Dent* 2C **107**
Thornhill Rd. *Droy* 1D **75**
Thornholme Clo. *M18* 1B **104**
Thorniley Brow. *M4* . . . 1C **69** (4C **6**)
Thornlea. *M9* 4A **24**
Thornlea. *Droy* 2A **74**
Thornlea Av. *Oldh* 1D **43**
Thornlea Av. *Swin* 4D **29**
Thornleigh Rd. *M14* 3C **101**
Thornley La. N. *Stoc* 1B **106**
Thornley La. S.
Stoc & Dent 2B **106**
Thornmere Clo. *Swin* 4C **13**
Thorn Pl. *Salf* 1B **66**
Thorn Rd. *Swin* 1A **46**
Thornsett Clo. *M9* 2C **39**
Thorns, The. *M21* 2B **114**
Thornton Av. *Aud* 3D **75**
Thornton Av. *Urm* 2A **92**
Thornton Clo. *M16* 3C **83**
Thornton Cres. *P'wich* 1D **17**
Thornton Pl. *Stoc* 4B **120**
Thornton Rd. *M14* 2C **101**
Thornton St. *M40* 3A **54**
Thornton St. N. *M40* 3A **54**
Thorntree Clo. *M9* 3C **39**
Thornwood Av. *M18* 4A **90**
Thorold Gro. *Sale* 4C **113**
Thorpe Av. *Swin* 1A **30**
Thorpebrook Rd. *M40* 4A **40**

Thorpe Gro. *Stoc* 3D **121**
Thorpeness Sq. *M18* 2D **89**
Thorpe St. *M16* 4C **83**
Thorpe Vw. *Salf.* 4C *67* (4A *8*)
     (off Ordsall Dri.)
Thorp Rd. *M40* 4A **40**
Thorp St. *Eccl.* 3B **60**
Thorsby Clo. *M18* 3A **90**
Thorverton Sq. *M40* 2B **40**
Three Acres Dri. *Stoc.* 4A **122**
Thruxton Clo. *M16* 1A **100**
Thurlby Av. *M9* 1C **23**
Thurlby St. *M13* 4B **86**
Thurlestone Dri. *Urm* 1C **93**
Thurloe St. *M14* 1A **102**
Thurlow St. *Salf.* 3D **65**
     (in three parts)
Thurlston Cres. *M8* 3D **37**
Thurlwood Av. *M20* 2C **117**
Thurnley Wlk. *M8.* 2B **52**
Thursby Av. *M20* 3C **117**
Thursfield St. *Salf* 2B **50**
Tib La. *M2.* 2B **68** (1B **10**)
Tib St. *M4.* 2C **69** (5D **7**)
Tideswell Av. *M40* 4B **54**
Tideswell Rd. *Droy.* 4A **58**
Tideway Clo. *Salf.* 2D **33**
Tidworth Av. *M4.* 1B **70**
Tiefield Wlk. *M21* 2A **116**
Tilbury Wlk. *M40* 4B **54**
Tilehurst Ct. *Salf* 3B **34**
Tilgate Wlk. *M9* *3C 23*
     (off Haverfield Rd.)
Tilney Av. *Stret.* 3C **97**
Tilshead Wlk. *M13* *2A 86*
     (off Dilston Clo.)
Timber Wharf. *M15.* 4D **67** (4C **8**)
Timothy Clo. *Salf.* 4D **47**
Timperley Av. *M11* 3C **73**
Timson St. *Fail.* 3B **42**
Tindall St. *Eccl.* 3B **60**
Tindall St. *Stoc.* 1B **106**
Tindle St. *Wors* 3A **12**
Tinningham Clo. *M11.* 1A **90**
Tinshill Clo. *M12* 3A **88**
Tinsley Clo. *M40* 1C **71**
Tintern Av. *M20* 4B **116**
Tintern Av. *Urm* 4A **92**
Tintern St. *M14* 2D **101**
Tiptree Wlk. *M9* 2C **39**
Tirza Av. *M19.* 1D **119**
Titterington Av. *M21.* 2B **98**
Tiverton Ho. *Salf.* 4C **47**
Tiverton Rd. *Urm* 4A **78**
Tivol St. *M3.* 2A **68** (1F **9**)
Tixall Wlk. *M8* 4A **20**
Toad Pond Clo. *Swin* 1C **45**
Tobermory Clo. *M11.* 2D **73**

Todd's Pl. *M8.* 1A **38**
Todd St. *M3* 1C **69** (3C **6**)
Todd St. *Salf* 1D **51**
Toft Rd. *M18* 4C **89**
Toledo St. *M11* 2D **73**
Tollard Av. *M40* 2B **54**
Toll Bar St. *M12.* 2C **87**
Tollesbury Clo. *M40* 3B **54**
Toll Ga. Clo. *M13.* 4C **87**
Tolworth Dri. *M8.* 3D **37**
Tomlinson St. *M15.* 2A **84**
Tomlinson St. *M40.* 3C **25**
Tom Lomas Wlk. *M11* 1B **72**
Tommy Browell Clo. *M14* . . . 1C **101**
Tommy Johnson Wlk.
   M14 . . . . 1C **101**
Tommy Taylor Clo. *M40* 2C **57**
Tonbridge Rd. *M19* 1B **120**
Tonbridge Rd. *Stoc* 1B **122**
Tonge St. *M12.* 4B **70**
Tongley Wlk. *M40* 4D **25**
Tong St. *Kear.* 1C **13**
Tonman St. *M3* 3A **68** (2F **9**)
Tontin St. *Salf* 1B **66**
Tooley Ho. *Eccl* 3D **61**
Tootal Dri. *Salf & M5* 1A **64**
Tootal Gro. *Salf* 1A **64**
Tootal Rd. *Salf.* 1A **64**
Topfields. *Salf.* 3D **35**
Topley St. *M40.* 1B **54**
Top o' th' Grn. *Chad.* 2D **27**
Topsham Wlk. *M40* 2D **57**
Torah St. *M8* 3C **53**
Torbay Rd. *M21* 1C **115**
Torbay Rd. *Urm* 3A **94**
Torcross Rd. *M9* 1D **21**
Torkington Av. *Swin* 1B **30**
Torksey Wlk. *M9* 1D **21**
Torness Wlk. *Open.* 2B **72**
Torpoint Wlk. *M40.* 1C **41**
Torquay Clo. *M13.* 2B **86**
Torrax Clo. *Salf.* 1D **47**
Torrens St. *Salf* 2B **48**
Torrington Av. *M9* 4A **24**
Torrington Rd. *Swin* 4D **31**
Torside Way. *Swin* 4B **14**
Totland Clo. *M12* 1B **104**
Totnes Rd. *M21* 1C **115**
Totnes Rd. *Sale* 4D **109**
Tottington La. *P'wich* 1C **17**
Tottington St. *M11* 1C **73**
Totton Rd. *Fail.* 3B **42**
Towcester Clo. *M4* 2B **70**
Tower Grange. *Salf.* 2D **35**
Tower Sq. *M13* 2A **86**
Towey Clo. *M18.* 2D **89**
Towncliffe Wlk. *M15* 2D **83**
Townfield. *Urm* 3B **92**

Townfield Wlk. *M15* 2D **83**
Towngreen Ct. *M8* 4B **20**
Town Hall La. *M2* 5B **6**
Townley Dri. *M8* 2B **52**
Townley St. *M11* 3D **71**
Towns Cft. Lodge. *Sale* 3A **110**
Townsend Rd. *Swin* 1B **30**
Town Sq. *Sale* 4D **111**
Towton St. *M9* 2C **39**
Towyn Av. *Salf* 1A **66**
Toxteth St. *M11* 4A **74**
Tracey St. *M8* 1C **37**
Traders Av. *Urm* 2A **78**
Trafalgar Av. *Aud* 4D **75**
Trafalgar Bus. Pk. *M8* 3A **52**
Trafalgar Ct. *M16* 2A **100**
Trafalgar Gro. *Salf* 2D **51**
Trafalgar Pl. *M20* 4C **117**
Trafalgar Rd. *Sale* 3A **110**
Trafalgar Rd. *Salf* 4C **47**
Trafalgar St. *Salf* 2A **52**
Trafalgar Wlk. *Hulme* 3A **84**
Trafalgar Wlk. *Open* 3A **72**
Trafford Athletic Stadium 3D **97**
Trafford Av. *Urm* 1A **94**
Trafford Bank Rd. *M16* 3C **83**
Trafford Boulevard. *Urm* 2C **77**
Trafford Cen., The. *Urm* 2D **77**
Trafford Ct. *M15* 2D **83**
Trafford Ecology Pk. 4A **64**
Trafford Enterprise Cen.
  Traf P 3B **80**
Trafford Gro. *Stret* 3B **96**
Trafford Ho. *Stret* 3D **81**
Trafford Mans. *M16* 2B **98**
Trafford Park 3A **80**
Trafford Pk. Heritage Cen. 2A **80**
Trafford Pk. Rd. *Traf P* 3D **63**
Trafford Pl. *M15* 2D **83**
Trafford Retail Pk. *Urm* 3C **77**
Trafford Rd. *Eccl* 3D **61**
Trafford Rd. *Salf* 2A **82**
Trafford St. *M3* 3A **68** (3F **9**)
Trafford Water Sports Cen. 3C **113**
Trafford Way. *Urm* 1C **77**
Trafford Wharf Rd. *Traf P* 4B **64**
Trail St. *Salf* 1C **65**
Tram St. *M11* 3C **73**
Tranmere Clo. *M18* 2B **88**
Transvaal St. *M11* 2D **73**
Travis St. *M1* 3D **69** (3F **11**)
Tree Av. *Droy* 4C **59**
Treelands Wlk. *Salf* 2B **82**
Trees St. *M8* 2B **36**
Tree Wlk. *Stret* 3A **96**
Tremain Wlk. M9 . . . . *3B* ***38***
  (off Stockwood Wlk.)
Trenam Pl. *Salf* 1B **66**

Trenant Rd. *Salf* 2B **48**
Trenchard Ct. *M11* 1D **73**
Trent Bri. Wlk. *M16* 1A **98**
Trent Clo. *Stoc* 4D **123**
Trent Ct. *M15* 2D **83**
Trentham Gro. *M40* 1A **40**
Trentham Lawns. *Salf* 3B **50**
Trentham Rd. *M16* 1A **98**
Trentham St. *M15* . . . 1C **83** (5B **8**)
Trentham St. *Swin* 1A **30**
Trent Wlk. *Droy* 2D **75**
Trent Way. *Kear* 1B **12**
  (in two parts)
Tresco Av. *Stret* 3C **97**
Trevelyan St. *Eccl* 1C **63**
Trevor Dri. *M40* 4A **26**
Trevor Rd. *Eccl* 4B **44**
Trevor Rd. *Swin* 4D **29**
Trevor Rd. *Urm* 1A **92**
Trevor St. *Open* 4A **74**
Triangle, The. *M4* 1B **68** (4B **6**)
Trimdon Clo. *M11* 1B **72**
Trimley Av. *M40* 2B **54**
Tring Wlk. *M9* 3D **21**
Trinity Ct. *Salf* 1D **67** (4D **5**)
Trinity Gdns. *Salf* 1D **67** (3D **5**)
Trinity Sports Cen. 3C **85**
Trinity Wlk. *M14* 1D **101**
Trinity Way. *Salf* 2D **67** (5D **5**)
Trippier Rd. *Eccl* 3A **60**
Triscombe Way.
  M16 . . . . 1A **100**
Tristam Clo. *M13* 2A **86** (5F **11**)
Trojan Gdns. *Salf* 2C **51**
Trongate Wlk. *M9* 3C **39**
Troutbeck Av. *M4* 1A **70**
Trowbridge Dri.
  M40 . . . . 1C **41**
Trowtree Av. *M12* 2C **87**
Troydale Dri. *M40* 1A **56**
Troy Wlk. *Salf* 1B **82**
Trumpet St. *M1* 3B **68** (3A **10**)
Truro Av. *Stoc* 4D **123**
Truro Av. *Stret* 2C **97**
Trust Rd. *M18* 1C **105**
Tudbury Way. *Salf* 4D **51** (3D **5**)
Tudor Av. *M9* 1C **39**
Tudor Av. *Chad* 3D **25**
Tudor Clo. *Stoc* 2A **122**
Tudor Ct. M16 . . . . *3C* ***83***
  (off Stanley Rd.)
Tudor Ct. *P'wich* 3C **19**
Tudor Ct. *Wors* 2A **28**
Tuer St. *M13* 2C **85**
Tufton Wlk. *M9* 3B **38**
Tugford Clo. *M16* 4A **84**
Tuley St. *M11* 4D **71**
Tulip Clo. *Sale* 4C **109**

Tulip Wlk. *Salf*	3D **51** (1C **4**)
Tulketh St. Ind. Est. *M40*	2D **39**
Tulle Ct. *P'wich*	2A **18**
Tully St. *Salf*	3A **36**
Tully St. S. *Salf*	1A **52**
Tumbling Bank. *M9*	3B **22**
Tunbridge Sq. *Salf*	1A **66**
Tunstall St. *M11*	4A **74**
Tunstead Av. *M20*	3B **116**
Turf La. *Chad*	3B **26**
Turfnell Way. *Wors*	2A **44**
Turley St. *M8*	1D **53**
Turnberry Wlk. *M8*	2A **38**
Turnbull Rd. *Gort*	4B **90**
Turnbull Rd. *Long*	2D **103**
Turnbury Clo. *Sale*	3D **111**
Turner Av. *Fail*	4A **42**
Turner Dri. *Urm*	2B **94**
Turner St. *M4*	1C **69** (4D **7**)
Turner St. *M11*	2C **73**
Turner St. *M16*	2C **83**
Turner St. *Gort*	3D **89**
Turner St. *Salf*	3A **36**
Turn Moss Rd. *Stret*	4D **97**
Turnpike Ct. *M16*	1D **99**
Turnpike Grn. *Salf*	4D **49**
(off Nursery St.)	
Turnpike Wlk. *M11*	2D **71**
Turton La. *P'wich*	1D **17**
Turton St. *Open*	4D **73**
Tuscany Vw. *Salf*	2B **34**
Tutbury St. *M4*	2B **70**
Tuxford Wlk. *M40*	2B **54**
(off Monsall St.)	
Tweedale Av. *M9*	1A **22**
Tweedale Way. *Oldh*	4B **26**
Tweedle Hill Rd. *M9*	2D **21**
Twillbrook Dri. *Salf*	4A **52** (2F **5**)
Twining Rd. *Traf P*	3A **62**
Tyersall Clo. *Eccl*	3A **46**
Tyldesley St. *M14*	1C **101**
Tymm St. *M40*	2C **41**
Tyndall Av. *M40*	1A **40**
Tynedale Clo. *Stoc*	4A **122**
Tynwell Wlk. *M40*	2A **54**
Tyrol Wlk. *M11*	3D **71**
Tyrrell Rd. *Stoc*	3B **106**
Tysoe Gdns. *Salf*	1D **67** (3D **5**)
Tyson St. *M8*	2B **36**
Tytherington Dri. *M19*	3D **105**

U

Ukraine Rd. *Salf*	4B **34**
Ullswater Wlk. *M9*	3C **23**
(off Rockmead Dri.)	
Ulverston Av. *M20*	2B **116**

UMIST Hardy Farm	
Sports Ground	3A **114**
Underhill Wlk. *M40*	3B **56**
Under La. *Chad*	3D **27**
Under St. *Chad*	3D **27**
Underwood Clo. *M18*	2B **90**
Unicorn St. *Eccl*	3B **60**
Union St. *M4*	1C **69** (4D **7**)
Union St. *M14*	1D **101**
Union St. *Abb H*	2A **90**
Union St. *Ard*	4A **70**
Union St. *Chad*	2D **27**
Union St. *Salf*	3A **50**
Union St. *Swin*	2A **30**
(Chorley Rd.)	
Union St. *Swin*	2C **31**
(Hilton St.)	
Union Ter. *Salf*	2B **36**
United Trad. Est. *M16*	3C **81**
Unity Dri. *Salf*	1A **52**
Universities	2C **85**
University of Manchester	2D **85**
University of Manchester Institute of Science & Technology, The.	
	3D **69** (3E **11**)
University of Salford	1D **67** (3C **4**)
(Adelphi Campus)	
University of Salford	1C **67** (3A **4**)
(Cockcroft Rd.)	
University of Salford	4B **50**
(Frederick Rd. Campus)	
University of Salford	2C **67** (5A **4**)
(Humphrey Booth Ho.)	
University of Salford	4C **51** (2B **4**)
(Meadow Rd.)	
University Rd. *Salf*	4B **50** (1A **4**)
University Rd. W. *Salf*	1B **66** (4A **4**)
Unsworth Av. *M18*	4D **89**
Unwin Ct. *Salf*	1D **65**
Upavon Ct. *M7*	4B **36**
Up. Brook St.	
M13 & M14	1D **85** (5E **11**)
Up. Camp St. *Salf*	2D **51**
Up. Chorlton Rd. *M16*	2C **99**
Up. Conran St. *M9*	2C **39**
Up. Cyrus St. *M40*	1C **71**
Up. Gloucester St. *Salf*	4A **50**
Up. Helena St. *M40*	1C **71**
Up. Kent Rd. *M14*	1B **102**
Up. Kirby St. *M4*	2A **70**
Up. Lloyd St. *M14*	1C **101**
Up. Medlock St. *M15*	2B **84**
Up. Monsall St. *M40*	1C **55**
Up. Moss La. *M15*	2A **84**
Up. Park Rd. *M14*	4A **86**
Up. Park Rd. *Salf*	1D **35**
Up. West Gro. *M13*	3B **86**
Up. Wharf St. *Salf*	2C **67** (5B **4**)

Up. Wilton St. *P'wich* 2C **19**
Upton Clo. *Midd* 1A **24**
Upton St. *M1* 2D **69** (2E **11**)
Upwood Wlk. *M9* 3C **23**
Urbis 1C **69** (3C **6**)
(Museum)
Urmston 2D **93**
Urmston La. *Stret* 3C **95**
Urmston Leisure Cen. 2A **92**
Urmston Pk. *Urm* 2A **94**
Uvedale Ho. *Eccl* 2D **61**
(off Adelaide St.)
Uxbridge Av. *M11* 1C **73**

V

Valance Clo. *M12* 2A **88**
Vale Av. *Sale* 4C **113**
Vale Av. *Swin* 1C **31**
Vale Dri. *P'wich* 4A **18**
Vale La. *Fail* 3C **59**
Valencia Rd. *Salf* 4B **34**
Valentia Rd. *M9* 2B **22**
Valentine St. *Fail* 3A **42**
Vale Pk. Ind. Est. *M8* 3A **38**
Valerie Wlk. M15 . . . . . 1B **84** (5B **10**)
(off Loxford St.)
Vale Rd. *Droy* 4D **59**
Vale St. *M11* 1C **73**
Va. Top Av. *M9* 3D **39**
Valetta Clo. *M14* 4D **101**
Valiant Wlk. *M40* 1A **42**
Valley Pk. Rd. *P'wich* 1D **17**
Valley Wlk. *M11* 2D **71**
Vancouver Quay. *Salf* 1D **81**
Vandyke Av. *Salf* 4D **47**
Vane St. *Eccl* 1D **61**
(in two parts)
Vanguard Clo. *Eccl* 4A **60**
Varey St. *M18* 3D **89**
Varley St. *M40* 3B **54**
Varna St. *M11* 1D **89**
Vauban Dri. *Salf* 4D **47**
Vaughan Av. *M40* 2A **40**
Vaughan Ind. Est.
M12 . . . . 1D **87**
Vaughan Rd. *M21* 4D **99**
Vaughan St. *M12* 1D **87**
Vaughan St. *Eccl* 4B **44**
Vauxhall Ct. M40 . . . . 3A **54**
(off Hamerton Rd.)
Vauxhall Ind. Est. *Stoc* 3A **122**
Vauxhall St. *M40* 3D **53**
Vega St. *M8* 3A **52**
Vela Wlk. *Salf* 4C **51** (2B **4**)
Velmere Av. *M9* 1C **21**
Velour Clo. *Salf* 4D **51** (1C **4**)

Velvet Ct. *M1* 3C **69** (3D **11**)
(off Granby Row)
Velvet Sq. *M1* 3C **69** (3D **11**)
(off Bombay St.)
Vendale Av. *Swin* 1D **45**
Venesta Av. *Salf* 3D **47**
Venetia St. *M40* 2C **57**
Venice Ct. *M1* 3C **69** (3D **11**)
(off Samuel Ogden St.)
Venice Sq. *M1* 3C **69** (3D **11**)
Venice St. *M1* 3C **69** (3D **11**)
Ventnor Av. *M19* 1B **120**
Ventnor Av. *Sale* 3D **111**
Ventnor St. *M9* 2B **38**
Ventnor St. *Salf* 2B **50**
Ventura Clo. *M14* 3C **101**
Venture Scout. *M8* 2B **52**
Venwood Ct. *P'wich* 4D **17**
Venwood Rd. *P'wich* 4D **17**
Verdant La. *Eccl* 3A **60**
Verdon St. *M4* 4C **53** (2C **6**)
Verdun Av. *Salf* 4D **47**
Verdun Rd. *Eccl* 3B **44**
Verdure Clo. *Fail* 3D **43**
Vere St. *Salf* 2D **65**
Verity Clo. *M20* 3D **117**
Verity Wlk. *M9* 3D **21**
Verne Av. *Swin* 2A **30**
Vernon Av. *Eccl* 1B **62**
Vernon Av. *Stret* 3B **96**
Vernon Ct. *Salf* 1C **35**
Vernon Dri. *P'wich* 4A **18**
Vernon Rd. *Droy* 1A **74**
Vernon Rd. *Salf* 1C **35**
Vernon St. *Harp* 3C **39**
Vernon St. *Old T* 3D **83**
Vernon St. *Salf* 2D **51**
Vernon Ter. *M12* 3D **87**
Verona Dri. *M40* 3C **57**
Vesper St. *Fail* 2C **43**
Vesta St. *M4* 2A **70**
Vestris Dri. *Salf* 4D **47**
Viaduct St. *M12* 3C **71**
Viaduct St. *Salf* 1A **68** (3F **5**)
Vicarage Clo. *Salf* 4D **47**
Vicarage Gro. *Eccl* 1B **62**
Vicarage Rd. *Swin* 2A **30**
Vicarage Rd. *Urm* 4B **76**
Vicarage St. *Oldh* 3D **27**
Vicars Rd. *M21* 1A **114**
Vicars St. *Eccl* 4B **46**
Vicker Clo. *Swin* 4B **14**
Vicker Gro. *M20* 4B **116**
Vickers St. *M40* 4C **55**
Victoria Av. *M9* 1C **21**
Victoria Av. *Eccl* 4B **46**
Victoria Av. *Lev* 4A **104**
Victoria Av. *Swin* 2C **31**

Victoria Av. E. *M9 & M40* 2C **23**
Victoria Bri. St. *Salf* 1B **68** (4A **6**)
Victoria Building, The. *Salf* 3D **65**
Victoria Ct. *Stret* 2A **96**
Victoria Cres. *Eccl* 4B **46**
Victoria Gro. *M14* 2A **118**
Victoria Gro. *Stoc* 4C **121**
Victoria Hall. M15 . . . . 2C **85**
(off Higher Cambridge St.)
Victoria Ho. *Eccl* 1B **62**
Victoria Ho. *Open* 3C **73**
Victoria Ho. *Salf* 3C **47**
Victoria Ind. Est. *M4* 2B **70**
Victoria La. *Swin* 2D **29**
Victoria Lodge. *Salf* 2C **51**
Victoria Pde. *Urm* 2D **93**
Victoria Park. 4B **85**
Victoria Pk. *M14* 4C **87**
Victoria Pl. *Traf P* 3D **81**
Victoria Rd. *Eccl* 4A **46**
Victoria Rd. *Fall* 4D **101**
Victoria Rd. *Lev* 3D **103**
Victoria Rd. *Salf* 3C **47**
Victoria Rd. *Stret* 2B **96**
Victoria Rd. *Urm* 2B **92**
Victoria Rd. *Whal R* 2D **99**
Victoria Sq. *M4* 1D **69** (3F **7**)
Victoria Sta. App. *M3* 1C **69** (3B **6**)
Victoria St. *M3* 1B **68** (4B **6**)
Victoria St. *Fail* 4D **41**
Victoria St. *Open* 3C **73**
Victoria Ter. *M12* 4D **87**
Victoria Trad. Est. *Chad* 3D **27**
Victor Mann St. *M11* 4C **75**
Victor St. *M40* 3A **54**
Victor St. *Oldh* 1D **43**
Victor St. *Salf* 1D **67** (4D **5**)
Victory Gro. *Aud* 4D **75**
Victory St. *M14* 1A **102**
Viewfield Wlk. M9 . . . . 3C **39**
(off Nethervale Dri.)
Viking Clo. *M11* 2D **71**
Village Circ. *Traf P* 2B **80**
Village Ct. *Traf P* 2A **80**
Village St. *Salf* 2C **51**
Village Wlk. *Open* 2C **73**
Village Way. *M4* 1C **69** (3F **7**)
Village Way. *Traf P* 2D **79**
Villemoble Sq. *Droy* 2C **75**
Villiers St. *Salf* 3D **49**
Vinca Gro. *Salf* 1D **51**
Vincent Av. *M21* 3A **98**
Vincent Av. *Eccl* 3D **45**
Vincent St. *M11* 3C **73**
Vincent St. *Salf* 3D **35**
Vine Av. *Swin* 2D **31**
Vine Clo. *Sale* 4C **109**
Vine Ct. *Stret* 3B **96**

Vine Fold. *M40* 1B **42**
Vine St. *M11 & M18* 4A **74**
Vine St. *Chad* 3D **27**
Vine St. *Eccl* 2C **61**
Vine St. *P'wich* 1C **19**
Vine St. *Salf* 2B **34**
Viola St. *M11* 1D **73**
Violet St. *M18* 2B **90**
Virgil St. *M15* 2C **83**
Virgina Ho. *M11* 4B **72**
Viscount St. *M14* 1A **102**
Vivian Pl. *M14* 4C **87**
Vixen Clo. *M21* 2D **115**
Voltaire Av. *Salf* 4D **47**
Vulcan Works. *M4* 2B **70**
Vyner Gro. *Sale* 3B **110**

W

Wadcroft Wlk. *M9* 2C **39**
Wade Clo. *Eccl* 2D **61**
Wadeford Clo. *M4* 4A **54**
(in two parts)
Wade Ho. Eccl 2D **61**
(off Wade Clo.)
Wadesmill Wlk. *M13* . . . 1D **85** (5E **11**)
Wadeson Rd. *M13* 4D **69** (4F **11**)
Wade Wlk. *Open* 3A **72**
Wadhurst Wlk. *M13* 3A **86**
Wadlow Clo. *Salf* 4D **51** (2E **5**)
Wadsworth M. *Droy* 2B **74**
Waggoners Ct. *Swin* 3B **30**
Wagstaff Dri. *Fail* 3B **42**
Wain Clo. *Eccl* 1B **60**
Wainman St. *Salf* 2B **50**
Wainwright Av. *Dent* 1B **106**
Wakefield Dri. *Swin* 1D **13**
Wakefield St. *M1* 4C **69** (4C **10**)
Walcott Clo. *M13* 3B **86**
Wald Av. *M14* 2C **119**
Waldeck Wlk. M9 . . . . 3C **23**
(off Ravenswood Dri.)
Walden Clo. *M14* 4C **101**
Walderton Av. *M40* 3A **40**
Walford St. *M16* 4A **84**
Walker Av. *Fail* 1D **59**
Walker Grn. *Eccl* 2B **44**
Walker Ho. *Eccl* 2D **61**
Walker Rd. *M9* 2C **23**
Walker Rd. *Chad* 4B **26**
Walker Rd. *Eccl* 3A **44**
Walkers Bldgs. *M1* 1F **11**
Walker's Cft. *Salf* 1B **68** (3B **6**)
Wallace Av. *M14* 1B **102**
Wallasey Av. *M14* 3C **101**
Walled Garden, The. *Swin* 4D **29**
Waller Av. *M14* 4A **102**

Wallingford Rd. *Urm* 1A **94**
Wallis St. *M40* 2C **57**
Wallis St. *Chad* 2C **27**
Wallis St. *P'wich* 1A **18**
Wallness . . . . **4B 50 (2A 4)**
Wallness La. *Salf* . . . . . . **3B 50 (1A 4)**
Wall St. *Salf* 1D **65**
Wall Way. *M18* 4A **90**
Wallwork St. *Open* 3A **74**
Wallwork St. *Stoc* 2B **106**
Wallworth Av. *M18* 3D **89**
Wally Sq. *Salf* 1A **52**
Walmersley Rd. *M40* 4A **26**
Walmer St. *Abb H* 2A **90**
Walmer St. *Rush* 1D **101**
Walmer St. E. *Rush* 1A **102**
Walmsley Gro. *Urm* 2D **93**
Walnut Clo. *Swin* 2D **13**
Walnut Gro. *Sale* 4C **111**
(Ashlands)
Walnut Gro. *Sale* 4C **111**
(Oakfield)
Walnut Rd. *Eccl* 3A **44**
Walnut St. *M18* 2D **89**
Walnut Wlk. *Stret* 3A **96**
Walsall St. *Salf* 2A **50**
Walsden St. *M11* 1C **73**
Walsh Av. *M9* 4B **22**
Walshaw Dri. *Swin* 3B **30**
Walsingham Av. *M20* 4B **116**
Walsingham Av. *Midd* 1A **24**
Walter Greenwood Ct. Salf 4A **50**
(off Belvedere Rd.)
Walter St. *M9* 2B **38**
Walter St. *Abb H* 2A **90**
Walter St. *Old T* 4C **83**
Walter St. *P'wich* 2D **17**
Waltham Rd. *M16* 3A **100**
Walton Hall Dri. *M19* 3D **105**
Walton Ho. *Fail* 2B **42**
Walton Rd. *M9* 1B **22**
Walwyn Clo. *Stret* 3C **97**
Wandsworth Av. *M11* 1D **73**
Wanley Wlk. *M9* 3C **23**
Wansbeck Clo. *Stret* 3C **97**
Wansbeck Lodge. *Stret* 3C **97**
Wansfell Wlk. *M4* 1B **70**
Wansford St. *M14* 1C **101**
Wanstead Av. *M9* 3B **24**
Warbeck Clo. *Stoc* 2C **107**
Warbeck Rd. *M40* 4D **25**
Warbrick Dri. *Urm* 3B **92**
Warburton St. *Eccl* 2A **62**
Warburton St. *Salf* 2B **82**
Warden La. *M40* 1B **56**
Warden St. *M40* 1B **56**
Warde St. *M15* 2A **84**
Wardle Clo. *Stret* 2C **97**

Wardle Rd. *Sale* 4A **112**
Wardle St. *M40* 4C **55**
Wardley 4C **13**
Wardley Av. *M16* 3A **100**
Wardley Hall La. *Wors* 2A **28**
(in two parts)
Wardley Hall Rd.
Wors & Swin 1B **28**
Wardley Ho. *Salf* 3A **48**
Wardley Ind. Est. *Wors* 1C **29**
Wardley St. *Swin* 2B **30**
Wardle Rd. *Droy* 2D **75**
Wardsend Wlk. *M15* 2D **83**
Ward St. *M9* 4A **22**
Ward St. *Fail* 2A **42**
Ward St. *Most* 2D **39**
Wareham Gro. *Eccl* 4C **45**
Wareham St. *M8* 1D **37**
Warfield Wlk. *M9* 3C **23**
Warford St. *M4* . . . . 3D **53 (1E 7)**
Warley Rd. *M16* 1A **98**
Warmington Dri. *M12* 2C **87**
Warner Wlk. M11 . . . . 2D **71**
(off Hopedale Clo.)
Warnford Clo. *M40* 3D **57**
Warp Wlk. M4 . . . . 1A **70**
(off Jackroom Dri.)
Warren Bank. *M9* 3B **22**
Warren Bruce Rd. *Traf P* 2B **80**
Warren Dri. *Swin* 2D **45**
Warren Rd. *Traf P* 2D **79**
Warren St. *M9* 4A **22**
Warren St. *Salf* 2B **36**
Warrington Rd. *M9* 2A **22**
Warstead Wlk. M13 . . . . 3A **86**
(off Plymouth Gro.)
Warwick Av. *M20* 4B **116**
Warwick Av. *Swin* 4D **13**
Warwick Ct. *M16* 1A **98**
Warwick Dri. *Urm* 4B **76**
Warwick Gro. *Aud* 3D **75**
Warwick Ho. *M19* 2A **104**
Warwick Rd. *Chor H* 3B **98**
Warwick Rd. *Fail* 2B **58**
Warwick Rd. *Old T* 3D **81**
Warwick Rd. S. *M16* 1A **98**
Warwick Rd. *M1* . . . . . 1D **69 (4E 7)**
Warwick St. *M15* 3B **84**
Warwick St. *Oldh* 2D **27**
(in two parts)
Warwick St. *P'wich* 2A **18**
(in two parts)
Warwick St. *Swin* 1B **30**
Wasdale Av. *Urm* 1B **92**
Wash Brook. *Chad* 2D **27**
Washbrook Ct. *Chad* 2D **27**
Washbrook Dri. *Stret* 2D **95**
Washway Rd. *Sale* 4C **111**

Wasnidge Wlk. *M15* 3B **84**
Waterbridge. *Wors.* 2A **44**
Waterfield Way. *Fail.* 4C **43**
Waterfront Ho. *Eccl* 4C **45**
Waterfront Quay. *Salf.* 1D **81**
Waterhouse Rd. *M18* 4A **90**
Water La. *Droy.* 2A **74**
(in two parts)
Waterloo Ct. *M20* *4C 117*
(off Lapwing La.)
Waterloo Est. *M8* 1C **53**
Waterloo Pde. *M8* 3B **52**
Waterloo Rd. *M8* 2B **52**
Waterloo St. *M1* 3C **69** (2C **10**)
Waterloo St. *M8 & M9* 2A **38**
Watermans Clo. *M9* 2D **39**
Waterpark Hall. *Salf* 1A **36**
Waterpark Rd. *Salf.* 2A **36**
Waters Edge Bus. Pk.
  Salf 2B **82**
Waterside. *Traf P* 2D **81**
Waterside Clo. *M21* 4D **115**
Waterside Ho. *Wors.* 2A **44**
Waterslea. *Eccl* 1C **61**
Watersmeet. *Stret* 4B **80**
Waterson Av. *M40* 3A **40**
Waters Reach. *Traf P* 2D **81**
Water St. *M3.* 3D **67** (3C **8**)
(in three parts)
Water St. *M9* 2B **38**
Water St. *M12* 3A **70**
Water St. *Aud* 4D **91**
Waterway Enterprise Pk.
  Traf P 2D **81**
Watfield Wlk. *M9* *3B 38*
(off Foleshill Av.)
Watford Av. *M14* 2D **101**
Watford Rd. *M19* 3A **120**
Watkin Clo. *M13* 2A **86**
Watkins Dri. *P'wich* 3A **20**
Watkin St. *Salf* 4D **51** (1D **5**)
Watson St. *M3* 3B **68** (3A **10**)
(in two parts)
Watson St. *Eccl* 1C **61**
Watson St. *Swin* 1B **30**
Watton Clo. *Swin* 4B **14**
Watts St. *M19* 1B **120**
Waugh Av. *Fail.* 4B **42**
Waverley Av. *Stret* 1C **97**
Waverley Ct. *M9.* 1C **21**
Waverley Cres. *Droy.* 4C **59**
Waverley Rd. *M9* 3D **39**
Waverley Rd. *Sale* 3A **112**
Waverley Rd. *Swin.* 3A **32**
Waverley Rd. W. *M9* 3D **39**
Waverton Av. *Stoc* 2D **121**
Waverton Rd. *M14.* 3C **101**
Wavertree Rd. *M9* 2A **22**

Waybridge Ind. Est. *Salf* 3B **64**
Wayfarers Way. *Swin* 3A **30**
Wayford Wlk. *M9.* *3A 38*
(off Hendham La.)
Wayland Rd. *M18* 4D **89**
Wayland Rd. S. *M18* 1D **105**
Wayne St. *Open* 3A **74**
Weald Clo. *M13* 2A **86** (5F **11**)
Weardale Rd. *M9* 1D **21**
Wearhead Row. *Salf.* 2D **65**
Weaste 1B **64**
Weaste Dri. *Salf.* 4B **48**
Weaste La. *Salf & M5.* 4A **48**
(in two parts)
Weaste Rd. *Salf.* 1B **64**
Weaste Trad. Est. *Salf.* 1B **64**
Weatherall St. N. *Salf* 3B **36**
(in two parts)
Weaver Ct. *M15.* 2D **83**
Weaverham Clo. *M13.* 1D **103**
Weaver Ho. *Salf.* 2C **51**
Weaver Wlk. *Open* 4D **73**
Webdale Dri. *M40* 3A **40**
Webster Gro. *P'wich* 4D **17**
Wedgewood St. *M40* 3D **55**
Wedgwood Rd. *Swin* 4A **16**
Weedall Av. *Salf.* 2A **82**
Weft Wlk. *M4.* 2A **70**
Weir St. *M15.* 3A **84**
Weir St. *Fail.* 3A **42**
Welbeck Av. *Chad* 3D **25**
Welbeck Av. *Urm* 1A **94**
Welbeck Gro. *Salf.* 3A **36**
Welbeck Rd. *Eccl.* 3A **46**
Welbeck Rd. *Stoc.* 3B **106**
Welbeck Rd. *Wors.* 4B **28**
Welbeck St. *M18.* 2D **89**
Welby St. *M13.* 4B **86**
Welcomb St. *M11.* 4B **72**
Weldon Dri. *M9.* 1B **22**
Weld Rd. *M20* 2B **118**
Welford Grn. *Stoc* 4B **122**
Welford Rd. *M8* 3B **20**
Welford St. *Salf* 3B **50**
Welland Clo. *M15* 2D **83**
Welland St. *Open* 3D **73**
Welland St. *Stoc* 3B **106**
Wellbank. *P'wich* 3D **17**
Wellbrow Wlk. *M9* 3C **23**
Weller Av. *M21* 2D **115**
Weller Gdns. *M21* 2D **115**
Wellesley Av. *M18* 2D **89**
Wellfield Rd. *Crum* 2C **37**
Wellgate Rd. *M19* 1B **120**
Wellhead Clo. *M15.* 3C **85**
Wellhouse Dri. *M40* 3C **25**
Welling Rd. *M40* 2A **42**
Wellington Av. *M16* 2D **99**

Wellington Bri. *Salf* 4B **52** (2A **6**)
(off Trinity Way)
Wellington Clo. *Sale* 3A **112**
Wellington Cres. *M16.* 1C **99**
Wellington Gro. *M15* 2D **83**
Wellington Ho. *Stret* 3A **96**
Wellington Pl. *M3* . . . 3A **68** (2E **9**)
Wellington Rd. *M20 & M14* . . . 2A **118**
Wellington Rd. *Crum* 2D **37**
Wellington Rd. *Eccl* 1A **62**
Wellington Rd. *Swin.* 2B **30**
Wellington Rd. *Whal R.* 2A **100**
Wellington Rd. N. *Stoc* 2B **120**
Wellington St. *M18* 3D **89**
Wellington St. *Fail* 1C **43**
Wellington St. *Salf* 1D **67** (3D **5**)
Wellington St. *Stret* 3A **96**
Wellington St. E. *Salf* 3D **35**
Wellington St. W. *Salf* 1D **51**
Wellington Ter. *Salf* 1B **64**
Wellmead Clo. *M8* 2B **52**
Wellock St. *M40* 1D **55**
Wellpark Wlk. *M40.* 2C **57**
Wells Av. *P'wich.* 4C **19**
Wells Clo. *Fail* 3B **74**
Wellside Wlk. *M8.* 1C **53**
Well St. *M4.* 1C **69** (4C **6**)
Wellwood Dri. *M40* 3A **40**
Welney Rd. *M16* 1B **98**
Welwyn Clo. *Urm.* 3B **76**
Welwyn Dri. *Salf* 2C **47**
Welwyn Wlk. *M40* 1B **70**
Wembley Gro. *M14* 4A **102**
Wembley Rd. *M18* 1C **105**
Wembury St. *M9* 2C **39**
Wembury St. N. *M9.* 2C **39**
Wem St. *Chad.* 2C **27**
Wemyss Av. *Stoc.* 3B **106**
Wendover Ho. *Salf.* 2A **66**
Wendover Rd. *Urm* 2C **93**
Wenfield Dri. *M9* 3B **24**
Wenlock Ct. *M12.* *2D **87***
(off Wenlock Way)
Wenlock St. *Swin.* 2D **29**
Wenlock Way. *M12* 2D **87**
Wensley Ct. *Salf.* 1A **34**
Wensley Dri. *M20* 4D **117**
Wensley Rd. *Salf* 2A **34**
Wensley Rd. *Stoc.* 4B **122**
Wentworth Av. *M18* 2A **90**
Wentworth Av. *Salf.* 4A **48**
Wentworth Av. *Urm* 3B **92**
Wentworth Ct. *Fail.* 4B **42**
Wentworth Dri. *Sale* 4B **110**
Wentworth Rd. *Eccl* 3B **46**
Wentworth Rd. *Stoc.* 3B **106**
Wentworth Rd. *Swin* 3D **29**
Werneth Av. *M14.* 2D **101**

Wesley Dri. *Wors* 2A **28**
Wesley Grn. *Salf* 3B **66**
Wesley Sq. *Urm* 2A **92**
Wesley St. *M11* 3A **72**
Wesley St. *Eccl* 1C **61**
Wesley St. *Fail* 1C **43**
(in two parts)
Wesley St. *Stret* 1C **97**
Wesley St. *Swin* 2B **30**
W. Ashton St. *Salf* 2D **65**
West Av. *Abb H* 3A **90**
West Av. *Burn* 2D **109**
West Av. *New M* 2D **41**
West Bank. *Open* 1C **91**
Westbank Rd. *M20.* 4B **118**
W. Bank St. *Salf.* 3C **67** (2A **8**)
Westbourne Av. *Swin* 1D **13**
Westbourne Gro. *M9* 2B **38**
Westbourne Gro. *Stoc* 1B **122**
Westbourne Gro. *Wthtn* 3C **117**
Westbourne Pk. *Urm* 1D **93**
Westbourne Range. *M18* 4B **90**
Westbourne Rd. *M14* 1B **118**
Westbourne Rd. *Eccl* 4B **44**
Westbourne Rd. *Urm* 2D **93**
Westbrook Ct. *M18* 1A **106**
Westbrook Rd. *Swin* 3A **30**
Westbrook Rd. *Traf P.* 1A **80**
Westbrook Sq. *M12* 2B **88**
Westbrook Trad. Est. *Traf P* . . . 1B **80**
Westbrook Wlk. *M20* 1C **117**
Westbury Rd. *M8.* 1D **37**
W. Central Dri. *Swin.* 3D **31**
W. Charles St. *Salf.* . . . 2B **66** (5A **4**)
Westcott Av. *M20.* 3C **117**
Westcourt Rd. *Sale* 3B **110**
W. Craig Av. *M40.* 3C **25**
W. Craven St. *Salf* 4B **66**
Westcroft Rd. *M20 & M19* 4B **118**
W. Crown Av. *Salf* 3B **66**
Westdale Gdns. *M19* 4A **120**
Westdean Cres. *M19* 4D **119**
W. Dean St. *Salf* 2C **67** (1B **8**)
West Didsbury **4B 116**
West Dri. *Droy.* 2B **74**
West Dri. *Salf.* 1C **49**
West Dri. *Swin.* 3D **31**
W. Duke St. *Salf* 2D **67** (1C **8**)
W. Egerton St. *Salf.* 2B **66**
W. End Trad. Est. *Swin* 1A **30**
Westerham Av. *Salf* 2A **66**
Westerling Way. *M16* 1A **100**
Western Av. *Swin.* 4B **16**
Western Circ. *M19.* 3D **119**
Western Pk. *Salf.* 3C **65**
Western St. *M18* 2A **90**
Western St. *Salf.* 4C **49**
Westfield. *Salf.* 3C **49**

Westfield Rd. *M21* 3B **98**
Westfield Rd. *Droy.* 1A **74**
Westfield St. *Salf.* 1D **35**
Westgate. *Urm.* 3B **92**
Westgate Av. *M9* 4A **22**
Westgate Dri. *Swin.* 1B **46**
Westgate Rd. *Salf.* 3A **48**
West Gorton 2D **87**
West Gro. *M13* 3B **86**
Westhide Wlk. *M9* 1D **39**
W. High St. *Salf.* 1A **66**
Westholm Av. *Stoc.* 2B **120**
Westholme Rd. *M20* 4D **117**
W. Hope St. *Salf.* 2B **66**
Westhorne Fold. *M8.* 4A **20**
Westinghouse Rd. *Traf P.* 2D **79**
W. King St. *Salf.* 1A **68** (3E **5**)
Westland Dri. *M9.* 2B **22**
Westlands, The. *Swin.* 4D **31**
Westlea Dri. *M18* 1D **105**
Westleigh Dri. *P'wich.* 3D **19**
Westleigh St. *M9* 1C **39**
W. Marwood St. *Salf.* 1A **52**
West Meade. *M21* 2A **114**
West Meade. *P'wich.* 4D **19**
West Meade. *Swin.* 4A **30**
West Mdw. *Stoc.* 3C **107**
Westmere Dri. *M9* 4A **38**
Westminster Av. *M16* 2C **99**
Westminster Av. *Stoc.* 2A **122**
Westminster Ho. *Salf.* 2E **5**
Westminster Rd. *Eccl.* 4A **46**
Westminster Rd. *Fail.* 2D **43**
Westminster Rd. *Urm.* 4D **77**
Westminster St. *M15* 5B **8**
Westminster St. *Lev.* 3B **104**
Westminster St. *Swin.* 1D **29**
Westmorland Clo. *Stoc.* 3D **123**
Westmorland Dri. *Stoc.* 3D **123**
Westmorland Rd. *Eccl.* 2C **47**
Westmorland Rd. *Urm.* 3C **93**
W. Mosley St. *M2* 3B **68** (2B **10**)
(in four parts)
Westmount Clo. *M40* 1A **54**
Weston Av. *M40.* 1A **42**
Weston Av. *Swin.* 2B **14**
Weston Av. *Urm.* 3B **92**
Weston Ct. *M14.* 2B **102**
W. One Retail Pk. *Salf.* 2C **63**
Weston Gro. *Stoc.* 3C **121**
Westover Rd. *Urm.* 1C **93**
Westover St. *Swin.* 1B **30**
W. Park St. *Salf.* 4B **66** (4A **8**)
West Pl. *M19.* 2D **119**
West Point. *M16* 3C **83**
W. Point Enterprise Pk. *Traf P.* . 1B **78**
W. Point Lodge. *M19.* 4D **103**
Westray Cres. *Salf.* 2C **65**

Westray Rd. *M13* 2C **103**
West Rd. *P'wich* 1D **17**
West Rd. *Stret.* 4C **79**
West Rd. *Urm.* 1A **78**
West Row. *P'wich.* 1D **33**
West St. *M9.* 3C **21**
West St. *M11.* 1B **72**
West St. *Droy.* 1D **73**
West St. *Fail.* 3B **42**
W. Towers St. *Salf.* 2D **65**
Westville Gdns. *M19.* 4C **119**
Westway. *Droy.* 4C **75**
Westwood Av. *M40.* 1A **42**
Westwood Av. *Salf.* 2A **36**
Westwood Av. *Urm.* 3B **94**
Westwood Cres. *Eccl.* 3A **44**
Westwood Dri. *Swin.* 4A **32**
Westwood Park **3B 44**
Westwood Rd. *Stret.* 2D **95**
Westwood Rd. *M14.* 4B **84**
Wetherall St. *Lev.* 3B **104**
Wetherby St. *M11* 1A **90**
Weybourne Av. *M9.* 4A **24**
Weybridge Rd. *M4.* 1A **70**
Weybrook Rd. *Stoc.* 2B **120**
Weylands Gro. *Salf.* 2D **47**
Weymouth Rd. *Eccl.* 4B **44**
Whalley Av. *Chor H.* 2C **115**
Whalley Av. *Lev.* 2B **104**
Whalley Av. *Sale.* 4A **112**
Whalley Av. *Urm.* 1A **94**
Whalley Av. *Whal R.* 1D **99**
Whalley Gro. *M16.* 2D **99**
Whalley Range **1D 99**
Whalley Rd. *M16.* 1C **99**
Wharf Circ. *Traf P.* 1A **80**
Wharf Clo. *M1.* 2D **69** (1F **11**)
Wharfedale Av. *M40.* 1A **40**
Wharfedale Rd. *Stoc.* 4A **106**
Wharf End. *Traf P.* 2A **82**
Wharf Rd. *Sale.* 4A **112**
Wharfside Av. *Eccl.* 3D **61**
Wharfside Bus. Cen. *Traf P.* . . 2D **81**
Wharfside Way. *Traf P.* 2C **81**
Wharf St. *Chad.* 3D **27**
Wharton Av. *M21.* 2D **115**
Wharton Lodge. *Eccl.* 4A **46**
Wheat Clo. *M13.* 3A **86**
(in two parts)
Wheater's Cres. *Salf.* 3C **51**
Wheater's St. *Salf.* 3D **51**
Wheater's Ter. *Salf.* 3D **51**
Wheatley Rd. *Swin.* 4D **13**
Wheatley Wlk. *M12* 2D **87**
Wheatsheaf Ind. Est. *Swin.* . . . 1D **31**
Wheeldon St. *M14.* 1C **101**
Wheler St. *M11.* 3D **73**
Whernside Av. *M40* 1A **40**

Whickham Clo. *M14* 1D **101**
Whiley St. *M13* 4D **87**
Whimberry Clo. *Salf* 4B **66** (4A **8**)
Whimberry Way. *M20* 3B **116**
Whingroves Wlk. *M40* 3A **40**
Whinmoor Wlk. *M40* 3B **40**
Whirley Clo. *Stoc* 4D **121**
Whiston Rd. *M8* 2D **37**
Whitburn Av. *M13* 2C **103**
Whitby Av. *Fall* 1C **119**
Whitby Av. *Salf* 4A **48**
Whitby Av. *Urm* 2A **94**
Whitby Av. *Whal R* 1D **99**
Whitby Rd. *M14* 1B **118**
Whitchurch Dri. *M16* 3D **83**
Whitchurch Rd. *M20* 2B **116**
Whitchurch St. *Salf* 4A **52** (1F **5**)
Whiteacres. *Swin* 3C **29**
Whiteacre Wlk. M15 . . . . *3A **84***
     (off Shearsby Clo.)
Whitebeam Clo. *Salf* 4A **50**
Whitebeam Ct. *Salf* 4A **50**
Whitebeam Wlk. *Sale* 4D **109**
Whitebeck Ct. *M9* 2A **24**
Whitebrook Rd. *M14* 3D **101**
Whitecar Av. *M40* 1A **42**
White City Circ. *M17 & M16* 3A **82**
White City Retail Pk.
  M16 . . . . 3A **82**
White City Way. *M16* 3A **82**
Whitecliff Clo. *M14* 1A **102**
White Ct. *Swin* 3C **29**
Whitecroft Gdns. *M19* 4C **119**
Whitefield. *Salf* 1B **48**
Whitefield Rd. *Sale* 4C **111**
White Friar Ct. *Salf* 4A **52** (2E **5**)
White Gate 3C **27**
Whitegate Av. *Chad* 2B **26**
Whitegate Clo. *M40* 1A **42**
Whitegate Dri. *Salf* 4B **48**
Whitegate Dri. *Swin* 4D **15**
White Gate End 3A **26**
Whitegate La. *Chad* 2B **26**
     (in two parts)
Whitegate Rd. *Chad* 3D **25**
Whitehead Rd. *M21* 1D **113**
Whitehead Rd. *Swin* 4D **15**
Whitehill Dri. *M40* 3A **40**
Whitehill Ind. Est. *Stoc* 4A **122**
Whitehill St. *Stoc* 4A **122**
     (in two parts)
Whitehill St. W. *Stoc* 4D **121**
White Horse Gdns. *Swin* 1C **45**
White Ho. Av. *M8* 3A **20**
Whitehouse Ter. *M9* 1D **39**
Whitehurst Rd. *Stoc* 4D **119**
Whitekirk Clo. *M13* 2D **85** (5F **11**)
Whitelake Av. *Urm* 2A **92**

Whiteley St. *M11* 1B **72**
Whiteley St. *Chad* 2D **27**
Whitelow Rd. *M21* 1A **114**
White Meadows. *Swin* 3B **30**
White Moss Av. *M21* 4C **99**
White Moss Gdns. *M9* 4A **24**
White Moss Rd. *M9* 3C **23**
White Moss Rd. E. *M9* 2D **23**
Whiteoak Ct. *M14* 1A **118**
Whiteoak Rd. *M14* 1A **118**
Whites Cft. *Swin* 2B **30**
Whiteside Clo. *Salf* 1B **64**
Whitestone Wlk. *M13* 3B **86**
White St. *M15* 2D **83**
White St. *Salf* 2C **65**
White Swallows Rd. *Swin* 4C **31**
Whitethorn Av. *Burn* 2D **119**
Whitethorn Av. *Whal R* 1D **99**
Whitewater Dri. *Salf* 3D **33**
Whiteway St. *M9* 3C **39**
Whitewillow Clo. *Fail* 4C **43**
Whitfield St. *M3* 4C **53** (1C **6**)
Whitfield Wlk. *M40* 4B **54**
Whitland Dri. *Oldh* 4D **27**
Whit La. *Salf* 1D **49**
     (in two parts)
Whitley Rd. *M40* 3A **54**
Whitman St. *M9* 2D **39**
Whitmore Rd. *M14* 3D **101**
Whitnall St. *M16* 1A **100**
Whitsbury Av. *M18* 1D **105**
Whitstable Rd. *M40* 1C **41**
Whitswood Clo. *M16* 1A **100**
Whittaker Clo. *P'wich* 2C **19**
Whittaker La. *P'wich* 2C **19**
Whittaker St. *M40* 2D **39**
Whittle Brook 4A **12**
Whittle's Cft. *M1* 2D **69** (1F **9**)
Whittle St. *M4* 1D **69** (4E **7**)
Whittle St. *Swin* 3A **30**
Whitwell Wlk. *M13* 4C **87**
Whitwell Way. *M18* 3C **89**
Whitworth Art Gallery, The 4D **85**
Whitworth La. *M14* 3B **102**
Whitworth Pk. Mans.
  M14 . . . . 4C **85**
Whitworth St. *M1* 3C **69** (3C **10**)
Whitworth St. *Open* 4A **72**
     (in two parts)
Whitworth St. E. *M11* 4C **73**
Whitworth St. W. *M1* 3B **68** (3F **9**)
Whixhall Av. *M12* 2C **87**
Wickenby Dri. *Sale* 4C **111**
Wickentree La. *Fail* 1B **42**
Wicket Gro. *Swin* 2A **14**
Widecombe Clo. *Urm* 4B **76**
Widgeon Clo. *M14* 4D **101**
Wiggins Wlk. *M14* 1A **102**

Wigley St. *M12* 1C **87**
Wigmore Rd. *M8*. 3D **37**
Wigsby Av. *M40* 4C **25**
Wilberforce Clo. *M15* 3A **84**
Wilbraham Rd. *M16 & M14* . . . 3B **100**
Wilbraham Rd. *M21* 3A **98**
Wilburn St. *Salf* 3D **67** (2C **8**)
(in two parts)
Wilby St. *M8*. 1D **53**
Wilcock St. *M16* 4A **84**
Wilcott Dri. *Sale* 4A **110**
Wildcroft Av. *M40* 1A **40**
Wilderswood Clo. *M20* 4A **118**
Wileman Ct. *Salf* 1A **64**
Wilfred Rd. *Eccl* 3A **60**
Wilfred St. *M40* 2A **40**
Wilfred St. *Salf* 3A **52** (1F **5**)
Wilfred St. *Swin* 2B **30**
Wilham Av. *Eccl* 2D **61**
Willan Ent. Cen. *Traf P.* 2A **80**
Willan Ind. Est. *Salf.* 2D **65**
Willan Rd. *M9* 2A **22**
Willan Rd. *Eccl* 1A **62**
Willaston Clo. *M21* 2A **114**
Willdale Clo. *M11* 1A **72**
Willerby Rd. *M8* 2A **52**
Willert St. *M40* 2B **54**
Willesden Av. *M13*. 1C **103**
Will Griffith Wlk. *M11* 3C **71**
William Chadwick Clo.
M40. . . . . 4A **54**
William Clo. *Urm* 3C **93**
William Coates Ct. *M16*. 1D **99**
William Jessop Ct.
M1. . . . . 2A **70** (1F **11**)
William Kay Clo. *M16* 4A **84**
William Lister Clo. *M40*. 3D **57**
William Murray Ct. *M4* 1A **70**
(off Winder Dri.)
Williams Cres. *Chad* 3B **26**
Williamson La. *Droy*. 3D **75**
Williamson St. *M4* 4D **53** (1E **7**)
Williamson St. *Stoc*. 2B **122**
Williams Rd. *Gort* 3C **89**
Williams Rd. *Most*. 3B **40**
Williams St. *M18*. 3C **89**
William St. *M12*. 3B **70**
William St. *Fail* 1C **43**
William St. *Salf*. 1A **68** (4E **5**)
Willingdon Dri. *P'wich* 1B **18**
Willoughby Clo. *Sale* 4C **111**
Willow Av. *Stoc* 4B **122**
Willow Av. *Urm* 2A **94**
Willow Bank. *M9*. 2C **39**
(off Church La.)
Willow Bank. *M14*. 1A **118**
Willowbank. *Swin* 4C **15**
Willowbrook Av. *M40* 3A **40**

Willow Ct. *M14* 3B **102**
(Mosley Rd.)
Willow Ct. *M14* 1A **118**
(Willow Bank)
Willow Ct. *Sale* 4C **113**
Willowdene Clo. *M40* 2A **54**
Willow Fold. *Droy* 3D **75**
Willow Gro. *M18*. 4A **90**
Willow Hill Rd. *M8* 4C **21**
Willow Pk. *M14*. 1A **118**
Willow Rd. *Eccl* 3A **44**
Willows Dri. *Fail* 3B **58**
Willows Rd. *Salf* 1B **64**
Willows, The. *M21* 2A **114**
Willow St. *M11* 2A **72**
Willow St. *Fail*. 3D **41**
Willow St. *Salf*. 3A **52**
Willow St. *Swin*. 2D **45**
Willow Tree Ct. *Eccl*. 2C **61**
Willow Wlk. *Droy* 1D **75**
Wilma Av. *M9* 2A **22**
Wilmcote Rd. *M40* 3B **54**
Wilmington Rd. *Stret* 2D **95**
Wilmott St. *M15*. 1B **84** (5B **10**)
(Hulme St.)
Wilmott St. *M15*. 2C **85** (5C **10**)
(Knowles Pl.)
Wilmslow Rd. *M14* 4A **86**
Wilmslow Rd. *M20* 4D **117**
Wilmur Av. *Salf* 4A **36**
Wilpshire Av. *M12* 1B **104**
Wilson Av. *Swin* 4D **15**
Wilson Pk. *M40* 2C **55**
Wilson Rd. *M9* 1B **38**
Wilson St. *M11* 3A **72**
Wilson St. *M13* 2A **86**
Wilson St. *M40* 3C **55**
Wilson St. *Sale* 4D **111**
Wilson St. *Stret*. 4C **81**
Wilsthorpe Clo. *M19* 3C **121**
Wilton Av. *M16* 1A **98**
Wilton Av. *P'wich* 4D **19**
Wilton Av. *Swin*. 3A **32**
Wilton Ct. *M9* 3C **21**
Wilton Ct. *Dent* 4C **91**
Wilton Gro. *Dent* 4C **91**
Wilton Paddock. *Dent* 4C **91**
Wilton Pl. *Salf* 1D **67** (4C **4**)
Wilton Polygon. *M8*. 1B **36**
Wilton Rd. *Chor H.* 1B **114**
Wilton Rd. *Crum* 4B **20**
Wilton Rd. *Salf* 3D **47**
Wilton St. *M13* 2D **85**
Wilton St. *Chad*. 3D **27**
Wilton St. *P'wich*. 2C **19**
Wilton St. *Stoc* 2B **106**
Wiltshire Rd. *Chad* 1D **27**

Wiltshire Rd. *Fail* 1C **59**
Wiltshire St. *Salf* 4A **36**
Wimbledon Rd. *Fail* 2D **43**
Wimbledon Ter. *M40* 3B **56**
Wimborne Av. *Urm* 4D **77**
Wimborne Wlk. *Salf* 1A **66**
Wimpory St. *M11* 1D **89**
Wincham Clo. *M15* 2D **83**
Winchester Av. *P'wich* 4C **19**
Winchester Rd. *Eccl* 2C **47**
Winchester Rd. *Salf* 3A **48**
Winchester Rd. *Urm & Stret*. . . 1D **93**
Wincombe St. *M14* 2D **101**
Windcroft Clo. *M11* 3D **71**
Winder Dri. *M4* 1A **70**
Windermere Av. *Dent* 2C **107**
Windermere Av. *Swin* 3C **31**
Windermere Clo. *Open* 3A **72**
Windermere Clo. *P'wich* 1D **17**
Windermere Clo. *Stret*. 1A **96**
Windermere Rd. *Urm* 3C **93**
Winders Way. *Salf* 3B **50**
Windle *M8*. 3B **20**
Windmill Av. *Salf* 4B **66** (4A **8**)
Windmill Clo. *Dent* 2D **107**
Windmill La. *Stoc* 3B **106**
Windmill La. Ind. Est.
    Dent. 1D **107**
Windmill St. *M2*. 3B **68** (2A **10**)
Windrush Dri. *M9* 3B **38**
Windsor Av. *Chad* 2C **27**
Windsor Av. *Fail* 2D **43**
Windsor Av. *Sale*. 3D **111**
Windsor Av. *Swin* 4C **15**
Windsor Av. *Urm*. 2A **92**
Windsor Ct. *M8*. 1B **20**
Windsor Ct. *Sale* 4B **110**
Windsor Cres. *P'wich* 3A **20**
Windsor Ho. *Dent* 1C **107**
Windsor Rd. *Dent* 4C **91**
Windsor Rd. *Droy*. 1D **73**
Windsor Rd. *Harp*. 3C **39**
Windsor Rd. *Lev* 3A **104**
Windsor Rd. *Newt H* 3A **58**
Windsor Rd. *P'wich*. 4A **20**
                                    (in two parts)
Windsor St. *Fail*. 2C **43**
Windsor St. *Gort*. 4C **89**
Windsor St. *Newt H*. 3A **58**
Windsor St. *Salf* 2B **66**
Winfell Dri. *M40* 4B **54**
Winfield Av. *M20*. 3B **118**
Winfield Dri. *M18* 2D **89**
Winford St. *M9* 2C **39**
Wingate Rd. *Stoc* 4C **121**
Wingfield Dri. *Swin* 1C **47**
Wingfield St. *Stret* 4B **80**
Wingrave Ho. *Salf* 2A **66**

Winifred Rd. *M40* 3B **40**
Winifred Rd. *Urm* 2D **93**
Winifred St. *Eccl* 2B **60**
Winnall Wlk. *M40* 1C **57**
Winnie St. *M40*. 2A **40**
Winning Hill Clo. *M18*. 4D **89**
Winnipeg Quay. *Salf* 4D **65**
Winscombe Dri. *M40* 3A **54**
Winser St. *M1* 3C **69** (3C **10**)
Winsford Rd. *M14*. 3C **101**
Winslow Pl. *M19*. 3D **119**
Winslow St. *M11*. 3A **72**
Winstanley Clo. *Salf* 2B **48**
Winstanley Rd. *M40* 4B **54**
Winstanley Rd. *Sale* 4A **112**
Winster Av. *M20* 4A **116**
Winster Av. *Salf*. 4B **34**
Winster Av. *Stret* 1C **95**
Winster Grn. *Eccl* 3B **60**
Winster Rd. *Eccl* 3B **60**
Winston Clo. *Sale* 4B **110**
Winston Rd. *M9* 1D **39**
Winston St. *M9*. 2D **39**
Winswell Clo. *M11* 1B **72**
Winterburn Av. *M21* 4C **115**
Winterdyne St. *M9* 3C **39**
Winterford Av. *M13*. 3B **86**
Winterford Rd. *Salf* 3B **36**
Wintermans Rd. *M21* 2D **115**
Winterton Rd. *Stoc* 3C **107**
Winthrop Av. *M40* 2B **54**
Winton **1B 60**
Winton Av. *M40* 1D **41**
Winton Rd. *Salf* 1B **48**
Wirral Clo. *Swin* 4C **15**
Wiseley St. *M11* 3C **71**
Wiseman Ter. *P'wich* 2C **19**
Wishaw Sq. *M21*. 2A **116**
Wisley Clo. *Stoc* 4B **106**
Wistaria Rd. *M18* 3D **89**
Withies, The. *Eccl* 1B **60**
Withington **3C 117**
Withington Pool
    Fitness Cen. 3D **117**
Withington Rd.
    M21 & M16. . . . . 1D **115**
Withington St. *Salf* 4B **50**
Withins Rd. *Oldh* 4D **27**
Withycombe Pl. *Salf* 2A **50**
Withy Gro. *M4* 1C **69** (4C **6**)
Witley Dri. *Sale* 3D **109**
Witterage Clo. *M12* 2D **87**
Witton Wlk. *M8* 1B **52**
Woburn Rd. *M16*. 1A **98**
Woburn St. *M16* 1B **100**
Woden's Av. *Salf*. 3C **67** (3A **8**)
Woden St. *Salf*. 4C **67** (4B **8**)
Wolfreton Cres. *Swin* 3C **15**

Wolseley Ho. *Sale* 3A **112**
Wolseley Pl. *M20* 4D **117**
Wolseley Rd. *Sale* 3D **111**
Wolverton St. *M11* 4D **71**
Woodacre. *M16* 3A **100**
Woodbank Ct. *Urm* 1B **92**
Woodbine St. *M14* 4C **85**
Woodbourne Rd. *Stoc* 3C **121**
Woodbray Av. *M19* 4C **119**
Woodcliffe Lodge. *P'wich* 4B **18**
Woodcote Rd.
   Dun M & M31 . . . . . . 4A **108**
Woodcote Wlk. *M8* *2A 38*
      (off Crescent Rd.)
Woodcroft Av. *M19* 4C **119**
Woodfield Gro. *Eccl* 2C **61**
Woodfield Gro. *Sale* 3C **111**
Woodfield Rd. *M8* 1C **37**
Woodfield Rd. *Salf* 3B **48**
Woodfold Av. *M19* 2A **104**
Woodford Av. *Eccl* 1B **60**
Woodford Ct. *Droy* *3D 75*
    (off Williamson La.)
Woodford Dri. *Swin* 4A **14**
Woodford Rd. *Fail* 2C **43**
Woodgarth Av. *M40* 2D **57**
Woodgarth Dri. *Swin* 1A **46**
Woodgate Rd. *M16* 3A **100**
Woodgrange Clo. *Salf* 1C **65**
Woodhall Av. *M20* 2C **117**
Woodhall Cres. *Stoc* 4C **123**
Woodhall Rd. *Stoc* 4B **122**
Woodhall St. *Fail* 2B **42**
Woodhalt Rd. *M8* 2C **37**
Woodhead St. *M16* 4A **84**
Woodheys St. *Salf* 2D **65**
Wood Hill Clo. *M12* 4B **88**
Woodhill Dri. *P'wich* 3B **18**
Woodhill Gro. *P'wich* 3B **18**
Woodhouse Ct. *Urm* 4A **76**
Woodhouse Rd. *Urm* 4A **76**
     (in two parts)
Woodhouses 4D **43**
Woodhouse St. *M18* 3A **90**
Woodhouse St. *M40* 2D **55**
Woodland Av. *M18* 4B **90**
Woodland Cres. *P'wich* 4B **18**
Woodland Rd. *Burn* 1A **120**
Woodland Rd. *Gort* 4A **90**
Woodlands. *Fail* 3A **58**
Woodlands. *P'wich* 1D **33**
Woodlands. *Urm* 1C **93**
Woodlands Av. *Eccl* 3A **60**
Woodlands Av. *Stret* 3B **98**
Woodlands Av. *Swin* 1C **45**
Woodlands Rd. *M8* 2C **37**
Woodlands Rd. *Sale* 4A **112**
Woodlands Rd. *Whal R* 3A **100**

Woodlands St. *M8* 2C **37**
Woodlands, The. *Droy* 4A **58**
Woodlands, The. *Swin* 3D **31**
Woodland St. *M12* 3B **88**
Woodland St. *Salf* 2A **52**
Woodland Ter. *Salf* 2D **51**
Woodlark Clo. *Salf* 2D **67** (5D **5**)
Woodlea. *Eccl* 3C **45**
Woodlea Av. *M19* 3C **119**
Woodleigh St. *M9* 1D **39**
Woodliffe St. *M16* 3C **83**
Woodlinn Wlk. *M9* 3B **38**
Woodmere Dri. *M9* 3C **23**
Wood Newton Clo. *M18* 4C **89**
Wood Rd. *M16* 1C **99**
Wood Rd. N. *M16* 1C **99**
Woodrow Wlk. *M12* 2D **87**
Woodside Av. *M19* 4D **119**
Woodside Av. *Wors* 4A **12**
Woodside Dri. *Salf* 4A **48**
Woodside Rd. *M16* 2B **98**
Woodsmoor Rd. *Swin* 3D **29**
Wood Sq. *Droy* 3C **75**
Woodstock Av. *Stoc* 4B **122**
Woodstock Dri. *Swin* 1C **47**
Woodstock Dri. *Wors* 2A **44**
Woodstock Grn. *Stoc* 3C **123**
Woodstock Rd. *Most* 1C **41**
Woodstock Rd. *Old T* 1B **98**
Wood St. *M3* 2A **68** (1F **9**)
     (Manchester)
Wood St. *M3* 1A **68** (4F **5**)
     (Salford)
Wood St. *Eccl* 2B **62**
Wood St. *Open* 3B **72**
Woodthorpe Ct. *P'wich* 4D **19**
Woodthorpe Grange. *P'wich* . . . 4D **19**
Woodvale Wlk. *M11* *2D 71*
    (off Redfield Clo.)
Woodview Av. *M19* 4D **119**
Woodville Dri. *Sale* 4C **111**
Woodville Gro. *Stoc* 3B **122**
Woodville Rd. *Sale* 4C **111**
Woodville Ter. *M40* 1D **39**
Woodward Ct. *M4* 1B **70**
Woodward Pl. *M4* 1A **70**
Woodward Rd. *P'wich* 4D **17**
Woodward St. *M4* 1A **70**
Woolden St. *Eccl* 4B **44**
Woolden St. *Swin* 4A **14**
Woolfall Clo. *M12* 2D **87**
Woollam Pl. *M3* 3D **67** (2D **9**)
Woolley St. *M8* 3B **52**
Woolpack Grn. *Salf* 4D **49**
Woolston Ho. *Salf* 3A **48**
Woolton Clo. *M40* 4C **25**
Worcester Clo. *Salf* 3A **48**

Worcester Rd. *Salf* 3A **48**
Worcester Rd. *Swin* 4D **13**
Worcester St. *Oldh* 1D **27**
Wordsworth Av. *M8* 1C **53**
Wordsworth Av. *Droy* 1C **75**
Wordsworth Gdns. *P'wich* 3D **17**
Wordsworth Rd. *M16* 1B **98**
Wordsworth Rd. *Stoc* 3D **105**
Wordsworth Rd. *Swin* 1D **29**
Wordsworth St. *Salf* 3C **51**
Workesleigh St. *M40* 2C **57**
World Trade Cen. *Salf* 2A **82**
Worrall St. *M40* 1A **56**
Worrall St. *Salf* 4C **67** (4A **8**)
Worsefold St. *M40* 2A **40**
Worsley 3A **28**
Worsley Av. *M40* 1D **39**
Worsley Ct. *M14* 2A **102**
Worsley Gro. *M19* 3A **104**
Worsley Rd. *Eccl* 3A **44**
Worsley Rd. *Wors & Swin* 2A **44**
Worsley St. *M3* 3A **68** (3F **9**)
. . . . (Manchester)
Worsley St. *M3* 2A **68** (4F **5**)
. . . . (Salford)
Worsley St. *M15* 4D **67** (4C **8**)
Worsley St. *Swin* 4B **14**
. . . . (Devon St.)
Worsley St. *Swin* 3C **31**
. . . . (Victoria Av.)
Worthenbury Wlk. *M13* 1C **103**
Worthing St. *M14* 2D **101**
Worthington Ct. *Sale* 4C **113**
Worthington Dri. *Salf* 1D **35**
Worthington St. *M40* 2C **41**
Worthington St. *Old T* 4C **83**
Wortley Av. *Salf* 4A **48**
Wortley Gro. *M40* 4B **24**
Wraysbury Wlk. *M40* 3A **40**
. . . . (off Hugo St.)
Wren Av. *Swin* 3D **15**
Wrenbury Av. *M20* 2B **116**
Wrexham Clo. *Oldh* 4D **27**
Wright Robinson Clo.
. . . *M11* 3C **71**
Wright St. *M16* 2C **83**
Wright St. *Chad* 1D **27**
Wright St. *Fail* 2B **42**
Wrigley Cres. *Fail* 3B **42**
Wrigley Head. *Fail* 2B **42**
Wrigley Head Cres.
. . . *Fail* 2B **42**
Wroe St. *Salf* 2D **67** (5C **4**)
Wroe St. *Swin* 3B **14**
Wroe Ter. *Swin* 3B **14**
Wrotham Clo. *Salf* 2A **66**
Wroxeter Wlk. *M12* 2D **87**
. . . . (off Wenlock Way)

Wroxham Av. *Dent* 1C **107**
Wroxham Av. *Urm* 1B **92**
Wroxham Rd. *M9* 3D **21**
Wyatt Av. *Salf* 4B **66** (4A **8**)
Wychbury St. *Salf* 1C **65**
Wycliffe Ct. *Urm* 2C **93**
Wycliffe Rd. *Urm* 2C **93**
Wycliffe St. *Eccl* 1C **61**
Wycombe Av. *M18* 2A **90**
Wycombe Clo. *Urm* 3C **77**
Wye Av. *Fail* 3B **42**
Wykeham St. *M14* 1C **101**
Wylam Wlk. *M12* 1B **104**
Wyndale Dri. *Fail* 2B **58**
Wyndham Av. *Swin* 3B **14**
Wynford Sq. *Salf* 2D **65**
Wynne Av. *Swin* 3B **14**
Wynne Clo. *M11* 3D **71**
Wynne St. *Salf* 3B **50** (1A **4**)
Wynnstay Gro. *M14* 4A **102**
Wynnstay Rd. *Sale* 4D **111**
Wynn St. *M40* 1A **42**
Wyre St. *M1* 3D **69** (3F **11**)
Wythburn Av. *M8* 1A **54**
Wythburn Av. *Urm* 1B **92**
Wythburn St. *Salf* 1C **65**
Wythop Gdns. *Salf* 2A **66**
Wyvern Av. *Stoc* 4A **122**
Wyverne Rd. *M21* 3D **99**
Wyville Dri. *Salf* 4D **49**
Wyville Dri. *Swin* 1A **46**

X

XS Superbowl 2C **29**

Y

Yarburgh St. *M16* 1A **100**
Yardley Av. *Stret* 2C **95**
Yardley Clo. *Stret* 2C **95**
Yarn Wlk. *M4* 2A **70**
Yeadon Rd. *M18* 1D **105**
Yelverton Wlk. *M13* 2A **86**
. . . . (off Copeman Clo.)
Yeomanry Ct. *M16* 1D **99**
Yeoman Wlk. *M11* 2D **71**
Yeovil St. *M16* 1B **100**
Yewdale. *Swin* 4D **15**
Yew Dale Dri. *Fail* 2D **43**
Yewlands Av. *M9* 1B **22**
Yew St. *M15* 3A **84**
Yew St. *Salf* 1C **51**
Yew Tree Av. *Fall* 2C **101**
Yew Tree Av. *Lev* 3A **104**
Yew Tree Cres. *M14* 3D **101**

Yew Tree Dri. *P'wich* 2B **18**
Yew Tree Dri. *Sale* 4C **113**
Yew Tree Dri. *Urm* 4A **76**
Yew Tree Rd. *M14* 1D **101**
York Arc. *M1* 1D **11**
York Av. *M16* 2C **99**
York Av. *P'wich* 4D **19**
York Av. *Sale* 4D **111**
York Av. *Swin* 4D **13**
York Av. *Urm* 1A **94**
York Ho. *Sale* 4D **111**
York Rd. *M21* 4B **98**
York Rd. *Droy* 4B **58**
York Rd. *Sale* 4C **111**
York Rd. *Stoc.* 4B **120**
York Rd. E. *Midd* 1C **25**
York Rd. W. *Midd.* 1C **25**
Yorkshire St. *Salf* 1A **68** (4F **5**)

York St. *M1* 3C **69** (3C **10**)
                 (in two parts)
York St. *M2.* 2C **69** (5C **6**)
York St. *M9* 2C **39**
                 (in two parts)
York St. *M13.* 1C **85** (5D **11**)
York St. *Lev.* 4A **104**
York Ter. *Sale.* 3C **111**
Young St. *M3.* 2A **68** (1F **9**)
Yulan Dri. *Sale.* 4C **109**

Z

Zebra St. *Salf.* 3B **36**
Zeta St. *M9* 3D **39**
Zetland Rd. *M21* 1B **114**
Zyburn Ct. *Salf.* 4C **47**

HOSPITALS and HOSPICES
covered by this atlas

with their map square reference

N.B. Where Hospitals and Hospices are not named on the map,
the reference given is for the road in which they are situated.

ALEXANDRA BMI HOSPITAL
(VICTORIA PARK) —4B **86**
110-112 Daisy Bank Rd.
MANCHESTER
M14 5QH
Tel: 0161 2572233

BOOTH HALL CHILDREN'S HOSPITAL
—3D **23**
Charlestown Rd., MANCHESTER
M9 7AA
Tel: 0161 7957000

CHRISTIE HOSPITAL —3D **117**
550 Wilmslow Rd.
MANCHESTER
M20 4BX
Tel: 0161 4463000

HOPE HOSPITAL —4D **47**
Stott La., SALFORD
M6 8HD
Tel: 0161 7897373

MANCHESTER BUPA HOSPITAL —1D **99**
Russell Rd., MANCHESTER
M16 8AJ
Tel: 0161 2260112

MANCHESTER CHILDRENS HOSPITAL
—3A **32**
Hospital Rd., Pendlebury
Swinton, MANCHESTER
M27 4HA
Tel: 0161 7944696

MANCHESTER ROYAL EYE HOSPITAL
—3D **85**
Nelson St., MANCHESTER
M13 9WH
Tel: 0161 2765526

MANCHESTER ROYAL INFIRMARY
—3A **86**
Oxford Rd., MANCHESTER
M13 9WL
Tel: 0161 2761234

MENTAL HEALTH SERVICES FOR
SALFORD —1D **17**
Bury New Rd., Prestwich
MANCHESTER
M25 3BL
Tel: 0161 7739121

NORTH MANCHESTER GENERAL
HOSPITAL —1D **37**
Delaunays Rd.
MANCHESTER
M8 5RB
Tel: 0161 7954567

OAKLANDS HOSPITAL —4D **47**
19 Lancaster Rd., SALFORD
M6 8AQ
Tel: 0161 7877700

ST MARY'S HOSPITAL FOR WOMEN &
CHILDREN —4A **86**
Hathersage Rd.
MANCHESTER
M13 0JH
Tel: 0161 2761234

STRETFORD MEMORIAL HOSPITAL
—1B **98**
226 Seymour Gro., MANCHESTER
M16 0DU
Tel: 0161 8815353

TRAFFORD GENERAL HOSPITAL —1A **92**
Moorside Rd., Urmston
MANCHESTER
M41 5SL
Tel: 0161 7484022

UNIVERSITY DENTAL HOSPITAL —2C **85**
Higher Cambridge St., MANCHESTER
M15 6FH
Tel: 0161 2756666

WITHINGTON HOSPITAL —3B **116**
Nell La., MANCHESTER
M20 2LR
Tel: 0161 4458111

RAIL & METROLINK STATIONS

with their map square reference

Anchorage Station. Met —3A **66**
Ardwick Station. Rail —4B **70**
Ashburys Station. Rail —4A **72**

Belle Vue Station. Rail —3C **89**
Bowker Vale Station. Met —3B **20**
Brinnington Station. Rail —3D **123**
Broadway Station. Met —3D **65**

Chassen Road Station. Rail —3B **92**
Clifton Station. Rail —4A **16**
Cornbrook Station. Met
—1C **83** (5B **8**)
Crumpsall Station. Met —1C **37**

Dane Road Station. Met —3A **112**
Dean Lane Station. Rail —4B **40**
Deansgate Station. Rail
—3A **68** (3F **9**)

Eccles Station. Rail —1B **62**
Eccles Station. Met —1B **62**
Exchange Quay Station. Met —2A **82**

Failsworth Station. Rail —2A **42**
Fairfield Station. Rail —1C **91**

G Mex Station. Met —3A **68** (3F **9**)
Gorton Station. Rail —2D **89**

Harbour City Station. Met —3D **65**
Heaton Chapel Station. Rail
—4C **121**
Heaton Park Station. Met —2C **19**
Hollinwood Station. Rail —4C **27**
Humphrey Park Station. Rail
—1C **95**

Ladywell Station. Met —1C **63**
Langworthy Station. Met —2C **65**
Levenshulme Station. Rail —3A **104**

Market Street Station. Met
—2C **69** (4D **7**)
Mauldeth Road Station. Rail
—3C **119**
Moorside Station. Rail —1D **29**
Mosley Street Station. Met
—2C **69** (5C **6**)
Moston Station. Rail —4D **25**

Old Trafford Station. Met —4A **82**
Oxford Road Station. Rail
—4B **68** (3C **10**)

Patricroft Station. Rail —1C **61**
Piccadilly Gardens Station. Met
—2C **69** (5D **7**)
Piccadilly Station. Rail & Met
—3D **69** (2F **11**)
Pomona Station. Met —2B **82**
Prestwich Station. Met —1A **18**

Reddish North Station. Rail
—2B **106**
Reddish South Station. Rail
—2B **122**
Ryder Brow Station. Rail —4D **89**

St Peter's Square Station. Met
—3B **68** (2B **10**)
Sale Station. Met —4D **111**
Salford Central Station. Rail
—2A **68** (5E **5**)
Salford Crescent Station. Rail
—1B **66**
Salford Quays Station. Met —1A **82**

Shude Hill. Met —1C **69** (4C **6**)
Stretford Station. Met —3B **96**
Swinton Station. Rail —1B **30**

Trafford Bar Station. Met —3B **82**
Trafford Park Station. Rail —1A **96**

Urmston Station. Rail —2D **93**

Victoria Station. Rail & Met
—4C **53** (2C **6**)

Weaste Station. Met —2B **64**
Woodlands Road Station. Met
—3D **37**

The representation on the maps of a road, track or footpath is no evidence of the existence of a right of way.

The Grid on this map is the National Grid taken from Ordnance Survey mapping with the permission of the Controller of Her Majesty's Stationery Office.